Pila (2012)

Copyright, Communication and Culture

For André

Copyright, Communication and Culture

Towards a Relational Theory of Copyright Law

Carys J. Craig

Associate Professor of Law, Osgoode Hall Law School, York University, Toronto, Canada

Edward Elgar

Cheltenham, UK • Northampton, MA, USA

Published by
Edward Elgar Publishing Limited
The Lypiatts
15 Lansdown Road
Cheltenham
Glos GL50 2JA
UK

Edward Elgar Publishing, Inc.
William Pratt House
9 Dewey Court
Northampton
Massachusetts 01060
USA

A catalogue record for this book
is available from the British Library

Library of Congress Control Number: 2011925706

MIX
Paper from
responsible sources
FSC® C018575
FSC
www.fsc.org

ISBN 978 1 84844 839 1

Typeset by Servis Filmsetting Ltd, Stockport, Cheshire
Printed and bound by MPG Books Group, UK

Contents

Acknowledgements

My thanks to Abraham Drassinower for the many challenging and thought-provoking discussions we had as this book took shape. Thanks also to Jennifer Nedelsky, both for her support and for her wonderful work, which has informed and inspired my own. I also owe a debt of gratitude to Ariel Katz and Myra Tawfik for their thoughtful feedback and suggestions. I am further indebted to the numerous people who have read or responded to portions of this work along the way, offering inspiration, encouragement and critique. These include Anne Bartow, Dan Burk, Julie Cohen, Rosemary Coombe, Giuseppina D'Agostino, Christine Haight Farley, Michael Geist, Wendy Gordon, Peter Jaszi, David Lametti, Jacqueline Lipton, Dennis Magnusson, Teresa Scassa, Sam Trosow, Kim Weatherall, Margaret-Ann Wilkinson, Julie Cromer Young and Lior Zemer.

I would not have been able to undertake this project without the generous financial support of Queen's University, the University of Toronto and the Centre for Law and Innovation Policy.

Finally, thanks to my husband, Conor Fitzpatrick, my family (the Scottish and Canadian contingents), friends and colleagues for their unerring encouragement and support.

Certain portions of this work have previously been published elsewhere: 'Digital Locks and the Fate of Fair Dealing in Canada: In Pursuit of "Prescriptive Parallelism"' (2010) 13(4) *Journal of World Intellectual Property* 503–39; 'Resisting Sweat and Refusing Feist: Rethinking Originality after CCH' (2007) 40:1 *University of British Columbia Law Review* 69–120; 'Reconstructing the Author-Self: Some Feminist Lessons for Copyright Law' (2007) 15:2 *American University Journal of Gender, Social Policy, and the Law* 207–68; 'Putting the Community in Communication: Dissolving the Conflict Between Freedom of Expression and Copyright Law' (2006) 56 *University of Toronto Law Journal* 75–114; 'The Evolution of Originality in Canadian Copyright Law: Authorship, Reward and the Public Interest' (2005) 2 *University of Ottawa Law & Technology Journal* 425–45; 'The Changing Face of Fair Dealing in Canadian Copyright Law: A Proposal for Legislative Reform' in Michael Geist (ed.), *In the Public Interest: The Future of Canadian Copyright Law*

(Toronto: Irwin Law, 2005); 'Locke, Labour, and Limiting the Author's Right: A Warning Against a Lockean Approach to Copyright Law' (2002) 28 *Queen's Law Journal* 1–60.

1. Introduction

This is a critical moment in our cultural life. The ownership and control of information resources is one of the most important forms of power in contemporary society.[1] Digital technologies therefore have the potential to alter and subvert power structures by changing the ways in which we access, engage with, and participate in the creation of these resources. By the same token, intellectual property laws have the capacity to shore up existing power structures and limit creative practices by enforcing and expanding traditional proprietary norms in the digital environment. Networked technologies present unprecedented opportunities for creative expression and participation in public discourse; but these technologies, and the activities they facilitate, are subject to legal regimes that allocate exclusive rights over information resources, restricting their creation, dissemination and development.

Copyright law, which creates exclusive rights over intellectual expression, is one such regime. Copyright attaches to original literary, dramatic, musical and artistic expression, granting authors and subsequent owners the power to control the production, reproduction, publication and performance of their works. Fundamentally, copyright is no more than 'the right to multiply copies of a published work, or the right to make the work public and still retain the beneficial interest therein.'[2] But through the powers of control that it grants to authors and subsequent owners, copyright regulates the production and exchange of meaning and information, and shapes social relations of communication. Writers, artists, musicians, performers, software programmers, publishers, students, researchers, librarians, teachers, readers, movie-goers, music fans – and so, one might say, all of us – exist in a web of cultural relations subject to the law of copyright.

The emergence of the digital world has rapidly generated a new public idea of communication, discourse, participation and production – one that values networking over singularity, and relationships over individuation. Most importantly, however, this new public idea favours a collaborative model of shared and cumulative cultural dialogue over a proprietary model of cultural production. Within this model, epitomised by social media, fan sites, digital sampling and file sharing, conventional ideas of individual ownership are swept aside. This explains why the recent focus of intellectual property policy-makers around the globe has been predominantly on the threats rather than the promises of digital technology. Copyright appears to have arrived at a crossroads: it increasingly seems that a choice is being made between maximising the potential of the digital revolution and reinforcing the traditional norms of the analog world. Thankfully, this is a false dilemma: as I will argue, copyright contains *within it* the norms and aspirations that not only permit but necessitate the development of a robust cultural landscape[3] in which citizens freely participate – a social space made more open, accessible, democratic and vital by the advances of network technologies.

From a utilitarian or instrumental perspective, the exclusive rights that copyright grants are justified as a means by which to maximise cultural production and exchange by encouraging the production of intellectual works. The underlying rationale is that such works will be under-produced unless authors are given sufficient opportunity to exploit them for financial return.[4] Rationalised in these terms, the exclusive rights of authors might be said to 'encourage learning'[5] and to 'promote the progress of the useful arts'.[6] From this it should follow that the rights granted to authors under the copyright system affirm the value that we as a society place in the cultural exchange and interaction represented by the production and dissemination of intellectual works.

Many utilitarian versions of copyright theory presuppose but fail to explain this initial premise. A pure economic theory can justify copyright in terms of the economic incentive it offers for authors *qua* rational economic actors, but economics alone cannot explain the nature of the societal benefits that flow from this incentive. This requires us to understand the public interest that resides in the creation and exchange of intellectual expression. From a public interest perspective, the encouragement of cultural production should be understood as the creation of opportunities for improved communication between members of society. The copyright system should be regarded as one element of a larger cultural and social policy aimed at encouraging the process of cultural exchange that new technologies facilitate. The economic and other incentives that copyright offers to creators of original expression are meant to encourage a participatory and interactive society, and to further the social goods that flow through public dialogue. Copyright's purpose is to create opportunities for people to speak, to develop relationships of communication between author and audience, and to fashion conditions that might cultivate a higher quality of expression.

However, the role that copyright plays as a cultural and social policy tool is rarely appreciated. Rather, copyright is widely regarded as a system whose purpose is the protection of private, proprietary rights. Notwithstanding the intangible and communicative nature of intellectual expression, its categorisation as a species of so-called 'intellectual property', compounded by a particular understanding of the nature of authorship, causes copyright to be commonly conceptualised as just another form of private property. Viewed through the proprietary lens, the intellectual expression of the author is an object that is owned like any other. In the context of a market economy, it is simply a commodity to be freely transferred and exploited in the marketplace. However, the language of 'ownership', 'property' and 'commodity' obfuscates the nature of copyright's subject matter, and cloaks the social and cultural implications of copyright protection. As history reveals, it also appears to result in the continuous strengthening and expansion of the private rights that copyright affords. As such, the way that we traditionally think about copyright – particularly in the modern digital age where works are created, shared, accessed and transformed more easily and efficiently than ever before – is inapposite to the task that we expect it to perform. Copyright is in desperate need of re-imagination.

My aim, in this book, is to provide a route towards the re-imagination of copyright law. This process of re-imagining copyright is not cast as a radical or revolutionary one: rather, it works from within the copyright system, using the concepts and components that constitute the current system, only reconceptualising them within a revised theoretical framework. Through this process, we are challenged to discard the loaded conception of the author as a bearer of rights and an owner of property, and to adopt in its place a vision of the relational author as a participant in a process of cultural dialogue and exchange. This, in turn, requires that we resist the notion of original expression as a stable, objectifiable thing, and instead embrace the idea of the work as a text, utterance or communicative act. Finally, this demands that we reject the characterisation of users of copyrighted works as actual or potential trespassers or pirates, and recognise them instead as active and equal participants in the very process of meaning-making and exchange that underpins copyright norms.

Ultimately, this route should lead us to an understanding of copyright as a system designed to further the public good by encouraging improved relations of communication between members of society, and maximising discursive engagement in a collective conversation. Viewed through this lens, author and text are no longer individualised and isolated from their social situation: it becomes possible for the contours of copyright protection to reflect the dialogic and inherently social nature of cultural expression.

As this suggests, the central concern of this book is the underlying philosophy or theory of copyright law. I argue that our current copyright model is premised upon the political and ontological assumptions of traditional legal liberalism, and the normative assumptions of possessive individualism. These political underpinnings guide courts' interpretation and application of copyright doctrine with the result that copyright law fails to adequately reflect the realities of cultural creativity, and frequently restricts the very communicative or expressive activities that it is meant to encourage. If copyright is to be a justifiable limitation upon the expressive activities of the public, it must increase opportunities for qualitative cultural production and exchange, ultimately furthering our communication ideals. The appropriate limits of copyright's protective sphere will become clear when we acknowledge that the copyright owner's rights exist only *through* this public interest and not in spite of it. Where copyright obstructs rather than facilitates relations of communication, it goes beyond the bounds of its justification.

The crux of this re-imagined theoretical framework for copyright is developed in Part I of the book, which challenges the liberal and neo-liberal theorising implicit in modern copyright discourse. This lays the foundation for the critique that builds throughout the book: namely, that the existing theoretical framework for copyright is responsible for the (mis) construction of its core concepts. The concepts of authorship, originality and ownership are defined and shaped by the philosophical assumptions that we bring to bear on the processes of cultural creativity and the legal system that we have built in its name. These concepts, in turn, affect the operation of copyright law and the extent to which it achieves its policy goals. The current copyright model, constructed as it is around the transcendent, rights-bearing author-self, is ill suited to the task of encouraging and maximising cultural creativity and the production and dissemination of new intellectual works.

I propose a relational model as a more appropriate framework within which to understand the processes of authorship, its significance for the author and the public, and consequently, the role and purpose of the copyright system. Chapter 2 critically examines the romantic conception of authorship that pervades copyright doctrine, and the power of this conception to obscure the connection between origination and imitation while individualising the author and commodifying his work. Chapter 3 suggests an alternative version of copyright's author-figure, drawing upon feminist theory to develop a notion of the author as a situated, relational self, and authorship as a dialogic and formative process.

I proceed in the following chapters to push towards copyright's re-imagination in these terms. I explore some of the principal concepts and convictions that have caused traditional copyright theory to misrecognise the nature of the author, the public and the copyright system, and show how a shift in thinking may alter the shape of copyright. Part II of this book challenges the pervasive view that the origin of the copyright interest (in both the moral and legal sense) can be found in the industry or labour of the author. My overarching proposition is that it is a mistake to look solely to the relation between the author and her work as the basis on which to justify the copyright system or to define the scope of the copyright interest. In so doing, we necessarily neglect the social and cultural goals of copyright, and so wrongly augment the scope of the rights conferred under copyright while failing to identify and draw the appropriate limits thereto.

Chapter 4 focuses primarily on the role of labour in defining the moral relation between the author and work by means of which the copyright interest is justified. In particular, it tackles the common conviction, grounded in Lockean theory, that the author as intellectual labourer has a natural right to own the fruits of his labour. Chapter 5 focuses on the role of labour and other elements of authorship in defining the legal relation between author and work – what the author must do to establish a legal right over her work.[7] I examine the doctrine of originality, which provides the defining characteristic of copyrightable expression, and therefore encapsulates many of the dominant misconceptions of modern copyright theory. I suggest that, by re-evaluating the originality threshold and its role in copyright disputes in light of a relational theory of authorship, the central doctrine of copyright law could be realigned with the public policy purposes of the copyright system.

The dialogic theory of authorship advanced in this book emphasises the cumulative nature of cultural creativity. This reveals the flaw inherent in the individualised account of original expression, but it also underscores the importance of downstream, meaning-generating uses of protected materials. To this end, it is essential that copyright leave space for the interactive, dialogic processes of cultural creativity if it is to enhance rather than obstruct relations of communication. As such, Part III focuses on the limits of the protection afforded to copyright owners to allow for the use, transformation and 'appropriation' of protected works as defined by user exceptions, defences and rights.

Chapter 6 takes critical aim at the restrictive fair dealing defence and other exceptions available to users, calling for a large and flexible defence to copyright infringement (even in the face of technical controls) that adequately reflects the dialogic nature of creative processes and the critical role of users in the copyright system. Chapter 7 explores the relationship between copyright protection and freedom of expression, employing relational theory to argue that both copyright and freedom of expression embody the values that we as a society attach to communication and discursive interaction between the members of our community: copyright's legitimacy therefore depends upon its capacity to accommodate and enhance the principles of free expression.

Much of the doctrinal analysis contained in these chapters is conducted in the context of Canadian jurisprudence. Recent developments in Canada, and in particular the Canadian copyright narrative that has emerged from the Supreme Court of Canada over the past decade,[8] make the Canadian context a fertile one in which to develop a far-reaching theory of copyright. Moreover, Canada occupies a unique position in the common law copyright world: it inherited its copyright system from the United Kingdom; it developed its copyright doctrine in the context of a 'mixed' common and civil law system, drawing in part on continental influences; and, with the United States as its only neighbour and largest trading partner, it is consistently reactive to US developments and political pressures.

In the United States, the analysis of copyright theory often starts and ends with the US Constitution and the power of congress under Article 1 to 'promote the Progress of Science and useful Arts, by securing for limited Times to Authors and Inventors the exclusive Right to their respective Writings and Discoveries.'[9] In the US Supreme Court decision of *Eldred v. Ashcroft*,[10] however, the practical force of this clause proved to be far less than many had hoped. Indeed, the US copyright narrative has largely fragmented over recent years into property-based discourse and anti-instrumentalist agendas, as evidenced by the enactment of the Digital Millennium Copyright Act 1998.[11] Meanwhile, in Britain, the copyright narrative has been disrupted, and policy-making largely dominated, by developments at the European Union level. Principled theorising proves difficult in a context where copyright laws are shaped by international obligations that derive from principles foreign to the jurisdiction.[12] Because Canada has lacked a concrete statement of copyright's purpose, and because it is (at least officially) free to shape its copyright law according to its own prerogatives (within the confines of its obligations as a member of the World Trade Organization[13]), the Canadian context offers greater space within which to contemplate the purposes, principles and potential of copyright law in the digital age. For these reasons, the Canadian legal experience affords an interesting and illustrative example from which larger general – indeed universal – lessons can be learned.

The overarching theme of this book is the need to discard notions of natural right, individual entitlement and private property in copyright theory, and to re-imagine copyright in relational terms of communication, community and cultural policy. Throughout the arguments that I have sketched in this introduction lies the unifying proposition: only by regarding copyright from a public interest perspective and recognising the social value of discursive engagement can we appreciate the system's incentivisation of cultural production as a means by which to enhance relations of communication. Furthermore, it is only by understanding the nature of the author-self as socially situated and intrinsically relational that we can appreciate the importance of communication and dialogue in the formation of human identity and community.

Individualising authorship and propertising intellectual expression causes us to miss what it is that matters about cultural creativity; and so it guarantees that we fail to recognise the real rationale behind the copyright system. The re-imagination of copyright is therefore essential if we are to fully comprehend the social goals that justify its existence – and if we are to have any hope of achieving them.

NOTES

1. James Boyle, 'A Politics of Intellectual Property: Environmentalism for the Net?' (1997) 47 Duke L.J. 87 at 87: 'Everyone says that we are moving to an information age. Everyone says that the ownership and control of information is one of the most important forms of power in contemporary society. These ideas are so well-accepted, such clichés, that I can get away with saying them in a *law review article* without footnote support.' The irony of this footnote is not lost on me.
2. *Underwriters' Survey Bureau Ltd v. Massie & Renwick Ltd* (1936) [1937] Ex. C.R. 15 at 20 (Maclean J.), varied [1937] S.C.R. 265 (S.C.C.). Cited in John S. McKeown, *Fox Canadian Law of Copyright and Industrial Designs*, 3rd edn (Scarborough, Ontario: Thomson Canada Ltd, 2000) at 1.
3. *Cf.* Julie E. Cohen, 'Copyright, Commodification, and Culture: Locating the Public Domain' in L. Guibault and P.B. Hugenholtz (eds), *The Future of the Public Domain* (Netherlands: Kluwer Law International, 2006) at 121–66.
4. See e.g. William M. Landes and Richard A. Posner, *The Economic Structure of Intellectual Property Law* (Cambridge, Mass.: The Belknap Press of Harvard University Press, 2003).
5. The first modern copyright statute, the *Statute of Anne 1709*, pronounced its purpose to be 'the *Encouragement of Learning*, by Vesting the Copies of Printed Books in the Authors or Purchasers if such Copies, during the Times therein mentioned.' For interesting discussion regarding the historical beginnings of copyright regulation see: L. Ray Patterson, *Copyright in Historical Perspective* (Nashville: Vanderbilt University Press, 1968); Mark Rose, *Authors and Owners: The Invention of Copyright* (Cambridge, Mass.: Harvard University Press, 1993).
6. Art. 1 §8, cl. 8 of the U.S. Constitution. This empowerment clause explicitly enshrines into the Constitution an instrumentalist account of copyright law.
7. The distinction between the legal and moral relation between author and work is explained by Christian G. Stallberg, 'Towards a New Paradigm in Justifying Copyright: A Universalistic-Transcendental Approach' (2008) 18 Fordham Intell. Prop. Media & Ent. L.J. 333 at 343–4.
8. See Daniel Gervais, 'A Canadian Copyright Narrative' (2008) 21 Intellectual Property Journal 269.
9. US Const., note 6 above.
10. 537 US 186 (2003).

11. Pub. L. No. 105-304, 112 Stat. 2860 (1998). See Gervais, note 8 above at 293–4.
12. A pertinent example is Directive 96/9/EC of the European Parliament and of the Council of 11 March 1996 on the Legal Protection of Databases [1996] O.J. L77/20, art 3.1 ('[D]atabases which, by reason of the selection or arrangement of their contents, constitute the author's own intellectual creation shall be protected as such by copyright'). *Cf.* Sections 3 and 3A of the British Copyright, Designs and Patents Act 1988 (as amended by the Copyright and Rights in Databases Regulations 1997 SI 1997/3032). This replaced the traditional 'labour and skill' threshold with an 'intellectual creation' threshold for copyright in data compilations.
13. Canada is therefore bound by the *Agreement on Trade Related Aspects of Intellectual Property* Marrakesh Agreement Establishing the World Trade Organization, 15 April 1994, Annex 1C, 1869 U.N.T.S. 299, 33 I.L.M. 1197 (1994).

PART I

Copyright and cultural creativity in context

2. Constructing authorship: The underlying philosophy of the copyright model

2.1 INTRODUCTION

The concepts of intellectual property – and the theoretical framework of copyright law in particular – are unmistakably premised upon liberal and neo-liberal assumptions. At the core of copyright's functionality are the concepts of private rights, property, ownership, exclusion and individualism. At the core of copyright's justifications are the concepts of individual entitlement or desert, on one hand, or economic rationality and self-interest on the other. Within this model, authors are individuated, proprietary personalities with a claim to ownership of their intellectual works; these works are the original, stable and propertisable results of authors' independent efforts.[1] Far from a situated, communicative act, the authorial activity presupposed by intellectual property is an individual act that produces a commodifiable thing and, of course, a right against all others in relation to that thing.

My aim, in Part I of this book, is to expose the weaknesses inherent in law's construction of authorship, and to identify the abstractions embraced by copyright's author-figure. Legal doctrine has a self-perpetuating power: the power to naturalise its constructions,[2] and to solidify its abstractions. I will argue that copyright's reduction and individualisation of authorial activity threatens to obscure the communicative function of authorship and to undermine its role in dialogic community. Copyright's construction of authorship, and its focus upon the abstract, individual rights-bearer, therefore threatens to obscure the social purposes of the copyright system and undermine its attempts to encourage cultural creativity.

This chapter examines the romantic conception of authorship that pervades the doctrinal constructs and application of copyright law: a conception that dichotomises origination and imitation while individualising the author and propertising his product. It also explores the post-romantic critiques to which this vision of authorship has been subjected. I will then identify some of the practical and political consequences of the romantic author in the copyright realm, focusing upon its tendency to support broad protection for 'original' authors, while chilling downstream uses and so restricting cultural exchange. In Chapter 3, I will attempt to establish a route towards re-imagining copyright's author figure, employing feminist literary and political theory to explain the notion of the author as a relational self, and the nature of authorship as a communicative and dialogic process. I will suggest that this theory of the author-self can pave the way towards a re-imagined copyright system justified in terms of the social good that resides in communication and cultural exchange of meaning.

2.2 AUTHORSHIP, ORIGINATION AND OBJECTIFICATION

Authorship is the foundation of copyright. It is authorship that brings into existence the copyrightable work, authorship that establishes the copyright interest, and authorship that determines its first owner.[3] Authorship is therefore a 'bedrock principle' of copyright, and yet, contrary to the immutability and solidity that this might suggest, it is 'one of the more elusive concepts in copyright law' [4] (which is full of elusive concepts). Recognising the centrality of the concept of authorship to the operation and application of copyright law reveals the extent to which our copyright model is guided and shaped by our interpretation of this elusive concept. This in turn reveals that an inquiry into the nature, processes and products of authorship affords the opportunity to rethink the shape of copyright protection.

In his seminal essay, 'What is an Author?', Michel Foucault insisted 'it would be worth examining how the author became individualized in a culture like ours . . . and how this fundamental category of "the-man-and-his-work" began.'[5] This challenge has since been taken up by intellectual property scholars, perhaps most notably Martha Woodmansee and Mark Rose, who have produced important texts on the development of the modern concept of authorship in eighteenth century Germany and England respectively.[6]

These examinations reveal the extent to which the modern concept of the author as the sole independent creator of an original work is profoundly ideological and historical. Through a process of contextualisation – locating modern concepts of assumed meaning within the 'worlds of significance' in which these meanings developed – such scholarship has brought attention to 'just how culturally specific and historically contingent such seemingly transparent terms actually are, and how complex the contexts in which they emerged, were contested, and gained legitimacy.'[7] This recent body of academic literature has provided an important route towards the doctrinal reconfiguration of copyright law by anatomising the author and demythologising copyright doctrine. I will explore this route – its justifications and implications – in the discussion that follows. In particular, I hope to show that copyright's current author-figure is both facilitative and symptomatic of its larger ideological framework, and to suggest that this figure/framework limits our ability to comprehend the cultural creativity central to copyright's claims. I will turn my attention, in the following chapter, to the task of reconfiguring copyright's author – retrieving the author from the myths that have defined him. Having set about understanding the past behind the modern conception of authorship, it should become possible to re-imagine its future.[8]

2.2.1 The 'Author'

Present-day copyright law emerged out of commercial struggles amongst interested parties, occurring at a time- and context-specific moment in the process of cultural and economic development.[9] It is against this picture of historical contingency that the connection between the romantic author and property theory becomes most evident. I do not pretend to offer here a comprehensive account of the formation of the modern representation of the author,[10] but it is crucial to recognise that, in spite of its apparent naturalness in the modern age, the modern author is 'a relatively recent invention.'[11] According to Woodmansee, the modern author is the product of the professionalisation of writing that accompanied the growth of public literacy in the eighteenth century. In Germany, writers who were unable to survive on writing alone sought to redefine the nature of writing to ameliorate their (financial) position in society. German theorists, elaborating upon the positions taken by English writers such as Edward Young and William Wordsworth,[12] attempted to dislocate the notion of the writer as a master of rules or a receptacle of sublime inspiration, in favour of the concept of internalised inspiration, or 'original genius.' The writer was thereby transformed into 'a unique individual uniquely responsible for a unique product. That is from a (mere) vehicle of preordained truths . . . the *writer* becomes an *author* (Lat. *auctor*, originator, founder, creator).'[13]

The exaltation of 'original' texts is also a relatively recent phenomenon: the idea of an 'author' as a 'maker' of an 'original' text would have been alien to literary thought in the classical period. Indeed, at this time, copying or imitating the great poets and writers that had gone before was considered to be a worthy objective and, if done successfully, an admirable achievement. Marilyn Randall explains that the eighteenth century saw a 'shift from a poetics of imitation to a valorization of originality', while prior to the eighteenth century 'imitation was the aesthetic norm.'[14] Aspirations of imagination, novelty, creativity and originality were of growing importance in the aesthetics of the Romantic period, which emphasised the individual author and the authority that flows from personal genius and sincere expression. At the heart of the Romantic ideal is the sanctity of individual creativity. The distinction between imitation and originality is therefore intricately tied to the perceived nature of man, such that true authorship represents the essence of human individuality. The human agent, as author, does not copy without sacrificing his authenticity and obscuring his intrinsic worth. From this perspective,

> [a]uthorship retains, in the eighteenth century, both the connotations of authority recast in the form of personal genius and inspiration, and the connotations of authenticity, born of the sincerity of expression of the individual and of the intimate connection between producer and product.[15]

In the nineteenth century, this concept of individual authorship was compounded by what Randall terms the 'great author' phenomenon. According to Randall, originality is the mark of an individual's genius and a greatness particular to him. Consequently, imitation signifies inferior or failed authorship, presumably by a lesser person. A great author is a 'great soul emitting inspired and universal truths',[16] while lesser humans can merely follow suit by learning, imitating and borrowing. The originator has a personal and moral claim to a right that is not shared by the imitator, and indeed, the imitator threatens to undermine the originator's claim: imitation is thus the 'scourge' of great literature.[17]

The valorisation of the individual author and his originality, and the resulting denigration of imitation that is captured in this description of nineteenth-century authorship, is axiomatic in modern copyright law. Copyright's subject is the author-as-originator. The 'author' is defined by, and rewarded because of, the 'originality' of his creation, with the essence of copyright's standard of originality being independent production. And, of course, the unworthy imitator is copyright's infringer.

It is true that copyright does not concern itself with questions of genius, quality or even creativity in the everyday sense of that word: it attaches to the most mundane of works; it resists inquiry into the objective value of the author's contribution; and it offers protection to works that demonstrate either the merest spark of creative effort, or in some cases, none at all. While these features of the modern copyright system would seem to imply on their face that copyright's author is in fact very far from the individual genius postulated in Romantic rhetoric, this apparent disparity simply reflects a divergence between copyright's reality and its guiding rationale.

In reality, the copyright system does not demand that the 'author' be the equivalent of the 'great man' eruditely writing in his garret, nor does it ask that the 'original' work represent his novel or brilliant musings.

Equally, the system does not deny the possibility of some copying and derivative use by authors and others. Indeed, as Jessica Litman has argued, the copyright fiction of 'original' authorship is sustainable precisely because copyright law concedes the concept of a public domain upon which authors are free to draw.[18] Litman's point is subtle but critical: on its surface, copyright law seems to acknowledge the need for some derivative use of protected works, but it does so only to the extent necessary to ensure a workable system while allowing the continuation of the myths and assumptions upon which that system operates. What is argued, then, is that these ideals of individual origination have nevertheless informed our sense of the author's right, and so have become engrained in the underlying rationale of the copyright system. This, in turn, defines the way in which that system works.

Let us return to the proposition that copyright's subject is the author-as-originator: irrespective of whether copyright doctrine requires creativity, skill or merely labour, the copyrightable work must be found to 'originate' from the author, and must not be copied from any other source. Only those elements of the downstream author's work that are said to be original to her in this sense shall fall within the monopoly that copyright provides. While none of these requirements in fact demands a demonstration of genuinely *de novo* origination, once a work is found to be 'original', the difference between reality and rhetoric is easily forgotten. We will see, in Part II, that the many ways in which the myths of authorship have become entwined with interpretations of copyright's originality doctrine.

And what of the second proposition – that the unworthy imitator is copyright's infringer? While copyright law permits insubstantial copying, the substantiality of the taking is determined not with reference to the totality of the downstream work, but instead with reference to the original protected work: no infringer can avoid liability by pointing to what she has created in addition to what she has copied. While the law permits the taking of 'ideas', the distinction between ideas and expression is a legal fiction, the meaning and effect of which is determined by the perceived equities of a particular case (as informed by a particular vision of author and authorship).[19] Even if we accept the principle at face value, it does not create the kind of room that is needed within the copyright system for creative engagement with protected works. Although ideas are an important vehicle for cultural exchange and downstream development, expression is also an indispensable component of the knowledge communicated through a protected work: the reutilisation of expression is as central to downstream users as is the sharing of ideas. And while even substantial copying of expression may be permitted in some circumstances, such circumstances are unduly limited, and defences for *prima facie* infringements are rarely successful. In Part III, I will explore in detail some of the limits imposed upon downstream expression in the name of the original authors' rights.

With these considerations in mind, it is suggested that the copyright system is built around an essentially moral divide between original (independent) authorship and downstream (derivative) expression. However, the moral divide between author and copier, between origination and imitation, is as untenable in today's 'post-modernity' as it was in the literary aesthetics of pre-Romantic eras. It captures and hypostasises a moment in the evolution of authorship; and that moment has passed.

In 1968, Roland Barthes famously declared the death of the author.[20] This pronouncement did not signal the death of the author concept *per se*, but rather the demise of its Romantic and post-Romantic conceptualisation. In repudiating this instantiation of the author-figure, post-structuralist literary theory undermined the significance of the 'biographical author-person' and 'the confidence placed in individual agency and control over discourse that involves, inevitably, a belief in the possibility of creative originality.'[21] The contemporary demystification of authorship insists upon the practical impossibility of independent creation and declares that all texts are necessarily reproductions of other texts: it is in the nature of expression and cultural development that the new builds upon the old. Regarded in this light, the act of writing involves not origination, but rather translation and recombination of 'raw material' taken from previously existing texts.[22] In Jessica Litman's words, authorship is essentially 'a process of adapting, transforming, and recombining what is already "out there" in some other form.'[23] What we hail as 'creativity' is really the result of 'a combination of absorption, astigmatism, and amnesia.'[24] In Barthes' vision, '[t]he text is a tissue of quotations drawn from the innumerable centres of culture. . . . [T]he writer can only imitate a gesture that is always anterior, never original. His only power is to mix writings, to counter the ones with the others, in such a way as never to rest on any one of them.'[25] If this is the essence of the creative process, the label of 'originality' does little more than legitimise (and valorise) texts that draw on a broad range of anonymous textual material over texts that draw only on one or a few identifiable sources.[26] This may appear to be an arbitrary basis upon which to determine a text's worth, but it is the gold standard in a copyright system that clings to the vision of the author as *creator ex nihilo*.

Upon such reasoning, it has become a fairly common feature of critical copyright scholarship to assert that the Romantic aesthetic is responsible for the shape of copyright law, and its conception of authorship in particular.[27] The extent to which modern copyright is committed to a Romantic ideology remains a subject for discussion,[28] but there is little doubt that copyright law reinforces an exclusionary ideal of the individual author that reflects a particular ideology and a particular locus in history. While copyright readily extends protection to the banal and commonplace – works that are undoubtedly far from the level of romantic aspiration – the label of 'author' and its concomitant romanticisation ensure that these uninspired works are nevertheless over-protected, and that such 'original authorship' is disproportionately valued against excluded forms of cultural expression. Indeed, the less copyright's subject-matter looks like the creation of a Romantic author, the more powerful is the role of Romantic ideology in maintaining the moral divide between author and copier.

It should be evident that there is nothing natural or necessary about the particular conception of authorship embraced by our copyright model. With this acknowledgement comes the space to ask about the appropriate conception of authorship for the purposes of copyright, and to inquire into the kinds of cultural creativity and communicative activity that the current concept excludes (or even precludes). Randall defines authorship as 'the attribution of a particular set of authorial functions to an agent of discourse.'[29] If this is the transhistorical significance of authorship, then the label of author performs a function; it does not state a fact. It must be asked, then, what function does copyright's version of authorship perform?

2.2.2 Propertisation and the Concept of the 'Work'

With the transformation from inspired imitator to original creator complete, it seems clear that 'the writer's claim to a property interest, particularly one based on natural rights, becomes more credible.'[30] As Randall notes, 'the theme of intellectual production as property is never very far from the concerns of those involved with defending literary ethics and aesthetics.'[31] While the triumvirate of authority, authenticity and originality make up the essential elements of authorship, a crucial fourth element is that of ownership.[32] The enduring relationship between authorship and ownership suggests a link to be explored between the emergence of the modern author-figure and the acceptance of proprietorship in the literary realm.

The valorisation of original genius lent weight to claims by 'authors' to property in their writings. Indeed, in the realm of law the emergent concept of author-genius was strategically developed to further commercial goals, lending its ideological power to economic self-interest:

> Although the concept of authorship was introduced into English law for the functional purpose of protecting the interests of booksellers . . ., the term took on a life of its own as individualistic notions of creativity, originality, and inspiration were poured into it. Authorship became an ideology . . .. As the authorship construct accumulated force and circumstantiality, the strategic manner in which the construct had been deployed was effaced.[33]

By the time that 'authorship' was adopted into the vocabulary of copyright law, the word 'author' had already acquired connotations of power or 'authority'. As the institution of copyright emerged in the eighteenth century, it thrived on the general philosophical discourse of the time, wherein concepts of 'author' and 'control' were associated with the 'individual' and 'property', and aspects of the 'vast complex of interdependent factors denoted by the term individualism.'[34] As Grantland Rice has argued, what was seen to be at stake in the literary-property debates of the time was no less than the underpinnings of liberal thought, or what C.B. Macpherson has denoted 'possessive individualism':[35] in other words, 'the enlightenment project of freeing the individual from dependence predicated on the possession of property.'[36] Thus, the theme of Lockean and Hobbesian possessive individualism that dominated social thought ensured that the word 'author' was invested with particular weight.

Foucault described the emergence of this notion of 'author' as 'the privileged moment of *individualization* in the history of ideas, knowledge, literature, philosophy and the sciences.'[37] Through this process of individualisation, the 'author' was said to acquire 'a role quite characteristic of our era of industrial and bourgeois society, of individualism and private property.'[38] The individuality and 'originality' of authorship in its modern form therefore established a simple route towards individual ownership and the propertisation of creative achievement. The elevation of the 'author' achieved through the notion of original genius legitimated writers' claims to property in their writings, allowing a shift in the author's role towards 'that of a professional trading in a new commodity.'[39] As Rosemary Coombe has aptly observed, this modern and highly individuated concept of 'authorship' possesses an 'alchemical power to transfer anything it can be made to adhere to into *property*, absolutely defined.'[40]

The individualisation of the author is both complimented and compounded by the propertisation of the author's product, and so the modern author, as an originator, became a proprietor, and his product became a 'special kind of commodity'.[41] Ownership claims flowed from the trope of origination as appropriation. This connection between the Romantic persona of the author-as-originator and the proprietary interest accorded to him in his 'work' is a major component of the 'the solid and fundamental unit of the author and the work';[42] it is the conceptual unit around which copyright is built.

Having complicated the operative assumptions of copyright's authorship concept, it is appropriate to reconsider the concept of the author's *product*: the original 'work' that is the result of authorship, so defined. The notion of a 'work' currently enshrined in copyright law is no more inevitable than that of the 'author', and has similarly been the subject of doctrinal reification or the 'naturalising' tendency of law. 'Work', as a term of art in modern copyright law, can be understood to represent the commodified version of a text produced by the Romantic figure of the professional 'author'. Put another way, the term 'work' solidifies the literary property notion, embracing the idea of creative production as an independent, identifiable and alienable object of personal property; the author's work is an object of appropriation.

Copyright dogma thus depicts the 'work' as an autonomous object with immutable characteristics and a fixed textual meaning: an abstraction that clearly facilitates its propertisation as an essential adjunct to the individualisation of the 'work's' 'author'. The idea of the 'work' as a discrete or free-standing entity differs greatly from the understanding of 'text' that existed from the classical period through the Renaissance, when, as Rose explains, 'the dominant conception of literature was rhetorical. A text was conceived less an object than as an intentional act, a way of doing something, of accomplishing some end such as "teaching and delighting".'[43]

From the late seventeenth century to the nineteenth century and the Romantic period, literary creations evolved into property and commodity; the 'text' became a 'work', an object of knowledge and meaning rather than a behavioural process of action and reaction.[44] The propertisation of literary creativity demanded this vision of the text as a stable object capable of commodification; a vision that paired easily with the Romantic understanding of originality and author-genius. Indeed, our continued attachment to the notion of the sole author and the solitary genius, in spite of the disaggregationist impulse of our post-modern age, could be regarded as a testament to the powerful vision of text as just another form of private property in our capitalist society.[45] In other words, our impulse to embrace text in the realm of private property can explain our persistent commitment to the individualised author-figure who legitimises the propertisation of text (and not merely vice versa).

Rice describes the debates in nineteenth century America over the corporeality of the literary product as reflective of 'the shift in legal thinking from the political accounts of the *activity* of authorship to economic formulations of the *materiality* of authorship.'[46] According to Rice, the efforts of lobbyists to recast authorial activity as the creation of material capable of ownership and appropriation caused the debate over copyright to be 'preoccupied with the object – rather than on the act of – public writing', with the result that it 'collapsed the intentional and communicative aspects of publication into an understanding of authorship that was no different than any other productive activity.'[47] When the results of authorship are cast as a stable, almost corporeal entity, the communicative and textual nature of the work is obscured. In the construction of the copyrightable work, then, the element of communication is sacrificed to commodification, and speech is mischaracterised as property (in the material and not just the relational sense).

In the latter half of the twentieth century, accompanying the demise of the modern author-figure, the concept of the static literary work was increasingly questioned through the lens of structuralist and post-structuralist thought. Structuralist thought considered the 'work' to be located within a broader context than that of a freestanding object with internalised significance, as a system of signs and conventions that acquire meaning only through the process of assimilation by the reader. Post-structuralist critique went further still, questioning the possibility of a fixed identity or meaning for any text, and understanding the reader and reading as determinative of a text whose identity must therefore be in a constant state of flux.[48] In 1979, Barthes announced the end of the literary 'work' as a fixed object of stable meaning to be passively consumed. In its place he proclaimed the literary 'text', an entity situated in language and suspended in a continual state of production in which readers are authorial collaborators, interpretation is 'intertextual', and meanings are fluid and infinite.[49] The boundaries between the 'author' and the reader are thereby disintegrated as the reader becomes 'an overt collaborator in an unending process of reading and writing . . . returning us to something like the expressly collaborative milieu of the Middle Ages and the Renaissance with which we began.'[50]

The poststructuralist challenge to the consensus generally surrounding copyright's characterisation of the 'work' highlights some critical fault-lines in the assumptions of our copyright model. As the concept of the freestanding 'work' is undermined by claims of 'inter-textuality' and 'audience recoding', copyright's 'thingification' of the text becomes increasingly apparent and problematic. Again, by problematising the object of copyright we can create an interpretative space within which to rethink the nature of the 'copyrightable work'.[51] Learning from the post-structuralist critique, we might begin this process by relinquishing the notion of the 'work' as a noun (a static object) and reconceptualising 'work' as a verb (a communicative activity).

2.3 THE PRACTICAL AND POLITICAL CONSEQUENCES FOR COPYRIGHT

Post-structuralism directly challenges many of the ideas central to the current system of copyright by throwing into confusion the copyright trinity of 'originality', the 'author' and the 'work'. As a result of interlocking dependencies, a challenge to any one of these concepts disrupts the delicate balance. To doubt any one, then, is to doubt all three; to dissolve one is to destabilise the foundations of modern copyright law. It is possible, however, to disaggregate the current meaning of these concepts without effecting the disintegration of the copyright system. To achieve this requires that we re-evaluate the foundations and justifications of copyright as a whole, and re-imagine the concepts around which modern copyright law is built. However, before we set about this task, it is important to understand the political and practical implications of the current theoretical model. While the issues addressed thus far may appear unduly abstract, they have very real consequences for the interpretation, application, and operation of copyright law.

2.3.1 The Author Function at Work

According to Mark Rose, '[m]uch of the notorious difficulty of applying copyright doctrine to concrete cases can be related to the persistence of the discourse of original genius and to the problems inherent in the reifications of author and work.'[52] Although the aesthetic theory surrounding the emergence of the Romantic author-figure may sound distinctly antiquated, I have suggested that the fetishisation of the individual and original author is still very much alive in our current construction of copyright and the policies that inform its development.

For example, as evolving technologies have presented new challenges for intellectual property policy, the authorship concept has been used to justify the extension of copyright's subject matter and the scope of the protection it affords. From early cases concerning the copyrightability of photographs[53] to controversies over the protection of computer software,[54] the spectre of Romantic authorship has been invoked and manipulated to support the claims of those who stood to benefit from the monopoly rights that copyright could confer. In recent debates over peer-to-peer technologies, the venerated author-figure has been reinvigorated by the appeals of recording industry stakeholders whose 'public education' and lobbying strategies point to the noble and deserving artist as a reason to stamp out online file sharing.[55] In the case of the computer software debate, appeals to authorship tended to obscure the actual practical and policy concerns posed by the protection of software for this burgeoning industry, and ultimately supported the interests of the large corporate bodies whose products (and profits) depended upon this putative authorship.[56] In the file-sharing debates, it is similarly the corporate actors who stand to benefit most from the regulation and commercialisation of music downloading.[57] The irony, of course, lies in the extent to which the Romantic notion of 'authorship' has served the commercial interests of publishers, employers and distributors, often at the expense of the people whose role in the 'creative' process was most similar to that of the Romantic author figure. Indeed, the manipulation of the author concept has achieved its most paradoxical result in the United States, in the contexts of works made for hire, where the claims of employers to direct ownership over the products of their employees have been rationalised in terms of a bizarre inversion of the 'authorship' concept.[58]

The persuasive force of Romantic authorship makes this an extremely powerful strategy for obtaining and strengthening copyright protection. As such, its function in copyright discourse has altered very little since the occasion of its first deployment in the eighteenth century literary-property debates, where it was an effective ideological instrument used to cloak the economic interests of the booksellers – 'a stalking horse for economic interests that were (as a tactical matter) better concealed than revealed.'[59] Indeed, as processes of creative production have come to resemble less and less the vision of creativity embodied in the Romantic author concept, the ideological function of 'authorship' has only grown correspondingly.

The persistent attachment to the vision of authorship as an independent process of original creation has significant implications for copyright policy. The animating presence of this vision in the legal subconscious can explain, at least in part, the sheer scope given to the rights of copyright owners, and the importance (moral, legal and cultural) accorded to them.[60] It supports calls for wide protection and generates complacency around the expanding domain of intellectual property and the corporate ownership that dominates the intellectual realm.

2.3.2 Authors and Imitators

Boyle argues that the myth of the Romantic author causes us to value some forms of 'creation' over others, and to underestimate the importance of external sources in the 'creative' process while overemphasising the claims of the identified 'author'.[61] Specifically, this conception of individuated authorship privileges the person identified as the 'original author' to the detriment of 'second generation' authors making downstream uses of the original work.

By way of example, a clear case of this primary-author bias can be found in the area of 'appropriation art',[62] which has its foundation in the post-modern aesthetic and anti-proprietary ethics. By definition, appropriation art challenges 'the viewer's ability to see beyond the link between notions of originality and art's commodity status.'[63] Predictably, because appropriation in the production of new artistic works is *prima facie* infringement in the eyes of copyright law, artistic appropriation practices have clashed with a copyright regime largely incapable of accommodating the expressive use of reproduced images:

> [T]he incorporation of recognizable visual images into new works of art . . . gives contemporary art its unique and irreverent flair. To the law, appropriation is simple copyright infringement, for which only minor infringements are allowed through the doctrine of fair use. Appropriationists have tried to avoid liability by invoking the defence of fair use, to little avail. The philosophical underpinnings of post-Modernism and intellectual property are fundamentally at odds.[64]

This would explain the infamous Second Circuit ruling in the US case of *Rogers v. Koons*.[65] The artist, Jeff Koons, mounted his *Banality* show in which appeared the sculpture known as *String of Puppies*, depicting a couple holding a string of (bright blue) German shepherd dogs. The large, three-dimensional sculpture was based upon a postcard reproduction of a black and white photograph taken by Art Rogers, but one that undermined the 'sentimental cuddliness' of the original and replaced it with a 'tacky, slightly disturbing and subtly hilarious image'.[66] Koons argued that the sculpture was a satire of society at large, and belonged to an artistic tradition that critiqued modern consumer culture through the incorporation of objects and media images drawn from contemporary, mass-produced culture. Nonetheless, Rogers was successful in his copyright infringement suit against Koons, whose work was regarded by the court to be intentionally exploitative, lacking in parodic value and beyond the scope of fair use.[67] The decision has been criticized as 'rife with ominous implications for the practice of artistic appropriation',[68] and the court has been criticized for basing its decision upon 'its distaste for Koons and his art [rather] than . . . any sound legal principle'.[69]

Rogers v. Koons offers a concrete example of the troublesome nature of author-based reasoning.[70] According to Keith Aoki, the court's conclusion resulted from the polarisation of the parties in light of a particular vision of worthy authorship: the pure artist was contrasted with the conniving art-world rook; the plaintiff's solo production was contrasted with the defendant's team of skilled labourers; and photo-from-life was contrasted with parodic treatment of pre-existing cultural material.[71] These polarisations converged to undermine the cultural and artistic contribution made by Koons' product. The court was unable to regard Rogers' work as a legitimate source of others' creativity because Rogers was so clearly an author, and his photograph so clearly an original copyrightable work. Similarly, it was unable to regard Koons as an author or creator of meaning because he failed to fit the template of an original author who creates independently. Viewed from this perspective, the case reveals 'copyright's bias toward rewarding clearly demarcated individual authorship with property rights enforceable against later deviant authors who attempt to trespass without "author-isation" on those rights.'[72]

The problem here is that the individual authorship trope can occlude discussion of the social, educational or cultural value of downstream or derivative uses of protected works. Because copyright's concept of the work resides in independent production, the work of a second-generation producer cannot compete equally as a 'work' of social value that merits protection; the social importance or the cultural value of the second text barely comes within the cognizance of the law. Add to this the subconscious and rhetorical impact of copyright's author construct: the idealisation of the author-originator entails the corresponding denigration of the author-user. Rather than regarding downstream users as authors who use prior texts to make new and important contributions to social dialogue, these authors are reduced to copiers from whom genuine authors must be protected. As a result of its commitment to fictional notions of 'creation' and 'creator', copyright fails to adequately appreciate alternative methods or actors. When they fall on the wrong side of the creator–imitator dichotomy, they are infringers, not worthy authors.

In contemporary culture there are many forms of art, music and intellectual endeavour that draw directly, consciously and explicitly from pre-existing and protected works (a practice that differs from other traditional forms of cultural 'creativity' only in the sense that such derivation is typically indirect, unconscious or implicit). An obvious example is digital sampling in rap and hip-hop music.[73] Although musical borrowing has a long history in the jazz and blues tradition, new technologies such as the digital sampler and online file sharing have expanded the creative possibilities of re-mixing pre-existing works and cultural artefacts. As Kembrew McLeod notes, the writings of Foucault and Barthes in a sense foreshadowed the creative realities of the digital age:

> [T]oday's young adults have been brought up reading and playing with fragmented, hyperlinked texts and images. The manner in which [they] use the Internet and editing software has severely damaged the myth of the individual genius author, for it gives them the tools to freely collage image, music, and text.

The controversy surrounding the *Grey Album* by underground hip-hop artist Danger Mouse, which combined instrumental fragments from the Beatles' White Album with *a cappella* rap vocals by Jay-Z, reflects this new reality.[74]

Network and digital technologies have, of course, brought with them innumerable challenges to the assumptions on which the traditional copyright system was built. For our purposes, however, perhaps the most significant of these is the challenge to the dichotomy between author and user – the shift from passive consumption to active engagement, which characterises 'use' of intellectual products in the digital age. It is crucial to understand that even as downstream author-users consume and re-present existing images and text, they are engaged in their own act of meaning making.[75] In a process of cultural dialogue, this re-presentation is a response to what has already been said: appropriation is therefore a technique in critical discourse. Indeed, the very act of appropriation can be politically symbolic to the extent that it openly resists proprietary structures and 'manifests a rejection of private property in favour of a more communitarian conception of society.'[76] If the communicative function of authorship was not lost beneath the commodified object of copyright, the significance of appropriation as communication would be evident, and the value of its contribution to cultural dialogue could be appreciated.

However, this is a message that copyright in its current form seems unable to absorb without thereby signalling its own demise. With respect to the legal commentators who critique *Koons*, Marilyn Randall insists:

> 'There is an unwitting irony in the suggestion that the institution specifically charged with the regulation of private-property rights according to financial incentives, should embrace a critique of those very rights and incentives to the point of "legalizing" those infractions that it is constituted to control.'[77]

The apparent irony dissipates, however, if we replace the idea of copyright as the regulation of private property rights with the idea of copyright as vehicle to encourage the creation of meaning and widespread engagement in social discourse. From this perspective the real unwitting irony would be that an institution entrusted with this public purpose should foreclose the very meaning-making it is supposed to encourage. If copyright cannot reflect the realities of cultural creation, then cultural creation may be forced to reflect the realities of copyright, to the detriment of us all.[78]

2.4 INTERIM CONCLUSIONS ON COPYRIGHT'S AUTHORSHIP CONSTRUCT

Our copyright regime is presently 'in the thrall of an idea [of authorship] that is taken as truth where it should be questioned as dogma.'[79] This chapter has suggested the need for a radical demystification of the 'work' concept and the notions of 'originality' and the 'author' that dominate copyright rhetoric but prove inhospitable to the public purposes of the copyright system. The societal function of copyright is to encourage participation in our cultural dialogue. Where the author is cast as a worthy producer of something from nothing, and the work is regarded as an owned object of fixed meaning, the dialogic and communicative nature of cultural creativity is hidden from view. The result is a copyright regime which propertises and over-protects the works of some authors while dismissing others as copiers and trespassers; which encourages some kinds of creativity while condemning others as unlawful appropriation; which values so-called original contributions but silences responses in the cultural conversation. Rather than creating an environment for communication and facilitating an exchange of meaning, the system creates a marketplace for intellectual products and rules for the exchange of commodities. By recognising these central tenets of copyright doctrine – authorship, originality and the work – as politically, socially and legally constructed metaphors lacking any essential meaning, it may be possible to reconsider their role and substance in a way that allows them to better serve their function in the furtherance of copyright's public purposes.

NOTES

1. Grantland S. Rice, *The Transformation of Authorship in America* (Chicago: University of Chicago Press, 1997) at 76 [Rice, *The Transformation of Authorship*].
2. Ibid. at 73.
3. E.g. s 13(1) of Canada's Copyright Act, R.S.C. 1985, c. C-42 [the Copyright Act] reads: 'Subject to this Act, the author of a work shall be the first owner of the copyright therein.' The Act provides no definition of 'the author'.
4. Alan L. Durham, 'The Random Muse: Authorship and Indeterminacy' (2002) 44 Wm and Mary L. Rev. 569 at 571, making reference to *Feist Publications, Inc. v. Rural Telephone Service Co.*, 499 U.S. 340 (1991) at 347 (quoting *Miller v. Universal Studios, Inc.*, 650 F.2d 1365, 1368 (5th Cir. 1981)) [Durham, 'The Random Muse'].
5. Michel Foucault, 'What is an Author?' in Paul Rabinow (ed.), *The Foucault Reader* (New York: Pantheon Books, 1984) at 101.

6. See Martha Woodmansee, 'The Genius and the Copyright: Economic and Legal Conditions of the Emergence of the "Author"' (1984) 17 *Eighteenth-Century Studies* 425 [Woodmansee, 'Genius and the Copyright']; Martha Woodmansee, *The Author, Art and the Market: Rereading the History of Aesthetics* (New York: Columbia University Press, 1994); Martha Woodmansee and Peter Jaszi (eds), *The Construction of Authorship: Textual Appropriation in Law and Literature* (London: Duke University Press, 1994), also published in (1992) 10 Cardozo Arts & Ent. L.J. 277; Mark Rose, *Authors and Owners: The Invention of Copyright* (Cambridge, MA: Harvard University Press, 1993) [Rose, *Authors and Owners*]; Mark Rose, 'The Author as Proprietor: *Donaldson v Becket* and the Genealogy of Modern Authorship' (1988) 23 *Representations* 51 [Rose, 'Author as Proprietor']; Mark Rose, 'The Author in Court: *Pope v Curl* (1741)' (1992) 21 *Cultural Critique* 197. See also Molly Nesbitt, 'What Was an Author?' (1987) 229 *Yale French Studies* 73; Carla Hesse, 'Enlightenment Epistemology and the Laws of Authorship in Revolutionary France, 1777–1793' (1990) 30 *Representations* 109 [Hesse, 'Enlightenment Epistemology'].
7. Rosemary Coombe, 'Challenging Paternity: Histories of Copyright' (1994) 6 Yale J.L. & Human. 397 at 398 [Coombe, 'Challenging Paternity']. See also Rosemary Coombe, 'The Properties of Culture and the Politics of Possessing Identity: Native Claims in the Cultural Appropriation Controversy' (1993) 6 Can. L.J. & Jurisprudence 249 at 285.
8. Peter Jaszi, 'On the Author Effect: Contemporary Copyright and Collective Creativity' (1991) 10 Cardozo Arts & Ent. L.J. 293 at 293 [Jaszi, 'Author Effect'].
9. See L. Ray Patterson, *Copyright in Historical Perspective* (Nashville: Vanderbuilt University Press, 1968).
10. For an excellent examination of the historical and ideological development of the idea of authorship, see Marilyn Randall, *Pragmatic Plagiarism: Authorship, Profit and Power* (Toronto: University of Toronto Press, 2001) [Randall, *Pragmatic Plagiarism*].
11. Woodmansee, 'Genius and the Copyright', note 6 above at 426.
12. See Edward Young, 'Conjectures on Original Composition' in Edmund D. Jones (ed.), *English Critical Essays: Sixteenth, Seventieth and Eighteenth Centuries* (London: Oxford University Press, 1975) at 274; cited in Woodmansee, 'Genius and the Copyright', note 6 above at 446. See also William Wordsworth 'Essay, Supplementary to the Preface', in Paul M Zall (ed.), *Literary Criticism of William Wordsworth* (Lincoln: Univ. of Nebraska Press, 1966) at 182; cited in Rose, *Authors and Owners*, note 6 above at 110.
13. Woodmansee, 'Genius and the Copyright', note 6 above at 429.
14. Randall, *Pragmatic Plagiarism*, note 10 above at 47, 72.
15. Ibid. at 51.
16. Ibid. at 54.
17. According to Pierre Larousse, *Grand dictionnaire universel du 19ème siècle.* (Paris: Administration du Grand dictionnaire universel, 1866): it is 'the most fertile source of literature' which is 'also its scourge' ['la source la plus féconde de la littérature' which 'en est aussi le fléau']; cited in, and trans. by, Randall, *Pragmatic Plagiarism*, note 13 above at 51.
18. Litman, 'The Public Domain' (1990) 39 Emory L.J. 965.
19. 'Nobody has ever been able to fix that boundary, and nobody ever can.' *Nichols v. Universal Pictures Corp. et al.*, 45 F.2d 119 (2d Cir. 1930), L. Hand J. See also, Allen Rosen, 'Reconsidering the Idea/Expression Dichotomy' (1992) 26 U.B.C. L. Rev. 263; Abraham Drassinower, 'A Rights-Based View of the Idea/Expression Dichotomy in Copyright Law' (2003) 16 Can. J.L. & Jur. 3.
20. Roland Barthes, 'The Death of the Author'(1968) in *Image, Music, Text* (New York: Hill & Wang, 1997).
21. Randall, *Pragmatic Plagiarism*, note 10 above at 24.
22. See Robert H. Rotstein, 'Beyond Metaphor: Copyright Infringement and the Fiction of the Work' (1992/93) 68 Chicago-Kent L. Rev. 725 [Rotstein, 'Beyond Metaphor']; Durham, 'Copyright and Information Theory', note 4 above.

23. Litman, note 18 above at 967.
24. Ibid. at 1011.
25. Barthes, 'The Death of the Author', note 20 above at 137.
26. Rotstein, note 22 above at 757.
27. This line of argument has been most famously pursued by James Boyle. See e.g. James Boyle, *Shamans, Software and Spleens: Law and the Construction of the Information Society* (Cambridge, Mass.: Harvard University Press, 1996) [Boyle, *Shamans, Software and Spleens*], and James Boyle, 'The Search for an Author: Shakespeare and the Framers' (1988) 37 Am. U.L. Rev. 617 [Boyle, 'The Search for an Author']. See also Peter Jaszi, 'Towards a Theory of Copyright: The Metamorphoses of "Authorship"' (1991) 2 Duke L.J. 455 [Jaszi, 'Towards a Theory of Copyright'].
28. See e.g. Anne Barron, 'Copyright Law and the Claims of Art' (2002) 4 I.P.Q. 368.
29. Randall, *Pragmatic Plagiarism*, note 10 above at 58.
30. Durham, 'The Random Muse', note 4 above at 615.
31. Randall, *Pragmatic Plagiarism*, note 10 above at 71.
32. Ibid. at 28.
33. Jaszi, 'Toward a Theory of Copyright', note 27 above at 470–1.
34. Ian Watt, *The Rise of the Novel: Studies in Defoe, Richardson and Fielding* (Berkley: University of California Press, 1957) at 60, cited in Jaszi, 'Towards a Theory of Copyright', note 27 above at 469.
35. C.B. Macpherson, *The Political Theory of Possessive Individualism: Hobbes to Locke* (Oxford: Oxford University Press, 1962).
36. Rice, *The Transformation of Authorship*, note 1 above at 89.
37. Foucault, 'What Is an Author?', note 5 above at 101.
38. Ibid. at 119.
39. Rosemary Coombe, 'Challenging Paternity', note 7 above at 405.
40. Rosemary Coombe, 'Authorial Cartographies: Mapping Proprietary Borders in a Less-Then-Brave-New-World' (1996) 48 Stan. L. Rev. 1357 at 1358, discussing Keith Aoki, '(Intellectual) Property and Sovereignty: Notes Toward a Cultural Geography of Authorship' (1996) 48 Stan. L. Rev. 1293.
41. Rose, *Authors and Owners*, note 6 above at 1.
42. Foucault, 'What is an Author?', note 5 above at 101.
43. Rose, 'Author as Proprietor', note 6 above at 63.
44. Rotstein, 'Beyond Metaphor', note 22 above at 33–5.
45. See Holly A. Laird, *Woman Coauthors* (Chicago: University of Illinois Press, 2000) at 2.
46. Rice, *The Transformation of Authorship*, note 1 above at 91.
47. Ibid. at 91–2.
48. Rotstein, 'Beyond Metaphor', note 22 above at 35–6. See generally on the postmodernist critique of modernism, Stephen Connor, *Postmodernist Culture*, 2nd edn (Oxford: Blackwell, 1997).
49. Roland Barthes, 'From Work to Text' in Josué V. Harari (ed.), *Textual Strategies: Perspectives in Post-Structuralist Criticism* (Ithaca: Cornell University Press, 1979) at 73–81.
50. Martha Woodmansee, 'On the Author Effect: Recovering Collectivity' (1991–92) 10 Cardozo Arts & Ent. L.J. 279 at 290.
51. For an interesting discussion of how a copyright system could incorporate this radically deconstructed concept of the 'work', see Rotstein, 'Beyond Metaphor', note 22 above at 39 *et seq*. *Cf.* Keith Aoki, 'Adrift in the Intertext: Authorship and "Recoding" Rights – Comment on Robert H. Rotstein, "Beyond Metaphor: Copyright Infringement and the Fiction of the Work"' (1993) 68 Chicago-Kent L.R. 805 [Aoki, 'Adrift in the Intertext'].
52. Rose, *Authors and Owners*, note 6 above at 141.
53. See e.g. Nottage v. Jackson (1883) 11 Q.B. 627 at 635 (Cotton L.J.): '"[A]uthor" involves originating, making, producing, as the inventive or master-mind, the thing which is to be protected.' See also Ibid. at 637 (Bowen L.J.): '[T]he true definition of

"author" . . . was the man who really represents or creates, or gives effect to the idea or fancy or imagination.' See also, Burrow-Giles Lithographic Co. v. Sarony (1884), 111 U.S. 53 at 54–5, allowing copyright in a photograph: '[T]he plaintiff made [the picture] entirely from his own original mental conception. . . . [F]rom [the] disposition, arrangement, or representation, made entirely by the plaintiff, he produced the picture in suit.'

54. See e.g. *Whelan Assocs., Inc. v. Jaslow Dental Laboratory, Inc.*, 797 F.2d 1222 (3d Cir. 1986), cert. denied, 479 U.D. 1031 (1987) at 1248, holding that copyright could extend to a computer program's 'structure, sequence and organisation'. Protection for computer programs is often justified by means of a comparison between the programmer and the literary 'author'. See e.g. Anthony L. Clapes, Patrick Lynch and Mark R. Steinberg, 'Silicon Epics and Binary Bards: Determining the Proper Scope of Protection for Computer Programs' (1987) 34 UCLA L. Rev. 1493 at 1510–45. (Cited by Jaszi, 'Towards a Theory of Copyright', note 27 above at 463, n. 23).
55. The website of the Recording Industry Association of America describes 'copyright' in the following terms: 'To all creative artists – poets, painters, novelists, dancers, directors, actors, musicians, singers, and songwriters – the term matters dearly. . . . It is a vital right, and over the centuries artists, such as John Milton, William Hogarth, Mark Twain, and Charles Dickens, have fought to preserve that right.'; see Karl Fogel, 'The Promise of a Post-Copyright World', available at: http://www.immagic.com/eLibrary/ARCHIVES/GENERAL/GENREF/C051019F.pdf (accessed 2 February 2011).
56. See Pamela Samuelson, 'Creating a New Kind of Intellectual Property: Applying the Lessons of the Chip Law to Computer Programs' (1985) 70 Minn. L. Rev. 471.
57. See David Nelson, 'Free the Music: Rethinking the Role of Copyright in an Age of Digital Distribution' (2005) 79 S. Cal. L. Rev. 559 at 576: 'When considering the normative arguments for copyrights it is important to remember that in the music industry it is almost always the record label and not the artist that controls the copyright.' See also Michael J. Madison, 'Where does Creativity Come From? And Other Stories of Copyright' (2003) 53 Case W. Res. L. Rev. 747 at 757–8.
58. See Jaszi, 'Towards a Theory of Copyright', note 27 above at 485–90, describing how the employer came to be seen as the originator of works, the source of the necessary inspiration and motivation, while the employee became a mere mechanic, following orders.
59. Jaszi, Ibid. at 500.
60. *Cf.* Mark A. Lemley, 'Romantic Authorship and the Rhetoric of Property' (1997) 75 Tex. L. Rev. 873 at 882–88, reviewing Boyle, *Shamans, Software and Spleens*, note 27 above. Lemley argues that the Romantic Author cannot explain much about intellectual property law, noting, for example, that intellectual property is heavily skewed to protect the interests of corporations as opposed to individual authors. However, romantic authorship may paradoxically support corporate ownership: in the US, it does this by simply recasting the corporation as 'author,' while in Canada, it achieves a similar result by providing a powerful ideological framework that simply overlooks the reality of corporate ownership and its implications for real (as opposed to mythic) authors.
61. See Boyle, *Shamans, Software and Spleens*, note 27 above.
62. This term is used to refer to the practice of incorporating, without the consent of intellectual property rights' owners, part or all of a protected image in the creation of a work of visual art by a person other than the owner. Relevant artistic practices include collage, montage and simulation. See Johnson Okpaluba, 'Appropriation Art: Fair Use or Foul?' in Daniel McClean and Karsten Schubert (eds), *Dear Images: Art, Copyright and Culture* (London: Ridinghouse, 2002) at 197–224 [Okpaluba, 'Appropriation Art']. See also John Carlin, 'Culture Vultures: Artistic Appropriation and Intellectual Property Law' (1988) 3 Colum.-V.L.A. J.L. & Arts 103, arguing for an expansion of fair use to permit the artistic appropriation of commercial images.
63. Peter Anderson, 'On the Legal Limits of Art' (1994) Arts & Ent. L. Rev. 70 at 73. Quoted by Okpaluba, 'Appropriation Art', Ibid. at 201.

64. Heather J. Meeker, 'The Ineluctable Modality of the Visible: Fair Use and Fine Arts in the Post-Modern Era' (1993) 10 U. Miami Ent. & Sports L. Rev. 195 at 195.
65. *Rogers v. Koons*, 960 F.2d 301 (2d Cir), cert. denied, 113 S. Ct. 365 (1992).
66. Kembrew McLeod, *Freedom of Expression: Overzealous Copyright Bozos and Other Enemies of Creativity* (Toronto: Doubleday, 2005) at 141.
67. 960 F.2d 301 at 309–10.
68. Martha Buskirk, 'Appropriation Under the Gun' (June 1992) *Art in America* at 37. Quoted by Randall, *Pragmatic Plagiarism*, note 10 above at 254.
69. Okpaluba, 'Appropriation Art', note 62 above at 207.
70. See Aoki, 'Adrift in the Intertext', note 51 above at 813–15, and Jaszi, 'Author Effect,' note 8 above at 305–12.
71. Aoki, 'Adrift in the Intertext', note 51 above at 813–14.
72. Ibid. at 814.
73. On the common characterisation of hip hop borrowings as theft, see O.B. Arewa, 'From J.C. Bach to Hip Hop: Musical Borrowing, Copyright and Cultural Context', (2006) 84 N.C.L. Rev. 547. See also McLeod, note 66 above at 30 *et seq.*
74. As Danger Mouse explained in an MTV interview: 'I thought it would be more challenging and more fun and more of a statement on what you could do with sampling alone. It's an art form. It is music. You can do different things, it doesn't have to be just what some people call stealing.' Quoted by McLeod, Ibid. at 153.
75. Rosemary Coombe, 'Objects of Property and Subjects of Politics: Intellectual Property Laws and Democratic Dialogue' (1991) 69 Tex. L. Rev. 1853 at 1863: 'the consumption of commodified representational forms is productive activity in which people engage in meaning-making to adapt signs, texts, and images to their own agendas.'
76. Patricia A. Kreig, 'Copyright, Free Speech and Visual Arts' (1984) 93 Yale L.J. 1565 at 1578–9. Kreig continues: 'Therefore the act of appropriation itself imparts a political message; it reveals that society (and its legal system) is laden with assumptions that financial incentives promote individual creativity, and that property interests supersede society's right of access to ideas and information.'
77. Randall, *Pragmatic Plagiarism*, note 10 above at 258.
78. Arewa warns: 'Such notions of music creation are often not conducive to the development of vibrant and living music traditions. As we apply such legal standards, we should . . . be alert to the . . . fact that musical production may in the end come to mirror the conceptions contained in the copyright standards applied to it.', note 73 above at 645.
79. James Boyle, 'A Theory of Law and Information: Copyright, Spleens, Blackmail, and Insider Trading' (1992) 80 Cal. L. Rev. 1415 at 1534.

3. Authorship and conceptions of the self: Feminist theory and the relational author

3.1 INTRODUCTION

In Chapter 2, I suggested that copyright law and its construction of authorship are premised upon the assumptions (both ontological and normative) of the Enlightenment and post-Enlightenment era, and in particular, the tenets of possessive individualism. The result is a copyright model that forces all intellectual production into doctrinal categories shaped by individualistic assumptions about the authorial ideal, producing the simplifying dichotomies of creation/reproduction, author/user, labourer/free-rider. Unless we problematise these binary oppositions, we risk hindering and preventing precisely the kinds of communicative activities that copyright is meant to encourage. I have suggested that, in order for copyright to embrace marginalised forms of creativity (especially those that explicitly rely upon prior works for their expression), we need to achieve a theoretical shift away from the liberal model upon which it is currently built.

In this chapter, I will argue that the legitimacy and success of copyright law depends upon a theoretical framework informed by feminist theory and capable of embracing the notion of the relational self/author, and the principles of dialogism. Identifying the liberalist foundations of the intellectual property system therefore opens a door for the re-imagination of copyright. Based as it is upon the legal structures and theoretical assumptions of liberal thought, the copyright model embraces liberal notions of the 'self': copyright's 'author' is liberalism's human subject. Once this connection is made, it can be seen that the impoverished subject of liberal thought entails an impoverished vision of the author. I hope to show that an ontological self that is complicated by liberalism's feminist critics can provide a route by which to see authorship in all its complexity.

My purpose in exploring the weaknesses of copyright's author-figure is not to proclaim the death of the original author; copyright needs the author (just as feminism needs the autonomous bearer of rights). Rather, the question is how we can reconceptualise authorship as a communicative and adaptive activity – as opposed to isolated and originating – without losing our capacity to differentiate authored and un-authored, original and unoriginal.[1] It is in the face of this dilemma that I turn to feminist theory. Employing the notions of dialogism and the relational self that have emerged from feminist scholarship, I hope to show how we can re-imagine the author not as source, origin or authority, but as participant and citizen. We can re-imagine authorship as the formation of individual identity and the development of self and community through discourse. These ideas illuminate the nature of authorship as a social and formative process, but they also offer the foundation for a coherent justification of copyright: if speech/dialogue constitutes us as social beings, copyright law, which aims to encourage creativity and exchange, thereby encourages meaningful relations of communication and participation with others. We have to understand the substance of copyright's goals before we can expect it to achieve them.

In the discussion that follows, I will explore the challenges faced by feminists in defining the nature of the 'subject' in literary and political theory, and some of the ways in which feminist scholarship has met these challenges. In doing so, my ultimate aim is to import some of the concepts and reasoning that has proved central to feminist theorising into debates about the reconstruction of authorship. In Section 2, I will briefly highlight the convergences I see between feminist theory, constructions of authorship and conceptions of selfhood. In Section 3, I will outline the dilemmas presented by competing constructions of authorship in the field of literary criticism, and suggest a possible route towards meeting these challenges with an appeal to 'dialogic feminism'. I will then consider, in Section 4, the similar challenges faced by feminists in political and legal theory in light of competing conceptualisations of selfhood. I will appeal to relational feminism, and the attendant concept of dialogue, as appropriate vehicles by which to resolve the debates and collapse the dichotomies that have characterised much of contemporary political theorising about the nature of the self. In Section 5, I will inquire into the potential for these feminist discourses to reshape our understanding of the processes and products of cultural creativity, and the nature of the rights granted by the copyright system.

3.2 FEMINISM, AUTHORSHIP AND CONSTRUCTIONS OF THE SELF

The paragon of independent original creation, discussed in Chapter 2, represents a naïve conception of the processes of authorship, and so provides the copyright system with an untenable and undesirable premise. To the extent that the truly original author-owner is conceptualised as an individual (and not merely a function or fiction), he depends upon Enlightenment ideals of individuation, detachment and unity.[2] The competing view sees the author as necessarily engaged in a process of adaptation, derivation, translation and recombination. This latter version of authorship coheres with a view of the individual as socially situated, as constituted by community, culture and society, thus constantly shifting and evolving: 'a "subject-in process" never unitary, never complete'.[3] Rather than meaning created out of nothing, the author's expression is the result of the complex variety of influences that have shaped her, and its meaning is essentially fluid, derived only from its interaction with other texts and discourses.

The tension between competing constructions of authorship has played out in feminist literary theory as a debate between recovering a strong and stable identity for women writers and their experiences, and deconstructing traditional notions of author and experience.[4] This tension in literary theory to some extent mirrors a tension that has been a critical subject of feminist scholarship in political and social theory: the tension between the individual, pre-social self of liberal theory, and the socially constituted, always-already encumbered self instated in communitarian critiques of liberalism. While these debates have generally been insulated from one another as a result of disciplinary divides, they are not unrelated and present similar challenges for feminism: namely, how can we escape a concept of the self that ignores relations, discourses and communities, without descending into a position where subjectivity and agency is overwhelmed by social situation?

The egalitarian rhetoric of feminist politics and its foundation in rights discourse weds feminism to the central premises of modernist theory. However, the historic exclusion of women from the benefits of rights and egalitarianism reveals as fictive the neutrality of modernism's philosophical paradigm and casts doubt upon the universalism of its putative meta-narratives.[5] Arguments about the nature of social theory's 'subject', and challenges to the liberal conception of the self in particular, have thus played a central role in the feminist struggle for genuine and substantive equality. Western liberal philosophy conceives of the self as an autonomous (independent) rational agent with the capacity for self-determination. This conception entails claims about the rights the agent must have if he is to be free to exercise this capacity: in particular, the right to own private property and to enter into voluntary, private contractual relations with other autonomous agents. As it is currently conceived, copyright – which takes the form of a private property right and is premised upon transferability through contract in a free market – relies squarely upon this liberal notion of the self as independent creator, individual owner and rational economic agent. It has been widely argued that liberalism's version of the self cannot accommodate, and so excludes or silences, those people whose experienced realities do not resonate with the individualised account of autonomy. Similarly, copyright's version of the author cannot accommodate, and so excludes or silences, those people whose communicative activities do not resonate within the individualised and originative account of authorship.

However, the simple refusal of a 'subject' is highly problematic for the feminist political project, just as the simple refusal of the 'author' would be highly problematic for copyright policy. It is not sufficient for feminist theory to radically deconstruct the modernist self, because with the evaporation of the self comes the evaporation of the concept of woman.[6] Feminists in literary, political and legal theory alike have therefore struggled to find a conception of the self that acknowledges connectivity without precluding individual autonomy, identity or voice. This struggle stems from awareness of the feminist ontological dilemma: 'it can fully embrace neither an unreconstructed modernism's subject nor postmodernism's rejection of the subject.'[7]

It has thus been observed that feminism 'constitutes both a critique of and a defence of modernity, so has a great stake in the modernity–postmodernity debates which are at heart about the possibility of a "subject" for social theory.'[8] In other words, it is 'the issue of agency and of subjectivity more generally, which lies at the heart of feminism's ambiguous "positioning" between modernity and postmodernity.'[9] Issues of agency and subjectivity are also critical to the construction of the author in copyright law: if we are to tackle the unreconstructed notion of the author as independent creator, but also refuse to deconstruct the author out of existence, then copyright theory has a similar stake in the modernity-postmodernity debates, which pertain to the possibility of an author-subject for the copyright system.

The re-imagination of copyright requires a challenge to the concept of autonomous selfhood that informs liberal political theory. It also requires a concept of self that affirms the centrality of relationships and community while acknowledging creative capacity and the agency to engage in social discourses. It seems to follow that feminist theory can inform copyright's search for an author-subject: it offers not only a critique of the atomised liberal individual, but its reconstitution as a rights-bearing, autonomous *and* relational self. It therefore holds the promise of a new theoretical model that can be brought to bear on the copyright system.

3.3 FEMINIST LITERARY CRITICISM AND THE AUTHOR-SELF

3.3.1 The Dilemma for Feminist Literary Theory

Foucault began his examination of the relationship between the text and the author by posing the question, 'What does it matter who is speaking?'[10] Since the 'fundamental unit of the author and the work' gives rise to the 'fundamental category of 'the-man-and-his-work criticism',[11] a feminist might answer that it matters precisely because the authoritative speaker is presumed to be a man. It certainly is arguable that, where authors belong to traditionally marginalised or unauthorised groups, the poststructuralist effacement of the author only compounds the historic invisibility of these stifled voices and denies them the authority to speak that traditionally attaches to authorship before it has even been acknowledged. And so Nancy K. Miller responds to Foucault's question:

> What does it matter who's speaking? I would answer that it matters, for example, to women who have lost and still routinely lose their proper name in marriage, and whose signature – not merely their voice – has not been worth the paper it was written on; women for whom the signature – by virtue of its power in the world of circulation – is *not* immaterial. Only those who have it can play with not having it.[12]

Miller's statement captures the feminist concern that the fragmentation of the author and her work forecloses the inquiry into the agency of the female subject, reduces her self-expression to a textual construction, and thereby reasserts hegemonic masculine meaning-making in the guise of intertextuality.[13] According to Miller, where the 'author' dissipates into textual free-play, there can be no acknowledgement of the 'author' *qua* 'woman'; disaggregating the author is therefore a luxury that belongs to those whose identities are not already experienced as decentred and fragmented.

Marilyn Randall defined authorship as 'the attribution of a particular set of authorial functions to the agent of discourse'.[14] This definition reveals, first, the agency implicit in the concept of authorship (a comparatively transhistorical constant), and second, the need to inquire into the nature and operation of these authorial functions (as fluid and historical contingencies). One relatively stable feature or function of authorship identified by Randall is the notion of the appropriation of the authority-to-speak. Feminist and post-colonial theorists have exposed the presupposition of such authority in their examinations of marginalised discourses, which reveal 'authorship' to be 'a privilege that must be acquired (constructed, earned or appropriated), even in the postmodern, "post-authorial" context.'[15] Furthermore, the notion of the 'appropriation' or 'misappropriation' of 'voice' across 'communities of identity', which is premised upon a concern with the 'authenticity' of the speaker's voice, has been a common component of contemporary gender, racial and post-colonial literary studies.

This presents a dilemma for critical theorists, pitting the 'authorizing authenticity of personal experience against the dangers of the essentialism that authority based on gender, race, or culture and sexuality seem to imply.'[16] It also suggests the root of a divide that emerged in the feminist literary criticism of the 1980s,

> between those pragmatically committed to the recovery of the woman writer and, with her, something usually called women's experience, and those concerned to explore the implications for feminism of postmodern theories that question the legitimacy of such constructs as the author and experience.[17]

The poststructuralist critiques of copyright's 'author' and 'work' encapsulate this feminist dilemma. I have argued that copyright theory has to complicate the author construct if it is to recognise the realities of cultural creativity. However, in the context of women's writing, and from the perspective of literary theory's 'gynocritics',[18] such a challenge to the author is a challenge to the assertion of women's experience and the project of recovering women's voices. But it is also more fundamentally a challenge to the male voice and the paternal nature of authorship that characterised Romantic and post-Romantic aesthetics, for 'the image of the "artist" underlying the works of the Copyright Act is that of the solitary *male* genius, isolated both spatially and temporally from his community and the background of the art in which he works.'[19] In other words, we should not be fooled into assuming that the original author-figure of copyright (and the target of poststructuralist critique) is gender-neutral.

The gendered nature of the authorial ideal is also evident in the aesthetic and cultural theories of value that determine the worth or import of intellectual contributions. In this regard, feminists have pointed to the exclusionary category of the literary canon that attributes greatness to predominantly (white, first-world) male authors. The equalising solution initially proposed was simply the discovery, re-evaluation and inclusion of worthy women writers who met accepted standards of excellence. The better solution, I think, is to challenge the traditional theories of value represented by the canon, and to 'interrogate the processes through which such values are produced, given authority, and disseminated within a particular historical and social formation', and the manner in which they 'reproduce the social formation that created them'.[20] One might ask, for example, why traditional aesthetic values favour originality over creative imitation, or sole authorship over collaborative creativity, and how these preferences emulate and perpetuate the solitary male authorial ideal. How is it that such contingent and contestable value judgments have come to seem 'natural, timeless, and self-evident',[21] and whose experienced realities or aspirations do they reflect? Examined in this light, it is not surprising that the relationship between the author and the work as concretised in copyright law should reflect 'a paternalistic or patriarchal relationship in that it emphasizes the importance of identifying the particular author responsible for creating a work and gives to him the absolute right to control and exploit the work for economic gain.'[22]

As feminists have learned, it is often a misguided strategy to attempt to fit women into patriarchal structures by showing the ways in which we are the same and so deserve to be included. The better approach is to challenge the structure itself and the putative universalisability of the attributes and values it represents. If we choose simply to assert the women writer as equally authentic, authoritative and original, we should be aware that this project presupposes 'a concept of stable identity and an authenticity and originality rooted in an ontological self.' In this respect, I share Finke's concern:

> [I]t has been the project of feminism to enable women to construct the same powerful sense of identity as men. But the search for "authentic" women's experience, for the woman writer who expresses herself authentically, grounds the female "self" in a Western mind/body dualism that ironically reinforces the very ideology of bourgeois individualism feminists wish to resist.[23]

Similarly, there is a danger that, by insisting upon the inclusion of certain women writers in the canon, we only subsume new works within the traditional definitions while continuing to portray value as inherent and objective rather than contingent and perspectival. Instead, we must cast doubt upon the ideological assumptions that have shaped conceptions of authorship, and question the attributes by which the value of literary achievement has been measured. Mary O'Connor explains this need to re-evaluate rather than integrate:

> Women's literature has been motivated by the imperative to know who we are and how to act on that knowledge, but our liberation comes belatedly as we discover that the "wholeness" of men is indeed a fabrication. . . . Freedom in this poststructuralist world must come from analyzing and subverting all constructed identities. . . . Women must still deconstruct the patriarchal image of ourselves as silent, . . . but problems arise when we start to construct our own identity.
>
> These issues have been debated in feminist literary theory – whether it is

> our job to establish a new identity, unified and strong . . ., or to forego this Romantic illusion and look for an identity that is based on the fluid process of history.[24]

Undoubtedly, this presents a challenging dilemma for feminist theorising. How can we resist the dominant (male) Romantic author-figure, while refusing to let go of the empowerment that the author-function affords? How can we reject the entirely fragmented, 'deceased' author of radical poststructuralism, which forecloses discussion about subjectivity and the agency/identity of the author-subject, while insisting upon the deconstruction of the author-label? How can we claim to value particular works of authorship, while repudiating the traditional criteria by which works have been evaluated and disavowing the concept of inherent or internal value?

3.3.2 Introducing Dialogism

These challenges present themselves as binary oppositions, asking us to choose between biographical author-person and historical author-function; between a stable pre-existing self, and a radically fragmented subject; between universal value systems, and an aesthetic relativism that precludes value judgments.[25] A feminist literary theory needs to dissolve these dichotomies if it is to arrive at a concept of authorship capable of acknowledging the identity of the author, her subjectivity, and the value of her contribution. According to Finke and O'Connor, the notion of dialogism, drawn from the work of Michel Bakhtin (and ostensibly reworked to overcome the male-centredness of Bakhtin's critique), is capable of bridging these poles and offering a space within which to contest them.[26]

While a comprehensive or critical account of Bakhtin's dialogic theory is beyond the scope this work, it is important to highlight the central characteristics of Bakhtinian dialogism that have been harnessed by feminist critics in the face of these challenges. The appeal to dialogism has provided a critical rhetoric with which feminists have sought to empower suppressed voices and discourses, while revealing the otherness hidden within dominant, ostensibly monologic discourse. In particular, Finke draws upon Bakhtin's portrayal of discourse as inherently dialogic and multivocal: every utterance exists in relation to other utterances, with the result that all utterances must be understood as interactive and inter-animating.[27] Every utterance contains within it myriad voices (*heteroglossia*) that stand in dialogic relationship with one another: a notion that emancipates subordinated voices while discrediting formalistic, ahistorical analyses of language and literature.[28] For Bakhtin, language is always a struggle between competing codes and constructions, and literature only magnifies the struggle. Language (and so literature) therefore exists in the 'realm of cultural activity, where it participates in the historical, social, and political life of its speakers . . . as both a production and a producer of social relations.'[29]

The concept of dialogism captures the clash and struggle of different languages and allows us to see the social significance of discourse and the relational nature of every utterance. Bakhtin's theory offers a critique of the transcendental self by attributing to the speaker a sociolinguistic point of view, and arming him only with a language already saturated with the voices of others.[30] However, it also promises the power and agency to actively respond to the dominant discourses, and 'the opportunity to engage in a productive, complex exchange with the others' words.'[31] Hence the attraction of Bakhtin's theory for feminist critics:

> [Bakhtin's] dialogism . . . takes into account the various determining and producing historical factors in our lives and at the same time allows for the idea of an active response on the part of the subject to these various discourses and other subject positions. Thus, his theories allow for a model of intersecting ideologies, in other words, a connection with history in society, as well as a model of connecting with others. Finally, they allow for process and change.[32]

3.3.3 Dialogism, Authorship and Copyright

Furnished with the concept of the dialogic, we can return to some of the dilemmas that have challenged feminist literary criticism. The desire to hold onto a concept of authorship – and the accompanying notions of authority, authenticity and identity – had caused some feminists to resist the 'death of the author', or the Foucauldian insinuation that it may not matter who speaks. Finke notes, however, that Foucault did not go so far as to state that the speaker's identity does not matter; rather, he invited us to consider whether it matters, and if so, why. Finke finds an answer in Foucault's work and expresses it in terms that seem to draw together Foucault's scepticism of the author-figure and Bahktin's optimistic dialogism:

> It matters [who is speaking] but for different reasons than those we have in the past supposed: not because a fixed, preexisting self expresses itself through discourse but because discourses – historically situated discourses – are part of the evolving, open-ended, and shifting process of becoming a subject.[33]

It follows, for Finke, that '[t]he contemporary theoretical concern with destabilizing subjectivity must be theorized relationally and historically rather than categorically.' The binary opposition between the wholly unified and the irretrievably fragmented author can be dissolved when we recognise the author-subject as existing at the 'nexus of material, social and historical practices through which [her] subjectivity has been constructed.'[34] Historically situated discourses shape the author's subjectivity, while the author shapes those discourses by contributing her voice to the dialogue. That the contribution is 'hers' matters not because she is the authoritative source of meaning, but because 'language cannot be cut loose from person, time, and place to float freely in some ideal, impersonal, non-time, non-space.'[35] By adding her voice to the dialogue, the speaker *qua* author engages in the complex arena of struggle and exchange with other dynamic voices and discourses in the cultural realm: a discursive interplay which operates at the levels of the text, society and the self.

If subjectivity does not transcend history, neither does the author. The author necessarily writes from within a 'complex network of . . . social relations that fracture the author's apparent solidity as the locus of meaning in her texts.'[36] A dialogic account of the author therefore repudiates the notion of the highly individualised or atomised self, but it also acknowledges the discursive agency of the author (albeit within the constrictions of inherited social discourses). While the subjectivity is constituted through discourses, it is also contested within discourses.[37] From this perspective, the historical and situational contingency of the author-as-subject category does not detract from the agency of the author-as-speaker, nor does it undermine the significance of the author's discourse. The author is socially situated and necessarily dependent upon the texts, languages and discourses already at play in the cultural domain. However, because the utterance is always imbued with the particular situation of the speaker and the addressee, its significance is always critical, interactive and novel. The embedded nature of the author-self does not preclude originality, but rather affirms it: 'It is the context, a particular social and cultural situation, that creates the sign's provisional, local meaning.'[38] This is not originality in its conventional sense, but a complex notion of originality whose significance is not rooted in the independence of the author and text.

This understanding of the author implies a concomitant revision of the concept of authorship: authorship is about interacting with the meanings and texts and discourses that are already out there – already shaping our ideologies, communities and ourselves – and adding to them something of ourselves and our (socially constituted) subjectivity. Others' speech is always present in our own, but this reality does not stultify our attempts to create meaning:

> [we] take it into new contexts, attach it to new material, put it in new situations in order to wrest new answers from it, new insights into meaning, and even

> wrest from it new words of our *own* (since another's discourse, if productive, gives birth to a new word from us in response).[39]

The dialogic approach thus casts authorship as something very different than the Romantic ideal that flows from a socially dislocated account of the author-self: authorship is not originative but participative; it is not internal but interactive; it is not independent but interdependent. In short, a dialogic account of authorship is equipped to appreciate the derivative, collaborative and communicative nature of authorial activity in a way that the Romantic account never can.

At another level, this dialogic theory of authorship can also assist with the feminist interrogation into the theories of value that have defined the worthy attributes of intellectual works. Value judgments themselves are revealed to be utterances existing in dialogic relationship with other judgments, meaning that value is not intrinsic to the text, or self-evident, but is contingent and so dependent upon external ideals and agendas. This acknowledgement should lead us to inquire into alternative discourses cloaked behind the monologic claims of the dominant discourse. We could ask, for example, whether originality merits its centrality in the valuation of literary works, and what dialogical response this statement of value anticipates. Who might argue that value resides in originality, in what conditions, and to what end? Who might disagree, and what circumstances or purposes would cause them to do so?[40] While a dialogic approach reveals the importance of agency, function and condition in theories of value, these dynamic concepts are hidden behind the abstract universalism of copyright's author-figure, and the intrinsic value of copyright's original intellectual work. Dialogism forces copyright theory to address the contingent nature of its assumptions about the copyrightable work and the discourses it privileges.

Where a property-rights oriented account of copyright fails to capture the nature of copyright as speech regulation, a focus on dialogicality illuminates the institutional role that copyright plays in shaping discourses. As Finke explains:

> every utterance about value forms part of a discourse on value, forming a class of judgments, a speech genre governed by rules that determine the authority (or lack thereof) of the speaker or the receiver and the particular historical, social, or institutional context in which an utterance is given force.[41]

The copyright system is an institution that attributes value to particular utterances, and thereby determines the authority of the speaker (author), as well as the lack of authority of the receiver (user). The dialogic approach provides a lens through which to view the influence of copyright in structuring (and suppressing) dialogic processes by virtue of its reinforcement of dominant discourses about value and authority. Central to this analysis is the unearthing of the power relationships that establish where that authority should lie: 'The notion of the dialogic requires precisely an investigation of the power relations that inform and shape any discourse. It calls for an investigation of the social institutions that control who speaks, in what situation, and with what force.'[42]

Copyright is one such institution. The notion of the dialogic therefore calls for an investigation into copyright, the power relations that it sustains and perpetuates, and the discourses of value and authority that it informs and replicates. In a culture such as ours, characterised by corporate ownership of cultural texts and images, it is not hard to imagine where such an investigation would lead.

As it relates to the core concepts of copyright theory – constructions of the author, the processes authorship, the value of works, and the institution of copyright as a whole – this discussion demonstrates the role that feminist theory can play in the re-imagination of copyright. Feminist literary theorists have met the challenges presented by the author-subject and its de/re-construction with an appeal to dialogism and the constant interplay of voices, texts and discourses that create the cultural noise in which we exist and upon which our subjectivity depends. Copyright theory, which also needs to survive the de/re-construction of the Romantic author, can learn from this approach; it should acknowledge the historical contingency of the author-figure, the social situation of the author-speaker, and the dialogic nature of the authored text. It should also examine the role that the institution of copyright plays in silencing counter discourses, attributing authority to speakers, and allocating power over speech.

3.4 FEMINIST THEORY AND THE ATOMISTIC SELF

3.4.1 Political Theory, Copyright and the Self

As suggested above, the tension in literary theory between competing versions of authorship parallels a similar tension between competing conceptualisations of selfhood in social and political theory. The liberal theory of the self as an autonomous self-determining subject has been widely accused of denying the social and interdependent nature of the human self; the competing communitarian vision of the socially constituted and encumbered self has also been criticised, in this case for foreclosing possibilities of genuine agency, autonomy and change. Feminist legal theorists have sought to resolve the dilemma by dissolving the binary opposition between social construction and individual agency.[43] In this section, I will outline the core concepts of relational feminism that have provided a route towards this end, and explore their possible implications in the field of copyright law.

It is important, at this juncture, to underscore the connection between conceptions of authorship and conceptions of selfhood *per se*. The following passage by Shelley Wright captures this relationship and is worth reproducing in full:

> The existing definition of copyright as both economic and personal within a political or civil context presupposes that individuals live in isolation from one another, that the individual is an autonomous unit who creates artistic works and sells them, or permits their sale by others, while ignoring the individual's relationship with others within her community, family, ethnic group, religion – the very social relations out of which and for the benefit of whom the individual's limited monopoly rights are supposed to exist. The community has only the most tenuous identity. Society itself is seen as an aggregate of anomic individuals, each separate, segregated, fragmented, and existing only as subjects of circumscribed civil rights, including the right to consume what others produce or create within limited "fair dealing" or "fair use" provisions. This vision undercuts to a large extent the social justification for monopoly rights as they exist in copyright and places the emphasis on the individual rights of the artist as a "creator" and the artist, or her publisher, as a producer of saleable commodities.[44]

Highlighted here is, first, that the construction of the author reflects a particular vision of the self, and second, that this individualised vision of the self inevitably undermines the social reasons for which the copyright system exists. Wright continues: '[I]ndividuals . . . are the products of their community, culture and society. The production of artistic works assists in creating this culture, this sense of community, and the psychological content of individuals themselves both as creators and as communicants of creation.'[45] Reframing the self within the community complicates the individualised self that plays the role of copyright's original author. The subject matter of copyright is not the independently produced and individually owned work-as-object, but rather a contribution to the continually evolving culture in which the author exists, and by which she is constituted.

Built upon the ontological assumptions that inform liberal thought, and the normative ideals that inform possessive individualism, the current copyright model is not well equipped to recognise either the communal and communicative nature of cultural expression or the significance of that expression to the society and the communicator. If copyright is to encourage such cultural expression while also respecting the interests of the public to access and engage with the expression, it must first be capable of recognising the nature and significance of its subject matter. The re-imagination of copyright therefore necessitates a challenge to the robust individualism of the pre-social, liberal self.

3.4.2 Political Theory and the Feminist Dilemma

Perhaps the greatest challenge to liberalism's conception of selfhood in recent decades has come from the school of thought categorised as communitarianism. While communitarianism resists any attempt at sweeping definition, it has more or less crystallised around a critique of liberal individualism premised upon social constructionism and the public good.[46] Unifying communitarian thought is the rejection of a liberal theory of the self as essentially pre-social, and the community as merely contingent and instrumental.[47] According to communitarians, the self can be understood only in the context of his or her community, culture and values, and in light of the social processes and institutions that have shaped them; the self is not 'unencumbered' but always-already situated, identity is not innate but intersubjective, and the community is not external but constitutive. As Michael Sandel explains:

> For [its members], community describes not just what they *have* as fellow citizens but also what they *are*, not a relationship they choose (as in a voluntary association) but an attachment they discover, not merely an attribute but a constituent of their identity.[48]

Communitarian concern with the metaphysics of social construction is not limited to a methodological claim – it translates into a normative discourse. It makes sense that the socially situated individual is concerned for the kind of society in which she exists, that she might hold obligations to other members of the community (as opposed to merely rights wielded against them), and that the values, norms and goals of the community might be shared and regarded as her own.[49] Thus, the social construction theory of the self flows into a social constructionist approach to political and moral value, and a concern with 'public goods' often lacking in the liberal landscape.

Of course, feminists have expressed a similar disenchantment with the liberal conception of personhood.[50] Because it overlooks the socially situated nature of the self, liberalism's individual is essentially disembodied, and social relations such as sex, class, and race are rendered invisible. This precludes sufficient acknowledgement of social injustice experienced as a result of group identity, legitimises the problematic public–private distinction behind which myriad oppressions lurk,[51] and simply denies the connected sense of self that many women experience in their lives.[52] Thus, it is a common thread amongst much feminist theory that '[a] person's critical, political consciousness can only be explained in terms of this socially situated conception of the self in which individual agency is not fully analysable in pre-social terms.'[53]

There may appear to be a neat convergence between the feminist critique of degendered, universalisable conceptions of the self, and communitarian objections to the ahistorical and atomistic individual of liberal political theory.[54] The communitarian conception of the constitutive community is attractive to feminists and other critical social theorists who take issue with the isolated rights-bearing individual. However, while it may be 'a commonplace amongst communitarians, socialists and feminists that liberalism is to be rejected for its excessive "individualism" or "atomism",'[55] feminists cannot simply appeal to communitarianism as an adequate solution to the shortcomings of modern political thought.

The crux of the problem is the apparent absence of political potential within communitarian scholarship: '[A]lthough communitarians take on board a critique of liberal individualism and purport to recognise the constitutive role of the social in our identity, they have so far stopped short of any genuinely political analysis or critique of the very community institutions whose importance they acknowledge.'[56] At best, the failure of communitarianism to generate any substantive political critique of the community institutions that constitute our identities leaves it disappointingly impotent.[57] At worst, this failure is merely symptomatic of a distinctly conservative undertone in communitarian thought, manifested in a propensity to idealise even oppressive communities, and so to rationalise the status quo.[58]

Feminism needs a critique of individualistic social ontology, but it also demands a critical capacity to evaluate and denounce the communities, traditions and institutions that it recognises as constitutive. Perhaps most importantly, it must be fully capable of perceiving the power relations that exist within and between these various communities;[59] questions of comparative disadvantage and power disparity are underemphasised in the works of prominent communitarians such as MacIntyre or Sandel.[60] Communitarianism therefore fails to provide a foundation for feminist critique at a political level; indeed, it largely fails to provide an account of how women, in the context of their communities, can develop a critical consciousness at all:

> On this communitarian view of personhood, the woman who lives in a sexist and patriarchal culture is peculiarly powerless. For she cannot find any jumping-off point for a critique of the dominant conception of value: her position as a socially constructed being seems to render her a helpless victim of

> her situation. . . . How is she to attain any measure of critical consciousness, so as to move towards the formation of alternative communities, alternative definitions . . .?[61]

Once again, feminism encounters its dilemma. The challenge for feminists who believe in the socially situated self is to provide a coherent account of selfhood that permits sufficient subjectivity for a person to comprehend her situation in critical terms, and sufficient agency for her to engage with and shape the community that shapes her.[62] Feminism has therefore tackled head-on the 'difficulties inherent in building a theory (and practice) that adequately reflects both the social and the individual nature of human beings.'[63]

3.4.3 Relational Feminism: Rethinking the Self

I cannot hope to canvas all of the ways in which feminist political and legal theorists have attempted to address this dilemma. Rather, I have chosen to appeal to the notion of 'relational feminism' as one potential route towards resolving the tension between individualism and communitarianism.[64] While feminist scholarship generally insists upon the intersubjective nature of being, it is concerned with freeing women to shape their own lives, to write their own narratives, to create themselves. Rather than emphasising only situatedness, feminists therefore stress the need to renegotiate our gendered identities and the terms of our subjectivity. For relational feminists, the key to this renegotiation lies in the very network of relations and cultural narratives that are commonly perceived as a threat to our subjectivity; according to relational feminism, they are also the route towards autonomy and self-identity.[65]

3.4.3.1 The relational self

The starting point for a relational account of the self is 'an attention both to the individuality of human beings and to their essentially social nature.'[66] The aspirational society is one that structures relations in such a way that communities and relationships foster, rather than undermine, self-worth and individual autonomy. Thus, the concepts of autonomy and individuality survive the rejection of atomistic individualism and the appeal to social constructionism.

The re-imagination of autonomy provides the centrepiece of relational feminism. The need for a genuine conception of autonomy is essential to the feminist political project, but the traditional liberal portrayal of autonomy as freedom, independence and self-determination misses the mark: if we take as a starting point the intrinsic sociality of human beings, then interdependence is not the antithesis of autonomy, but its precondition.[67] If interdependence is a 'constant component of autonomy', genuine autonomy is only realisable through the human interactions that allow it to develop and flourish.[68] An adequate theory of autonomy must therefore understand autonomy in relational and not individualistic terms: 'It is relationships, from child-parent, to student-teacher, to client-state, as well as patterns of relationship among citizens, that make actualisation of the human potential for autonomy possible.'[69]

In the context of constructive relationships, Jennifer Nedelsky casts the agency and autonomy of the relational self in terms of a human capacity for self-creation: 'a capacity that means we are never fully determined by our relationships or our given material circumstances . . .. We are always in a creative process of interaction, of mutual shaping, with all the dimensions of our existence.'[70] Susan Williams understands this creative process as narrative agency – the capacity to engage in an ongoing process of evaluation, interpretation and reinterpretation of one's experiences and life-story. In other words, 'the self is a creature in and of the world, but one capable of at least partially transforming herself through thought, criticism, and self-interpretation.'[71] With its commitment to interdependence, community, agency and individuality, relational theory provides the solution to feminism's political and ontological dilemma:

> The notion of the relational self . . . nicely captures our empirical and logical interdependence and the centrality to our identity of our relations with others and with practices and institutions, whilst retaining an idea of human uniqueness and discreteness as central to our sense of ourselves. It entails the collapse of any self/other or individual/community dichotomy without abandoning the idea of genuine agency and subjectivity.[72]

3.4.3.2 Rights as relationship

The notion of the relational self challenges the liberal conception of the autonomous individual as an independent bearer of rights to be wielded against others and the state. The role of rights in feminist discourse is therefore another facet of the dilemma that feminists face in the liberal-communitarian debate. This rights-bearing individual is the protagonist of liberalism, and the epitome of individualism. However, in the context of a struggle for substantive equality, feminists generally refuse to abandon the notion of rights as a political tool, even while rejecting the rights-fetishism of the liberal political order. As with autonomy, the concept of right must be retained but re-imagined.

In liberal thought, rights take the form of limits to democratic outcomes, constraints upon collective choices, and boundaries between citizens. Rights are portrayed as innate to the individual, and human relations are cast in terms of clashing rights and interests. In contrast, from a relational perspective, human interaction is seen primarily 'in terms of the way patterns of relationship can develop and sustain both an enriching collective life and the scope for genuine individual autonomy.'[73] Rights, in this picture, do not simply mediate the boundaries of individual self-interest: they encapsulate collective choices about the values that we, as members of this society, hold most dear. These values are neither innate nor trans-temporal, but evolve with society over time. As such, they are best understood in terms of relationships, because 'the shifting quality of those basic values makes more sense when our focus is on the structure of relations that fosters those values.'[74]

In liberal thought, property rights epitomise the role attributed to rights in general. Property represents the boundaries of the individual's private sphere and a limit upon the powers of the state and fellow citizens.[75] The symbolic power of traditional property probably flows in part from its apparent concreteness, which lends materiality to the personal space claimed by the rights bearer, and makes it easy to identify violations and resultant harm.[76] As lawyers know, however, this conceptual tendency to physicalise property belies its nature. Property rights are primarily about relations between persons and not the material thing that is owned.[77] Moreover, there is nothing about property rights that make them intrinsic or pre-social: their significance is entirely dependent upon the rules and guarantees of the state. Like any other right, then, property rights represent a collective, democratic choice about structuring relations of power and responsibility in society. Property rights may give the owner protection against the collective, but they have their source in the collective.

Relational feminism thus recasts individual rights as relational: rights are not things to be wielded by individuals in defence of their personal sphere, but are instead vehicles that 'construct relationships – of power, of responsibility, of trust, of obligation.'[78] Debates about the substance or scope of rights should not begin and end with the claim or denial of right (which only obfuscate the underlying issues) but should instead focus upon the kinds of human relationships the right would structure, and the values that would be furthered by its guarantee.[79]

3.4.3.3 Dialogic communitarianism

In light of the role played by 'dialogism' in feminist literary criticism and the collapse of structure/agency dichotomies, it is interesting to note the significance accorded to dialogue in relational feminism's theory of selfhood. This is perhaps best captured in the work of Nicola Lacey and Elizabeth Frazer, who appeal to the concept of 'dialogic communitarianism'[80] as a means by which to move beyond the binary oppositions of the liberal-communitarian debate:

> This ideal is dialogic in the sense that it assumes democratic institutions providing real access to political processes for all citizens. It is both dialogic and communitarian in the sense of proceeding from the relational theory of the self, recognising the importance of both dialogue and identification with various 'communities' in the constitution of subjectivity and human identity, and it is communitarian in the sense of placing questions of both public goods and the institutions needed to support them, and the ideal of collective life based on mutual acceptance and recognition, at the heart of politics.[81]

Taking as their starting point a theory of the 'relational self', Frazer and Lacey argue that a commitment to dialogue is essential for the ongoing scrutiny and negotiation of power relations within communities and social structures. This necessitates both an awareness of the power that inheres in practices and discourses, and attention to the value and audibility of members' voices. Substantive access to informed political debate and the capacity to be heard are central to the dialogic communitarian ideal.[82]

According to dialogic communitarianism, subjectivity requires discursive engagement: the capacity to listen to the claims of others and to articulate one's own. Feminism's appeal to the practice of interactive consciousness-raising is an example of transformative politics through dialogic process.[83] The collective practice of exchanging personal accounts and experiences is intended to generate a critically reflective capacity, creating opportunities for women to better understand themselves and their social condition. Related to this practice is the similar but more self-conscious art form of 'narrative' creation.[84] The creation of narrative is essentially 'story-telling', which aims to give voice to women's experiences, but also, through the processes of communication and sharing, to facilitate human connection across difference. Narrative is self-evidently situated and perspectival, but also creative (in its construction and interpretation), and potentially reconstructive (in its political power). As such, it is another tool with which feminists have tempered the implications of social constructionism:

> [T]here is enough of a story-teller in all of us to create a coherent, if unstable self. Yet the narrative speaker is not simply an outspoken incarnation of the pre-existing, bounded individual of modernist thought; she must contend with the social forces that continually threaten to destroy her carefully crafted sense of self.[85]

The use of narrative is also said to temper the postmodern deconstruction of Woman by recreating a meaningful connection amongst women through their gendered realities: 'Narrative thus straddles the postmodern divide between a unified, essentialist meaning of womanhood and no meaning at all; the narrating self is a woman-in-process.'[86]

At the foundation of consciousness-raising, narrative creation and dialogic communitarianism more broadly, is the understanding that identity and subjectivity are constituted by dynamic interaction with others in a process of dialogic exchange, both interpersonal and intrapersonal. It is through this dialogic process of interpreting and ordering experiences, discourses, and social forces that the socially-situated subject of feminist ontology is able to exercise the agency demanded of her by feminist politics.

3.4.4 Relational Theory, Authorship and Copyright

My aim, in exploring these elements of relational feminism, has been to reveal the potential for a notion of subjectivity that acknowledges the connectedness of the human subject without engulfing it within its social situation and so denying individuality, difference and creative capacity. My purpose, of course, is to draw from this some lessons for the law of copyright. Authorship is an essentially human project, and constructions of authorship are thus essentially bound to conceptions of the human self. I have argued that the author in copyright law is postulated in unequivocally liberal terms. It is my suggestion that copyright theory can draw upon the lessons of relational feminism to re-imagine the nature of the author-self (which will entail the re-imagination of copyright itself).

3.4.4.1 The relational author

As Nedelsky has noted, there is 'inherent tension between the idea of autonomy as both originating with oneself and being conditioned and shaped by one's social context. Those tensions are the tensions of feminism, and they come from feminism's recognition of the nature of human beings.'[87] Similarly, I would suggest, there is an inherent tension between the idea of authorship as both originating within oneself and being derived from the social and cultural context within which the author creates. These are the tensions of copyright. Copyright's failure to adequately recognise the essentially social nature of human creativity obscures these tensions, and so misrepresents the processes of authorship. Copyright needs a relational theory of the author-self.

Far from than the individualised, self-determining author of modern copyright law, the 'relational author' is always already situated within, and constituted by, the communities in which she exists, and the texts and discourses by which she is surrounded. Far from creating independently and choosing relationships through the vehicle of copyright *qua* private property, the author necessarily creates from within a network of social relations: she is not individualisable, and her works of authorship cannot be regarded in isolation. It follows that the author's works are not 'independent' creations and they do not originate from the author alone.

However, this does not mean that author and authorship are illusory or obsolete. A relational theory of authorship recognises the social dimension of the author, but also her duality: she encapsulates both our connectedness and our capacity for critical reflection. As we have seen, relational feminism regards the self as continuously engaged in a 'creative process of interaction, of mutual shaping, with all the dimensions of her existence.'[88] When we conceive of autonomy as the freedom and ability to construct one's own narrative, and to project this narrative of the self into the world, the self takes on the role as both actor and author. The scene is set, and the role is given, but the relational self has the creative capacity to improvise, to refuse direction, to re-write the ending. It is easy to find, in the creative process of authorship, an instantiation of this capacity for creative agency upon which relational feminism insists.

In an effort to explain the duality of the relational self as both socially constituted (determined) and possessing narrative autonomy (creative), Susan Williams' words provide insight into the duality of the *author*-self:

> [T]he difference between creativity and determinism may simply be a difference in the degree of complexity in the causal sequence. It is not that anything is uncaused, but that the influences on a given human being are so many, varied, and interacting that at some point it becomes meaningless to ascribe causality to any useful subset of those influences.[89]

Similarly, in the processes of authorship, the texts, discourses, experiences and relationships that constitute the author are combined, interpreted, reinterpreted and retold. What emerges from the authorial process is not original in the sense of having been created *ex nihilo*; but it is nonetheless the author's creation in the only sense that matters. When Williams describes narrative autonomy, she might equally be describing authorship:

> [T]he activity of narrative construction – of interpretation and reinterpretation – begins, of course, from the materials at hand. That is, a person works with her own experiences and the stories, values, and concepts that are available to her in whatever culture(s) she inhabits. These materials are always, and from the beginning, both given and created. They are given in that they are shaped by forces beyond any individual's control; they are created in that each new repetition of such cultural and personal artefacts is always a reinterpretation rather than merely a replication.[90]

In the same way, the materials of authorship are both given and created. The relational author must always create from the materials around her, but the authorial process is one of reinterpretation, recombination and so transformation. The influences upon the author are so many, and the sources so various, that we can call this process authorial creativity.

3.4.4.2 Relational copyright

A relational theory of the author has implications for the nature of copyright. In the relational model, copyright cannot be allowed to play the role attributed to traditional property rights in liberal political theory. Due to the ubiquitous property analogy, copyright lends itself to similar reification (in spite of its intangible nature) and so threatens to occupy an equivalent role in an individual rights-based analysis. Also, because copyright is so often rationalised in Lockean terms (whereby the author's right is just reward for intellectual labour), it lends itself to categorisation as a 'natural right.' Applying the lessons of relational feminism, the individual liberty and natural rights-based accounts of copyright are untenable.

The author's right is not reducible to an individual entitlement that limits the actions of others. Although few would dispute this broad claim, its implications have yet to be grasped in principle or realised in practice. Copyright must be understood in relational terms: it structures relationships between authors and users, allocating powers and responsibilities amongst members of cultural communities, and establishing the rules of communication and exchange. To assess the nature of copyright with reference only to the copyright owner's private sphere of entitlement is to undermine its normative significance. The importance of copyright lies in its capacity to structure relations of communication, and also, to establish the power dynamics that will shape these relations. Its purpose is to maximise communication and exchange by putting in place incentives for the creation and dissemination of intellectual works. Relational feminism can teach us that an individualised account of the copyright holder's right will disregard the significance of the relationships affected by copyright, and will be blind to the power dimensions and social implications of the copyright system. It is therefore imperative that copyright is not regarded as just another brick in 'the wall (of rights) erected between the individual and those around him.'[91]

Relational feminists do not ascribe to the notion of the individual as possessor of rights and interests that precede her entrance into civil society as an embodied person. Such rights or interests as she has under the law and against the collective are only the culmination of collective choices that have been made about the kind of society in which she should live, and the kind of relationships and values that should therefore be fostered.

From this perspective, it makes no sense to talk of the author's natural right to own the fruits of her intellectual labour, nor to compare the authorial act to the picking of acorns in the state of nature. There is no prior, transcendent entitlement here that must be respected by the political powers that be in the name of legitimate government; there is only a choice to be made about the kind of intellectual creativity and exchange that we want to see in our society, and the relations of communication that are likely to foster it. Copyright exists only because it is created and defined by the state, and only to the extent that it is enforceable through state mechanisms. A relational theory of copyright thus repudiates any notion of copyright as a natural right of the author – it is simply the result of democratic, political decision-making, and subject to revision as a result of shifting values, changing circumstances, or the need to redress imbalances of power.

It follows that the claim to authorial right only obfuscates the real issues underlying policy debates about the strength and scope of copyright. The language of copy*right* and intellectual *property* is unfortunate because it contains a rhetorical power to foreclose debate,[92] and like any invocation of right or entitlement, has the tendency to 'obscure rather than clarify what is at issue, what people are really after'.[93] The lessons of relational feminism reveal that the copyright system, as the result of a collective choice, always requires evaluation and re-evaluation. In particular, we must be attentive to the relationships of power and responsibility that it generates, and ask ourselves whether they foster the kind of creativity that we value. By regarding copyright as relational and resisting its reification in the form of property, we open the door to debate about its subject matter, its scope, its goals and its consequences. At this moment in history, where traditional copyright concepts are critically challenged by new technologies and the activities they facilitate, the future direction of copyright depends upon our readiness to debate these issues.

3.4.4.3 Authorship as dialogic process

The final lesson to be drawn from a relational-feminist inquiry into copyright relates to the dialogic nature of the authorial creation. As we have seen, relational feminism stresses the central role of dialogue and narrative in the process of shaping social practices, institutions, discourses and, of course, the self. A relational theory of copyright should regard authorship as participatory and dialogic. When the author creates original expression in the form of literature, art, drama or music, she is engaged in an *intra*-personal dialogue (developing a form of personal narrative by drawing upon experience, situation and critical reflection) and an *inter*personal dialogue (drawing upon the texts and discourses around her to communicate meaning to an anticipated audience). Authorship – like the feminist conception of narrative – is a way to develop one's voice, to communicate, and so to interact with others in and across communities. It is a way to generate meaning and establish one's individuality, but also to connect with others in relations of communication. This is the dual nature of authorship.

By understanding authorship as a dialogic process rather than a single unitary act, we can recognise facets of authorship that copyright law has, traditionally, either neglected or undermined. The author's works must be understood in their social context, and her acquired rights must be examined in relation to her audience and other members of her communicative communities. There is no vacuum around the creative process, and no wall surrounding the author and her expression. With her original expression the creative author is entering a cultural conversation that has been going on long before she appeared, and one that will continue long after she leaves. Whatever she adds will therefore incorporate and respond to that which has already been said; and she must trust that her contribution will inform what others say after her. In other words, the dialogic nature of authorship reveals the cumulative nature of cultural creativity.

It becomes clear that the author can only generate meaning using the texts, discourses and experiences that she has encountered, and that all original expression is, in this sense, derivative. The creation of meaning through imitation, incorporation or transformation of pre-existing texts should, therefore, be recognisable as a central component of original authorship. This does not 'diminish the merit' of authorship, but accurately describes the creative process that copyright is meant to encourage.[94] A copyright system shaped by a dialogic theory of authorship would, therefore, embrace creative forms that are currently marginalised, chilled or declared unlawful because of the use that they make of pre-existing, protected works. It follows that the rights we establish over intellectual expression must leave room for others to engage in a similar communicative process; when others enter the cultural conversation they must be free to acknowledge, respond to, and build upon the contribution the author has made. A dialogic theory of authorship thus reveals the necessary limitations of copyright's protective sphere if it is to facilitate authorial contributions to the cultural conversation.

3.4.5 A Feminist Theory of Authorship and Copyright

Copyright's conception of the author is dependent upon a particular conception of the self. In calling for a re-imagination of the author-figure that occupies the protagonist's role in modern copyright, I am appealing to the de-/reconstruction of selfhood that has been a central component of (post-)modern political philosophy and theorising, but from which the structures of intellectual property have remained stubbornly immune. As a member of groups, communities and society, and a participant in cultural and political dialogue, the author cannot be individualised without being stripped of the very characteristics that make her an author. Authors exist within, and create out of communities, culture and society. In turn, through their creative capacity, their works shape that culture and community. Authorship must therefore be understood within the context of cultural dialogue and participative processes, and in recognition of the audience and the public as a whole.

Attempts to recast the author as something other that originating individual tend to have taken the form of criticisms of romantic authorship, usually drawing upon poststructuralist accounts of the 'death of the author'. These important contributions to copyright scholarship have not had the desired impact, most likely because the notion of the author is clearly alive and well. From a policy perspective, insisting upon the death of the author is a non-starter; from a theoretical perspective, any attempt to assimilate the author's death into copyright law can only spell the death of copyright itself. Copyright needs the author, but it is not sheer pragmatism that allows copyright's author-figure to survive her brush with death: there is something intuitive about the idea of the author as, in some sense at least, the source of the words, notes, actions and images that she creates. There is something about the idea of creativity, individuality, ability, that we are unwilling to discard. Even in the face of social constructionism and the fragmentation of the stable, unified self, something that looks like author/authorship persists. The task for copyright theory is to begin to define that something in the absence of the masks and metaphors traditionally employed.

Feminist theory, both literary and political, has taught us that the simplifying dichotomies of liberal thought (self/other, public/private, individual/community, autonomy/dependence) create false dilemmas that impede our ability to engage in genuine debate, and obstruct our path towards nuanced solutions. By regarding the self as both an individual and a member of multiple, shifting communities – an autonomous agent *and* socially constituted – feminism provides the route by which we can break down the simplifying dichotomies that pervade copyright theory (author/user, creator/copier, labourer/free-rider). As an autonomous but socially constituted individual, the author is the product of her community and culture, but capable of developing her own voice, constructing her own narrative, and making her own meaning out of the discourses that constitute her. Her works are therefore the product of her communities, her culture and herself.

This route leads us to a new understanding of authorship and so to a new appreciation of copyright's task. Employing a feminist theory of dialogism, we can rediscover the significance of authorship that adopts and adapts prior texts to create new meaning. We can appreciate the nature of copyright as an institution that attributes value and authority to certain texts and speakers while silencing others, and inquire into the power dynamics that inform it. We can also perceive the importance of authorship as a dialogic process with the power to shape speakers, listeners and communities, even as it reproduces established languages and discourses. Employing relational feminism, we can question the individualised account of the author by locating her (and her expression) within the communities and relationships in which she creates. We can appreciate the nature of copyright as an institution that constructs relationships of communication between authors, users and the public by allocating powers and responsibilities. We can also perceive the nature of authorship as a form of dialogue through which individuals actively participate in a cultural conversation. All of these lessons culminate to underscore one essential proposition: a copyright system designed to encourage authorship must be capable of recognising *and valuing* the derivative, collaborative and communicative nature of creativity. Only then will the rights that it grants be means – and not obstacles – to that end.

3.5 CONCLUSION: A RELATIONAL THEORY OF COPYRIGHT

The notion of discursive engagement as central to the formation of human identity and community provides a route towards a teleological justification for the copyright system. I have described the purpose of copyright as the encouragement of communication and exchange by putting in place incentives for creativity and the dissemination of intellectual works. The rationale behind this purpose, and the significance it holds for society, can be properly understood only in the context of a theory that recognises the social value of the development, communication and exchange of intellectual expression.

A utilitarian, economic justification for copyright – which typically justifies copyright in terms of its capacity to incentivise intellectual productivity, and defines the optimal contours of copyright in terms of its ability to balance the costs and benefits of exclusionary interests[95] – is not capable of providing a normative explanation for why such creativity and exchange really matters. The starting premise for economic theorising about copyright is that authors should have sufficient economic incentive to create intellectual products, thus requiring proprietary interests over informational goods to permit recoupment in the marketplace of the 'cost of expression'.[96] The rationale: 'In the absence of copyright protection . . . the work may not be produced in the first place because the author and publisher may not be able to recover their costs of creating it.'[97] What economic theory cannot satisfactorily explain is why this matters. What is it about intellectual expression that makes us want to create the conditions necessary for its proliferation?

The concept of economic efficiency is ill equipped to capture the nature of intellectual expression as a social good.[98] As Charles Taylor states: '[T]he modern philosophy of utilitarianism is from its very foundations committed to atomism. From within this philosophy it just seems self-evident that all goods are in the last analysis the goods of individuals.'[99] As Shelley Wright warned, where society and community is presented as 'an aggregate of anomic individuals', the social justification for copyright is undercut and the benefits it provides are obscured or distorted.[100] I hope this chapter has shown how a theory of dialogic communitarianism and the notion of the relational self provide a fundamental basis for understanding the importance of authorship to the author, the audience and the public in a way that traditional, individualistic copyright theories, framed in the discourses of legal liberalism, cannot.

In this book, my overarching claim is that, when we think about copyright law, a focus upon communication and culture in the place of property and entitlement can lead us towards the re-imagination of the copyright system. In its re-imagined form, protected works are not objects of property but moments of speech; authors are not individual rights-holders but contributors to a collective conversation; original expression is not independently produced but derived from the texts and discourses that make up our culture; users are not trespassers but participants in a public dialogue. Reconfigured as such, the copyright system is one way through which the State aims to maximise social engagement, dialogic participation and cultural contributions, all of which are aspects of the public good inherent in participatory community. The value attributed to these goals is premised upon an understanding of human associations as constitutive and essential to genuine human agency and fulfilment.

I submit that such a re-imagination of copyright could have significant consequences for the shape and scope of copyright protection. Recent years have seen the progressive expansion and proliferation of copyright, extending it to new subject matters and reinforcing it with new powers of control. This re-imagined framework reveals as false the notion that more and stronger protection produces more and better intellectual production. The cumulative nature of creativity means that contributors must be free to make meaning from pre-existing works; we must leave space within the legal framework for these interactive, dialogic processes of cultural engagement, ensuring room for learning, sharing, interpreting, responding, and not just passively consuming. This framework also reveals as flawed the current emphasis upon the author as owner and natural bearer of rights. Instead, we can recognise the author in her role as communicator, while similarly valuing the communicative activities of users of cultural products, from students and educators to historians, biographers, journalists, hip-hop artists and post-modern sculptors.

Such expressive participation in cultural dialogue lies at the heart of copyright's public purpose. It follows that the rights protected by copyright law – and their reach – must be justifiable in relation to this purpose. In short, the re-imagination of copyright entails the re-evaluation of the rights that it grants to authors and the burdens that it imposes upon the public.

Part I has examined the nature of the author-figure in copyright law, and the philosophical assumptions that inform his current characterisation as independent, individual originator of meaning. I have explored critiques that have been launched in copyright and literary scholarship against this romanticised conception of the author. I have argued that copyright needs a new understanding of the processes of cultural creativity capable of embracing expression that does not fit within this inapposite, historically and politically contingent mould. In search for a route towards this new understanding of authorship, I have turned to the work of feminist theorists whose philosophical positions and political goals have forced them to retrieve a meaningful conception of subjectivity from the postmodern ruins of atomistic individualism. I have suggested that an appropriate route can be forged using the concepts of dialogism and the relational self. This will lead us towards an improved understanding of the socially situated author, the relational nature of copyright, and the dialogic processes of authorship. This will, in turn, allow us to re-imagine copyright as an institution designed to encourage relations of communication and participation in the name of the public good.

Parts II and III continue to push towards copyright's re-imagination in these terms. I will critically examine some of the concepts and convictions that have caused traditional copyright theory to misrecognise the nature of cultural creativity and copyright's purpose. I will show how a shift in thinking or a departure from these notions might alter the shape and scope of copyright law and allow it to better perform its social function.

NOTES

1. *Cf.* Alan Durham, 'Copyright and Information Theory: Toward an Alternative Model of "Authorship"' (2004) B.Y.U.L. Rev. 69 at 71 [Durham, 'Copyright and Information Theory']. As Julie Cohen reminds us, 'talking about creativity and inspiration need not entail philosophical commitment to discredited romantic ideals of individual authorship and related notions of the natural rights of authors.' See J.E. Cohen, 'Copyright, Commodification, and Culture: Locating the Public Domain' in Lucie Guibault and P. Bernt Hugenholtz (eds), *The Future of the Public Domain* (Netherlands: Kluwer Law International, 2006) 121.
2. See Thomas D. Barton, 'Troublesome Connections: The Law and Post-Enlightenment Culture' (1998) 47 Emory L.J. 163.
3. B.L. Marshall, *Engendered Modernity – Feminism, Social Theory and Social Change* (Cambridge: Polity Press, 1994) at 108.
4. Laurie A. Finke, *Feminist Theory, Women's Writing* (Ithaca: Cornell University Press, 1992) at 1 [Finke, *Feminist Theory*].
5. As Jennifer Nedelsky writes: '[I]n the realm of both political theory and legal history, . . . women and other subordinated groups were excluded from the underlying [liberal] conception of selfhood and from the corresponding legal rights. The important point here is not just the fact of historical exclusion, but the arguments that such exclusion was built into these paired conceptions of self and rights. If these arguments are persuasive, then it is not possible simply to use these exclusionary concepts to include everyone.' Nedelsky, 'Citizenship and Relational Feminism' in Ronald Beiner and Wayne Norman (eds), *Canadian Political Philosophy* (Oxford: Oxford University Press, 2001) 131 at 132.
6. See T. de Lauretis, 'Upping the Anti [*sic*] in Feminist Theory' in S. During (ed.), *The Cultural Studies Reader* (New York: Routledge, 1993) at 83.
7. Marshall, note 3 above at 148, cited in Anne Brooks, *Postfeminisms: Feminism, Cultural Theory and Cultural Forms* (New York: Routledge, 1997) at 15–16. Marshall goes on to explain: '[W]oman as subjects have never been accorded the coherence, autonomy, rationality or agency of the subject which undergirds an unreconstructed modernism, and which postmodernism has deconstructed out of existence.'
8. Marshall, note 3 above at 148, cited in Brooks, Ibid. at 13.
9. Brooks, Ibid. at 15.
10. Michel Foucault, 'What Is an Author?' in Paul Rabinow (ed.), *The Foucault Reader* (New York: Pantheon Books, 1984) 101.
11. Ibid.
12. Nancy K. Miller, 'The Text's Heroine: A Feminist Critic and Her Fictions' (1982) 23:3 *Diacritics* 48 at 53, cited in Finke, *Feminist Theory*, note 4 above.
13. See Finke, *Feminist Theory*, note 4 above at 109. Finke notes (Ibid. at 194, n. 1): '[A]s it proliferated in American universities in the 1980s, deconstruction seemed to lose the force of this ideological agenda and political mission. The death of the author served more to aggrandize the (male) critic than to expose the pernicious effect of patriarchal order as an ideological formation.'
14. Marilyn Randall, *Pragmatic Plagiarism: Authorship, Profit and Power* (Toronto: University of Toronto Press, 2001) [Randall, *Pragmatic Plagiarism*] at 58.
15. Ibid. at 59.
16. Ibid. at 56. See also Judith Roof and Robyn Wiegman, *Who Can Speak: Authority and Critical Identity* (Urbana: University of Illinois Press, 1995).

17. Finke, *Feminist Theory*, note 4 above at 1.
18. This term was coined by Elaine Showalter, 'Feminist Criticism in the Wilderness' (1981) 8 Crit. Inquiry 179.
19. Shelley Wright, 'A Feminist Exploration of the Legal Protection of Art' (1994) 7 C.J.W.L. 59 at 62.
20. Ibid. at 154. See Lillian Robinson, *Sex, Class and Culture* (London: Methuen, 1983); Christine Froula, 'When Eve Reads Milton: Undoing the Canonical Economy' (1983) 10 Crit. Inquiry 321; Jane Tompkins, *Sensational Designs: The Cultural Work of American Fiction, 1790–1860* (New York: Oxford University Press, 1985).
21. Finke, *Feminist Theory*, note 4 above at 154.
22. Wright, note 19 above at 77–8.
23. Finke, *Feminist Theory*, note 4 above at 110.
24. Mary O'Connor, 'Subject, Voice, and Women in Some Contemporary Black American Women's Writing' in David M. Bauer and Susan Jaret McKinstry (eds), *Feminism, Bakhtin and the Dialogic* (Albany: State University of New York Press, 1991) 199 at 200.
25. Finke, *Feminist Theory*, note 4 above at 111, 155.
26. See e.g. Michel Bakhtin (ed.), *The Dialogic Imagination: Four Essays*, trans. Caryl Emerson and Michael Holquist (Austin: University of Texas Press, 1981) [Bakhtin, *Dialogic Imagination*]; Tzvetan Todorov in Bakhtin, *Rabelais and His World*, trans. Helene Iswolsky (Bloomington: Indiana University Press, 1984) at 60. See also Michael Holquist, *Dialogism: Bakhtin and his World*, 2nd edn (New York: Routledge, 2002). On the feminist reworking of Bakhtin's dialogism, see Patricia Yaeger, 'Afterword' in Bauer and McKinstry, note 24 above at 240: '[F]eminist dialogics . . .overcome the male-centeredness of Bakhtin criticism and replace its fallacies with new forms of textual and cultural critique – providing the resistance from the margins that Bakhtin applauded but refused to gender.' See also, Patricia Yaeger, '"Because a Fire Was in My Head": Eudora Welty and the Dialogic Imagination' (1984) 99 P.M.L.A. 955; Wayne Booth, 'Freedom of Interpretation: Bakhtin and the Challenge of Feminist Criticism' (1982) 9 Crit. Inquiry 45; Dale Bauer, *Feminist Dialogics: A Theory of Failed Community* (Albany, N.Y.: State University of New York Press, 1988).
27. Bakhtin, *Dialogic Imagination*, note 26 above at 354; Finke, *Feminist Theory*, note 4 above at 12.
28. Bakhtin uses the term 'heteroglossia' (or untranslated: *raznojazychie*) to capture the dynamic complexity and clamorousness of this contested field of multivocal utterances. Ann Shukman (ed.), *Bakhtin School Papers* (Oxford: RPT Publications, 1983) at 4, cited by O'Connor, note 24 above at 199.
29. Finke, *Feminist Theory*, note 4 above at 13, citing Bakhtin, 'Discourse in the Novel', in Bakhtin, *Dialogic Imagination*, note 26 above at 276
30. See Bakhtin and V.N. Vološinov, *Marxism and the Philosophy of Language*, trans. Ladislav Matejka and I.R. Titunik (Cambridge, Mass.: Harvard University Press, 1986) at 85: 'Utterance, as we know, is constructed between two socially organized persons. . . . The *word is oriented toward an addressee*, toward who that addressee might be. . . . There can be no such thing as an abstract addressee, a man unto himself, so to speak.' See also Bakhtin, *Dialogic Imagination*, note 26 above at 293: 'each work tastes of the context and contexts in which it has lived its socially charged life. . . . Contextual overtones . . . are inevitable in the work.'
31. Finke, *Feminist Theory*, note 4 above at 14.
32. O'Connor, note 24 above at 201.
33. Finke, *Feminist Theory*, note 4 above at 111. *Cf.* Foucault, 'What is an Author', note 10 above at 119–20.
34. Ibid. at 111.
35. Gale M. Schwab, 'Irigarayan Dialogism: Play and Powerplay' in Bauer and McKinstry, note 24 above, 57 at 58.

36. Finke, *Feminist Theory*, note 4 above at 194.
37. *Cf.* Janet Ransom, 'Feminism, Difference and Discourse: The Limits of Discursive Analysis for Feminism' in C. Ramazanoglu (ed.), *Up Against Foucault: Explorations of Some Tensions Between Foucault and Feminism* (New York: Routledge, 1993) 123 at 134.
38. Finke, *Feminist Theory*, note 4 above at 13–14.
39. Bakhtin, *Dialogic Imagination*, note 26 above at 346–7.
40. Finke writes, in *Feminist Theory*, note 4 above at 159: '[V]alue is always "value-for" because it is through selection, classification, and ordering (hierarchies) that we confer value upon objects . . . . If value is value-for, then we must ask of any valued object, value for whom? Under what circumstances and conditions? And for what purpose?'
41. Ibid. at 156.
42. Ibid. at 17.
43. See e.g. Elizabeth Frazer and Nicola Lacey, *The Politics of Community: A Feminist Critique of the Liberal-Communitarian Debate* (Toronto: University of Toronto Press, 1993) at 174: '[T]he resolution, or at least weakening of the agency/structure dichotomy is of first importance from a feminist perspective. For if this cannot be achieved, we are stuck with an unenviable choice. We can have a disembodied conception of selfhood which implicitly excludes or problematises women and marginalizes women's experiences. . . . Or we can have a determined if embodied conception of the socially situated self which seems to take away with one hand the possibility of critical thinking, social struggle and radical politics just as it gives us the possibility of contextualized political theory with the other.'
44. Wright, note 19 above at 73–4.
45. Ibid. at 74.
46. Frazer and Lacey, note 43 above at 102. See e.g. Alasdair MacIntyre, *After Virtue: A Study in Moral Theory* (Notre Dame, Ind.: University of Notre Dame, 1981); Michael Sandel, *Liberalism and the Limits of Justice*, 2nd edn (New York: Cambridge University Press, 1998); Michael Walzer, *Spheres of Justice: A Defense of Pluralism and Equality* (New York: Basic Books, 1983); Charles Taylor, 'Atomism' in Shlomo Avineri and Avner de-Shalit (eds), *Communitarianism and Individualism* (New York: Oxford University Press, 1992) 29; Roberto Unger, *Knowledge and Politics* (New York: Free Press, 1975). But see also, C. Taylor, 'Cross-Purposes: The Liberal-Communitarian Debate' in Nancy L. Rosenblum (ed.), *Liberalism and the Moral Life* (Cambridge, Mass.: Harvard University Press, 1989) 159; Michael Walzer, 'The Communitarian Critique of Liberalism' (1990) 18 Pol. Theory 6.
47. *Cf.* Seyla Benhabib, *Situating the Self: Gender, Community and Postmodernism in Contemporary Ethics* (New York: Routledge, 1992) at 70 [Benhabib, *Situating the Self*]: 'As a political theory, "communitarianism" must primarily be identified via negative, that is less in terms of the positive social and political philosophy it offers than in light of the powerful critique of liberalism it has developed.'
48. Sandel, note 46 above at 150 [emphasis in original].
49. Avineri and de-Shalit, note 46 above at 6–7.
50. See e.g. Benhabib, *Situating the Self,* note 47 above ; Drucilla Cornell, 'The Doubly Prized World: Myth, Allegory and the Feminine' (1990) 75 Cornell L. Rev. 644; Sarah Hoagland, *Lesbian Ethics: Toward New Value* (Palo Alto: Institute for Lesbian Studies, 1988); Jennifer Nedelsky, 'Reconceiving Autonomy: Sources, Thoughts and Possibilities' (1989) 1 Yale J.L. & Feminism 7 [Nedelsky, 'Reconceiving Autonomy']; Lorraine Code, *What Can She Know? Feminist Theory and the Construction of Knowledge* (Ithaca: Cornell University Press, 1991).
51. See Frazer and Lacey, note 43 above at 54, 125. See also, Penny A. Weiss, 'Feminism and Communitarianism: Comparing Critiques of Liberalism' [Weiss, 'Feminism'] in Penny Weiss and Marilyn Friedman (eds), *Feminism and Community* (Philadelphia: Temple University Press, 1995) 161 at 172–3.

52. See e.g. Mari J. Matsuda, 'Liberal Jurisprudence and Abstracted Visions of Human Nature: A Feminist Critique of Rawl's Theory of Justice' (1986) 16 N.M.L. Rev. 613 at 627; Nedelsky, 'Citizenship and Relational Feminism', note 5 above at 134–41, examining the claims of 'maternal feminism'; Virginia Held, 'Non-Contractual Society: A Feminist View' (1987) 13 Can. J. Phil. 124.
53. Frazer and Lacey, note 43 above at 57.
54. *Cf.* Seyla Benhabib and Drucilla Cornell, 'Introduction' in Seyla Benhabib and Drucilla Cornell (eds), *Feminism as Critique: On the Politics of Gender* (Minneapolis, Minn.: University of Minnesota Press, 1987).
55. Will Kymlicka, 'Liberalism and Communitarianism' (1988) 18 Can. J. Phil. 181 at 181 cited in Weiss, 'Feminism and Communitarianism', note 51 above at 164.
56. Frazer and Lacey, note 43 above at 137.
57. See Weiss, 'Feminism', note 51 above at 175: 'Women's roles have frequently meant obliteration and sacrifice of the self, or redefinition of one's self and self-interest predominantly in terms of and in relation to others. The communitarian solution to liberalism's impoverished social life fails, however, to solve or even seriously address this enforced self-abnegation.'
58. See Ibid. at 141.
59. See Iris Marion Young, 'The Ideal of Community and the Politics of Difference,' in Weiss and Friedman, note 51 above at 233–57.
60. See Weiss, 'Feminism', note 51 above at 165–6: '[The communitarian notion of social context] omits such traditions and practices as sexism and racism. . . . Such forces . . . not only often create distinct communities . . . but also establish relations that pervade and structure all communities'.
61. Ibid. at 151.
62. Ibid. at 151, 175.
63. Nedelsky, 'Reconceiving Autonomy', note 50 above at 8.
64. See e.g. Martha Minow, *Making All the Difference: Inclusion, Exclusion and American Law* (Ithaca: Cornell University Press, 1990); Nedelsky, 'Reconceiving Autonomy', Ibid.; and Jennifer Nedelsky, 'Reconceiving Rights as Relationship' (1993) Rev. Const. Stud. 1 [Nedelsky, 'Reconceiving Rights']. See also Catherine Keller, *From a Broken Web: Separation, Sexism, and Self* (Boston: Beacon Press, 1986); Carol Gilligan, *In a Different Voice: Psychological Theory and Women's Development* (Cambridge, Mass.: Harvard University Press, 1982); Robin West, 'Jurisprudence and Gender' (1988) 55 U. Chicago L. Rev. 1; and Mary Becker, 'Patriarchy and Feminism: Toward a Substantive Feminism' (1999) U. Chicago Legal. F. 21.
65. See e.g. Nedelsky, 'Reconceiving Autonomy', note 50 above at 21: 'The collective is not simply a potential threat to individuals, but is constitutive of them, and thus is a source of their autonomy as well as a danger to it.'
66. Ibid. at 22.
67. See Nedelsky, 'Reconceiving Autonomy', note 50 above at 12. See also, Susan H. Williams, 'A Feminist Reassessment of Civil Society' (1997) 72 Ind. L.J. 417 at 427 [Williams, 'A Feminist Reassessment'] at 435; Diane T. Meyers, *Self, Society, and Personal Choice* (New York: Columbia University Press, 1989) at 40.
68. See Nedelsky, 'Reconceiving Autonomy', Ibid. at 21. See also, Frazer and Lacey, note 43 above at 180.
69. Nedelsky, 'Citizenship and Relational Feminism', note 5 above at 133.
70. Ibid.
71. Richard H. Fallon, 'Two Senses of Autonomy' (1994) 46 Stan. L. Rev. 875 at 887–8, cited in Williams, 'A Feminist Reassessment', note 67 above at 437.
72. Frazer and Lacey, note 43 above at 178.
73. Nedelsky, 'Reconceiving Rights', note 64 above at 8.
74. Ibid. at 9.
75. See Nedelsky, 'Reconceiving Autonomy', note 50 above at 15–18.
76. Ibid. at 23.

77. See Joseph William Singer, 'The Reliance Interest in Property' (1988) 40 Stan. L. Rev. 577.
78. Nedelsky, 'Reconceiving Rights', note 64 above at 13. See also Iris Marion Young, *Justice and the Politics of Difference* (Princeton: Princeton University Press, 1990) at 25: 'Rights are relationships, not things; they are institutionally defined rules specifying what people can do in relation to one another.'
79. Nedelsky, 'Reconceiving Rights', Ibid. at 14–15.
80. See Seyla Benhabib, 'Liberal Dialogue Versus a Critical Theory of Discursive Legitimation' in Rosenblum, note 46 above, 143; Seyla Benhabib, 'Autonomy, Modernity and Community,' in Benhabib, *Situating the Self*, note 47 above, 68; Drucilla Cornell, 'Beyond Tragedy and Complacency' (1987) 81 Nw. U.L. Rev. 693; Drucilla Cornell, 'Two Lectures on the Normative Dimensions of the Community in the Law' (1987) 54 Tenn. L. Rev. 327; Drucilla Cornell, *The Philosophy of Limit* (New York: Routledge, 1992). Nedelsky, 'Citizenship and Relational Feminism', note 5 above at 143, also stresses the importance of public participation in ongoing debates and collective decision-making 'both as an intrinsic part of human autonomy and expression, and in order to ensure that the structures of relationship are such that they foster the autonomy of all.'
81. Frazer and Lacey, note 43 above at 203.
82. Ibid. at 192–3.
83. See Ibid. at 208. Consciousness-raising is an 'interactive and collaborative process of articulating one's experiences and making meaning of them with others who also articulate their experiences.' Katharine T. Bartlett, 'Feminist Legal Methods' in Katharine T. Bartlett and Rosanne Kennedy (eds), *Feminist Legal Theory: Readings in Law and Gender* (Oxford: Westview Press, 1991) at 381.
84. See Anne C. Dailey, 'Feminism's Return to Liberalism' (1993) 102 Yale L.J. 1265 at 1274 *et seq.*
85. Ibid.
86. Ibid. at 1276.
87. Nedelsky, 'Reconceiving Autonomy', note 50 above at 11.
88. Nedelsky, 'Citizenship and Relational Feminism', note 5 above at 133.
89. Williams, 'Utopianism, Epistemology, and Feminist Theory' (1993) 5 Yale J.L. & Feminism 289 at 308–9.
90. Williams, 'A Feminist Reassessment', note 67 above at 430–31.
91. Nedelsky, 'Reconceiving Autonomy', note 50 above at 12.
92. Nedelsky speaks of the conclusory quality of claims such as 'it's my property,' and warns that proprietary language can do harm by 'treating as settled what should be debated.' Nedelsky, 'Reconceiving Rights', note 64 above at 16.
93. Ibid. at 15.
94. *Cf.* Litman, 'The Public Domain' (1990) 39 Emory L.J. 965 at 1011: 'My characterization of authorship as a combination of absorption, astigmatism, and amnesia is not intended to diminish its merit. Indeed, my position is that this mixture is precisely the process that yields the works of authorship we wish to encourage through the copyright law . . .. If this description is accurate, it implies that the romantic model of authorship, taken seriously, would do grave disservice to the authors it seeks to describe.'
95. See e.g. William M. Landes and Richard A. Posner, *The Economic Structure of Intellectual Property Law* (Cambridge, Mass.: The Belknap Press of Harvard University Press, 2003); Landes and Posner, 'An Economic Analysis of Copyright Law' (1989) 18 J. Legal Stud. 325; Stephen Breyer, 'The Uneasy Case for Copyright Protection: A Study of Copyright in Books, Photocopies, and Computer Programs' (1970) 84 Harv. L. Rev. 281; Mark A. Lemley, 'The Economics of Improvement In Intellectual Property Law' (1997) 75 Tex. L. Rev. 989; and R. Polk Wagner, 'Information Wants to Be Free: Intellectual Property and the Mythologies of Control' (2003) 103 Colum. L. Rev. 995.

96. Landes and Posner, *The Economic Structure of Intellectual Property Law*, Ibid. at 37.
97. Ibid. at 40.
98. *Cf.* Neil Weinstock Netanel, 'Copyright and a Democratic Civil Society' (1996) 106 Yale L.J. 283 at 288: '[N]eoclassicism cannot serve as the basis for copyright doctrine because copyright's primary goal is not allocative efficiency, but the support of a democratic culture.'
99. Charles Taylor, *Philosophical Arguments* (Cambridge, Mass.: Harvard University Press, 1995) at 128.
100. See note 44 above and accompanying text.

PART II

The origin of copyright: Locke, labour and limiting the author's right

4. Against a Lockean approach to copyright

4.1. INTRODUCTION

Copyright law has been the subject of many theories that purport to explain or justify its existence, its scope and its limitations. The particular species of justification we offer in turn defines the extent of the rights that copyright confers, and the kinds of limits that naturally evolve to demarcate those rights. My aim, in Part II of this book, is to challenge the pervasive view that the origin of the copyright interest (in both the moral and legal sense) lies in the industry or labour of the author. Chapter 4 focuses primarily on the role of labour in defining the moral relation between the author and work by means of which the copyright interest is justified, while Chapter 5 focuses on the role of labour and other elements of authorship in defining the legal relation between author and work – what it is that the author must do in order to establish a legal right over her work.[1] My proposition is that it is a mistake to look to the relation between the author and her work as the basis on which to justify the copyright system. In so doing, we necessarily neglect the social and cultural goals of copyright, and so wrongly augment the scope of the rights conferred under copyright while failing to identify and draw the appropriate limits thereto.

The language of property and entitlement pervades copyright rhetoric. In the common law world, at least, the notion of entitlement that underlies a property-based theory of copyright is commonly derived, consciously or unconsciously, from a Lockean-type labour acquisition approach. Rights conferred on authors under the copyright system are strengthened in scope and form by the persistent presence of this approach. As such, my purpose in this chapter is to explore the weaknesses and the dangers of a theory of intellectual property grounded in a Lockean vision of property entitlement and focused upon the link between the author and her original intellectual work – particularly where that link is conceptualised in terms of the investment of labour. My argument is that deontological explanations for copyright law framed in Lockean natural rights rhetoric, and loaded with presumptions of moral entitlement, inevitably distort rather than facilitate a nuanced understanding of the copyright system.

I will begin by briefly introducing the conceptual and normative tensions of the copyright system, in terms of the relationship between the author, the public and the work. The distinction between two competing justificatory frameworks for copyright – one centred around the public–work link and the other around the author–work link – will provide the context for the argument that follows. Sections 2 and 3 will set out the foundational tenets of Locke's theory of acquisition through labour and the significance of this theory in the copyright context. In Section 4, I present what I call the 'internal critiques' of a Lockean approach to copyright, contesting the extent to which the shape and scope of copyright law can be explained by the labour model. I raise the 'external critiques' of the Lockean copyright model in Section 5, arguing that attempts to formulate a Lockean explanation for the copyright system are not only unconvincing but also misplaced, potentially threatening the system's legitimacy by undermining its rationale. From both within and outside of Locke's model, my analysis aims to reveal the inappropriateness of labour theory in the copyright realm and the need to reorient our focus towards the relationship between the public and the intellectual work. This departure from a natural rights theory of copyright protection is an essential step towards the reimagination of copyright.

4.2 THE PUBLIC, THE AUTHOR AND THE WORK: JUSTIFYING COPYRIGHT

4.2.1 Author–work or Public–work?

Copyright can be conceived of as a triadic relationship between the author, the intellectual work and the public: the author has an exclusionary interest over the intangible work; the public has an interest in the author's work as an intellectual expression; and the author has a relationship with the public through the work. One possible angle from which to justify copyright protection is to focus upon the relationship between the author and the work, and to identify within that author–work link the reason why we protect the author's intellectual product through copyright. From this angle, the authorship process itself establishes the right of the author to own the results of that process. This, in turn, defines the relationship between the author and the public (in relation to the owned work), and between the public and the work (as restricted by the author's ownership).

Compare this line of reasoning to a justification for copyright framed in terms of the public-work link. According to this approach, it is only by virtue of the relationship between the public interest and the products of intellectual creativity (which Chapter 3 described in terms of the social value of cultural dialogue) that we can explain the relationship of control created between the author and the work in the form of copyright. This relationship in turn defines the relationship between author and public (in terms of rights and duties, but also in recognition of a larger, and mutually constitutive, cultural conversation).

At its most fundamental level, this public interest approach justifies copyright in light of its public purpose of encouraging intellectual creativity. Rights are granted to authors in the belief that intellectual works will be underproduced unless there is sufficient opportunity to exploit them for financial return. But as I have argued, it is only if we appreciate the role that intellectual creation plays in our society that we can recognise this underproduction as a danger that public policy should seek to avert. Copyright, as the chosen policy tool, must therefore be rationalised in light of the relationship between the public and intellectual works. The subject matter of copyright – literary, artistic, dramatic, and musical expression – is a social good that furthers a shared cultural value.

By advancing a copyright concept premised upon the relationship between the public and the author's intellectual product, I am appealing to the role of cultural production and communication in society. My concern is that, if we understand copyright as based upon some conception of the author-work link, we fail to see the relationship between the public and the work as anything other than the consequence of the author–work relationship. An effective and justifiable copyright system requires that the copyright interest (the link between author and work) be structured with deference to the public-work link. The copyright interest must then be understood as the consequence of the relationship between the public and the work. The appropriate relationship between the author, the public and the work can only be achieved through the copyright system if we make our policy decisions and choose our metaphors with a focus upon the connection between the public and the products of cultural and intellectual creativity.

4.2.2 Authorship and Entitlement

The popular rhetoric of copyright law embraces author-oriented reasoning, or a focus upon the author–work link. Two major facets of prevailing copyright philosophy are grounded in the author–work relationship: first, the vision of romantic authorship (and the convergent concepts of 'originality' and the independent 'work') criticised in Part I; and second, the theory of private property and natural right addressed in this chapter. It is important to note that these facets of copyright theory are not discrete but are mutually facilitative and, arguably, mutually dependent. As I have already argued, the individualisation of authorship establishes a simple route towards propertisation of creative achievement: a text can achieve the level of objectification necessary for it to be cast as the appropriate subject matter of a property right, while at the same time the author becomes the worthy owner of the fruits of her labour. Indeed, Rosemary Coombe notes, the concept of 'authorship' possesses an 'alchemical power to transfer anything it can be made to adhere to into *property*, absolutely defined'.[2]

Author-based reasoning, compounded by theories of private entitlement, gives rise to a rights-based vision of copyright, which affects both our basic characterisation of the copyright regime and the extent of the rights that we expect it to accord. Notions of reward, desert and natural right give copyright holders' claims a substantial and unmerited normative force that pervades copyright rhetoric, culminates in the overprotection of copyrightable works, and in so doing, threatens to undermine the coherence of the copyright system. Rather than searching for or presupposing deontological explanations for intellectual property rights, we should be struggling to understand doctrinal concepts such as authorship and originality – and copyright itself – as politically and socially constructed metaphors. It may then become possible to recognise and reconfigure the foundations and motivations of copyright law, enabling it to better serve the social goal of encouraging creative expression and exchange.

4.3 THE ROLE OF LOCKEAN LABOUR THEORY

4.3.1 Locke's Theory of Acquisition of Property

The desire to link a theory of intellectual property back to Locke probably has much to do with reasons of ideological legitimacy; Locke remains a powerful totem.[3] The extent to which Lockean theory has entrenched itself within our society's ideological framework is often underestimated. Perhaps because the notion of 'fruits of one's labour' appeals intuitively to our sense of justice, it has a solid grip upon our basic assumptions about property entitlement, even when it seems obvious that labour is not, simply as a matter of fact, constitutive of property. Since a natural rights approach to copyright grounds a strong version of property rights, it is not surprising that those whose interests will be furthered by an expansive copyright system are the quickest to stress the author's natural right to reap the benefit of her labour. However, there is cause to suspect that the ideological force of Locke's theory in this area has come to outweigh its ability to actually disentangle and resolve the issues at stake in copyright policy. After all, as Peter Drahos has observed, the theory is itself disputable in meaning and result, offering a 'hermeneutical free play' for those who would make a strategic appeal to the Lockean model.[4]

The Lockean justification for copyright rests upon the assertion that the original author is entitled to the exclusive rights in her work, having exerted mental labour in its creation. This assertion depends upon the 'root idea' of Lockean theory that 'people are entitled to hold, as property, whatever they produce by their own initiative, intelligence, and industry.'[5] According to Locke, the right to acquire private property can be derived from natural law principles. All persons have the liberty to use the commons, given to mankind by God for their support and comfort.[6] Men have the right of self-preservation, and because things cannot be of any use until they are appropriated, without private appropriation the Earth cannot serve the purpose for which it was given.[7] With this foundation for a divine authority to privately appropriate, the remaining question is *how* one 'come[s] to have a property in any thing'. The answer lies in Locke's labour-to-property equation.

Man can acquire property in the products of his labour, because 'the *Labor* of his Body, and the *Work* of his Hands . . . are properly his.'[8] The theory of acquisition begins with the assumption that everyone has a natural right of property in his or her own body, and it follows, according to Locke, that whenever a person mixes or annexes or joins one's labour to a thing, that thing becomes the property of that person. As there is a prior obligation not to harm another 'in his Life, Health, Liberty, or Possessions',[9] all persons have the duty not to interfere with the resources that another individual has legitimately appropriated or produced by labouring on the common. The person who takes a labourer's property does so because he 'desired the benefit of another's Pains, which he had no right to.'[10] Property rights, Locke seems to suggest, are a just reward for the industrious.[11]

However, according to Locke's theory of acquisition, labour does not alone determine the existence of a property right over the product of labour. The labour-to-property equation will only apply where two fundamental conditions are met. The first condition requires that there be 'enough, and as good left in common for others'.[12] The second condition, often called the 'no-spoilage proviso', requires that no person take from the common more than he can use.[13] This is based on the understanding that God made things for people to enjoy, and not to spoil or destroy.

4.3.2 Lockean Labour Theory in Copyright Discourse

Is there any need for a critique of the Lockean justification for copyright? We could argue that the time has long since passed when we believed in an author's entitlement, as a matter of natural right, to property in the creative product. As long ago as 1774, the House of Lords declared that the entirety of an author's interest in his work was contained in the copyright statute, and the nature of copyright as a creature of statute continues to be widely acknowledged.[14] However, rights-based author-reasoning remains very much a part of modern day copyright discourse. The interpretation and application of copyright law in the courts is frequently incongruous with its purported nature as a utilitarian construct.[15] While the Lockean influence is not always detectable on the face of judicial pronouncements, Lockean concepts of entitlement and desert often exist as a subterranean presence that provides a particular sense of justice or fairness, thereby exerting significant power over the development and application of copyright doctrine.

In the copyright context, natural rights discourse begins and ends with a proprietarian focus. Although an emphasis on the property rights of copyright owners could be consistent with a utilitarian conception of copyright,[16] the property rights dogma employed by courts and governments often reveals an unmistakably moralistic edge. According to a Canadian government report on the revision of copyright, '[o]wnership is ownership is ownership. The copyright owner owns the intellectual works in the same sense as the landowner owns land.'[17] Following this logic, infringement of copyright becomes analogous to an invasion of property – a conclusion with important ramifications for the way in which the courts enforce copyright law. [18] It is however most important to note that this property-oriented vision of copyright affects how we rationalise the copyright system; copyright is not about manipulating expressive activity but is rather a means to protect authors' private property rights. The importance of this rationale is that, unless entirely tautological, it presupposes the existence of rights that require protection.

The property-based starting point therefore tends toward the conclusion that statutory copyright 'is *based on* . . . the *recognition* of the property of authors in their creation',[19] with copyright's purpose being 'to protect and reward the intellectual effort of the author'.[20] In *Bishop v. Stevens*, McLachlin J. insisted that '[t]he *Copyright Act*, 1911, was passed with *a single object*, namely, *the benefit of authors* of all kinds.'[21] Similarly, in *CCH Canadian v. Law Society of Upper Canada*, Gibson J. opined at trial level that '[t]he object and purpose of the *Copyright Act is to benefit authors*, albeit that in benefiting authors it is capable of having a . . . broader-based public benefit . . . for the advancement of learning.'[22] The implication is that any benefit the public might derive from the copyright system is merely a fortunate by-product of private entitlement. In the *Michelin* case, which will be examined in detail in Part III, Teitelbaum J. refused to question the 'usual characterization of copyright as private property' with a 'private nature', and proceeded to define the purpose of the Copyright Act as being the '*protection of authors* and ensuring that they are *recompensed* for their creative energies.'[23] In 1985, a Canadian Sub-Committee produced a report that characterised copyright as a 'reward system', under the politically unambiguous title: *A Charter of Rights for Creators*.[24] When copyright is regarded as a species of private property, it is typically justified in terms of the individual copyright owner's entitlement to own and control.

One might, of course, distinguish between a concern for the copyright holder's property rights and a more powerful understanding of those rights as the author's moral and natural entitlement. But the distinction turns out to be a vulnerable one, difficult to maintain in practice. Certainly, property need not depend upon a Lockean explanation either for its existence as a right, or for its justification. Nonetheless, there is a strong tendency, often beneath the conscious level, for us to conceive of a property right in Lockean terms. The property right conferred by copyright legislation is understood as a reward for intellectual labour and effort, and that reward is in turn regarded as something 'deserved'. What is deserved becomes an entitlement,[25] a heavily loaded concept that carries with it a normative force ill-suited to copyright theory. As the language of private property combines intuitively with Lockean assumptions, copyright is transmogrified into individual entitlement.

Ample evidence of Lockean rhetoric can be found in copyright cases. It is not uncommon for explanations of copyright protection to emphasise the importance of ensuring 'that men of ability . . . may not be deprived their *just merits* and the *reward* of their ingenuity and *labour*.'[26] The principle at work was famously stated in *Hogg v. Scott*: '[T]he defendant is not at liberty to use or avail himself of the labour which the plaintiff has been at for the purpose of producing his work, that is, in fact, merely to take away the result of another man's labour, *or, in other words, his property*.'[27]

In the English case of *Walter v. Lane*,[28] which reveals perhaps better than any other the tensions and uncertainties that pervade copyright's central doctrine of originality, Lockean concepts were invoked to rationalise copyright protection. According to Lord Halsbury, the state of the law must not permit 'one man to make profit and to appropriate to himself the labour, skill and capital of another.'[29] In order to prevent such an occurrence, it was necessary to find that 'the *labour* of reproducing the spoken words . . . makes the person who has so acted . . . an author.'[30] Since there was labour to be protected, there was authorship and, hence, copyright. Lord Davey found copyright in the plaintiff's work by asserting the 'sound principle that a man shall not avail himself of another's skill, labour, and expense by copying the written product thereof.'[31] The reasoning was syllogistic; *because* the defendants 'desire[d] to reap where they [had] not sown', the plaintiff had copyright in a verbatim report, which the defendants had infringed. In this way, the relationship between the author and the work (the author laboured to produce the work) results in a copyright interest over the work that is then enforceable against the unentitled interloper (the unlicensed public).

In the context of the determining the originality of a work, Lockean labour theory has provided support for the copyrightability of intellectual products involving only labour on the part of the author, as opposed to some broader element of skill, judgment or creativity. The Supreme Court of Canada drew this connection when it explained, 'the "sweat of the brow" or "industriousness" standard of originality . . . is premised on a natural rights or Lockean theory of "just desserts", namely that an author deserves to have his or her efforts in producing a work rewarded.'[32] The same reasoning seems to underlie the 'rough practical test that what is worth copying is worth protecting';[33] if something is worth copying, some effort must have gone into its production, and that effort therefore deserves protection against those who would attempt to benefit from the producer's pains. From the natural rights-based perspective, it is the industry and effort of the producer that the law must protect, even above the expressive activity (or indeed the labour) of the user. Fortunately, as I will discuss in detail in Chapter 5, Canada's originality standard no longer extends copyright protection to the results of mere labour.[34] However, Canadian copyright jurisprudence and policy continues to reflect unwillingness on the part of the judiciary, the legislature and perhaps the public at large to depart from the notion that the labourer deserves to own the product of his intellectual labour.[35]

Inevitably, the notion that intellectual labour translates into ownership guides decisions about every aspect of copyright law: what subject matter to protect; how to separate protectable expression from non-protectable ideas; to whom to attribute authorship; when to recognise substantial similarity; and in what circumstances to allow fair dealing. How we choose to understand the rights held by authors will affect how we define the extent of the rights that copyright confers and the limits that will demarcate those rights.

In Canada, it might be suggested that the Supreme Court ruling in *Théberge v. Galerie D'Art du Petit Champlain Inc.*[36] in which the Court articulated the need for balance in the copyright system, indicated a shift away from the traditional rights-based reasoning typical of Anglo-Canadian copyright jurisprudence. Although the case shifted Canadian copyright jurisprudence away from a pure author-orientation, the Court's articulation of copyright's balance falls short of a departure from natural rights-based reasoning: it is 'a balance between promoting the public interest in the encouragement and dissemination of works of the arts and intellect and *obtaining a just reward for the creator* (or more accurately, to prevent someone other than the creator from *appropriating* whatever *benefits* may be generated).'[37]

It is notable that this '*Théberge* balance' requires that we first '*recogniz[e] the creator's rights*',[38] making 'an awkward amalgamation' of a utilitarian and natural rights model for copyright.[39] It is not particularly surprising, then, that the balance has since been explained in distinctly Lockean language, revealing the powerful grip of Locke's premise: 'The person who sows must be allowed to reap what is sown, but the harvest must ensure that society is not denied some benefit from the crops.'[40] Courts purporting to implement the *Théberge* copyright balance can still be guided by a conviction that that 'to deprive authors of the fruits of their labour is unjust.'[41]

Even in the United States, where copyright law is generally regarded as a utilitarian system whose purpose is 'to promote progress in the science and useful arts',[42] natural rights-based reasoning is easy to find. In *Wheaton v. Peters*, Thompson J. stated in dissent: 'The great principle on which the author's rights rests, is, that it is the fruit or production of his own labour, and which may, by the labour of the faculties of the mind, establish a right of property.'[43] In *Mazer v. Stein*, the court reasoned: '*sacrificial days* devoted to such creative activities *deserve rewards* commensurate with the services rendered.'[44] In *Harper & Row v. Nation Enterprises*, the Supreme Court said: '[t]he rights conferred by copyright are designed to assure contributors to the store of knowledge a *fair return for their labours*.'[45] In *Childress v. Taylor*, the court sought to guard against 'spurious claims by those who might otherwise try to *share the fruits of the efforts* of a sole author.'[46] And, of course, in *International News Service v. Associated Press*, 'hot news' was declared 'quasi-property' so that the defendant could not 'reap where it has not sown', 'appropriating to itself the harvest' of the plaintiff's labour.[47] US courts, like their British and Canadian counterparts, regularly display concern for protecting the original creator's 'substantial investment of time, money and labour'[48] and the 'author's right to compensation.'[49] While economic theory could explain many decisions along these lines in terms of the need to ensure adequate incentive, the moral disapprobation with which 'free-riding' is viewed, together with the value attached to the original labourer and his efforts, is often more indicative of a commitment to the 'if labour, then right' equation.

The rhetoric of natural right has a strength and pervasiveness that overwhelms the utilitarian, incentive-based explanations generally offered for copyright protection. Instead of copyright being an instrument subordinate to a broad social purpose, moral claims of an implicit right infiltrate the doctrinal framework, allowing Lockean perceptions of natural right to shape copyright policy. These perceptions are detectable throughout the copyright system, from 'sweat of the brow' notions of originality, to 'reaping where one did not sow' condemnations of infringement.

Scholarly writing in the area of copyright law frequently lends weight to the natural rights approach to copyright. As is the case with judicial pronouncements, scholarly appeal to Locke's acquisition theory is often implicit, simply taking the author's right to own as the foundational assumption. Particularly interesting, however, is the relative frequency with which academic literature directly invokes Lockean labour theory as axiomatic in the copyright realm.[50] This body of literature, whether ultimately supporting or challenging a Lockean justification for copyright, is evidence in itself of the powerful grip of this theory over the legal imagination in this area. Indeed, Locke's labour theory is so commonly invoked in examinations of copyright doctrine that one might be forgiven for believing that he explicitly defended intellectual property rights, or for that matter, that copyright legislation explicitly affirmed Lockean theory.

4.4 AN 'INTERNAL CRITIQUE' OF LOCKEAN COPYRIGHT THEORY

If Lockean concepts of natural entitlement do indeed play a role in our understanding of intellectual property and its justification, what impact does this have on our interpretation and application of copyright law? It is not my aim in this section to provide an overarching critique of Locke's property model as a whole.[51] What I do wish to do is highlight some of the possible limitations and inadequacies of Lockean theory in the area of intellectual property. I want to shed light on some of the stumbling blocks that advocates of a Lockean account of copyright must encounter in the world of intangibles.

The following discussion is divided into the 'internal' criticisms, discussed in this section, and the 'external' criticisms, discussed in Section 5. In essence, the internal critique asks whether Locke's theory *can* inform or legitimate our notion of intellectual property, and the external critique asks whether that theory ought to be so employed. Ultimately, I hope to show that the application of Lockean theory to intellectual property is at best unhelpful, and at worst harmful, to the development of a sound and effective copyright system.

4.4.1 Applying the Provisos to Copyright

Due to the wide acceptance of Locke's 'labour-mixing' metaphor, it seems to be generally assumed that Locke's model provides unambiguous support for intellectual property rights. Indeed, it has been suggested that the theory of original acquisition is more readily applicable to intellectual property than to the physical property it was intended to legitimate.[52] The basis for such an assertion is the conviction that the 'enough and as good' proviso is most easily satisfied in the case of acquisition of *intellectual* property.

4.4.1.1 Copyright and the 'enough and as good' proviso

The 'enough and as good' proviso is effectively a 'no loss to others' precondition for property acquisition. It requires that a labourer must not worsen others' position by her appropriation from the commons. Ideas, unlike physical property, are 'non-rivalrous', thus it is generally thought that this condition is easily met when intangibles are privately appropriated. In contrast to physical objects, ideas can be used by any number of individuals without ever being 'consumed', and consequently, possession and use of an intellectual work cannot cause loss to anyone else.[53] Moreover, because there are conceivably an infinite number of ideas 'out there', there will always be enough ideas available for others to possess and use. No one can claim harm as a result of another's intellectual property appropriation because everyone is equally free to write, compose, draw, develop and invent.

There is room to dispute this application of the proviso. Peter Drahos suggests:

> '[E]ven where the stock of abstract objects is infinite, the human capacity to exploit that stock at any given moment is conditioned by the state of cultural and scientific knowledge which exists at that historical moment . . . The set of usable abstract objects may also be further reduced because some ideas or knowledge may be necessary gateways to others.'[54]

The possibility of exploiting abstract objects will always be limited by human capabilities. In this sense, the notion of a more or less infinite set of abstract objects can be distinguished from the realities of social development and the process of knowledge accumulation. A process of gradual, incremental accretion is very different from the individual and ad hoc exploitation of infinite, discrete ideas that the no-harm argument calls to mind. Even if there are an infinite number of ideas, it can never be said that they are all within our grasp at any one time. It is a key facet of progress and development that any one idea can act as a gateway to another. If social progress is fundamentally dialogic, every idea is dependent upon ideas that went before and will form the gateway for ideas yet to come. In this sense, it could follow that an individual's appropriation of the 'gateway idea' from the intellectual commons contravenes the no loss requirement by diminishing the number or quality of 'usable' ideas.

We should also ask whether it makes sense to talk about an infinite supply of something when we attribute some character of 'uniqueness' to each of the things belonging to that category, which in turn means that each has its own value. The labourer may appropriate one acorn, but presumably all acorns are capable of fulfilling the same function and therefore the remaining supply of acorns will equally do for others. The same can be said of taking a drink from a river. The difficulty in the case of 'ideas' is that, where an idea has a meaning or purpose of its own, it will simply not be true that any other idea can perform the same function. It is arguable that the removal of something *unique* from the common necessarily causes harm.

Justin Hughes argues that one person's use of some ideas does not deplete the common; in fact, the common actually expands with use. Idea X makes possible ideas Y and Z, which could not have come into being without someone first having used X, thereby increasing the accessible common.[55] However, if we take 'idea' to refer to the 'ideational entity' that is copyright's intangible work, then the harm caused by private appropriation remains clear: if A obtains a property right in X, that property right can exclude B and C from X, and so can prevent them from developing ideas Y and Z. An obvious example of this restriction is the control the copyright owner enjoys over the derivative works that B and C may wish to author. Does this mean that B and C have suffered a loss as a result of A's private appropriation? Arguably not: A's use of X has caused no hardship to B and C because they are no worse off than if A had not created X in the first place. Yet, in practical terms it seems that B and C *are* worse off as a result of A's exclusionary right. This follows, again, from understanding the nature of culture as dialogic. Granting a property right in X has precluded others from using X in whatever way they choose: responding to X, transforming it, critiquing it and building upon it to produce Y and Z. Without A, X might not have been available for B and C to use. However, once X has made its contribution to the cultural discourse, preventing B and C from using it not only excludes them from X itself, but also prevents them from engaging in the social dialogue, from responding to the message conveyed by X. They are therefore worse off because they cannot make their contribution to the 'drive to meaning' of cultural life. If a certain musical phrase is introduced into the world by one composer, preventing a second composer from incorporating that phrase into his music may leave him ostensibly no worse off than had the phrase never been written.[56] However, the first composer *did* write it, and it is now 'out there'. To deny the second composer the possibility of developing or interpreting it worsens his situation, because he cannot write what he wants to write, respond to the external stimulus that he encounters, or add what he wants to add to the cultural conversation.[57]

We do not evaluate our loss by reference to constant baselines or to comparable loss in competing scenarios. To find a gateway that is closed to you is a very different experience from never finding the gateway. It results in a harm that is not cognisable in evaluations of basic 'but for . . .' hardship. To say that B and C are no worse off as a consequence of A's property right is to ignore the nature of cultural development and the basic human drive to participate in the social conversation.

Hughes addresses this problem in terms of 'added labour'.[58] He points to copyright principles that accord property ownership to a labourer where his labour is sufficiently separate from the 'parent idea', and awards ownership to the owner of the 'parent idea' where the new work bears too much resemblance to the original. The person who truly has something to 'add' to the cultural discourse (as opposed to merely reproducing another's prior contribution) will benefit from the same rules of acquisition as the first labourer. However, where a defendant's work is, as a result of copying, substantially similar to the plaintiff's, *prima facie* infringement will be established regardless of the 'labour added'. In a copyright infringement action, we ask whether the defendant's work is substantially similar to a 'substantial part' of the plaintiff's work, rather than whether the work taken from the plaintiff constitutes a substantial part of the defendant's work.[59] The additional labour of the second author will generally not save her from liability for, as noted by Judge Learned Hand, 'no plagiarist can excuse the wrong by showing how much of his work he did not pirate.'[60]

To show that copyright law does indeed balance the claims of first and second generation author-labourers and so corresponds to the labour theory and the no loss requirement, Hughes points to the leeway given to parodies by the US law, which he explains in terms of the second user's 'independent labour or creativity'. Notably, parodies are not currently given such leeway in Britain or Canada. In the United States, as illustrated by the famous Supreme Court case of *Campbell v. Acuff-Rose Music, Inc.*,[61] parodies are indeed given some leeway, but this is not well explained in terms of the additional labour expended (which would arguably translate into a finding of no infringing substantial similarity); rather, this leeway depends on the principle that someone may fairly use the fruits *of another's* labour in spite of their ownership claim.

Hughes' parody example appears to appeal to the significance attributed to 'transformative' use in the fair use inquiry. In assessing the 'purpose and character' of the allegedly infringing use, US courts are to have regard to whether the second work 'alter[s] the first with new expression, meaning, or message'.[62] However, the degree to which a use is transformative is only one of many considerations in the fair use inquiry, and 'such transformative use is not absolutely necessary for a finding of fair use.'[63] Fair use protects many uses that do not involve additional intellectual labour, such as photocopying an article for the purposes of research, and does not protect many truly laborious uses, such as rewriting a novel as a screenplay or creating an exact replica of an original masterpiece. The function of fair use is not to reward B and C for their added labour, but to allow the productive social and cultural dialogue that A's property right might otherwise preclude. The reason for the incongruence of fair use and independent or added labour is precisely that the two considerations are not inherently related.

Even if we were to understand the concept of added labour in its most expansive light – referring not only to the added intellectual labour of original or transformative expression, but including the productive or socially useful labour or added value involved in studying or reviewing others' expression, for example – the characterisation of fair use in terms of the user's labour remains unsatisfactory; it overlooks the social significance of the user's activity by reducing it to an individual (and exceptional) act. The normative justifications for fair use offered by the US Supreme Court depend not upon the added value of the individual act of copying, but upon its significance as an example of a positive social practice: fair use 'makes sense only if a given fair use problem is characterized in social terms as well as in individual terms.'[64]

What we may infer from this discussion, however, is that the justifiability of copyright – even in purely Lockean terms – depends upon two conditions: first, the narrow construction of 'substantial similarity', such that 'added labour' by the second author might also be protected, and second, the existence of a broad fair use exception at least capable of embracing parody and other transformative uses of protected works, such that the 'no loss' requirement is actually met. Taking into account the breadth of the rights accorded to copyright owners and the narrowness of exceptions to copyright infringement, when the 'enough and as good' proviso is taken seriously, there are real grounds for doubting the justifiability of the copyright system even in purely Lockean terms. Copyright, at least in its present form, does not appear to leave enough and as good. The proviso is implicated notwithstanding the non-crowdable nature of copyrightable subject matter, and at the very least it would take a radical reshaping of the copyright system to meet even this burden. However, if the concept of harm is understood in experiential terms, and the cultural, social and political importance of participation and dialogue is fully appreciated, the bigger question might be whether a system of private property rights over the cultural subject matter of copyright could ever be said to leave 'as good' for others.

4.4.1.2 Copyright and the 'no-spoilage' proviso

Like the 'enough and as good' proviso, it is easy to assume that the 'no-spoilage' proviso does not present a great hurdle in the appropriation of *intellectual* property. Writings, songs or films do not spoil in the way that an unused basket of plums might. In that sense, one could say that they are non-perishable. However, it would be reductionist to assume that the acquisition of objects of intellectual property cannot violate the no-spoilage proviso simply because of their abstract nature. In some sense ideas can spoil: once appropriated, their time span of useful application might be limited. New stories become old news, literature may become dated, and criticisms may become irrelevant, outdated or obvious. Hughes identifies such forms of spoilage as examples of decline in the *social value* of an idea. There is, in this sense, 'waste in a social context', but not 'waste for the individual organism', because the internal value of the idea itself remains constant.[65] Moreover, even the perceived social loss can only be speculative; if ideas do not 'perish' as such, they retain the possibility of future value. Hughes argues that the kind of purely social loss resulting from the waste of an idea is therefore very different from the kind of loss (present and future, social and individual) that results from Locke's food spoilage.

But to what extent should we be concerned with 'internal value' when ideas and language and knowledge are most cognisable and valuable through communication, development and application? The true value of an idea can only be fully appreciated in light of its social value. Drahos observes: '[a]s abstract objects ideas cannot spoil, but the opportunities that they confer may.'[66] The unrealised 'opportunities' should be understood in terms of wasted potential for dialogue and development. Even if such loss can be seen only against a social backdrop, as Hughes suggests, it is primarily the social backdrop with which the Lockean proviso is concerned. Moreover, waste in the 'social context' is simultaneously situated in the 'individual' because, as a member of society, the individual has deprived herself of the optimal social value of the idea.

Perhaps plums are not as different from ideas as we might imagine. When the owner retains a basket of plums until it spoils, they can no longer be consumed. They might still *exist*, and conceivably for some reason the owner is satisfied to hold on to a basket of rotting plums. This is still *wasteful* because the plums are no longer fit to be used in the manner in which they ought to have been used: rotten plums can no longer be consumed. Is it the internal value, or is it the social value that decreases when plums spoil? If their value lies in the fact that members of society can eat them, then the no-spoilage proviso is violated at the moment when the plums become inedible. Similarly, when ideas can no longer fulfill their social purpose or potential, there has been waste and the proviso has been violated. Just as the appropriator wastes the plums by failing to eat them or leave them available for others to eat, so too does the intellectual property owner waste the idea by preventing its communication and development.

It seems to follow that those who appropriate ideal objects with a view to doing nothing with them violate Locke's spoilage proviso. Whenever the copyright owner shelves a work without publication or asserts a copyright interest to achieve a pure anti-dissemination result, the proviso has not been satisfied. Understanding 'waste' from a social perspective certainly casts doubt upon Lockean appropriation in the particular scenario where the object of the copyright is purposefully withheld from the public. Indeed, bearing in mind that the proviso is essentially concerned with avoiding wastefulness, there is considerable weight to the argument that appropriations of intellectual property are *generally wasteful*. According to Hettinger:

> 'Since writings . . . are nonexclusive, this requirement prohibiting waste can never be completely met by intellectual property. When owners of intellectual property charge fees for the use of their expressions . . ., certain beneficial uses of these intellectual products are prevented. This is clearly wasteful, since everyone could use and benefit from intellectual objects concurrently.'[67]

Because of the non-crowdable nature of abstract objects, intellectual property rights will almost always cause waste (and never leave enough and as good), because they always deprive others of something to which they would have had free access but for the artificial scarcity manufactured by the copyright system.

Those who wish to invoke Lockean theory to justify strong intellectual property rights too readily assume that the provisos are easily satisfied simply because of the intangible and non-rivalrous nature of ideal objects. In fact, there seems to be plenty of room to argue that, by its very nature, intellectual property falls afoul of either one or both of the provisos. As part of an internal critique, applying the provisos to the current copyright system is perhaps the least controversial way to criticise the Lockean argument for property rights in abstract objects. There are, however, larger problems with the application of Locke's appropriation theory to copyright protection.

4.4.2 Identifying the Labourer and the Product of Her Labour

Perhaps the first question we should ask is whether labour is actually involved in the act of idea-making at all.[68] Certainly, the type of labour differs considerably from the physical labour envisaged by Locke. However, it does seem fairly easy to characterise abstract objects as the products of labour, not least because copyright protects only the expression of the idea and not the idea itself. More problematic is the question of how much of the final product can actually be attributed to the labourer.

The natural rights thesis, which awards a property right to the labourer in his intellectual product, ignores the contributions that have been made by those who preceded him.[69] Thoughts and ideas are not free-standing, but are inherently linked to the thoughts and ideas that went before. The fact that mental labour is involved in the development and expression of an idea does not mean that the entire value of the resulting work is attributable to that labour. If a labourer has a right to the fruits of her labour, this right can only entitle her to the *value added* through her own labour.[70] The myths of romantic authorship and the assertion of private property entitlement as a reward for intellectual labour are closely related. Hettinger writes:

> 'Given this vital dependence of a person's thoughts on the ideas of those who came before her, intellectual products are fundamentally social products. Thus even if one assumes that the value of these products is entirely the result of human labor, this value is not entirely attributable to *any particular laborer* (or small group of laborers).'[71]

When the creative process is recharacterised as collective rather than individual, it becomes difficult to explain how a property right can be accorded to an individual on the basis of individual labour. Granting a property right over the abstract object overlooks the historical, social and cultural components of that object. Once it is recognised that every ideal object is necessarily the 'joint product of human intellectual history',[72] the simple claim to a right over the fruits of one's labour is emptied of meaning: the fruit of intellectual labour has no definable boundary, and the results of an individual's 'added labour' become impossible to demarcate. This reveals not only a practical difficulty in the application of Lockean theory to intellectual property, but also an important weakness in the deontological justification of property acquisition. As Horacio Spector explains: '[i]f the labour employed by a person does not offer an explanation for the total value of a commodity – and only explains the added value – then Locke's theory does not justify ownership over the whole commodity.'[73] Paradoxically, by focusing on individual labour, the rationale for individual ownership over intellectual creations dissipates. The interdependent nature of human culture means that intellectual works (including the copyright-protected original expression and not merely the unprotected ideas) are necessarily the products of collective labour.[74]

One may argue that individual labourer's right should be defined, not in relation to the object upon which he laboured, but to the market value of his contribution. The market value claim seems untenable when we remember that Locke's theory entitles a labourer only to the product of her own labour; market value is a 'socially created phenomenon' dependent upon the subjective demand of others. Because this value depends on variables far beyond the labourer's control, it cannot be attributed to her.[75]

4.4.3 The Question of Liberty

A final line of internal critique concerns the question of liberty.[76] Tom Palmer has argued that, by virtue of the specific nature of ideal objects and their relationship to individual liberty, Lockean theory does not support the acquisition of private property rights in the products of intellectual as opposed to physical labour. Rights ought to be considered with reference to the correlative duties that they entail. The power to exclude others from something means the power to alter another's liberty, rights and duties with respect to that thing.[77] Although this is the case with all property rights, Palmer sees an important difference: where tangible property rights restrain action, intellectual property rights restrict liberty. He explains:

> 'Liberty and intellectual property seem to be at odds, for while property in tangible objects limits actions only with respect to particular goods, property in ideal objects restricts an entire range of actions *unlimited by place or time*, involving *legitimately owned property* . . . by all but those privileged to receive monopoly grants from the state.'[78]

Palmer provides an example to shed more light on the distinction: while a property right in an abacus prevents others from using the owner's abacus, an intellectual right prevents them from making their own abacus through their own labour and with their own wood.[79] Similarly, my tangible property right can prohibit you from using my piano, but my intellectual property right can restrict your liberty to hit particular notes in a particular order on your own piano. Palmer's concern is with the restriction that intellectual property imposes upon others' liberty to use resources to which they have a moral and legal right. In what way does this differ from the legal restrictions imposed upon the use of an individual's private property, which might dictate how hard a person can push on the gas pedal of his or her legitimately owned car, or when a person can pull the trigger of his or her legitimately owned gun? Perhaps there is no real difference, except that speed restrictions and gun laws do not purport to rely upon Lockean theory for their justification; they are restrictions imposed and justified in the interests of public safety or social policy but are external to the logic of property ownership. Palmer is questioning the internal *coherence* of the Lockean account of intellectual property on the grounds that the justification must rely upon a premise that it essentially contravenes.

The first and most fundamental pillar of Locke's theory is the belief that there is a right to self-ownership. Given that ownership over our body can readily be understood to include our mind, it might be assumed that Locke's theory can extend to the appropriation of the intangible fruits of intellectual labour. However, if there is a tension between intellectual property and the liberty premise, the extension of Locke's theory is less obvious, disrupting the natural rights-based case for intellectual property. Self-ownership is the foundation for ownership of alienable objects, but if we accept the distinctions Palmer draws, ownership of copyright contradicts the argument from self-ownership. If liberty, the cornerstone of Lockean theory, is undermined in the protection of intellectual property, then there is reason to question the congruence of intellectual property rights with a Lockean concept of private property.

4.5 AN 'EXTERNAL CRITIQUE' OF LOCKEAN COPYRIGHT THEORY

The internal critiques examined in Section 4 lend support to the claim that a Lockean theory of intellectual property is *descriptively* unsound. My purpose in Section 5 is to establish that, more importantly still, this theory is *prescriptively* undesirable.

4.5.1 The Effects of a Property Rights Theory for Copyright

Copyright has continually been referred to and has gradually become understood in rights-based terms, to the extent that it now appears solidly entrenched in private property discourse. Keith Aoki notes that the proliferation and strengthening of intellectual property within the discourse of natural proprietary rights is somewhat ironic: while political and legal theorists have 'disaggregated' the concept of private property itself, the notion of private property rights in relation to abstract objects appears somehow to have emerged unscathed.[80] In the area of traditional private property legal theorists, such as Robert Hale,[81] have insisted upon the analytical error of conceptualising property rights as pre-political or absolute. They have argued for the re-imagination of property as imbued with political and economic considerations, socially produced and amenable to alteration or modification by government and judiciary.[82] Once the institution of private property is re-imagined in this way, it cannot be confined to the 'private' domain presumptively beyond the control of the state; its creation, protection and promotion is inherently dependent upon the state. This insight deserves to be taken seriously in the field of intellectual property where the notion of copyright as private property, and private property as a right with pre-institutional existence, appears deeply entrenched. Should we continue to accept the subtle but persistent invocation of traditional property theory in the realm of intellectual property? What damage is the background hum of property rhetoric doing to the copyright system?

The characterisation of 'authors' rights' as some natural entitlement, or some pre-social phenomenon, creates a false bifurcation between the public and private domains. Deontological justifications for the copyright interest, which cast copyright as inhering naturally and necessarily in the author by virtue of her individual actions, can close down debate about which laws, rights and exceptions will further the public goals that we hope to achieve. The powerful claim to a pre-political natural right obscures the political force of the law and disguises the dynamics of the relationship between property owners and non-owners. When we become hypnotised by the label of property, we fail to question categories, to make distinctions, and to adequately acknowledge social and political context.

The label of natural entitlement therefore constrains policy-making; if the author's right is private and pre-political as opposed to socially produced, then it is not amenable to pragmatic or principled alteration in the name of a broader public interest. Property rights are conceived of as entrenched and fundamental, so property interests are accorded a legal and moral primacy over other kinds of rights and interests. This constraint is certainly a problem when the basic coherence of the copyright system, not to mention its success, relies upon a pro-active stance by the state toward the creation and dissemination of cultural objects. As the copyright system is meant to provide incentives to maximise cultural production, copyright policy by its nature requires an unambiguously functional approach. As soon as we subordinate public interest concerns, we depart from the policy foundations of the copyright system.

Propertising copyright not only relocates it in the private domain but more importantly still, redefines it along individualistic lines. In the shift from the concept of a socially determined privilege to an individualistic explanation for copyright, we inevitably stumble upon 'the natural tendency to reify rights even when they are set up and justified purely on utilitarian grounds.'[83] Due to this process of reification, and under the influence of what might be termed 'rights-fetishism', rights to the products of intellectual labour come to be regarded as independent absolutes, as an end in themselves. What began as a matter of social policy – desirable to the extent that it provided an incentive to authors – becomes firmly defined as an individual moral entitlement.

The endorsement of property rights rhetoric goes hand in hand with the departure from social justification and a move towards individualistic justification for copyright. The gradual loosening of a community-based rationale for copyright law paves the way for an individualistic approach. Locating the copyright rationale in the individual author clears the path for a proprietary conception of the individual's interest. At the moment of propertisation we become bound to the individualistic account and so relegate still further into the background the community concerns that provided the initial justification.

In copyright rhetoric, we often see the 'pairing' of social interest and private entitlement accounts of copyright. Waldron observes that the co-existence of both justifications for copyright is due in large part to the belief that the two are not opposed, and perhaps even converge.[84] The operative assumption behind the dualistic approach is that the interests of the author and those of the public are always/already balanced in the protection of copyright. While this is clearly a popular starting point in copyright analysis, I want to stress the threat posed for the development of copyright policy when it is taken for granted. Although it might be pleasing to think that two separate and equally meritorious sets of interests coincide in one legal doctrine, the convenient picture of an exact overlap is difficult to maintain. As a consequence, when the interests are gradually perceived to diverge, they eventually appear to be (at least potentially) in conflict, requiring a 'balance' to be found and maintained by the law.[85] The initial appearance of a convenient coincidence of interests confuses the social policy objectives by conceding that copyright has a role in protecting authors' natural rights to the fruits of their labour. By definition, natural private rights will appear to have priority over conflicting interests. Thus it is hardly surprising that a simultaneous focus on the interests of author and public has often led to the elevation of private rights over public interest whenever a choice must be made.[86]

Justifying the copyright system from a social policy perspective, or in light of the public-work link, does assume that the interests of individual authors in the protection of their intellectual works will generally coincide with the interests of the public; only this can explain the copyright given to authors under a system whose purpose is to further the public interest. But we must resist conflating these two sets of interests. The rationale for copyright protection dissipates at the point at which authors' rights contravene the broader public interest. This becomes crucial when considering claims by or against 'second generation authors' or productive users of copyrighted material whose activities further the public interest goals that copyright ought to serve.

Conflating the interests of authors and the public leads to the assumption that strong authors' rights will serve the long-term public policy goals of the copyright regime. This is not the case. Limits upon the rights given to the copyright owner are nothing less than fundamental to the very purposes of copyright. The goal of maximising cultural production and exchange will be realisable only when we acknowledge that cultural production, circulation, transformation and consumption all play a part in furthering this goal. From this should follow an appreciation of the socially valuable, productive or transformative uses made of copyrighted works by others, and the need to protect these uses as integral to the copyright framework.

There is much to be lost by overprotecting the 'original author'. The boundaries that copyright doctrine places upon the copyright holder's monopoly reflect this concern. Concepts such as originality, the idea–expression dichotomy, independent creation and fair use limit the kinds of abstract objects to which copyright attaches and the scope of the rights it accords. However, interpreting and applying these concepts to the processes and products of intellectual activity is a complex task that brings into tension the author's private interests in maximum protection and the public interest in maximum creation and access. It is my argument that, from the moment this tension appears, the language of natural rights skews the debate in favour of the author. Copyright law requires us to draw lines between the public and private domain. A natural law approach draws lines that tend to favour the latter. Indeed, it seems that this is often the very purpose of natural rights rhetoric.

It has been convincingly argued elsewhere that concepts of natural right and property for labour were introduced into the debate over authors' rights as a means of rhetorical leverage, ideal for furthering the interests of the booksellers.[87] As it did in eighteenth-century England, Lockean labour theory can add ideological legitimacy to the economic goals of copyright holders. It is largely towards this end that Lockean rhetoric is employed and endorsed by the courts. When confirming a copyright interest, finding infringement or refusing a defence, it is not uncommon for a court to preface its argument with a sentimental passage depicting the author's position in terms of entitlement, effort and labour, and to juxtapose this depiction against a portrayal of the defendant as lazy, opportunistic, parasitic or merely inconsequential. Diane Conley has described this kind of author-hierarchy as 'the producer/user and scholar/chiseller dichotomies.' She explains: 'The original author is held up as one who brings to life an important new work, while the author-user is continually relegated to the position of a nonproductive interloper.'[88]

The 'nonproductive interloper' thus characterised is not 'contributing to the store of knowledge', so her actions become trespass or thievery[89] as opposed to participation in cultural dialogue and the production of meaning. In *Harper & Row*, where copyright's purpose was articulated in terms of a 'fair return for labours',[90] the defendant's (or author-user's) action was 'plagiarism' and 'piracy', and the author's manuscript was, as an unexamined statement of fact, 'purloined'. This rhetoric exemplifies the reality of natural rights discourse in copyright law: it obscures issues of communication and social discourse behind the overwhelming concern with private property and entitlement.

When we approach copyright questions with a focus on the proprietary relationship between the author and her work, we fixate on demarcating and protecting the boundaries of original authorial property. As the dialogic processes of cultural production fade in significance, so too do the claims of those who seek to make use of this property in their own communicative activity. The relationship between public and work is determined by the author–work link. For example, in the *Michelin* case mentioned above, we saw an unerring adherence to the analogy of naïve private property, an appeal to the Lockean concern with the 'fruits of one's labour', and a clear sense of the moral supremacy of the original creator.[91] It is no coincidence that we also saw a broad approach to finding substantial similarity regardless of the transformative value of the defendants' use, and a very narrow approach to the fair dealing defence regardless of the social and political value of that transformative use. When we disengage public interest demands from the copyright system, we radically weaken the copyright doctrines responsible for delimiting the copyright owner's rights.

4.5.2 Re-Imagining the Lockean Right?

Having set out my concerns with Lockean rights theory in the copyright context, it is now worth asking whether a Lockean approach *inevitably* entails these results or whether they are merely one possible and perhaps mistaken consequence of rights-based reasoning.

One possible starting place for this discussion is to assert that Locke's theory has been misunderstood and misapplied. If we situate this theory within the context and purpose for which it was undertaken, it is not entirely clear that Locke drew the libertarian conclusion attributed to him. Locke's purpose was to show how a common donation could be individuated. With this purpose as a starting point, Barbara Friedman argues that Locke was willing to (and indeed intended to) undo the power of private property rights after they had served this polemical purpose.[92]

According to Friedman's interpretation of Locke, absolute property rights acquired through labour do not survive the transition to civil society. In support of this position, Friedman cites a generally neglected provision of Locke's *Second Treatise*: '[E]very Man, when he at first incorporates himself into any Commonwealth, he, by his uniting himself thereunto, annexes also, and submits to the Community, those Possessions which he has or shall acquire.' Having entered civil society, property acquired in the state of nature 'which was before free', is now 'to be regulated by the Laws of Society'. In civil society, the government is responsible for 'the regulating of Property between the Subjects one amongst another', and such government authority is to be exercised 'as the good of Society shall require'.[93]

The departure from the state of nature may therefore mark the end of the role of deontological private property in Lockean theory. The 'good of society', or the common good, was the criterion against which the legitimacy of a government was to be measured in determining whether revolt was warranted. On this basis Friedman argues that, within civil society, a person's property consists only of 'goods, which by the law of the Community are theirs.'[94] What begins as a deontological explanation for the acquisition of private property from the common becomes a consequentialist theory for the regulation of property in a modern society.

This line of argument is interesting for two reasons. First, it situates Lockean theory – so often decontextualised and misstated by ardent supporters of private property – within a purposive framework that dilutes the force of the strong natural rights approach. Second, the argument adds strength to a teleological approach to private property (and intellectual property in particular), by recasting the role of the common good as pivotal in the development of positive law in this area. In Friedman's words: 'The advantage of taking this tack is that it does not express the concern for human well-being in deontological formulations that preclude the investigation of which laws will, as an empirical matter, advance the common good.'[95]

It is certainly true that a strong justificatory form of the labour theory is not the only kind of theory for intellectual property that we can extract from Locke's thesis. Various versions of Lockean theory take the position that private property institutions are matters of positive law and convention, regulated on the basis of utilitarian concerns and with a view to maximising the welfare of the community.[96] While this discussion is interesting, it does not offer a complete solution to our problem. Perhaps most fundamentally, this reading does not coincide with our general understanding of Locke's theory of acquisition, according to which the difference between the 'State of Nature' and 'Civil Society' is the presence of judges in the latter who are positioned to interpret the law of nature and to adjudicate upon conflicting claims. Civil society is thus formed precisely because its authorities will provide security for natural rights on behalf of its members, and its failure to do so is precisely what legitimises civil revolt.[97] While Locke's writings have no doubt been simplified and distorted by supporters of strong property rights, Locke was not a socialist thinker, and attempts to recast him as such probably do a disservice to Lockean adherents and dissenters alike. Moreover, one has to doubt whether the interpretive debate about Locke's actual meaning can significantly affect the meanings attributed to him. Lockean rhetoric may not be true to Locke's writings, but it is in the rhetoric that the power lies.

Another approach to re-imagining the force and effect of Lockean theory does not question the deontological nature of Lockean rights *per se*, but rethinks the scope of the rights that Locke's theory is capable of justifying. This approach begins from the position that Lockean theory, properly understood, creates a form of private property imbued with its own inherent limits; natural property rights as described by Locke are self-limiting, ensuring the protection (or even the maximisation) of the public interest. The provisos always look to the public interest and, if given their proper force, significantly limit the rights conferred upon the copyright holder. Taking this approach, it might be said that the limit upon duration of copyright, the idea–expression dichotomy, and the fair dealing exception are already examples of the limits imposed upon property rights by the norms and demands of natural rights theory. In the above discussion, I argued that copyright law may not be capable of justification through Locke's acquisition theory because it contravenes the provisos. Perhaps, then, the copyright system *should* be held up to Lockean standards of property acquisition. This would arguably result in a more just and measured approach to copyright, with clear limits upon copyright holders' rights, and with sufficient user rights to ensure that the standards of 'enough and as good' and 'no waste' are met.

Wendy Gordon, applying a comprehensive account of Locke's theory to intellectual property, arrives at this conclusion: '[C]reators should have property in their original works, only provided that such grant of property does no harm to other persons' equal abilities to create or to draw upon the preexisting cultural matrix and scientific heritage.'[98] According to Gordon, Locke's theory can be transposed into the realm of intangibles without doing violence to his analysis. The central criteria remain constant: everyone has the right to use the common, and everyone needs to use the common for sustenance. The 'common' in this instance is the intangible common or the 'public domain', made up of intellectual creations not privately owned and incapable of being owned under Lockean principles. Gordon offers 'ideas' as an example of intangibles incapable of appropriation though labour. The non-protectability of ideas is fundamental to the modern copyright system, such that establishing the congruence of natural law and copyright law requires an explanation for the system's failure to protect the labour invested in idea creation. Responding to this challenge, Gordon shifts the focus of Lockean copyright theory from establishing rights to defining their limits. She explains: 'The [no-harm] proviso prohibits a creator from owning abstract ideas because such ownership harms later creators. . . . To give ownership in such fundamentals would deprive future creators of a meaningful opportunity otherwise open to them.'[99]

Another example of this effort to recast natural rights theory as a limiting force is found in Alfred Yen's work. According to Yen, natural law – which embraces Lockean labour theory and Roman doctrines of possession – vests property rights in the author who labours to create an original work, but prohibits the creation of proprietary interests in things inherently incapable of possession.[100] Thus the non-protectability of ideas, for example, is said to be rooted in the dictates of natural law. Lior Zemer's recent efforts to recast Lockean theory in its application to copyright are also noteworthy. Zemer proposes a reimagined Lockean copyright theory that embraces the collectivist and social constructionist aspects of Locke's writings, and so imposes limits on copyright ownership in recognition of 'authorial collectivity' or, in other words, the public as Lockean labourer contributing to intellectual works.[101]

I appreciate the attempts made by Gordon, Yen and Zemer to encompass within the notion of natural property rights the limits upon those rights, which are prescribed by the very same assumptions on which the rights are grounded. Yen notes that because our general intuition about property is heavily influenced by Lockean philosophy, 'the courts' unguided intuition often involves an uncritical use of natural law principles in which property follows labour.'[102] In a similar vein, Gordon criticises judges in copyright cases for 'mistakenly finding a warrant for strong "authors' rights" in a philosophy of natural law . . . [when] [n]atural rights theory . . . is necessarily concerned with the rights of the public as well.'[103] The shared premise here is that natural rights theory can and ought to be critically employed to problematise the claims to right advanced by copyright owners. In Yen's words, 'a better way [than economic instrumentalism] to prevent copyright's unlimited expansion is the careful development of a natural law copyright jurisprudence.'[104] In this sense, Yen and (at least arguably) Gordon and Zemer, appear *first* to perceive the need to limit copyright with regard to subject matter and the scope of the rights, and *then* to posit natural law as a means of achieving these essential limits.

From this perspective, the project appears in essence to be a consequentialist one. To the extent that deontological theories of copyright are employed as *means to an end*, critiques of this approach need not be based upon a challenge to the proposed deontology of intellectual property rights or the ontological nature of intellectual creations; it is enough simply to argue that natural law is neither a necessary nor appropriate way to achieve the desired end. If the natural rights approach is not, pragmatically or strategically, an effective means to achieve the limits on copyright that these authors have in mind, the argument loses its force.

The question I have posed is whether Lockean property theory can be re-imagined to shape a copyright system that furthers the social policy goals I have identified, namely, the maximum creation and dissemination of intellectual works and engagement in cultural dialogue. Using natural rights to this end is not only ineffective, but it in fact compounds the problems identified by Gordon, Yen and Zemer. It carries the same threat of copyright expansionism that they hope to counteract. Gordon is clear in stating that her arguments 'turn to the very arguments that proponents of intellectual property use to defend more extensive owner control',[105] but with the intent to reveal the error of this application of Lockean theory. What is not clear, however, is exactly why we should force ourselves to stumble through the assumptions and unnecessary restrictions imposed by the invocation of natural law reasoning, rather than avoiding them and being honest about the end-point that is sought. This critique goes back to the above discussion of Friedman: it makes little sense to tie up an instrumentalist agenda with deontological reasoning, particularly where the deontological approach advanced is far from self-evident and riddled with ambiguities.

Certainly, the common oversimplification of Lockean theory is responsible for a version of labour-acquisition theory that discounts the role and importance of the provisos and the 'common good' in the process of property acquisition. While I am willing to concede that Locke's theory could be understood in a manner that supports restrictions upon the individual owner's rights and upholds the interests of the public in avoiding harm and waste, I do not consider this construction to be viable in any real sense. Firstly, as discussed, if the provisos are understood sufficiently broadly to ensure protection of the public interest in access to and dissemination of copyrighted works, it seems doubtful that an intellectual property regime could ever adequately meet the no-harm and no-waste requirements. But secondly, and most importantly, the normative force of labour-acquisition theory simply does not lie in the protection or furtherance of the public interest: it is almost trite to say that a theory of natural property entitlement to the product of one's intellectual labour makes its normative claims in respect of the rights of the copyright owner. Therefore, however theoretically plausible or attractive the alternative approach to this theory might be, it is simply not the way that Lockean rhetoric is deployed in copyright discourse.

Natural law has a powerful normative and legitimising force, which comes into play at the moment when copyright is recast in individualistic, rights-based terms. The inevitable result is the widening of copyright protection and the concomitant undermining of the public interest. Copyright attaches to an ever-increasing pool of 'creations'. The duration and scope of the author's rights increase, protecting the author from more uses over a greater period of time. Defences to infringement actions are marginalised, and are given increasingly restrictive interpretations. The consequence is that copyright begins to defeat its own ends in favour of furthering the economic and proprietary interests of copyright holders (who are, incidentally, rarely the 'authors' as commonly understood).[106]

Perhaps this description does not do justice to Locke or to his concern for the public welfare. But ultimately, no matter how forcefully we insist that Locke, properly understood, prescribed enough inherent limitations on the acquisition of private property to protect the public interest adequately, common law copyright jurisprudence reveals the extent to which private property, natural rights and Lockean rhetoric are invoked in support of the copyright owner's rights, to the neglect of the public interest. If we have any hope of avoiding the expansionist consequences of a rights-based approach, we must first avoid the evocative rhetoric of the Lockean approach.

4.6 CONCLUSION: ESCAPING THE INFLUENCE OF ENTITLEMENT DISCOURSE

My purpose here has been to draw to the fore the natural law based assumptions that underlie copyright and that tend to subtly – and sometimes not so subtly – inform our understanding of the role and function of the copyright system. The propertisation of the author's work has formed the basis for a flawed and inappropriate application of labour-acquisition theory and natural rights rhetoric. The presence of this rhetoric in intellectual property theory has entailed an author-oriented reasoning that distorts our understanding of copyright and privileges the economic and 'private property' interests of the author over the social goals that explain the existence of a copyright system. The Lockean analysis of copyright forces us to justify as counter-norms the very public policy purposes that lie at the heart of copyright's rationale. By identifying and resisting the distorting influence of natural law assumptions, we can reassert a teleological copyright theory rooted in the relationship between the public and the work rather than the relationship between the author and the work. With this theory as our starting point, we will be better placed to comprehend and articulate the social aims and imperatives of copyright law and the proper route to their attainment.

The nature of language and law means that we are always dealing with metaphorical constructs. There is nothing vicious about this in itself, but by failing to recognise legal conceit in the realm of intellectual property we are placing the social goals of the copyright system in jeopardy. We must be cognisant of the metaphorical nature of the legal concepts with which we are dealing, and constantly re-evaluate their appropriateness for the purposes they are intended to further. Without such scrutiny, there is a serious risk (which has largely been realised in the case of copyright law) that metaphor will take over our analysis, constraining and distorting it, until we find ourselves far removed from the goals we first sought to achieve. As Laurie Stearns warns: 'all too often legal metaphors are not used in combination to enlarge our understanding, but in isolation to constrict it. A metaphor can distort our analysis by squeezing it into a mould for which it is not suited. The power of a metaphor to shape our understanding is profound.'[107]

In the copyright context, this warning is particularly apt. The powerful and mesmerising badge of 'property', whose force is compounded by the natural law tradition's labour-to-property equation, is not a helpful model for copyright. Instead of facilitating our analysis, it constricts our understanding and distorts our policy decisions. Copyright must operate in furtherance of the public interest in maximising production and communication of intellectual works. Lockean deontological analyses serve only to steer us away from this course. Even when, on rare occasions, Locke's theory is not used to expand copyright protection, it entangles us in a normative web of rights-based reasoning from which there is no easy or theoretically convincing escape.

The methodology entailed by a natural law approach begins with the author's entitlement and reasons backwards to defend its limits. If, in contrast, our analysis were to begin with the public interest in the production and exchange of knowledge, ideas and intellectual works (the public–work link), and reason backward to defend the author's right of control in terms of encouragement (the author–work link), then the presumptive force would lie with the freedom to use and not the right to exclude. As Neil MacCormick explains: 'There is a public benefit to be produced by encouraging certain kinds of investment, and the minimum encouragement necessary for the maximal benefit is all that can be justified or that should be accepted by way of positive law.'[108]

Jennifer Nedelsky reminds us that the choice of legal category is, essentially, a strategic one.[109] Natural rights talk avoids the question of whether the legal category is apposite by establishing simply that 'it is so'. If a natural rights approach to copyright obstructs progress towards shared policy goals, restricts the role of the public interest and produces a pattern of expanding protection, then the property rights category is not a facilitative one. Nedelsky advises:

> 'In choosing a legal category perhaps the most important starting point of inquiry is what the presumptions are, what will require justification, what norms will have to be argued against, what values will be taken as given. . . . [W]e need legal tools that will not divert our energies (and skew our perceptions) by requiring us to rebut presumptions that were never appropriate in the first place.'[110]

Where the natural proprietary rights of the author form the starting point of our copyright inquiry, the presumption is an unqualified right to the 'fruits of her labour', the norm is one of exclusive control, and the values assumed are those that favour maximum protection for intellectual creations. Users' rights, limits on the copyright owner's control and restrictions on copyright protection will all require justification as derogations from general copyright policy. A more nuanced understanding of 'property' may indeed embrace users' rights and limits upon the author's right, and such a shift of focus would certainly be welcome. However, given the reality of absolutist conceptions of property and the pervasiveness of market ideology, if the grand term of 'property right' is standing in the way of this discussion, then we must escape its grasp.[111]

Of course, choosing legal categories is easier than escaping them once they have become entrenched in our imagination. With the intellectual property metaphor so engrained into how we think and speak about the copyright system, the task of extricating copyright from the clutches of property is not a simple one. This is why it will take more than the simple and popular appeal to the need for 'balance' between the individual right and the public interest. This balancing act typically leaves intact the author's right to reward, such that Lockean conceptions of individual entitlement persist.[112] For so long as the copyright owner wears the shoes of the author, and the author wears the shoes of the labourer entitled to reap the fruits of his labour, the public interest will remain a secondary consideration. And for so long as the author-as-labourer is the owner of copyright-as-property, copyright will misrecognise the nature of cultural production and participation, and impede the communication that it is supposed to encourage.

At the outset of this chapter, I stated that author-based reasoning produces theories of private entitlement and a rights-based vision of copyright whose normative force disrupts the public purposes of the copyright system. Throughout the chapter, I have attempted to expose and critically examine the moral assumptions responsible for this vision of copyright. I hope I have succeeded in demonstrating the need to remove the notion of individual entitlement from copyright's theoretical framework. Without this overwhelming diversion, courts, commentators and policy-makers would be free to focus instead on the social role and communicative nature of intellectual creativity, and to define the shape and boundaries of the copyright interest with this in mind. The chapters that follow will address the extent to which our understanding of the processes of authorship, the author's right and the public interest influences the construction of copyright doctrines such as originality and fair dealing, and the scope of the copyright interest more generally.

NOTES

1. *Cf.* Christian G. Stallberg, 'Towards a New Paradigm in Justifying Copyright: A Universalistic-Transcendental Approach' (2008) 18 Fordham Intell. Prop. Media & Ent. L.J. 333 at 343–44.
2. Rosemary J. Coombe, 'Authorial Cartographies: Mapping Proprietary Borders in a Less-Than-Brave New World' (1996) 48 Stan. L. Rev. 1357 at 1358, discussing Keith Aoki, '(Intellectual) Property and Sovereignty: Notes Toward a Cultural Geography of Authorship' (1996) 48 Stan. L. Rev. 1293 [emphasis in original] [Aoki, '(Intellectual) Property and Sovereignty'].
3. Peter Drahos, *The Philosophy of Intellectual Property* (Aldershot: Dartmouth Publishing Company Ltd, 1996) at 48 [Drahos, *Philosophy of IP*].

4. Ibid. at 44.
5. Lawrence C. Becker, *Property Rights: Philosophic Foundations* (London: Routledge and Kegan Paul, 1977) at 32 [Becker, *Property Rights*].
6. John Locke, 'Second Treatise of Civil Government' in P. Laslett (ed.), *Locke: Two Treatises of Government*, 3rd edn (Cambridge: Cambridge University Press, 1968) §26 [Locke, 'Book II'].
7. Ibid. §26: '[B]eing given for the use of men, there must of necessity be a means to appropriate [the earth's fruits and beasts] before they can be of any use, or at all beneficial to any particular man.' See also §28: without a right of private appropriation 'man had starved, notwithstanding the plenty that God had given him.' Locke saw labour and appropriation are part of a divine command to 'subdue the Earth.' Ibid. §32.
8. Ibid. §27.
9. Ibid. §6. Locke presents this no-harm obligation as the first element of natural law; see Wendy J. Gordon, 'A Property Right in Self-Expression: Equality and Individualism in the Natural Law of Intellectual Property' (1993) 102 Yale L.J. 1533 [Gordon, 'Property Right in Self-Expression'].
10. Locke, 'Book II', Ibid. §34.
11. Drahos, *Philosophy of IP*, note 3 above at 44, noting that, although Locke does not invoke the language of 'just deserts,' he does refer to 'just *Property*' in §46 of Locke, 'Book II''. For a discussion of desert-for-labour arguments with respect to intellectual property, see Lawrence C. Becker, 'Deserving to Own Intellectual Property' (1993) 68 Chicago-Kent L. Rev. 609 [Becker, 'Deserving to Own IP'].
12. Locke, 'Book II', note 6 above §27.
13. Ibid. §31: 'As much as any one can make use of to any advantage of life before it spoils; so much he may by his labour fix a Property in.'
14. *Donaldson v. Becket* (1774), 4 Burr. 2408, 1 E.R. 837 (H.L.). But see Lyman Ray Patterson, *Copyright in Historical Perspective* (Nashville: Vanderbilt University Press, 1968) at 15, arguing that the overruled *Millar v. Taylor* (1769), 98 E.R. 201 decision had 'firmly fix[ing] the idea of copyright as an author's right.' *Cf. Compo Co. Ltd v. Blue Crest Music et al.* [1980] 1 S.C.R. 357 at 372, 105 D.L.R. (3d) 249 [*Compo* cited to S.C.R.] per Estey J.: '[C]opyright law is neither tort law nor property law in classification, but is statutory law . . . . Copyright legislation simply creates rights and obligations upon the terms and in the circumstances set out in the statute'.
15. Jeremy Waldron observes: 'although the official line about copyright is that it is a matter of social policy, judicial and scholarly rhetoric on the subject retains many of the characteristics of natural rights talk.' Jeremy Waldron, 'From Authors to Copiers: Individual Rights and Social Values in Intellectual Property' (1993) 68 Chicago-Kent L. Rev. 841 [Waldron, 'Authors to Copiers'].
16. See e.g. Frank H. Easterbrook, 'Intellectual Property is Still Property' (1990) 13 Harv. J.L. & Pub. Pol'y 108 at 112; Stephen L. Carter, 'Does It Matter Whether Intellectual Property is Property?' (1993) 68 Chicago-Kent L. Rev. 715; I. Trotter Hardy, 'Property in Cyberspace' (2001) 1996 U. Chicago Legal F. 217; Edmund W. Kitch, 'Patents: Monopolies or Property Rights?' (1986) 8 Res. L. & Econ. 31; and Edmund W. Kitch, 'The Nature and Function of the Patent System' (1977) 20 J.L. & Econ. 265.
17. Canada, Sub-Committee on the Revision of Copyright, *A Charter of Rights for Creators* (Ottawa: Standing Committee on Communications and Culture, 1985) at 9 [*Charter of Rights for Creators*].
18. See Mark A. Lemley, 'Property, Intellectual Property and Free-Riding' (2005) 83 Tex. L. Rev. 1031, critiquing a property rights-based economic rationalisation of intellectual property rights that tends towards absolute control.
19. Canada, Information Highway Advisory Council Copyright Sub-Committee, *Copyright and the Information Highway: Final Report of the Sub-Committee on Copyright* (Ottawa: Information Highway Advisory Council, 1995) at 28.
20. *Apple Computer Inc. v. Mackintosh Computers Ltd* (1986), 10 C.P.R. (3d) 1, 3 F.T.R.

118, cited in *CCH Canadian Ltd v. Law Society of Upper Canada* (1999), 2 C.P.R. (4th) 129 at 187, 169 F.T.R. 1 [*CCH (FCTD)* cited to C.P.R.].

21. *Bishop v. Stevens* [1990] 2 S.C.R. 467 at 477, 72 D.L.R. (4th) 97 [*Bishop* cited to S.C.R.] at 478–9 [emphasis added], citing Maugham J. in *Performing Rights Society, Ltd v. Hammond's Bradford Brewery Co.* [1934] 1 Ch. 121 at 127.
22. *CCH (FCTD)*, note 20 above at 187 [emphasis added].
23. *Compagne Générale des Établissements Michelin–Michelin & Cie v. National Automobile, Aerospace, Transportation and General Workers Union of Canada (CAW-Canada)* [1997] 2 F.C. 306, 71 C.P.R. (3d) 348 [*Michelin* cited to F.C.] at para. 109.
24. *Charter of Rights for Creators*, note 17 above, especially at 3–6.
25. Waldron, 'Authors to Copiers', note 15 above at 851–2.
26. *Sayre v. Moore* (1785), 102 E.R. 139 (Eng. K.B.) [emphasis added].
27. *Hogg v. Scott* (1874), L.R. 18 Eq. 444 at 458 [emphasis added].
28. [1900] A.C. 539 (H.L.).
29. Ibid. at 545.
30. Ibid. at 546.
31. Ibid. at 552.
32. *CCH Canadian Ltd v. Law Society of Upper Canada* [2004] S.C.J. No 12, 1 S.C.R. 339 at para. 15 [*CCH (SCC)*], McLachlin CJC.
33. *University of London Press, Ltd v. University Tutorial Press, Ltd* [1916] 2 Ch. 601 at 610.
34. See *CCH (SCC)* note 32 above at para. 23.
35. In *Robertson v. Thomson Corp.* [2001] O.J. No. 3868, 15 C.P.R. (4th) 147 at para. 34, the Ontario Court of Appeal therefore stated that originality after *CCH (SCC)* has 'both a labour component and a content component.'
36. 2002 SCC 34 [2002] S.C.R. 336 [*Théberge*].
37. Ibid. at para. 30 [emphasis added].
38. Binnie J. writes for the court, Ibid. at para. 31: 'The property balance . . . lies *not only in recognizing the creator's rights* but in giving due weight to their limited nature' [emphasis added].
39. Teresa Scassa, 'Interests in the Balance' in Michael Geist (ed.), *In the Public Interest: The Future of Canadian Copyright Law* (Toronto: Irwin Law, 2005) 41 at 44.
40. *CCH Canadian v. Law Society of Upper Canada* (2002), 18 C.P.R. (4th) 161 at para. 23 (F.C.A.) [*CCH (FCA)*] at para. 23 (Linden J).
41. *Robertson v. Thomson Corp.*, note 35 above at para. 51.
42. U.S. Const. art. I, §8 reads: 'Congress shall have the power . . . to promote the Progress of Science and the useful Arts, by securing for limited Times to Authors and Inventors the exclusive right to their respective Writings and Discoveries.' No equivalent statement exists in British or Canadian law.
43. 33 U.S. (8 Pet.) 591 at 669–70 (1834).
44. 347 U.S. 201 at 219 (1954) [emphasis added].
45. 471 U.S. 539 at 546 (1985) [*Harper & Row*] [emphasis added].
46. 945 F.2d 500 at 507 (1991) [emphasis added].
47. 248 U.S. 215 at 239 (1918).
48. See e.g. *Wainwright Sec. v. Wall Street Transcript Corp.*, 558 F.2d. 91 at 96 (2d Cir. 1977).
49. See e.g. *Triangle Publications v. Knight-Ridder Newspapers*, 626 F.2d 1171 at 1174 (5th Cir. 1980).
50. For discussion of Lockean natural rights philosophy in intellectual property law, see e.g. Justin Hughes, 'The Philosophy of Intellectual Property' in Adam D. Moore (ed.), *Intellectual Property: Moral, Legal, and International Dilemmas*, (Lanham, Md.: Rowman & Littlefield, 1997) 107; Drahos, *Philosophy of IP*, note 3 above at 41; Gordon, 'Property Right in Self-Expression', note 9 above; Tom G. Palmer, 'Are Patents and Copyrights Morally Justified? The Philosophy of Property Rights and Ideal Objects' (1990) 13 Harv. J.L. & Pub. Pol'y 817 [Palmer, 'Are Patents and

Copyrights Morally Justified?']; Dale A. Nance, 'Owning Ideas' (1990) 13 Harv. J.L. & Pub. Pol'y 757; Alfred C. Yen, 'Restoring the Natural Law: Copyright as Labour and Possession' (1990) 51 Ohio St. L.J. 517 [Yen, 'Restoring the Natural Law']; Horatio M. Spector, 'An Outline of a Theory Justifying Intellectual and Industrial Property Rights' (1989) 8 Eur. I.P. Rev. 270; Edwin C. Hettinger, 'Justifying Intellectual Property' (1989) 18 Phil. & Pub. Aff. 31; Lior Zemer, *The Idea of Authorship in Copyright* (Aldershot, UK: Ashgate, 2007).

51. For a concise critique of Locke's theory, see Becker, *Property Rights*, note 5 above at 36–56. For conflicting interpretations of Lockean theory on property acquisition, see James Tully, *A Discourse on Property: John Locke and His Adversaries* (Cambridge: Cambridge University Press, 1980), and C.B. Macpherson, *The Political Theory of Possessive Individualism: Hobbes to Locke* (London: Oxford University Press, 1979).
52. See Hughes, note 50 above at 141: 'Locke's unique theoretical edifice [may find] its firmest bedrock in the common of ideas.'
53. See e.g. Adam D. Moore, 'Toward a Lockean Theory of Intellectual Property' in Moore (ed.), *Intellectual Property: Moral, Legal, and International Dilemmas*, note 50 above, 81 at 98: 'The individual who takes a good long drink from a river does as much as to take nothing at all. The same may be said of those who acquire intellectual property'.
54. Drahos, *Philosophy of IP*, note 3 above at 51.
55. See Hughes, note 50 above at 130–32.
56. This is the example offered by Waldron as a possible application of the 'no hardship' argument: See 'Authors to Copiers', note 15 above at 864–5.
57. *Cf.* Gordon, 'Property Right in Self Expression', note 9 above at 1570, arguing that first creators' ownership over any aspect of the culture may make a later creator less well off.
58. Hughes, note 50 above at 131–32.
59. Falconer J., cited in *Michelin,* note 23 above at para. 54: 'The fact that the defendant in reproducing his work may have himself employed labour and produced something original is beside the point if none the less [*sic*] the resulting defendant's work reproduces without the licence of the plaintiff a substantial part of the plaintiff's work.' See also Ibid. at para. 57: 'The expenditure of some mental labour is not enough to trump the fact that there has been reproduction of a substantial part of a work.'
60. In *Sheldon v. Metro-Goldwyn Pictures Corp.*, 81 F.2d 49 at 56 (2d Cir, 1936).
61. 510 U.S. 569, 114 S. Ct. 1164 (1994) [*Acuff-Rose*].
62. Ibid. at 1171.
63. *Acuff-Rose*, note 61 above at 1171. Pursuant to s. 107 of the US Copyright Act of 1976 (17 USCS 107), factors for determining whether a particular use is fair 'shall include (1) the purpose and character of the use, including whether such use is commercial, (2) the nature of the copyrighted work, (3) the amount and substantiality of the portion used, and (4) the effect of the use on the potential market for the copyrighted work.' The transformative nature of a use is generally considered to be relevant with regard to the first and fourth factors. See Rebecca Tushnet, 'Copy This Essay: How Fair Use Doctrine Harms Free Speech and How Copying Serves It' 114 Yale L.J. 535 (2004), arguing that fair use serves expressive values wholly independent of transformative use.
64. Michael J. Madison, 'Rewriting Fair Use and the Future of Copyright Reform' (2005) 23 Cardozo Arts & Ent. L.J. 391 at 403. Madison continues: 'The idea of only comparing the value of the copyright owner's use to the value of the defendant's use is incoherent. . . . The second use wins only where society trumps the individual.'
65. Hughes, note 50 above at 139–40.
66. Drahos, *Philosophy of IP*, note 3 above at 51.
67. Hettinger, note 50 above at 44.
68. See Hughes, note 50 above at 117–18.

69. David Fewer, 'Constitutionalizing Copyright: Freedom of Expression and the Limits of Copyright in Canada' (1997) 55 U.T. Fac. L. Rev. 175 at 187 [Fewer, 'Constitutionalizing Copyright'].
70. Hettinger, note 50 above at 37.
71. Ibid. at 38 [emphasis in original].
72. Ibid.
73. Spector, note 50 above at 272.
74. See Drahos, *Philosophy of IP*, note 3 above at 52–3. See also Zemer, note 50 above, arguing that the collective nature of authorship should entail collective ownership of intellectual works under a 'new' Lockean theory of copyright.
75. Hettinger, note 50 above at 38–9. See also Fewer, 'Constitutionalizing Copyright', note 69 above at 187–8.
76. See Palmer, 'Are Patents and Copyrights Morally Justified?', note 50 above at 827–35.
77. See Becker, 'Deserving to Own IP', note 5 above at 621.
78. Palmer, 'Are Patents and Copyrights Morally Justified?', note 50 above at 830 [emphasis added]. *Cf. White-Smith Music Publishing Co. v. Apollo Co.*, 209 U.S. 1 at 19 (1908), Holmes J. [emphasis in original], cited in Laurie Stearns, 'Copy Wrong: Plagiarism, Process, Property, and the Law' (1992) 80 Cal. L. Rev. 513 at 537 [Stearns, 'Copy Wrong']: '[Copyright's] right to exclude is not directed to an object in possession or owned, but is *in vacuo* . . .. It restrains the spontaneity of men where but for it there would be nothing of any kind to hinder their doing as they saw fit. It is a prohibition of conduct remote from the persons or tangibles of the party having the right.' But *cf.* Richard Epstein, 'Liberty versus Property: Cracks in the Foundations of Copyright Law' (2005) 42 San Diego L.J. 1.
79. Palmer, 'Are Patents and Copyrights Morally Justified?', note 50 above at 831.
80. See Aoki, '(Intellectual) Property and Sovereignty', note 2 above at 1338.
81. See e.g. Robert L. Hale, 'Coercion and Distribution in a Supposedly Non-Coercive State' (1923) 38 Pol. Sci. Q. 470, cited Ibid. at 1320, n. 105.
82. Aoki, '(Intellectual) Property and Sovereignty', note 2 above at 1320. See also Kenneth Vandevelde, 'The New Property of the Nineteenth Century: The Development of the Modern Concept of Property' (1980) 29 Buff. L. Rev. 325 at 328–30.
83. Waldron, 'Authors to Copiers', note 15 above at 851. He explains further at 856: '[S]ocial policy arguments for intellectual property tend to get converted into individualist arguments, and thus to be assimilated much more closely to rhetoric associated with material property rights.'
84. Ibid. at 850, n. 28. Waldron cites the opinion of James Madison, expressed at the framing of the Constitution, that '[t]he public good fully coincides . . . with the claims of individuals'.
85. *Cf.* Stallberg, note 1 above at 356: '[T]he different moral perspectives on copyright expressed by the distinction between individualistic and collectivistic models cannot be reconciled in case of conflict. On the contrary, they ultimately make a decision between the author and society inevitable.'
86. *Cf.* Gordon, 'Property Right in Self-Expression', note 9 above at 1562, arguing that, in Locke's view, 'no natural right to property could exist where a labourer's claim would conflict with the public's claim in the common.'
87. For an account of the origins of modern copyright, see e.g. Mark Rose, *Authors and Owners: The Invention of Copyright* (Cambridge: Harvard University Press, 1993).
88. Diane Conley, 'Author, User, Scholar, Thief: Fair Use and Unpublished Works' (1990) 9 Cardozo Arts & Ent. L.J. 15 at 26 [Conley, 'Author, User, Scholar, Thief'].
89. See e.g. *Iowa State University Research Foundation, Inc. v. American Broadcasting Cos.*, 621 F. 2d 57 at 61 (2d Cir. 1980): '[T]he fair use doctrine is not a license for corporate theft.' Taking a strong rights-based view to its logical extreme, fair dealing can be regarded as a 'legitimised trespass[...] on human rights': Jeremy Phillips, 'Fair Stealing and the Teddy Bears' Picnic' (1999) 10 Ent. L. Rev. 57 at 57.
90. *Harper & Row*, note 45 above at 546. The rhetoric in this ruling is criticised by Conley,

note 88 above at 27–8.

91. *Michelin*, note 23 above and accompanying text.
92. See Barbara Friedman, 'From Deontology to Dialogue: The Cultural Consequences of Copyright' (1994) 13 Cardozo Arts & Ent. L.J. 157 at 164 [Friedman, 'Deontology to Dialogue'].
93. Ibid. at 162–3.
94. Ibid. at 164.
95. Ibid. at 167.
96. See e.g. K. Olivecrona, 'Locke's Theory of Appropriation' in Richard Ashcraft (ed.), *John Locke* (New York: Routledge, 1991).
97. Gordon, 'Property Right in Self-Expression', note 9 above at 1541, n. 42. See also Jeremy Waldron, 'Locke, Tully, and the Regulation of Property' (1984) 32 Pol. Stud. 98.
98. Gordon, 'Property Right in Self-Expression', note 9 above at 1563–4.
99. Ibid. at 1581.
100. Yen, 'Restoring the Natural Law', note 50 above at 537–8.
101. Zemer, note 50 above. See also, Zemer 'The Making of a New Copyright Lockean' (2006) 29 Harv. J. of L. & Pub. Pol. 892.
102. Yen, 'Restoring the Natural Law', note 50 above at 547.
103. Gordon, 'Property Right in Self Expression', note 9 above at 1535.
104. Yen, 'Restoring the Natural Law', note 50 above at 547.
105. Gordon, 'Property Right in Self-Expression', note 9 above at 1539.
106. Aoki, '(Intellectual) Property and Sovereignty', note 2 above at 1335 [footnotes omitted]: 'While we pay homage to John Locke and his theories of gaining a property right in unowned materials by adding one's labor, the average worker alienates his labor at a fairly low hourly wage and the products of his labor belong to the employer.'
107. Stearns, 'Copy Wrong', note 78 above at 538–9.
108. Neil MacCormick, 'On the Very Idea of Intellectual Property: an Essay according to the Institutionalist Theory of Law' (Paper presented at the SCRIPT Presidential Lecture, 2002), available at: http://www.law.ed.ac.uk/ahrc/files/74_maccormickide-aofipfeb02.pdf (accessed 2 February 2011).
109. Jennifer Nedelsky, 'Property in Potential Life? A Relational Approach to Choosing Legal Categories' (1993) 6 Can. J.L. & Jur. 343 at 354.
110. Ibid. at 353–4.
111. Compare Pamela Samuelson, 'Information as Property: Do *Ruckelhaus* and *Carpenter* Signal a Changing Direction in Intellectual Property Law?' (1988) 38 Cath. U.L. Rev. 365 at 371, n. 30:

> To say that copyright is 'property,' . . .would not be baldly misdescriptive if one were prepared to acknowledge that there is . . .property with few if any legal consequences extending uniformly to all species. . . . *But characterization in grand terms then seems of little value: we may as well go directly to the policies activating or justifying the particular determinations* [emphasis added].

112. See *Théberge*, note 36 above and accompanying text.

5. The evolution of originality: The author's right and the public interest

5.1 INTRODUCTION

I argued in Chapter 4 that the justification for copyright law should be found in the relationship between the society and the work. Building on Chapter 3, then, my argument is that the legal relationship between the author and her work is a means by which to achieve social goals. This does not remove the author and her interests from the copyright equation, but rather integrates the interests of a relational author into our conception of copyright's social goals. The public interest that justifies copyright embraces the value of authorship to individual authors, not as Lockean labourers, but as socially situated human beings engaged in a constitutive cultural dialogue. In Chapter 5, the argument turns towards the legal relationship between the author and her work, and in particular, that which is required to bring it into being – the creation of original expression. The moral relation (society/work) used to justify copyright is logically independent from the legal relation (author/work) established in its name.[1] However, any incongruence between these two relations casts doubt on the justifiability of the legal construct. The originality doctrine at the core of copyright law has, for many years, been defined and developed in a way that is congruent with a system justified in terms of the moral relation between author and work. In the discussion that follows, I will suggest ways in which the doctrine can be reconceptualised and redefined to better reflect the social values that justify copyright and so to better advance its social goals.

The recent evolution in the originality standard in Canadian copyright jurisprudence provides an illuminating context for this discussion. As such, much of the chapter will be devoted to tracing this evolution in Canada, and drawing connections between shifting definitions of originality and a larger normative shift in Canadian copyright theory. I hope that from this analysis will emerge a clearer picture of the interconnections between the justifications offered for the copyright system and the origin and scope of the legal rights that it accords. At a more concrete level, I hope to show the potential for a reconceptualisation of originality that sets aside labour-reward and romantic authorship assumptions and incorporates the public interest as a defining factor in determinations of copyrightability. Section 2 sets the scene by describing the concept of originality and its role in the copyright system. Section 3 explores the Canadian context against which the evolution of originality is to be evaluated, emphasising, in particular, the introduction of a public interest element in Canada's newly articulated originality standard. In Section 4, I will compare this new standard, which requires the exercise of non-trivial skill and judgment, to that of the UK and the US, attaching significance to the departure from both a 'labour' and a 'creativity' test. Finally, in Section 5, I will explain how the originality doctrine, reimagined in an instrumental and relational mode, could begin to rein in the scope of copyright protection and realign copyright with its social purposes.

5.2 ORIGINALITY AND ITS ROLE IN COPYRIGHT LAW

Copyright law offers protection for original works of artistic, literary, dramatic or musical expression. Originality is therefore precondition of copyright protection – its 'very premise'[2] – and is thus the defining characteristic of copyrightable expression. Like many aspects of intellectual property law, it is easy to state the basic need for originality, but it is far harder to ascertain what this means. How should originality be understood? It is trite to say that absolute originality is impossible: we are always already part of that which surrounds us and precedes us. We all stand on the proverbial shoulders of giants.

The search for the meaning of originality might appear wholly abstract – of interest to artists, philosophers and critics, but beyond the practical concerns of the law. To treat it as such is a mistake. Not only does copyright necessitate consideration of the creative processes that it aims to encourage, but the way in which we understand these creative processes and their results will determine how copyright functions. The limits of the copyright system lie in the meaning of originality, and so do its consequences. Far from being a matter of semantics, the structural and substantive formulation of the originality doctrine reverberates with theoretical perspectives, political implications and practical consequences; the foundations of the copyright interest and its justifications are encapsulated in the standard erected for copyright's subsistence. If copyright were to require absolute originality, it could function only upon a myth. If copyright were to require originality in the sense of inventiveness or imagination, it would be a very different creature: offering greatly restricted protection, perhaps requiring application and registration, and demanding determinations of prior art and comparisons across works. In short, it would look more like patent law. Copyright that vests automatically upon creation, requires no registration, and refuses to discriminate based upon the quality of a work, must ask for something less. But how much less can copyright demand before originality becomes a redundant criterion?

Irrespective of the particular formulation of originality adopted by different courts or in different jurisdictions, one attribute is required by all: namely, that the work is not copied. The fundamental characteristic, or *sine qua non*, of originality is that the work originates from the author; it must be independently produced and not copied from any other source.[3] The debate about appropriate formulations of the originality doctrine is concerned only with the question: 'what else?' On the need for independent origination, there is apparently no debate.

As addressed in Part I of this book, the presumption of independent origination represents a naïve conception of the processes of authorship, providing the copyright system with an untenable premise. Authorship is constructed in law as an individual moment of creation, where words or notes or actions are born of a largely internal, independent process, making them uniquely the author's. I have already argued that the processes of authorial creativity have to be examined, complicated and re-imagined, so that authorship can be recognised as a communal and communicative act that is transformative and adaptive, as opposed to isolated and originating. I have noted that, unlike literary theory, copyright law does not have the luxury of disaggregating the author entirely. If copyright law is to exist, it needs the author: the principal of authorship is all that can separate copyrightable works from the public domain. And so this is copyright's challenge:

> How can we conceptualize authorship as a largely transformative act – an elaboration and juxtaposition of existing materials – without losing our sense of what authorship is or how to distinguish between the original and unoriginal, or "authored" and "un-authored," aspects of a copyrighted work?[4]

The answer I propose is twofold. First, we must recognise the functional and metaphorical nature of the originality requirement. It is important to appreciate that, in our attempts to define the originality threshold, we are not engaged in a search for the actual attributes of independent original creation; rather, we are searching for a legal tool with which to define the copyrightable work in a way that will further the purposes of copyright law by encouraging the kind of intellectual exchange that we have identified as a social good. Second, we must rise to the challenge of defining the originality requirement in a way that respects the dialogic processes of authorship. With such a definition, the originality doctrine should be capable of appropriately performing the function demanded of it without distorting the scope and application of copyright on a false premise. Copyright needs viable conceptions of authorship and originality, but it is crucial that these do not find their foundation in traditional myths and misconceptions.

When it comes to recognising the metaphorical nature of copyright's originality doctrine, nobody has explained this better than Jessica Litman:

> [O]riginality is a legal fiction. . . . Because authors necessarily reshape the prior works of others, a vision of authorship as original creation from nothing – and of authors as casting up truly new creations from their innermost being – is both flawed and misleading. If we took this vision seriously, we could not grant authors copyrights without first dissecting their creative processes to pare elements adapted from the works of others from the later authors' recasting of them. This dissection would be both impossible and unwelcome. If we eschewed this vision but nonetheless adhered unswervingly to the concept of originality, we would have to allow the author of almost any work to be enjoined the by owner of the copyright in another.[5]

In other words, originality in the sense of independent origination is both impossible to determine and impossible to attain. The borders of the copyrightable work that originality constructs are 'entirely illusory', and the concept of originality itself is simply 'chimerical'.[6] Copyright law itself does not – and could never – take the concept literally without undermining its own structural integrity and operation. It is a legal fiction, and, according to Litman's analysis, the fiction is sustainable only because copyright law concedes the concept of a public domain upon which authors are free to draw. It appears, from Litman's account, that the common belief we seem to share in the possibility of absolutely independent creation manifests some sort of shared human neurosis. We are satisfied with the concept of originality, notwithstanding that it is a mere apparition, because it has 'enough symbolic power to subdue its vaporous reality'. This power flows from its ability to reflect 'what we would like to believe about authors and the authorship process.'[7] As with the concept of property, the concept of originality holds an intuitive appeal and is buttressed by common philosophical assumptions of the liberal tradition: not least, of course, the innate individuality of the self.[8]

However, as with the concept of property, it is essential that we let go of this refractory notion of the author-as-originator if we are to reimagine the copyright model. Mark Rose is correct to assert: 'Much of the notorious difficulty of applying copyright doctrine to concrete cases can be related to the persistence of the discourse of original genius and the problems inherent in the reifications of author and work.'[9] This certainly describes the difficulty courts have had developing and applying a coherent account of the originality doctrine. Applying to modern authorship a doctrine that assumes originality to be the very opposite of imitation will inevitably prove difficult if, in reality, 'originality is impossible, and . . . genius may in fact be a flair for creative imitation.'[10] The first step towards a solution for copyright is to shake off the discourse of original genius and deconstruct the reified author who continues to exist in the legal imagination. Originality as a legal concept will persist – as it must if copyright is to survive its re-imagination – and, if freed from these defining fictions, the originality doctrine will be better placed to do its job as the gatekeeper of copyright.

Recognising the metaphorical nature of 'originality' in copyright law is therefore one key to re-imagining copyright's concept of authorship. From this should follow the redefinition of originality in a way that respects the processes of authorship, properly understood; only then can the doctrine be used to encourage the kind of creative and communicative activities that are the *raison d'être* of the copyright system, as opposed to rewarding the labour of the putative author. When the originality construct is emptied of intrinsic substance, we can begin to fill it with an appropriate meaning: if 'originality' is a copyright metaphor, for what should it stand?

5.3 THE EVOLUTION OF ORIGINALITY IN CANADA: INTRODUCING THE PUBLIC INTEREST

5.3.1 The Background Battle

The originality doctrine provides the central requirement of copyright protection. A work is only protected by copyright if it consists of original expression, and copying will only amount to infringement if original elements of the protected work are copied. In this sense, the originality doctrine is responsible for delineating the nature and the scope of copyright's subject matter. Further, originality is the foundational concept that defines the relationship between an author and her work, for copyright in a work comes into existence at the moment when an author produces original expression. However, as with many or most of the foundational concepts in copyright law, the meaning of originality has long been a matter of doubt and a source of contention. The debate has evolved around two prominent schools of thought: the 'sweat school' and the 'creativity school'.

According to the 'sweat school', copyright's originality requirement demands only the 'sweat of one's brow'. To invest time, labour or effort into a work's production entitles one to protection against those who would seek to benefit from one's pains. Works that are not copied and that involve industry on the part of their creator are entitled to the protections afforded by copyright. In practical terms, this means that copyright is capable of extending to routine, mundane and functional works such as garden-variety compilations of information. Contrast this with the 'creativity school', whose adherents advocate the need for genuine authorship as evidenced by a creative spark: a modicum or scintilla of creativity or ingenuity in addition to not copying. Depending upon how the creativity standard is formulated and applied, it raises the bar for copyrightability, depriving garden-variety compilations of copyright on the rationale that industry is not the same as authorship.

In recent years, judicial determinations of originality in the Canadian courts swung unpredictably between the two schools of thought, reflecting the conflicts and contradictions underlying the originality doctrine, and causing uncertainty, confusion and controversy. As David Freedman explains:

> [A]rising in part from the tensions inherent in Canada's bijural tradition and the influence of American law on domestic doctrine, the most recent cases have tended to complicate matters by alternatively pulling towards and pushing away from conceptions of creative authorship in general and specifically in respect of compilation of factual material. In the process, the law has become uncertain both in doctrine and direction.[11]

Some courts remained vigorously aligned with the traditional British approach requiring only that a work be not copied and independently created,[12] while others, also drawing on UK precedent, spoke interchangeably of 'skill, judgment, or labour' and 'work, taste and discretion'.[13] Illuminating the tension in Canada between civil and common law principles, decisions in the Quebec courts spoke of 'a certain personal effort' accompanied by 'knowledge, skill, time, reflection, judgment and imagination.'[14] Others spoke of the importance of demonstrating a 'minimum of creativity', while nevertheless classifying as infringement the unauthorised adoption of another's 'labour or effort.'[15]

In 1995, in the *U&R Tax Services* case, the Federal Court stated, rather unequivocally, that 'industriousness ("sweat of the brow") as opposed to creativity is enough to give a work sufficient originality to make it copyrightable.'[16] Two years later, in the *Tele-Direct* case, the Federal Court of Appeal opined, almost as unequivocally, that the *U&R Tax* case and others like it had been misunderstood; the creativity standard was part of Anglo-Canadian copyright law (or at least, if it was not, it should have been).[17] According to *Tele-Direct*, the 'sweat of the brow' cases had never stood for the proposition that labour alone could be determinative of originality; apparently, 'skill, judgment *or* labour' had always meant 'skill, judgment *and* labour.'[18] If it were otherwise, the court opined, Canada would not be in compliance with its NAFTA obligations, which were said to impose standards of intellect and creativity.[19] In short, the Federal Court of Appeal in *Tele-Direct* purported to declare victory for the creativity school in the originality 'battle', finding that the NAFTA definition of protectable compilations as 'intellectual creations' had:

> decided the battle which was shaping up in Canada between partisans of the 'creativity' doctrine . . . and the partisans of the 'industrious collection' or 'sweat of the brow' doctrine – wherein copyright is a reward for the hard work that goes into compiling facts.[20]

The *Tele-Direct* case was widely understood to be an endorsement of the US approach to originality, which had been established by the US Supreme Court in the famous *Feist* decision,[21] and according to which a work must not be copied and must contain a modicum of creativity. Indeed, the Canadian Federal Court of Appeal expressly found assistance in the US experience. Several subsequent cases in Canada followed the *Tele-Direct* decision,[22] and the prevalent expectation at the time seems to have been that *Feist* or something resembling it would soon become the standard approach across the common law jurisdictions.[23] However, just five years after the ruling in *Tele-Direct*, the Federal Court of Appeal sought to clarify its position; anyone under the impression that it had embraced a creativity standard for Canadian originality was once again mistaken. According to the Court of Appeal in the *CCH* case, the only precondition to copyright in Anglo-Canadian law was that a work be 'independently produced and not copied from another person.'[24] Skill, judgment, labour, knowledge and so forth were all possible indicators or ingredients of originality, but none was required in order for an independently produced work to receive protection.

Compounding the confusion that already surrounded the doctrine, the Court of Appeal had now released two apparently contradictory decisions on the meaning of originality within five years, each purporting to settle the question. In the latest twist in this chain of cases, the Supreme Court of Canada overturned the Court of Appeal's ruling on the meaning of originality, finding that the answer lies in between the 'two extremes' of industriousness and creativity. An original, copyrightable work 'must be more than a mere copy of another work', but it 'need not be creative, in the sense of novel or unique'. Rather, in order to be protected, an author's expression must also involve a more than trivial amount of 'skill and judgment'. 'Skill' is defined as 'the use of one's knowledge, developed aptitude or practised ability in producing the work', while 'judgment' is 'the use of one's capacity for discernment or ability to form an opinion or evaluation by comparing different possible options in producing the work'.[25]

Nowhere is the pull between the extremes of creativity and industry better illustrated than in the progression of the *CCH* case through the Canadian courts. The history and outcome of this case encapsulate the dynamics that have shaped originality jurisprudence. As such, I will use this case as a platform from which to examine those dynamics and the significance of the apparent resolution achieved by Canada's Supreme Court in March 2004. My intention is to contextualise the formulation and application of the doctrine in light of the perceived purposes of copyright law, and correspondingly, the identification of copyright's intended beneficiaries. My argument is that some seismic shifting in the theoretical ground underlying copyright in Canada caused this movement in copyright's doctrinal structure. From the time that the Trial Division issued its ruling in *CCH* until the Supreme Court released the final decision, copyright in Canada evolved from a right existing solely for the benefit of authors into a system for achieving a balance between authors' rights and the public interest. Contextualising the *CCH* case within that shifting paradigm sheds light on the divergent approaches to originality taken by the various levels of court. My broad contention, in this section, will be that the Supreme Court's *CCH* ruling represents the first occasion in Canada in which originality was shaped with the public interest, and not simply the author's rights, in mind. It therefore illustrates the doctrinal significance of the theoretical model that is brought to bear in the justification of the copyright interest.

5.3.2 The *CCH* Case

At issue in the *CCH* case was the non-profit, custom photocopy service offered by the Great Library at Osgoode Hall. The Great Library reproduced and delivered legal materials upon request to members of the Law Society, the judiciary, students and researchers, as well as maintaining on-site self-service photocopy machines. The plaintiffs in the matter were legal publishers who sought a declaration of subsistence and ownership of copyright in certain works, and a declaration that copyright was infringed when the Great Library made copies thereof. The works at issue included case headnotes, summaries, a topical index and a compilation of reported judicial decisions. The publishers were ultimately successful in obtaining the declaration of copyright subsistence and ownership, but nevertheless failed to obtain an injunction against the Great Library, whose activity was found by the Supreme Court to be neither direct infringement (the dealing was fair), nor indirect infringement (there was no implied authorisation of infringing activity).

5.3.2.1 *CCH* at the Trial Division: the creative spark

The decision of the Trial Division on the issue of copyright's subsistence effectively confirmed and compounded the initial fears generated by the *Tele-Direct* decision that a 'creativity' standard would elevate the originality threshold beyond what was reasonable, and would cause judges to become subjective arbiters of literary value or worth. Refusing to find original expression in reported judicial decisions, including headnotes, catchlines, parallel citations and running heads, Justice Gibson concluded that such additions 'involved extensive labour, skill and judgment' but 'lacked the "imagination" or "creative spark" . . . essential to a finding of originality.'[26]

Resistance to a creativity standard has often been justified in terms its potential connotations. In the United States, Melville Nimmer famously – and successfully – objected to the proposed inclusion of the word 'creative' in the 1976 Act on the ground that the term would suggest a higher standard than required, implying the need for some degree of objective novelty.[27] In applying the *Tele-Direct* standard to the case headnotes, in particular, I would respectfully suggest that Justice Gibson drew this mistaken inference from the concept of 'creativity' when he found that skilful faithfulness to the original material precluded original expression.[28] Having denied copyright to many of the legal publications at issue in the case, and having endorsed a view of creative originality that required 'imagination' and 'creative spark' beyond basic skill and judgment, it seemed clear that the ruling was unlikely to survive on appeal. It was also clear, however, that this overly restrictive application of the creativity standard had put the standard itself in jeopardy.

For the purposes of my argument, it is important to examine this originality ruling in light of the copyright policy assumptions at play. The court began its analysis stating what it understood to be the object and the purpose of Canada's Copyright Act, namely:

> to benefit authors, albeit that in benefiting authors, it is capable of having a substantially broader-based public benefit through the encouragement of disclosure of works for the advancement of learning or, as in this case, the wider dissemination of law.[29]

As previously noted, the obvious implication of this statement is that any benefit enjoyed by the public as a result of the protection of the author's copyright is an incidental, if fortunate, by-product of upholding the private right. This vision of copyright's purpose echoed the position of the Supreme Court of Canada at that time. In the Supreme Court decision of *Bishop v. Stevens*, it was said: 'the Copyright Act . . . was passed with a single object, namely, the benefit of authors of all kinds'.[30]

Having thus identified the sole intended beneficiary of the copyright system as the rights-bearing author, the formulation of the originality standard in the *CCH* case at trial can be understood in terms of the court's explicit author focus. The Trial Division's ruling is best examined through the lens of a personality-based concept of copyright: original works of authorship are protected because and to the extent that they manifest the personalities or individuality of their authors, embodying their subjective choices and intellectual energy.[31] This argument is reinforced by Justice Gibson's approval of dictum from the *Tele-Direct* decision. Citing Justice Decary, Justice Gibson adopts the author-oriented perspective that seems to have informed the Federal Court of Appeal's articulation of a creativity standard in that case:

> One should always keep in mind that one of the purposes of the copyright legislation, historically, has been "to protect and reward the intellectual effort of the author . . . in the work". The use of the word "copyright" in the English version of the Act has obscured that fact that what the Act fundamentally seeks to protect is "*le droit d'auteur*". While not defined in the Act, the word "author" conveys a sense of creativity and ingenuity.[32]

The standard of creative originality that emerged from the Court of Appeal in the *Tele-Direct* ruling, and which was embraced by Justice Gibson in the *CCH* case at trial level, can therefore be seen to flow from an attempt to identify and protect 'true authors' – the intended beneficiaries of the Copyright Act. If originality defines true authorship, thus conceived, then some personal connection and subjective contribution to the work is required, for this connection is what underpins the right.[33] As I will argue, while these decisions were widely regarded as having adopted a *Feist*-like standard in Canada, this reading of the judgment would suggest a very different foundation for the creativity requirement than that upon which Justice O'Connor relied in the *Feist* decision.

5.3.2.2 *CCH* at the Court of Appeal: 'Not copied' and the labour-reward model

The ruling on the meaning of originality at the Federal Court of Appeal was, in my opinion, more problematic than the Trial Division's ruling.

According to Justice Linden, the trial judge had 'failed to conduct any substantive analysis of the American standard of originality', and thereby 'entangled the standard set out in *Feist* . . . with the Canadian touchstone of originality.'[34] Justice Linden's ruling emptied the originality concept of virtually all meaning, reducing the central requirement of copyrightability to the mere proposition that original works originate from the author.[35]

The standard as articulated is over-inclusive, and the scope of copyright protection is potentially widened beyond the kind of intellectual productions that require protection in furtherance of copyright's goals. There is, in this sense, no actual 'standard' to be met; anything not copied is worth protecting, and the only 'sweat' required is the effort it takes to distinguish a work from a mere copy. Under this view, originality determinations involve no consideration of the attributes of the work or the processes undertaken in its production, but are purely concerned with the existence of a single originating source.

Interestingly, the copyright policy articulated by Justice Linden also differs quite significantly from that espoused by Justice Gibson at the trial level. The Court of Appeal began its analysis with the following statement of copyright's goals:

> [T]he purposes of Canadian copyright law are to benefit authors by granting them a monopoly for a limited time, and to simultaneously encourage the disclosure of works for the benefit of society at large. . . . The person who sows must be allowed to reap what is sown, but the harvest must ensure that society is not denied some benefit from the crops.[36]

This position was in line with the most recent articulation by the Supreme Court on the matter of copyright's purposes. As we have seen in passing, the case of *Théberge v. Galerie D'Art du Petit Champlain Inc.*[37] saw a shift by the Canadian Court away from its previous author-orientation and towards the idea of copyright as a balance between two sets of interests:

> A balance between promoting the public interest in the encouragement and dissemination of works of the arts and intellect and obtaining a just reward for the creator. . . . The proper balance among these and other public policy objectives lies not only in recognising the creator's rights but in giving due weight to their limited nature. In interpreting the Copyright Act, courts should strive to maintain an appropriate balance between these two goals.[38]

The question then becomes whether the adoption of this policy goal played a significant role in the Court of Appeal's interpretation of originality. Was it somehow the search for an appropriate equilibrium between copyright's two purposes that resulted in the polar opposite approach to originality? In my view, the answer is no, not quite. The focus of the Court of Appeal for the purposes of determining originality was placed upon the first goal set out in *Théberge*: the need to provide just reward for the creator. The court noted: 'A more onerous standard of originality deprives owners of the copyright protection that the signatories to these [international] agreements intended to guarantee. Their purpose is frustrated, rather than promoted by implying additional requirements of creativity, imagination or creative spark into the Act.'[39]

As Daniel Gervais has observed, a focus upon the author – such as that which seems to have informed the courts in *Tele-Direct* and *CCH* at the Trial Division – is not always in the interests of those who would claim to be authors.[40] A personality-based notion of authorship might limit the works to which copyright protection extends. However, an author-orientation that defines the author's right in terms of the effort and labour invested will lower the threshold for protection in order to 'prevent someone other than the creator from appropriating whatever benefits may be generated', thereby ensuring 'just reward'.[41]

Justice Linden describes those who would be denied copyright protection due to additional creativity requirements as 'owners of the copyright' nonetheless. The premise must be that ownership does not flow from creativity, and so when creativity is a prerequisite for protection, true owners of copyright are denied protection. In lowering the threshold of originality, Justice Linden had regard to only one of the two goals identified: obtaining just reward (ownership) for the creator (labourer). This reward was measured in relation to the effort invested in its production. So what of the other goal and its implications for originality determinations? Justice Linden wrote:

> Admittedly, the public interest in the dissemination of works may be a policy reason to impose a high standard of "creativity" as a prerequisite to copyright protection. There is also the concern that overprotection of certain works will thwart social and scientific progress by precluding persons from building upon earlier works. However, . . . a fair interpretation of user rights can counteract the apparent imbalance potentially generated by a low threshold. For example, the fair dealing provisions of the Act provide a mechanism whereby user rights are better considered.[42]

In a Canadian context, as we will see, reliance on the fair dealing defence is of little comfort to those concerned with the over-inclusiveness likely to result from the minimal originality standard. But more importantly, to limit consideration of the public interest to infringement determinations, while excluding it from subsistence determinations, both relegates and distorts the nature of the public interest at stake. The public interest has a critical role to play in determining the subject matter to which copyright ought to attach. This is the moment at which the work becomes subject to the exclusionary interest and is set apart from the public domain; this is the basis upon which the legal relation between author and work is established. Clearly at this stage, perhaps more than any other, the public has interests at stake.

While the Court of Appeal posited, as a starting point, the balance articulated by the Supreme Court in *Théberge*, it failed to acknowledge the relevance of the public's side of that balance in arriving at its definition of originality. With this side of the balance neglected, the only relevant purpose that remained was that of protecting the author's reward, and thus ensuring that the author reaped what was sown. Consequently, the originality threshold was lowered to the point of virtual irrelevance, creating a real – and not merely 'apparent' – imbalance in favour of the author's right. This imbalance cannot be justified or rectified merely by an appeal to the limits of infringement liability.

5.3.2.3 *CCH* at the Supreme Court: 'skill and judgment' and the public interest

The Supreme Court's recent judgment in the *CCH* case provides a new standard for originality, one that requires independent production and the exercise of skill and judgment. However, as the history of the originality doctrine displays, sometimes the particular words used to define its meaning are less important than the policy reasons that inform its application. Notwithstanding the Chief Justice's attempt to ascribe meaning to the words 'skill' and 'judgment', they remain inherently vague, and necessarily open to subjective interpretation on a case-by-case basis. In attempts to interpret and apply the *CCH* standard, courts will have to appeal to the relevant policy considerations as they were articulated in Chief Justice McLachlin's judgment. Perhaps the most important implication of the ruling on originality flows not from the particular formulation of the standard, but rather from the acknowledgement that 'the public interest in promoting the encouragement and dissemination of works of the arts and intellect'[43] is a relevant consideration in the determination of copyrightability.

Like Justice Linden, Chief Justice McLachlin accepted the copyright balance formulated in *Théberge*, but in contrast to Justice Linden, she went on to apply that balance as a framework within which to assess the meaning of originality:

> When courts adopt a standard of originality requiring only that something be more than a mere copy or that someone simply show industriousness to ground

> copyright in a work, they tip the scale in favour of the author or creator's rights, at the loss of society's interest in maintaining a robust public domain that could help foster future creative innovation. . . .
>
> A "sweat of the brow" standard fails to allow copyright to protect the public's interest in maximising the production and dissemination of intellectual works.[44]

Having recognised the public interest at stake in the initial determination of a work's copyrightability, the Chief Justice decided that elevating the minimalist originality standard by requiring skill and judgment would achieve the appropriate balance between the public interest and that of the author. The importance of the Supreme Court's articulation of the purposes of copyright in *Théberge* thus became evident in its subsequent *CCH* ruling, where the notion of balance and the concern for the public interest pervaded the court's interpretation and application of the law. In the originality sphere, the acknowledgement of a relevant public interest and public goal for copyright law was a major development, and a significant improvement upon the author-orientation of past decisions concerning copyrightability.

On this basis, I would suggest that the *CCH* case is to Canada what *Feist* is to the United States – far more so, in fact, than the *Tele-Direct* decision ever was. The comparison is not premised upon the simple fact that *CCH* unambiguously rejected an industrious collection standard as *Feist* had done in the United States several years earlier. Purely in terms of the test adopted, *Tele-Direct* would indeed bear a closer resemblance to *Feist*. The basis for the analogy is rather the way in which both Courts, in establishing the meaning of originality, looked beyond the interests of the purported rights-bearer and made an appeal to the public policy goals of copyright law. In *Feist*, having asserted that originality in compilations of data requires 'a minimal degree of creativity' in the selection and arrangement, Justice O'Connor addressed the public purposes of copyright:

> It may seem unfair that much of the fruit of the compiler's labor may be used by others without compensation. . . . It is, rather, "the essence of copyright" and a constitutional requirement. The primary objective of copyright is not to reward the labor of authors, but "[t]o promote the Progress of Science and useful Arts". To this end, copyright assures authors the right to their original expression, but encourages others to build freely upon the ideas and information conveyed by a work.[45]

Similarly, in *CCH*, Chief Justice McLachlin justified the higher originality standard by way of an appeal to the public interest at stake:

> [W]hen an author must exercise skill and judgment to ground originality in a work, there is a safeguard against the author being overcompensated for his

> or her work. This helps ensure that there is room for the public domain to flourish as others are able to produce new works by building on the ideas and information contained in the works of others.[46]

Whereas the originality debate in Canada had previously been framed in terms of the search for the deserving author (the meritorious producer of something worthy of protection), the *CCH* case adopts an approach similar to that of the US Supreme Court: the meaning of originality is to be determined with a view to the primary objective(s) of copyright law, which necessitates consideration of the public interest and the appropriate limits of private appropriation. This kind of openly purposive, policy-infused analysis of a copyright concept represents a significant departure from previous Canadian jurisprudence, which tended to reify these concepts and so to deny their inherently malleable and therefore political nature.

5.3.3 Implications of *CCH* for Originality and Canadian Copyright Law

I am hopeful that the concept of balance between authors' reward and public's interest, as propounded in *Théberge* and developed in *CCH*, will provide a revitalising framework for assessing current controversies in the originality debate. Thus, for example, in the policy dilemma surrounding database protection, a concern for the public interest will ensure appreciation of the need for the dissemination of information and the freedom to build upon it. The unavoidable question of whether databases should receive protection, and if so to what extent, must therefore be answered in the context of the various policy considerations at stake, and not simply against the backdrop of a desire or perceived need to reward the labour, time or investment of a compiler/'author' or prevent its 'misappropriation'.

However, it is important to stress that the real implications of this development in the originality context have yet to be seen. The subject matter at issue in the *CCH* case did not present the degree of controversy that will inevitably be encountered elsewhere. The works at issue in *CCH* were not of the type involved in the *Feist*, *Tele-Direct* or the Australian *Telstra*[47] decisions. It will be interesting to see what happens to the balance sought by the *CCH* originality standard when a court is faced with allowing the unlicensed extraction of substantial amounts of information for commercial purposes from a garden-variety compilation of data, laboriously collected. Such a scenario will present the real challenge involved in striking the balance between rewarding author-compilers and allowing the free flow of information for the public interest.

With two goals to further in the pursuit of copyright's purposes, at a certain point, a choice will have to be made. Which right will prevail when the balance (or the illusion thereof) can no longer be convincingly maintained? Historically, faced with such choices, Canadian courts have erred in favour of protecting an author's perceived right. This highlights the vulnerability intrinsic to the *Théberge* balancing act, as well as revealing a crucial point of divergence between the reasoning in *Feist* and *CCH*. To reiterate: in *Feist*, the refusal to protect facts in a compilation was not 'unfair or unfortunate' for the compiler, but was the very means by which copyright advanced its '*primary* objective', which is not to reward authors but to promote progress. As Guy Pessach explains, underlying the Court's decision was 'the conviction that the requirement of creativity was the correct and desired way to implement copyright's policy of encouragement, and thus achieve the optimal result for promoting the public interest.'[48] By way of contrast, in *CCH*, copyright's objective was to 'promot[e] the encouragement and dissemination of works *and* to obtain[...] a just reward for the creator.'[49] Copyright has *two* goals. While, following the US approach, the author's private rights are ultimately a means to secure a public end, in the Canadian context, the author's rights are regarded at once as a means to an end and an end in themselves.

Indeed, when the US courts speak of the copyright balance, the nature of that balance differs significantly from the Canadian copyright balance employed in *CCH*. The US copyright balance is properly understood as internal to the public interest; it requires courts to establish whether the public interest in promoting progress of the useful arts has shifted from demanding the recognition of the author's copyright to necessitating its refusal. On one hand, recognition of a copyright interest will presumably incentivise production of such works to the ultimate benefit of the public, while on the other hand, refusing copyright protection will allow the work to be freely accessed and disseminated, thereby also serving the public interest. Within this framework, the question is not how one balances the conflicting interests of society on one hand and the owner on the other, but how one achieves a balance between protection and the public domain that will serve the interests of society at large.[50] This differs from the balancing act described in *Théberge*, which appears to leave intact the notion of the author's right to reap the rewards of her intellectual effort, with the caveat that these rights will be subject to necessary limitations when balanced against the relevant public interest.

It is worth remembering that the idea of 'balancing' competing interests is no more than a metaphor itself, albeit one that is pervasive in modern copyright discourse. It seems clear that competing interests cannot simply be weighed or balanced in an ideological vacuum: they have no intrinsic weight and there exists no essential scale by which to measure them.

Undeniably, '[t]he "weight" of an interest varies according to the objective in view.'[51] Is it enough, then, to say that our objective is to achieve a balance, or does that merely beg the question: a balance by what measure? If the overarching value or ideal that underlies copyright law, and by which the balance is gauged, remains the protection and promotion of authors' rights to a 'just reward', then less weight will be attributed to the public interest in access and dissemination of intellectual products than to the owner's rights in the copyright balance. As David Freedman has observed, 'the balancing exercise is unhelpfully complicated by the automatic entitlements that flow necessarily from a proprietary approach.'[52]

With the natural-rights based theory of copyright escaping any explicit critique, we should ask whether the Canadian balancing approach is truly equipped to generate the kind of outcome reached in *Feist*, where the existence of a copyright interest was dependent on, and so subject to, the requirements of progress for the benefit of the public. Chief Justice McLachlin appears satisfied that the exclusory application of a higher threshold for originality, established in the name of the public interest, can be consistent with the goal of rewarding authors. Whether this plays out in practice, however, will be determined by the weight attributed to each goal in the balance; the weight of these goals will be determined by the theoretical or justificatory principles that guide the balancer.

The development of Canada's originality standard over the past few years has unfolded against a shifting theoretical background. The interest that the public has in the protection of copyright – in who and what is protected and how much – has finally been recognised not simply as a secondary and incidental benefit potentially derivable from the enforcement of authors' rights, but as a primary goal of the copyright system. Until the Supreme Court of Canada's in *CCH*, originality determinations in Canada were overwhelmingly concerned with how to understand, identify and protect authors' rights. The conflict between the creativity standard and the sweat of the brow standard was fought on the basis of differing conceptions of the author's entitlement; in particular, the outcome depended upon whether a court favoured a personality-based or a labour-based understanding of authors' rights. Taken together, the Supreme Court's rulings in *Théberge* and *CCH* de-centred the notion of authorial entitlement, creating room for the public interest to play a far greater role in determinations of copyrightability. Notwithstanding the possible limitations or weaknesses inherent in the *Théberge* balancing act, the *CCH* case has situated the debate about the meaning of originality squarely within the newly acknowledged public policy purposes of the copyright system. The appropriate originality threshold is to be determined, not only with the author's interests in mind, but also taking into account the public interest that is at stake when exclusive rights are granted over intellectual works. The significance of including public interest considerations in originality determinations is therefore the first lesson that ought to be drawn from Canada's experience. This approach offers a substantially more nuanced framework within which to develop copyright policy, beginning with questions about the kind of subject matter that copyright should protect and, of course, the suitable limits of that protection.

5.4 PUTTING THE CANADIAN COMPROMISE IN CONTEXT

5.4.1 Parallels between *CCH* and *Walter v. Lane*

The various lines of reasoning about originality in the *CCH* case encapsulate the dynamics that have shaped Canadian originality jurisprudence, but they also reflect the tensions that have subsisted in the originality doctrine throughout its history and development. In this section, I will put the Canadian originality 'compromise' in context by comparing it to the UK and US originality standards. In doing so, I hope to tease out the true significance of Canada's new originality standard, but also to draw conclusions about the significance of the originality doctrine generally in its capacity to either support or undermine the theoretical model in which copyright is cast.

In the classic British originality case of *Walter v. Lane*,[53] the work at issue was a stenographer's report of a public speech delivered by Lord Rosebery. The House of Lords ruled that copyright could subsist in the verbatim report, and that the reporter was the author of the report for the purposes of copyright law. The judgments of the five Lords reveal three divergent theoretical approaches underlying the determination of originality: an authorship model, a labour model and a public interest model.[54] Arguably, these different paradigms mirror in large part the conflicting approaches that we have seen in the Canadian cases and in *CCH* in particular.

In *Walter v. Lane*, Lord Robertson decided that the plaintiff's work was not original given the meaning to be attributed to the term 'author'.[55] The same concern for defining 'authorship' informed the reasoning of Lord James, although it led to the opposite conclusion.[56] Arguably, a parallel can be drawn between this 'authorship model' and the reasoning employed by the *Tele-Direct* court and the Trial Division in the *CCH* case, where the meaning of originality was derived from the demands of genuine authorship. In stark contrast, the Earl of Halsbury in *Walter v.*

Lane chose to avoid the use of the word 'author' to describe the producer of the work in light of the 'confusion' it would create.[57] He spoke instead of the need to prevent one man from appropriating and profiting from another's labour.[58] The industriousness standard for originality espoused by Lord Davey was similarly underpinned by the desire to ensure that the plaintiff was permitted to reap what he had sown.[59] Here a parallel can be drawn between the approach of Lords Halsbury and Davey and the minimalist standard arrived at by the Court of Appeal in *CCH* and other Canadian sweat-of-the-brow cases, which looked for deserving effort and not meritorious authorship as the basis for protection.[60]

Taking a third tact, Lord Brampton in *Walter v. Lane* appeared to lend some credence to both authorship and labour considerations, but ultimately arrived at the conclusion that the work was original by making reference to the public interest at stake. It would appear that Lord Brampton found the work to be original because the report furthered access to, and dissemination of, the speech. In other words, recognising the public benefits of having reporters take down truthful records of public speeches meant awarding copyright protection to the writers engaged in this worthwhile activity.[61] Lord Brampton's approach to the originality question can be more or less aligned with the Supreme Court's ruling in *CCH*: the title of 'author' and the label 'original' are to be attributed not simply on the basis of an assessment of the process of production – the degree of authorship or effort displayed – but flow at least in part from consideration of the public interest served by protecting the work.

However, Lord Brampton's judgment in *Walter v. Lane* also highlights the central conundrum of a public interest analysis in copyright law: while protecting the work might have encouraged the accurate recording of important speeches, refusing protection would have further increased dissemination by allowing publication of the reported speech in the defendant's book. Lord Brampton did not address this second element of the public interest. This additional, neglected consideration demonstrates the need for the balancing act that I have described as 'internal' to the public interest. Taking the public interest seriously means acknowledging that there will be occasions when protecting the socially useful results of an individual's effort does not serve the interests of the public, and that on such occasions copyright protection should be denied.

By identifying the themes of authorship, labour and the public interest within the seminal *Walter v. Lane* case, we can see the source of divergent doctrinal approaches to originality in divergent theoretical conceptions of copyright's purpose. While both authorship and labour, as determining considerations in originality jurisprudence, have tended to focus on the individualist moral relation between author and work as the source of the legal right, the public interest consideration has defined the legal relation between author and work with regard to the moral relation between the purported author's work and society; the determination of originality thus depends, at least in part, on an assessment of how the public interest would best be served.

In the discussion that follows, I will argue that, by resisting a British 'sweat'-based approach to originality while also refusing to endorse a American *Feist*-like approach, the *CCH* ruling potentially freed the concept of originality from the kinds of 'labour' and 'creativity' conceits that have tended to define it in Anglo-American copyright jurisprudence. In doing so it has paved the way for the re-imagination of originality in an instrumental mode: originality not as the root of the author's entitlement, but as a functional doctrine, the meaning and application of which is guided by the purposes of the copyright system.

5.4.2 Resisting 'Sweat': a Comparison to Originality in the UK

Perhaps the best way to understand the 'skill and judgment' standard for originality is in light of the things it leaves out. Arguably, the most important point of departure in *CCH* from previous or alternative articulations of originality is the exclusion of the word 'labour' – or its common companion 'effort' – from the 'skill and judgment' test. The labour invested in the production of a work has traditionally had a significant role to play in determinations of originality in common law copyright, either as a sole requirement in the traditional 'sweat of the brow' standard, or at least as one component of an originality standard requiring, for example, 'skill, judgment and labour.' Implicit in its absence from the 'skill and judgment' test is the proposition that labour *per se* is simply not part of the copyright equation. In order to make this argument, I will show that the rejection of pure 'sweat of the brow' and the desire to leave information itself in the public domain did not necessitate the complete exclusion of labour. The 'skill and judgment' test should therefore be appreciated as important shift away from a labour-based justification for the copyright interest.

5.4.2.1 Protecting labour; protecting information

The primary basis for rejecting the 'sweat of the brow' approach appears to have been concern about its ability to extend copyright protection to facts contained in a protected work. In *Feist*, the US Supreme Court, rejecting a sweat of the brow approach, identified as its 'most glaring flaw' that:

> it extended copyright protection in a compilation beyond selection and arrangement – the compiler's original contributions – to the facts themselves.

> . . . "Sweat of the brow" courts thereby eschewed the most fundamental axiom of copyright law – that no one may copyright facts or ideas.[62]

When the Supreme Court of Canada rejected the sweat-based approach in *CCH*, Chief Justice McLachlin agreed that 'in Canada, as in the United States, copyright protection does not extend to facts or ideas but is limited to the expression of ideas.' On this basis, she found that 'O'Connor's J. concerns about the "sweat of the brow" doctrine's improper extension of copyright over facts also resonate in Canada.'[63]

The Canadian case of *B.C. Jockey* illustrates how a labour-based originality standard can confer exclusivity over facts to the detriment of downstream users and the public.[64] The plaintiffs produced a publication, 'Overnight', in advance of each day of horse racing, with information on the races, horses, jockeys and conditions for the day ahead. The defendant's publication adopted much of this information, but in a form that was 'not at all similar',[65] and included additional comments and preferences. The British Columbia Court of Appeal noted at the outset that '[a] good deal of work has to be performed before publication of the [plaintiff's] "Overnight," '[66] and ultimately affirmed 'the right of the Club to protect its compilation of information as a whole', notwithstanding that the defendant had 'adopted it to his own style'.[67] The court shared the trial judge's view that the defendant had taken 'a substantial part of this compilation made by the plaintiff at a great deal of cost and trouble to himself',[68] and that this was a sufficient basis on which to find infringement. It also approved the British authorities quoted by the judge, which appealed to the 'painstaking labour'[69] involved in compiling the facts, and stated that 'no man is entitled to avail himself of the previous labours of another for the purpose of conveying to the public the same information.'[70]

When the copyright in a factual work is based on the labour involved in compiling information, then taking the information gathered will amount to appropriating the very fruits of the labour that copyright protects.[71] The copyright interest may not confer a true monopoly over the information because the information can, in theory, be independently discovered and published without liability.[72] Thus, the number of milestones that separate two towns is factual information that cannot be exclusively owned. However, a sweat of the brow approach will protect the labour expended by the first person to count those miles against those who wish to rely upon his efforts to impart the same information.[73] The exclusive right therefore protects the information, although it remains independently discoverable. But where the source of the original compilation is the sole source of the information, as in *B.C. Jockey*, copyright confers a *de facto* monopoly; independent discoverability is no more than a fictional limit to the exclusivity conferred.

Granting control over information through copyright is troubling, not least because it obstructs the flow or exchange of information contrary to the public purposes of the copyright system. Furthermore, the 'count your own milestones' approach seems generally counterproductive, and arguably misconceived, to the extent that it requires a duplication of effort without producing any added value to the work or further benefit to the public.[74] It is hard to see in what way it furthers the purposes of copyright protection, unless those purposes are understood simply as providing a proprietary reward for labour.

Having explained her conclusion with reference to the dictum in *Feist*, the Chief Justice's rejection of a pure labour-based standard for protection should be seen as a rejection of any version of originality that would indirectly confer exclusive rights over information. The Court explained that a 'sweat of the brow' approach unduly favours owners' rights and 'fails to allow copyright to protect the public's interest in maximising the production and dissemination of intellectual works.'[75] It follows that the appropriate copyright balance is struck only where information remains in the public domain, free for the taking.[76] Future courts applying the originality doctrine to informational works should bear this conclusion in mind. Whatever scope of protection will be afforded to works such as data compilations in light of the 'skill and judgment' test, it should not permit effective control over information (even if the information itself is the result of the compiler's skill and judgment). In this sense, the protection given to informational works must be 'thin.'[77] As the Supreme Court appears to have understood, in order for this to happen, we have to discard the notion that copyright is an appropriate reward for the mere investment of labour.

Some recent Australian case law reveals the potential significance of drawing this strict distinction between information and its original expression. The Australian courts have found it unnecessary to arrive at a definitive originality standard in order to deny copyright protection to certain basic informational works.[78] Rather, the High Court has emphasised that the relevant intellectual effort, by whatever standard, must be 'directed to the originality of the particular form of expression'. The skill and labour involved in producing the work – making programming decisions for TV listings, for example – is not relevant to copyright's subsistence where it does not go to the expressive form of the work.[79] By acknowledging that information belongs in the public domain as a necessary condition of furthering copyright's public purposes, and insisting that copyright is not concerned with the misappropriation of skill and labour *per se*, the Australian courts have significantly limited the capacity of copyright to protect informational works.[80] In doing so, they have provided an example for British and Canadian courts to follow.[81]

5.4.2.2 Leaving labour aside

Although the Supreme Court of Canada in *CCH* apparently rejected 'sweat of the brow' in order to ensure the public nature of information, this is not sufficient, in itself, to explain the exclusion of labour from the Canada's new originality standard. Traditionally, 'labour' has said in the same breath as 'skill and judgment' and the resulting threshold has been at least as high as 'skill and judgment' alone. Such a 'sweat plus' threshold would not protect mere sweat, and nor need it protect facts. The significance of the Supreme Court's decision to exclude labour therefore becomes apparent only when viewed against the backdrop of the UK's originality jurisprudence and earlier Canadian case law.

A common formulation of the originality standard in Britain requires 'skill and labour' or 'skill, labour and judgment'. Applying this test, labour is not the sole basis of the right conferred: a mechanical expression should not be protected if it resulted from industry but required nothing in the way of skill or judgment. Both 'skill' and 'judgment' import additional ingredients into copyrightability, moving the test further along the originality spectrum, away from pure industry and towards creativity. The 'labour' component of the test is one ingredient in the mix of attributes that combine to constitute 'originality' in the UK jurisprudence.

While Britain is widely regarded as the archetypal 'sweat of the brow' jurisdiction, this is an oversimplification of the originality doctrine as it emerges from the British case law.[82] Support for the proposition that labour alone is sufficient could be found in the judgment of Lord Devlin in *Ladbroke*: '[T]he product must originate from the author in the sense that it is the result of a substantial degree of skill, *industry or* experience employed by him.'[83] Similarly, Lord Hodson in *Ladbroke*, required a showing of 'substantial labour, skill, *or* judgment'.[84] However, this position should be contrasted against other authorities require both skill *and* labour. One example is the case of *Football League Ltd v. Littlewoods Pools Ltd*:

> Copyright can only be claimed in the composition or language which is chosen to express the information or the opinion. . . . [W]here the facts are presented in some special way, it then becomes a question of fact and degree as to whether the *skill and labour* involved in such special representation of the information is entitled to copyright.[85]

Thus stated, it would seem that copyright in factual compilations in Britain did not always or necessarily flow from labour alone, and that (at least some) British courts have respected the distinction between facts and their expression. Indeed, a similar conclusion may be drawn from the older House of Lords case of *Cramp v. Smythson*,[86] in which the Lords' conception of original authorship was sufficient to exclude from copyright pure facts whose expression required nothing significant in the way of skill or judgment.[87] Having inquired into 'whether enough work, labour *and* skill is involved',[88] the Lords denied protection to a compilation of data, even in the face of 'slavish copying' by a competitor.

The fine distinction between a pure 'sweat' standard and the 'skill *and* labour' test that appears to be prevailing in Britain[89] has been brought into greater relief following the revisions to the British law required by the European Database Directive. With regard to data compilations, copyright law will now protect only those data compilations that are the author's own 'intellectual creation'.[90] This has been interpreted to mean that 'there must be something which has had the author's creativity stamped upon it. . . .There must be some "subjective" contribution. A "sweat of the brow" collection will not do.'[91] In the recent *Football Dataco* case, the Chancery Division ruled on the status of football league listings under the revised law.[92] It held that the listings were original literary works that could qualify as 'intellectual creations' because preparation of the fixture lists involved 'very significant skill and labour' and 'judgments . . . as to the relative importance of certain rules', such that the work was 'not mere sweat of the brow', but 'depends in part on the skill of those involved'.[93] In other words, the presence of skill, labour *and* judgment – the same attributes commonly associated with basic originality – was evidence that the data compilation constituted an 'intellectual creation' protectable by copyright.

Even this little dip into British case law reveals the complexity of the originality standard in the United Kingdom, which is so often characterized as a 'sweat of the brow' jurisdiction.[94] This in turn adds nuance to the common but overly stark dissection of originality into a sweat or creativity standard. It seems that the moment of departure comes somewhere closer to the middle of the spectrum, somewhere between 'skill, labour *or* judgment' and 'skill, labour *and* judgment'. If this is indeed the critical distinction, the degree of ambiguity presented by the case law cannot be overstated: many judgments refer to the need for an author to exercise 'skill, labour and/or judgment.'[95] While it might seem like a small concession to ambiguity, 'and/or' entirely collapses the doctrinal polarity, replacing it with interchangeable but critically opposed versions of original authorship: when 'or' is used, labour is enough; when 'and', something more is required.

The contours between 'and' and 'or' were explicitly addressed in

Canada's *Tele-Direct* case, in which the court surmised (in defence of its creativity standard) that 'whenever "or" was used instead of "and", it was in a conjunctive rather than in a disjunctive way.'[96] Of course, this suggestion was more convenient than it was compelling. Where 'or' is used, the standard is easily reduced to mere 'sweat', while 'and' should require something more in the way of intellectual effort. Where 'and' and 'or' are used interchangeably, however, a test that should require some additional feature of skill or judgment is easily reduced to a basic requirement of industry.

The British and Canadian jurisprudence evidences the overwhelming power of the 'labour' component. An originality standard that posits labour as a relevant consideration seems prone to metamorphose into a standard that requires nothing more. As one commentator has explained, courts applying the 'skill and labour' test

> have protected compilations that have displayed marginal skill in their selection or arrangement, but which have involved considerable labour or expense. Thus the application of the "skill and labour" test is a highly flexible one and it may operate as a pretext for protecting mainly investment.[97]

Because 'labour' is included in the test, courts can continue to regard copyright as a reward for labour, and can find copyright in anything independently produced, particularly in cases that involve some perceived element of unfair competition. When 'labour' is omitted from the test, however, merely industrious works must be refused protection. The 'skill and judgment' test should therefore be recognised as significantly different (in substance, if not always in application) from the British 'skill and labour' test. In Britain, '[t]he role of labour has not been segregated from the other components of the tests, namely skill and judgment.'[98] In Canada, that is precisely what has happened by virtue of the *CCH* ruling: 'labour' has been segregated and set aside.

The omission of 'labour' from Canada's new originality standard was neither obvious nor inconsequential; rather, it was a profound and potentially pivotal moment in the development of copyright policy. The Supreme Court made a subtle but critical departure from the minimalist formulations of originality that had 'shift[ed] the balance of copyright protection too far in favour of the owner's rights.'[99] The new standard for originality should be understood in light of this departure, which seems to suggest that labour, in its own right, should play no role in determining the subsistence of copyright.

Of course, given the pervasive force of the labour-reward equation, which has subsisted in common law copyright regimes practically since their inception, this will be easier said than done. There are already indications that that the departure from labour-based standard has been overlooked by lower courts interpreting the decision. In the case of *Robertson v. Thomson*,[100] the Ontario Court of Appeal described the Supreme Court's definition of original work as having, 'both a labour component and a content component. This approach falls between UK law, which extends copyright to cover any work produced through one's labour, and US law, which requires an element of creativity for copyright to apply.'[101] Because the Supreme Court cast the 'skill and judgment' test as a middle ground between sweat and creativity, 'labour' was no sooner removed than it was allowed to creep back in as a facet of the Court's compromise. Even if the new standard is appropriately conceived as a compromise position between two extremes, part of the compromise involved removing the labour component from the originality doctrine. Unless the doctrinal and political import of this decision is recognised, there is a risk that the potential of the *CCH* ruling will go unrealised.

It is no coincidence that the Ontario court in *Robertson* was expressly guided by a conviction that 'to deprive authors of the fruits of their labour is unjust.'[102] The Supreme Court's stand against a 'sweat' or 'sweat plus' originality test should have undermined the notion that copyright is a reward for labour. According to the Chief Justice, when copyright protects works that require only labour in their production, it risks 'overcompensating' the author.[103] The implication is that rewarding pure labour with copyright gives reward where reward is not due. Following this logic, copyright is not a reward for labour, but for something else. As a reward, it is deserved only when an author exercises skill and judgment in the creation of 'works of the arts and intellect'.[104] This should be conceptualised as the *quid pro quo* that society receives in return for granting the author's right.

The Supreme Court's ruling in *CCH* eludes the philosophical and practical implications of a sweat-based approach to originality. Philosophically, awarding copyright to works as a result of labour endorses a 'natural rights or Lockean theory of "just desserts", namely than an author deserves to have his or her efforts in producing a work rewarded.'[105] Practically, granting copyright to such works would permit the 'improper extension of copyright over facts'[106] and thereby diminish the public domain. By rejecting 'sweat of the brow', and by dropping 'labour' from the components that constitute originality, Canada's Supreme Court has taken a significant step: a step away from labour and the author's claim to right; away from the expansion of copyright's scope and the diminishment of the cultural commons; and towards the public interest, the public domain, and the purposive interpretation of copyright doctrine.

5.4.3 What Happened to 'Creativity'?

Having rejected the relevance of authorial 'sweat' in terms not dissimilar to those of the US Supreme Court in *Feist*, the Supreme Court of Canada also eschewed any need for 'creativity' in the originality requirement.[107] It agreed in principle that originality required more than merely independent production or pure labour; it sought to avoid extending protection to information; and it apparently decided that the 'skill, labour, and judgment' test was not appropriate. And so the question remains: why not adopt the ready-made solution offered by its US counterpart in the form of the 'creativity' standard? Once again, we will have to look beyond the Court's explicit rationale and understand the philosophical, political and pragmatic considerations that may have guided the Court's analysis. My argument is that the Court made a considered choice to avoid the term 'creativity', with its attendant civilian conceptions of authors' natural rights and its romantic connotations.

In arriving at its decision, the Court explicitly wished to avoid importing additional requirements into the originality doctrine that may involve substantive assessment of the novelty of copyrightable works. Chief Justice McLachlin dismissed a creativity requirement ostensibly on the basis that '[a] creativity standard implies that something must be novel or non-obvious – concepts more properly associated with patent law that copyright law. By way of contrast, a standard requiring the exercise of skill and judgment in the production of a work avoids these difficulties'.[108] Were novelty a requirement, copyright would protect only those works that in some sense departed from or improved upon the existing body of intellectual creations. It is axiomatic that copyright does not compare a work to others to determine eligibility, but inquires only into the personal processes of authorship. As the Chief Justice notes, objective novelty belongs to the realm of patent law, wherein independent production without copying is no defence to infringement, never mind a basis upon which to assert a separate and equal entitlement.[109] According to the Court's reasons, then, this is cause enough to resist any terminology that connotes a standard of objective novelty. In *Feist*, however, Chief Justice O'Connor made it perfectly clear that 'creativity' implied no such thing:

> Originality does not signify novelty; a work may be original even though it closely resembles other works so long as the similarity is fortuitous, not the result of copying. To illustrate, assume that two poets, each ignorant of the other, compose identical poems. Neither work is novel, yet both are original and, hence, copyrightable.[110]

As such, '[t]he Court's suggestion that the *Feist* creativity standard implies novelty is clearly mistaken.'[111] Creativity in copyright terms does not demand an assessment of the inherent characteristics of the work, but speaks only to the processes of its creation. The dispositive criteria are internal to the workings of the author's mind. The question is not one of objective newness – whereby a work differs to a specified degree from other, pre-existing works – but rather with *subjective* newness: the work is 'new' to the person who brought it into being, in the sense that it was not copied but was independently produced.[112]

If the Court was afraid of a judicial inclination to misunderstand or misapply a creativity standard, it could easily have elaborated on the intended meaning of creativity. The rejection of external considerations, such as literary merit or objective novelty, is fairly fundamental in the common law tradition, and does not offer much assistance in terms of defining what originality is, as opposed to what it is not. Meanwhile, nothing in the Supreme Court's critique would seem to undermine a creativity standard properly understood and correctly applied. Therefore the Court's reasoning falls short of an emphatic repudiation of the principles that underlie a *Feist*-like creativity standard. My suggestion is that the court chose to resist the *language* of 'creativity' rather than the practical implications of the creativity test itself, perhaps because the adoption of that language would have wider philosophical and political implications.

5.4.3.1 Creativity and the *droit d'auteur*

While the connection has been superficially muddied somewhat by the adoption of a creativity approach in the United States, there is a clear relationship between an elevated originality threshold requiring something in the way of creativity and the civilian copyright tradition. In France, for example, the standard of originality is relatively high and demands that copyrightable works are 'creations of the mind'.[113] The traditional understanding of this terminology was that copyrightability required the imprint of the personality of the author upon the work.[114] The search for originality is thus the search for the mark of the author's individuality as revealed in her expression: 'expressive self-articulation'[115] – the heart of true authorship – is achieved through the creative imagination. While such an approach imposes a more onerous standard for obtaining copyright than the traditional industriousness approach of the common law tradition, once the label of original authorship is awarded, it comports with a strong authors'-rights theory of copyright rooted in the notion of possessive personality.[116] Influenced by continental philosophy, the *droit d'auteur* that flows from original, creative authorship emanates from the 'inalienable personality of the author'.[117]

The divergence between civilian and common law principles of authorial right has a particularly critical relevance in Canadian copyright jurisprudence. Although the Federal Act ostensibly follows the British tradition and philosophy, Canadian case law and commentary manifests some degree of tension between Canada's two major legal systems. As was noted by Justice Binnie, writing for a majority in the Supreme Court's *Théberge* decision, the English and French versions of Canada's Copyright Act use the terms '*droit d'auteur*' and 'copyright' as though they were direct translations and equivalent terms, when in fact they are widely thought to encapsulate very different conceptions of the copyright interest:

> [T]he distinction between the copyright tradition and the "*droit d'auteur*" tradition is based on a question of terminology: where the followers of the first tradition, the British and their spiritual heirs, talk about "copyright" to refer to a right that derives from the existence of a "copy", an object in itself, the followers of the second tradition talk about "author's right" to refer to a right that stems from intellectual effort or activity brought to bear by an author, a creator.[118]

Whereas Justice Binnie was intent upon avoiding the confusion that led others to import *civiliste* concepts into Canadian copyright, the minority ruling, supported by the three judges from a civil law background, insisted that 'it is important to recall that Canadian copyright law derives from multiple sources and draws on both common law tradition and continental civil law concepts.'[119] In support of this minority position, Justice Gonthier explained that Canada 'inherited [the common law copyright] aspect while remaining receptive to the French doctrines, particularly because of Quebec's influence. This does great credit to our law since the Canadian Parliament is more inclined than any other legislature to stay attuned to external developments in order to mould its own rules.'[120]

The continuing pervasiveness of *civiliste* conceptions of the *droit d'auteur* in Canadian copyright likely had a bearing on the Court's chosen formulation of the original authorship standard. Certainly, the use of the term 'creativity' in this bi-juridical setting would present greater challenges in Canada than in the Anglo-American context. For one thing, due to the correspondence between a creativity standard and a personality-based conception of the copyright interest, it could readily be assumed that the former affirms the latter; the definition of the legal relation between author and work (the origin of which is creativity) would appear to confirm a theoretical model for copyright based on the moral relation between the author-as-creator and the work as the embodiment of her personality. Simply put, a creativity test that demands the reflection of the author's personality in the work would suggest that the resulting right flows from that investment of personality. Within this context, the creativity test could fortify a conceptualisation of copyright as an inalienable authorial right, which would, inevitably, have significant implications in terms of defining the form, scope and limit of the right.

'Creativity' as it exists in the United States does, of course, have its own ideological baggage. A great deal of US legal scholarship criticises the pervasiveness of romantic authorship tropes as they are revealed or compounded through the *Feistian* notion of original, creative authorship.[121] However, the personality theory underlying the civilian tradition places the romantic author-figure front and centre as the individual around whom the copyright system is built, and in whose interest it operates. The power of this philosophy was apparent in the *Tele-Direct* ruling at the Federal Court of Appeal. While the US creativity approach was justified in light of the 'public-oriented justification of copyright in American law',[122] the same approach was welcomed in Canada as the validation of a civilian philosophy of original authorship and an affirmation of the *droit d'auteur*. Abraham Drassinower has addressed this discrepancy:

> Justice Decary [in *Tele-Direct*] evoked the inherent dignity of authorial right as the central copyright concern par excellence, yet he did so by invoking a case, *Feist*, that affirms a radically instrumentalist understanding of the creativity requirement, an understanding for which the author is but a "secondary" consideration. . . . The evocations of authorial dignity obviously involved in the phrase, "*le droit d'auteur*", have little to do with the pure public interest instrumentalism of the American approach that Justice Decary went on to invoke immediately thereafter.[123]

Had the Supreme Court of Canada handed down a creativity standard for originality, it would have been susceptible to interpretation as the triumph of the civilian concept of author's right over the common law concept of copyright as an instrument to facilitate commercial exploitation. Understood in this light, a creativity standard would likely entail both the strengthening of copyright holders' rights and the increasing elevation of copyright's threshold to admit only works that display 'creativity and ingenuity' and bear the imprint of the author's personality. Apparently, the Court felt that neither result would further 'a balance between promoting the public interest in the encouragement and dissemination of works of the arts and intellect and obtaining a just reward for the creator.'[124]

To summarise, the primary difficulty posed by a 'creativity' standard in Canada is the philosophical assumptions that the term entails. The concept of authorial creativity cannot easily be recast as an instrumental requirement whose purpose is to further the goals of the copyright system. By the same token, if a creativity requirement were imported into such a setting, it would be hard to cast the author's right as anything other than a natural entitlement flowing from the investment of her personality in her work. Taking into account the rather unique dynamics of Canadian copyright law, the creativity standard, while justified in the United States in terms of copyright's incentive structure, has the potential in Canada to exacerbate a critical doctrinal division, to emerge as a full-blown personality-based standard, and to substantiate a philosophical conception of authorship ill suited to the common law context and the purposes of copyright identified by the Court.

With the exclusion of 'creativity' – as with the exclusion of 'labour' – the court resisted a formulation of originality that would define the copyright interest in terms of the author's individual investment and corresponding entitlement. In doing so, it took another step away from rights-based and author-oriented determinants of copyrightability, and towards an instrumental interpretation of copyright's scope.

5.4.3.2 Creativity and the legacy of *Feist*

I have argued that the Supreme Court's decision to exclude both 'labour' and 'creativity' from its originality test reveals a willingness to expunge from the originality doctrine labour-reward and personality theories of right, both of which have influenced its (mis)application in the Canadian courts. This conclusion still leaves open the question of how a 'skill and judgment' standard should be understood in the absence of such theories. The answer, I suggest, lies in the reconceptualisation of originality in an instrumental mode: it is not the foundation of an individual entitlement but a tool with which to further a social end. In order to make this case, I will briefly turn our attention back to the US position, before proceeding to draw out some larger conclusions about the appropriate shape, application and role of an instrumental originality doctrine in a copyright system premised on conceptions of relational authorship.

Notwithstanding the common conflation of creativity and civil law theory in Canada, the American creativity approach is not tantamount to the 'intellectual creation' standard invoked by Justice DeCary in *Tele-Direct*.[125] Describing the US originality standard that emerged from *Feist*, David Freedman has warned:

> The [US] creativity standard is not akin to the "author's own intellectual creation" standard in those civilian systems in which the personality of the author must be reflected in the work, but furthers the same policy goals that are familiar to British copyright: rewarding the judgement and taste of the author through the copyright grant, encouraging others to act likewise, but in no case making unavailable the general ideas or discrete matters of fact that ought to be available to them.[126]

It could be argued that the *Feist* standard, which requires only a minimal degree of creativity, does not go much – if any – further than the Canada's 'skill and judgment' test, and properly understood, does not raise the bar 'too high'.[127] This would reinforce the idea that the Court had other reasons for refusing to follow *Feist*, thereby making available some tools for interpreting the test adopted in its place.

In practice, a US standard requiring creativity may be less significant than it appears, given the kinds of works that it has proved capable of embracing. For example, in *Key Publications Inc. v. Chinatown Today Publishing Enterprises Inc.*,[128] a telephone directory listing businesses associated with New York City's Chinese-American community was protected in copyright. An interesting comparison can be made between the *Key Publications* case and that of *ITAL-Press Ltd v. Sicoli*[129] in the post-*Tele-Direct* Canadian context, where the court found copyright in a telephone directory that consisted only of Canadians of Italian origin. Generally, courts applying a creativity standard have not struggled to find a modicum of creativity even in highly functional or mundane works.[130] As the US Supreme Court insisted in *Feist*, 'the requisite level of creativity is extremely low; even a slight amount will suffice. The vast majority of works make the grade quite easily, as they possess some creative spark, "no matter how crude, humble or obvious" it might be.'[131] Certainly, it seems likely that the kind of works that would be excluded by a 'minimum degree of creativity' threshold will fall similarly short of the 'more than trivial skill and judgment' requirement.[132]

There is little, if any, likelihood that a 'skill and judgment' test will extend protection to a work that would fail to satisfy the US modicum of creativity test, properly applied.[133] Certainly, it should not. One might assume that a creativity standard would leave less room for the protection of data compilations on the *Feistian* logic that factual works minimally engage one's creative faculties, but may nonetheless call upon one's skill or judgment.[134] However, both tests are premised upon – and so must respect – the proposition that 'facts are free for the taking.'[135] Equally, both tests permit the protection of the selection or arrangement of information resulting from a more than mechanical or routine choice.[136] The minimal degree of creativity required in the United States is just enough to reveal some degree of authorial judgment or choice between possible alternatives that is not routine, commonplace, mechanical or dictated by functional considerations.[137] It thus demands no more than did Chief Justice McLachlin in her description of 'skill and judgment'. If this is accepted, then the 'creativity' test is not, in substance at least, any 'higher' a threshold than the 'skill and judgment' test, despite the Supreme Court's statements to that effect.[138] It seems fair to say that 'the Court can differentiate its own "skill and judgment" standard from the "creativity" standard only by mischaracterizing the latter as requiring something "novel", "unique", or "non-obvious".'[139] Avoiding such mischaracterisation, the difference between the standards is elusive – or indeed illusive.

If the creativity test as formulated in the *Feist* case does not necessarily impose a barrier that is too high or goes too far, it seems reasonable to suggest that something more was at play in the Supreme Court's decision to avoid use of the term 'creativity.' As well as the philosophical implications of the term addressed in the previous section, the Court's refusal to follow *Feist* may reflect a general reluctance to incorporate into Canadian copyright doctrine what has come to be recognised as an essentially American standard. In Canadian cases, warnings against the adoption of American principles abound, usually with reference to the words of Justice Estey in *Compo v. Blue Crest*: 'United States Courts decisions, even where the factual situations are similar, must be scrutinised very carefully because of some fundamental differences in copyright concepts which have been adopted in the legislation of that country.'[140]

It is common to see this wariness of US precedent justified in terms of the constitutional basis for the American copyright system, as though the context and stated purpose of American copyright law definitively sets it apart from the Canadian system.[141] Furthermore, the suggestion of misguided reliance on American authorities is a popular and effective ground for appeal. For example, when Justice Linden reversed Justice Gibson's earlier ruling in *CCH*, he criticised the trial judge for having 'mistakenly adopted' the American approach and having 'import[ed]' an 'American principle' into Canadian law.[142] Similar arguments have been given weight in other Canadian cases.[143]

When exploring the Supreme Court's decision not to use the language of 'creativity', it is wise to keep this dynamic in mind. Refusing to go as far as *Feist*, the Supreme Court referred to Compo and observed: 'U.S. copyright cases may not be easily transferable to Canada given the key differences in the copyright concepts in Canadian and American copyright legislation.'[144] Perhaps the 'skill and judgment' test was intended to resemble the creativity test both in substance and effect, albeit without going as far as to explicitly adopt the American terminology and thereby appear to overlook these supposedly 'key differences.' Indeed, one could take this even further and argue that the *CCH* test does a better job than America's 'modicum of creativity' test at achieving the normative objectives underpinning the US Supreme Court's ruling in *Feist*; it evades the quantitative (what is a 'modicum'?) and qualitative (what is 'creativity'?) conundrums that the US test entails. Moreover, by focusing on authorial, non-trivial choice, the 'skill and judgment' test captures the normative force and substance of *Feist* while avoiding the 'the colloquial notion of creativity'.[145]

An appreciation of the similarities between the US and Canadian originality standards is important in two respects. First, when interpreting the 'skill and judgment' standard, Canadian courts need not begin with the assumption that it catches more works than does the US standard.[146] If the prevailing assumption is that Canada has a lower standard, the temptation will be to reduce it to a point where, once again, everything makes the bar. If it is accepted that the Canadian standard will result in what is effectively a 'creativity' standard, there is a better chance that 'skill and judgment' will indeed further the purposes of copyright law while still ensuring that information remains free and the public domain has room to flourish.

Second, this should lend support to the argument that the instrumental role attributed to 'creativity' in *Feist* applies equally to the role of 'skill and judgment' in Canada. The ruling of the Supreme Court brought the Canadian position closer to the American approach, both by elevating the originality standard and by justifying that elevation on the basis that a higher standard is the best way to achieve copyright's purposes.[147] In this sense, the ruling is a subtle endorsement of the American approach to originality, albeit nominally reconfigured for the Canadian context within which a so-called 'creativity' standard could not have functioned in the same way. By recognising it as such, we can restore some substance to originality in Canada, and re-imagine it as instrumental to the goals of the copyright system. Other common law jurisdictions facing similar normative quandaries about the meaning of originality in the digital age, but reluctant to leap from one side of the great divide (labour) to the other (creativity), may choose to follow suit.

5.5 THE INSTRUMENTALITY OF ORIGINALITY

I began this chapter with the assertion that the originality doctrine, in any of its various forms, is no more than a legal construct – a metaphor for authorship whose only purpose is to define the appropriate subject matter for a system intended to further intellectual exchange. Emptied of any intrinsic substance, originality is a concept to be filled with meaning – a meaning determined by the purposes of the copyright system. I suggested that a common preoccupation with the interests and perceived entitlements of the author-owner has interfered with our ability to find originality's appropriate meaning. Rather than asking questions about the kinds of works we should protect and the kinds of works that should remain in the public domain, we have been occupied with questions about the origin and scope of the author's natural entitlement. The meaning given to the empty vessel of 'originality' has been guided by the notion of copyright as a reward for labour or as the right that flows from the investment of one's personality in the work. Instead, I have argued, the meaning of originality should be guided by our understanding of the public purposes that justify the interests that copyright grants. These public purposes should act as a compass in determining what originality means and when it is present. Finding that a work is original is, after all, another way of saying that the would-be author has done enough to warrant the monopoly that copyright grants.[148] This is, in turn, another way of saying that protecting this work will encourage the kind of expressive activity that we hope to stimulate by means of our copyright system.

In my view, the 'skill and judgment' standard, as articulated by the Supreme Court of Canada in *CCH*, has taken some significant steps towards reconceptualising originality in this instrumental mode. As I have argued, the recognition of the public as an intended and primary beneficiary of copyright was the seed from which the 'skill and judgment' test grew. With this development came a departure from the authorship tropes that have defined originality. By resisting a sweat of the brow approach, removing 'labour' from the subsistence determination and avoiding the language of 'creativity', Canada's originality standard no longer reverberates with the ring of natural rights. The new standard of non-trivial 'skill and judgment' is a good proxy for authorship in the sense that it demands something in the region of 'expressive self-articulation' by capturing a combination of personal attributes and choice in the expressive enterprise.

The act of authorship that crystallises into copyright, regarded in this light, is an intellectual effort to make meaning, to communicate, and not simply the investment of time and money. That being said, this version of originality is not romantic in its assumptions about authorship; the author who utilises skill and judgment is not cast as the creator of something new that flows from her individual self – she may simply be engaging with the information, ideas and expressions that she encounters. In this way, the 'skill and judgment' standard for originality is capable of embracing the idea of relational authorship without either romanticising the processes of creative expression or reducing them to a mechanical exercise. The kinds of works that it should capture are, therefore, the kinds of works that further the values that underpin a copyright system justified in terms of the encouragement of communication and cultural engagement, but without tying the copyright interest to the moral relation between the author and her work.

It will be important, however, that the application of the skill and judgment standard is not itself mechanical, but rather guided by a nuanced understanding of originality's instrumental role in the copyright system. Ultimately, the inquiry should involve consideration of the extent to which the protection of the work at issue serves the public purposes of copyright. Looking back to the nineteenth century and judgments such as that of Lord Halsbury in *Walter v. Lane*, Kathy Bowrey has argued that, contrary to modern day assumptions about jurisprudence from that period, the decision about whether or not to protect an author's right was typically recognised to be a matter of public policy, with protection being justified and measured with regard to the social good being served.[149] Whether this is an accurate reassessment of the body of British case law is less important than the light that this analysis can shed upon alternative approaches to modern day originality determinations. In particular, Bowrey emphasises the complex relationship between determinations of copyright's subsistence and consideration of infringement evident in nineteenth century copyright cases: 'The originality of one party was generally considered in light of the originality of the other. The worth of both efforts were considered in relation to each other, and reference to the community interest often explicitly informed that evaluation.'[150]

Resolving a copyright infringement case should involve a broad recognition of the 'significance or intrinsic value of the plaintiff's expression to the world at large',[151] not in terms of the quality of the contribution but its nature as expression. This inquiry cannot be satisfactorily undertaken in isolation, however: the originality of the plaintiff's expression should be assessed in relation to the defendant's originality. Originality is therefore best understood as a relational concept. This approach coheres with the concept of relational authorship, explored in Chapter 3, which views the work not as an isolated product/thing, but as a dialogic text/speech, such that the plaintiff's work can be seen to exist in dialogic relation to the defendant's work.

This more nuanced approach to originality can incorporate into the subsistence inquiry an awareness of the infringement inquiry that the finding of copyright will entail. Avoiding the strict bifurcation of subsistence and infringement determinations ensures that the public interest can be satisfactorily considered in the context of assessing originality. At present, there is a strict (but often artificial) division between the finding of copyright and the conclusion that copyright has been infringed. Doctrinally, these elements of a copyright case are typically approached and regarded in isolation, such that only the plaintiff's originality matters in the subsistence determination while the defendant's originality matters only to the determination of infringement (specifically, whether she has taken a substantial part of the plaintiff's work or whether she has a defence available to her).

As Bowrey notes, this division puts the defendant at a clear disadvantage, particularly where almost any work will pass the minimum threshold required for originality, and almost any use of that work will make use of the minimal amount required to constitute a 'substantial part' thereof. More often than not, once the existence of a right in the work has been established, the defendant who has engaged in an unlicensed use of the protected work is fighting a losing battle. By the stage in the proceedings where attention turns to the defendant's work, the defendant is already on the wrong side of a moral equation: she is the would-be free rider, playing opposite the meritorious producer of value. By failing to assess the plaintiff's work in dialogic relation to that of the defendant, the current approach supports the plaintiff's 'often meagre claims to originality at the expense of an equal consideration of the defendant's claim'.[152] In contrast, complicating the originality inquiry by maintaining a simultaneous awareness of the relative originality of the defendant's work permits courts to consider whose communicative act is more consistent with the social goals of the copyright system.

By way of example, consider the recent controversy over Shepard Fairey's 'Hope' poster, which became familiar during Barack Obama's 2008 presidential campaign. These posters depicted a stylised version of Obama's face in red, white and blue, but the image was based on a 2006 Associated Press news photograph taken of Obama at a Press Club event by one Mannie Garcia. Fairey sought a declaratory judgment alleging non-infringement, while Associated Press counterclaimed. The case, which has since stalled in light of controversies over Fairey's conduct and the actual photograph used, was generally thought to turn on the question of whether Fairey's use was fair use; but Joseph Scott Miller has raised another question, namely, whether the Garcia photographs ought to be protected by copyright at all. Struck by 'how conventional – how uncreative – the Garcia photos of the Press Club event are', Miller states, '[i]f conventional copyright doctrine tells us these photos are sufficiently original to earn the strong exclusion rights that copyright provides, so much the worse . . . for copyright law.'[153]

Miller suggests elevating the originality requirement as a means 'to stem the copyright flood', proposing that expression should be 'demonstrably atypical or unconventional', when compared to common expression in the genre at the time of authorship, in order for copyright to attach.[154] Roberta Kwall has agreed that originality should be 'hoisted', if only to require 'substantial creativity'.[155] My suggestion, however, is that originality should simply be viewed in relative terms, such that a holistic assessment of the originality of the plaintiff's and the defendant's works in a particular case can guide the court's analysis, bringing together the subsistence and infringement inquiries.

In the *Fairey v. Associated Press*[156] scenario, for example, a court would likely find that the Garcia photograph is original in light of the skill and judgment – or even the modicum of creativity – involved in choosing the subject, angle, lighting and moment at which the photograph was taken. The work is nonetheless only minimally original in the sense that it is merely an accurate, conventional representation of reality. Fairey's work, in contrast, is substantially creative; from the choice of image to the use of colours, contrast, style and tone, it powerfully expresses the message of optimism and patriotism through a visual medium. Indeed, the iconic image has been described as 'the most efficacious American political illustration since "Uncle Sam Wants You."'[157] When the two works are viewed in context and in relation to one another, then, an appreciation of the greater originality of Fairey's work comes to the fore. While the author of the photograph did just enough to attract copyright, the author of the poster made a significant contribution to American political and cultural conversation, furthering the social values of expression and exchange that underpin the copyright system.

Restricting consideration of the added expressive value of Fairey's work to the final issue of whether a defence is available does not sufficiently reflect copyright's purposes or the manner in which Fairey's work furthers those purposes. This is particularly true in jurisdictions, such as Canada and the UK, where a statutorily restrictive fair dealing defence does not create adequate breathing space for transformative uses. The relative originality and expressive value of Fairey's work should inform a judicial analysis throughout: the press photograph is minimally original, while Fairey's work is substantially original; Fairey's work copies a substantial part of the minimally original expression, but it contributes a far greater degree of original expression, giving the work a new meaning such that it is properly regarded as a new work and not a copy of the photograph; even if Fairey's work is a copy, the transformative nature of his use should mean that he incurs no liability; to impose liability in this case would be to restrict the kind of creative engagement and cultural dialogue that copyright ought to encourage in order to protect the author of a work demonstrating the very minimum of skill and judgment.

Some may argue that the concept of relational authorship should entail a more dramatic restructuring of the protection that copyright affords. Thus, for example, it has been suggested that a gradated version of copyright ought to be available to recognise the kind of contribution made by relational authors in its cultural context. Brian Fitzgerald and Xiaoxiang Shi propose dividing authorial contributions into 'first contributions' (wherein initiating authors open new dialogue or start new conversations) and 'post-first contributions' (which are directly and immediately derived from and dependent on the first contribution). Post-first contributors that do not destroy the commercial viability of first contributions would be immune from liability, but they should be granted more limited rights to the work generated by their contribution. In this way, 'the relational conception of authorship will give rise to a responsive and flexible copyright regime.'[158]

Gideon Parchomovsky and Alex Stein have similarly suggested a system of graduated originality that assesses creativity along a continuum and not merely as a threshold.[159] Their proposal is based not on the idea of relational authorship, but rather in recognition of the inefficiencies and unfairness that result from treating alike all works that meet the minimum threshold of originality. Under this model, for example, an author whose work is highly creative would be maximally protected and shielded from liability; meanwhile, an author whose work demonstrates average originality would be restricted to claiming only market value compensation from a defendant whose work is as or more original.

While, of course, I share the sentiments that underpin these proposals, as well as the sense that 'one's rights should correspond to the level of one's contribution',[160] a formally graduated system of originality seems to me to be distant and difficult to operationalise. Furthermore, once we accept the idea of originality and creativity as relative and contextual, it seems conceptually problematic to place works into static categories that classify works as inherently more or less creative. The better solution, I think – and one that is readily implementable from this moment – is simply for courts to assess originality in light of the purposes of copyright, the realities of authorship and the relational nature of expressive works. In any particular case, then, the differing level of authorial contribution can play a role in determining which work merits the protection that copyright affords, and the appropriate extent of that protection. Although this approach offers a less formalised solution, it would represent an important doctrinal and conceptual shift in the way that we think about originality and its role in copyright cases.

5.6 CONCLUSION: ON DETERMINING ORIGINALITY

Canada finally has a definitive standard by which works are to be measured and copyright conferred: only works demonstrating a more than trivial amount of skill and judgment will receive the benefits that copyright affords. This is a significant improvement upon the previously uncertain state of Canadian originality jurisprudence. However, there is no guarantee that the originality standard as formulated by the Supreme Court will advance the purposes of copyright; the test has the potential to slip towards an extremely low threshold or a relatively high threshold.[161] With such subjective concepts at play, courts must have regard to the larger legal principles and policies that emanate from the *CCH* judgment in arriving at their conclusions. The real substance of Canada's new originality is the spirit in which it was conceived, and the principles and purposes by which it appears to have been shaped.

First, the Supreme Court resisted a 'sweat-based' approach and excluded labour from its test. Courts applying the new standard should therefore appreciate that labour *per se* is no longer part of the originality inquiry in Canada, and that copyright is no longer to be granted as a reward for industriousness. As a related point, it should be borne in mind that a primary motivation behind the decision to exclude 'labour' was the desire to ensure that information itself remained in the public domain. Courts assuming that the 'skill and judgment' threshold is lower than the US equivalent should ensure that their interpretation of Canada's originality standard does not permit a *de facto* monopoly over information contained in a copyrightable work.

Second, courts should recall that the Supreme Court has explicitly rejected any requirement of 'creativity.' I have suggested that, implicitly, it sought to avoid the philosophical and political implications of the 'creativity' standard. In particular, I have argued that the Court meant to avoid 'creativity' in the sense used in the *Tele-Direct* case: as concomitant with the *droit d'auteur*. Therefore, it will be important for Canadian courts assessing copyrightability to put aside romantic authorship ideals and the personality-based theories of individual entitlement informed by the civilian tradition. The 'skill and judgment' test, however, retains the notion of authorship as involving some degree of self-expression through creative choice, and it is therefore well-suited to capture the notion of the relational author making new meaning through the re-interpretation and re-combination of pre-existing culture.

Finally, but most importantly, the Supreme Court's originality standard represents an attempt to strike the appropriate balance between authors' interests and the public's interests, and thereby further the stated purposes of copyright. This final consideration should operate as the fundamental principle that mediates between competing visions of copyrightability; the appropriate construction of copyright's central doctrine requires an appreciation of copyright's public purposes. The instrumental role of originality in furthering the encouragement of cultural dialogue has two important implications for the application of copyright doctrine. First, originality is not an absolute but rather a relational concept, and so it makes sense to assess a work's originality in relation to other works with which they have a dialogic relation. In the context of copyright litigation, this means complicating the traditional originality inquiry with a simultaneous awareness of the relative originality of the allegedly infringing work. Second, it means avoiding the rigid bifurcation of copyright subsistence and infringement determinations, allowing the relative originality of the works at issue to inform every stage of the analysis, thereby ensuring that significant contributions to cultural dialogue are not silenced in the name of minimally expressive works and contrary to the social goals of copyright.

With originality potentially freed from the assumptions and metaphors that have defined and disrupted it for so long, the approach taken by the Supreme Court of Canada in *CCH* has provided a much-needed opportunity for its re-imagination, not only in Canada but beyond. Originality determinations should be approached without misconceived notions of copyright as a natural entitlement of the author, whether born of the investment of labour or personality, but rather, with an eye to the goals of the copyright system.

NOTES

1. Christian G. Stallberg, 'Towards a New Paradigm in Justifying Copyright: A Universalistic-Transcendental Approach' (2008) 18 Fordham Intell. Prop. Media & Ent. L.J. 333 at 343.
2. *Feist Publications, Inc. v. Rural Tel. Serv. Co.*, 111 S. Ct. 1282 (1991), 499 U.S. 340 at 347 (1991) (quoting *Miller v. Universal Studios, Inc.*, 650 F.2d 1365, 1368 (5th Cir. 1981)) [*Feist*].
3. At its most minimal, originality 'does not require that the expression must be in an original or novel form but that the work must not be copied from another work – that it should originate from the author': *University of London Press Ltd v. University Tutorial Press Ltd* [1916] 2 Ch. 601 at 608–9 (Peterson J).
4. Alan L. Durham, 'Copyright and Information Theory: Toward an Alternative Model of "Authorship"' (2004) B.Y.U.L. Rev. 69 at 72.
5. Jessica Litman 'The Public Domain' (1990) 39 Emory L.J. 965 at 969.
6. Ibid. at 1006.
7. Ibid. at 1007.
8. See Charles Taylor, *Sources of the Self: The Making of Modern Identity* (Cambridge, Mass.: Harvard University Press, 1989) [Taylor, *Sources of the Self*]) at 376, describing how '[e]xpressive individuation has become one of the cornerstones of modern culture.'
9. Mark Rose, *Authors and Owners: The Invention of Copyright* (Cambridge, Mass.: Harvard University Press, 1993) at 141.
10. Marilyn Randall, *Pragmatic Plagiarism: Authorship, Profit and Power* (Toronto: University of Toronto Press, 2001) at 55.
11. David Freedman, 'Revising Canadian Database Protection: What Lessons from Europe?' (2002) 81 Can. Bar Rev. 563 at 593.
12. See e.g. *British Columbia Jockey Club et al. v. Standen* (1985) 8 C.P.R. (3d) 283 [*B.C. Jockey*].

13. *Slumber-Magic Adjustable Bed Co. Ltd v. Sleep-King Adjustable Bed Co. Ltd et al.* (1984), 3 C.P.R. (3d) 81, McLachlin J. (as she then was).
14. *Edition Hurtubise HMH Ltée v. Cégep André Laurendeau* [1989] R.J.Q. 1003 (Sup. Ct); approved in *Edutile Inc. v. Automobile Protection Assn.* (1997) 81 C.P.R. (3d) 338 (F.C.T.D.), Dubé J., and *CCH Canadian Ltd v. Law Society of Upper Canada* [1999] F.C.J. No. 1647 (F.C.T.D.), Gibson J. [*CCH (FCTD)*].
15. *Caron v. Association des Pompiers de Montréal Inc.* (1992) 42 C.P.R. (3d) 292 (FCTD) at 295, 297.
16. (1995) 62 C.P.R. (3d) 257 (FCTD) at 264 [*U & R Tax*].
17. *Tele-Direct (Publications) Inc. v. American Business Inc.* (1995), 76 C.P.R. (3d) 296 (FCA) at para. 17 [*Tele-Direct*], DeCary J.A.: 'The 1993 North American Free Trade Agreement [NAFTA] amendments simply reinforce in clear terms what the state of the law was, or ought to have been: the selection or arrangement of data only results in a protected compilation if the end result qualifies as an original intellectual creation.'
18. Ibid. at para. 29.
19. Ibid. at paras 15, 16 (referencing NAFTA, art. 1705).
20. Ibid. at para. 13.
21. Note 2 above.
22. *E.g. Prism Hospital Software, Inc v. Hospital Medical Records Institute* (1994), C.P.R. (3d) 129; *ITAL-Press Ltd v. Sicoli* (1999), 86 C.P.R. (3d) 129; *CCH (F.C.T.D)*, note 20 above; *Edutile inc. v. Ass'n pour la Protection des Automobilistes* [2000] 188 D.L.R. (4th) 132 (F.C.A.); *B & S Publications, Inc. v. Max-Contracts, Inc.* [2001] A.J. No. 143; *Robertson v. Thomson Corp.* [2001] O.J. No. 3868 [*Robertson*]. *Cf. Hager v. ECW Press Ltd et al.* (1998) 85 C.P.R. (3d) 289 (1998), rejecting the argument that *Tele-Direct* raised Canada's originality standard to require creativity.
23. See Daniel Gervais, 'Feist Goes Global: A Comparative Analysis of the Notion of Originality in Copyright Law' (2002) 49 J. Copyright Soc'y U.S.A. 949 at 951 [Gervais, 'Feist Goes Global']: 'A *Feist*-like standard is now applied or may soon emerge in key common law countries.'
24. *CCH Canadian Ltd v. Law Society of Upper Canada* [2002] F.C.J. No. 690 [*CCH (FCA)*] at.para. 36, Linden J.: 'The Trial Judge interpreted *Tele-Direct* as altering the classic Anglo-Canadian standard of originality and adding new requirements of 'imagination' and "creative spark". In this, he was mistaken.'
25. *CCH Canadian Ltd v. Law Society of Upper Canada* [2004] S.C.J. No 12 at para. 16 [*CCH (SCC)*].
26. *CCH (FCTD)*, note 14 above at para. 139.
27. 3 Omnibus Copyright Revision Legislative History: Copyright Law Revision, Part 3 at 42–6 (1976): cited in Timothy Young, 'Copyright Protection for Factual Compilations: The White Pages of the Phone Book are Not Original Enough to be Copyrighted – But Why?' (1992) 17 Dayton L. Rev. 631. *Cf. CCH (FCA)*, note 24 above at para. 58.
28. *CCH (FCTD)*, note 14 above at para. 140, Gibson J.: 'Here, faithfulness to the original, whether or not in the public domain, is the dominant editorial value and thus, the creative 'is the enemy of the true.'
29. Ibid. at para. 116.
30. [1990] 2 S.C.R. 467 at 478–9, McLachlin J. (as she then was).
31. See Jane Ginsburg, 'Creation and Value: Copyright Protection of Works of Information' (1990) 90 Colum. L. Rev. 1865 at 1881–8 [Ginsburg, 'Creation and Value'].
32. *CCH (FCTD)*, note 14 above at para. 131: quoting Decary J. in *Tele-Direct*, note 17 above at 37–8.
33. For more on the personality theory of copyright, see e.g. Justin Hughes, 'The Philosophy of IP' (1988) 77 Geo. L.J. 287; Hughes, 'Personality Interests of Artists and Inventors in Intellectual Property', (1998) 16 Cardozo Arts & Ent. L.J. 81; Peter Drahos, *A Philosophy of Intellectual Property* (Aldershot: Ashgate, 1996) at 73–4.

34. *CCH (FCA)*, note 24 above at para. 52.
35. Ibid. at para. 53.
36. Ibid. at para. 23.
37. 2002 S.C.C. 34 [2002] S.C.R. 336 [*Théberge*].
38. Ibid. at paras 30–31.
39. *CCH (FCA)*, note 24 above at para. 42.
40. See Gervais, 'Feist Goes Global', note 23 above at 957, noting with reference to *Feist*: 'Putting the author/creator at the center of the copyright picture by requiring evidence of human (intellectual) creativity does not necessarily stem from an author-friendly perspective or benefit authors.'
41. *Théberge*, note 37 above at para. 30.
42. *CCH (FCA)*, note 24 above at para. 59.
43. *CCH (SCC),* note 25 above at para. 23.
44. Ibid. at paras 23, 24.
45. *Feist,* note 2 above at 1289–90.
46. *CCH (SCC)*, note 25 above at para. 23.
47. *Desktop Marketing Systems Pty Ltd v. Telstra Corp. Ltd* [2002] F.C.A.F.C. 112 [*Telstra*]. The Australian Federal Court of Appeal found copyright in telephone directories 'because of the labour and expense involved in the compilation' (Ibid. at paras 438–9, Sackville J.).
48. See Guy Pessach, 'The Legacy of Feist Revisited – A Critical Analysis of the Creativity Requirement' (2002) 36 Isr. L.R. 19 at 43 (explaining the *Feist* standard in light of the 'public-oriented justification of copyright in American law').
49. *CCH (SCC),* note 25 above at para. 23.
50. Jeremy Waldron, 'From Authors to Copiers: Individual Rights and Social Values in Intellectual Property' (1993) 68 Chicago-Kent L. Rev. 841 at 848–9: 'The point is not merely that the individual rights of authors must be balanced against the social good. The Constitution stipulates that authors' rights are created to serve the social good, so any balancing must be done *within* the overall context of the public good.'
51. R.W.M. Dias, 'The Value of a Value-Study of Law' (1965) 28 M.L.R. 397 at 400, cited in Alan Story, 'Burn Berne: Why the Leading International Copyright Convention Must be Repealed' (2003) 40 Hous. L. Rev. 763 at 793.
52. In Freedman, note 11 above at 576. Freedman goes on to quote H. Perleman, 'Taking the Protection-Access Tradeoff Seriously' (2000) 53 Vand. L. Rev. 1831 at 1834: '[I]n the contest between property rights and access rights, property rights have the home field advantage. The incentives created by property rights are clear and the rhetoric is powerful.'
53. [1900] AC 539 (HL) [*Walter*].
54. *Cf.* Abraham Drassinower, 'Sweat of the Brow, Creativity and Authorship: On Originality in Canadian Copyright' (2003–04) 1 U. of Ottawa L. & Tech. J. 107 at 112–16.
55. *Walter*, note 53 above at 562: 'The word "author" . . . seems to me to present a criterion consistent with the widest application of the Act to all who can claim as *embodying their own thought*, whether humble or lofty, the letterpress of which they assert the authorship.'
56. Ibid. at 555: '[A] reporter of a speech under the conditions existing in this case is the meritorious producer of the something necessary to constitute him an "author" within the meaning of the Copyright Act.'
57. Ibid. at 547: 'The question here is solely whether this book . . . can be copied by someone else than the producers of it (I avoid the use of the word 'author')'.
58. Ibid. at 545: 'I should very much regret it if I were compelled to come to the conclusion that the state of the law permitted one man to make profit and to appropriate to himself the labour, skill, and capital of another.'
59. Ibid. at 552: 'It is a sound principle that a man shall not avail himself of another's skill, labour and expense by copying the written product thereof. To quote the language

of North J. in another case: "For the purposes of their own profit they desire to reap where they have not sown, and to take advantage of the labour and expenditure of the plaintiffs . . . for the purpose of saving labour and expense to themselves." '

60. See e.g. *B.C. Jockey Club.*, note 12 above at 286, approving the following statement from *Hogg v. Scott* (1874) Eq. 444 at 485: '[T]he defendant is not at liberty to use or avail himself of the labour which the plaintiff has been at for the purpose of producing his work; that is, in fact, merely to take away the result of another man's labour or, in other words, his property.'
61. *Walter*, note 53 above at 559: 'Without [the reporter's] brain and handiwork the book would never have had existence, and the words of Lord Rosebery would have remained unrecorded. . . . [B]y [the report] in *The Times* the thousands of the readers of that journal might be truthfully and accurately informed of those intellectual and interesting utterances of Lord Rosebery which they had not been privileged to hear. I think, for the reasons I have given, that the proprietors of *The Times* have copyright in the article and reports in question.'
62. Note 2 above at 1291.
63. *CCH (SCC)*, note 25 above at para. 22.
64. Note 12 above. See also *Weetman (c.o.b. Beta Digital Mapping) v. Baldwin*, 2001 BCPC 292; and *B & S Publications Inc. v. Max-Contracts Inc.*, note 31 above.
65. *B.C. Jockey*, note 12 above at para. 3.
66. Ibid. at para. 2.
67. Ibid. at para. 5.
68. Ibid. at para. 8.
69. Ibid. at para. 6, citing Laddie, Prescott and Vitoria, *The Modern Law of Copyright* (London: Butterworths, 1980) at para. 2.65; and Ibid. at para. 7, citing Harold Fox, *The Canadian Law of Copyright and Industrial Designs,* 2nd edn (Toronto: Carswell, 1967) at 329.
70. *B.C. Jockey*, Ibid. at para. 6, citing *Wood V.-C. in Scott v. Stanford* (1867), L.R. 3 Eq. 718 at 724 (cited in Laddie, Prescott and Vitoria, note 69 above at para. 2.65).
71. If copyright protects the author's industrious effort in compiling material, it follows that 'the copyright in such a work may be infringed by appropriating an undue amount of material.' Ibid. at para. 6, citing Laddie, Prescott and Vitoria, note 69 above at para. 2.65.
72. See Norman Siebrasse, '*Feist* Is Not and Should Not Be the Law in Canada' (1994) 11 C.I.P.R. 191.
73. As famously stated in the English case of *Kelly v. Morris* [1866] L.R. 1 Eq. 697 at 701–02: 'A subsequent compiler is bound to set about doing for himself that which the first compiler has done. In case of a road-book, he must count the milestones for himself.'
74. See *Feist*, note 2 above at 1292, stating that a 'sweat of the brow' standard means that 'authors are absolutely precluded from saving time and effort by relying upon the facts contained in prior works. In truth, "it is just such wasted effort that the proscription against the copyright of ideas and facts . . . [is] designed to prevent." '
75. *CCH (SCC)*, note 25 above at para. 24.
76. See Ibid. at para. 15: a higher standard 'helps ensure that copyright protection only extends to the expression of ideas as opposed to the underlying ideas or facts.' *Cf.* Ibid. at para. 23: '[It] helps ensure that there is room for the public domain to flourish as others are able to produce new works by building on the ideas and information contained in the works of others.'
77. See *Feist*, note 2 above at 1289: 'No matter how original the format, however, the facts themselves do not become original through association. . . . This inevitably means that the copyright in a factual compilation is thin. Notwithstanding a valid copyright, a subsequent compiler remains free to use the facts contained in another's publication to aid in preparing a competing work, so long as the competing work does not feature the same selection and arrangement.'

78. See *IceTV Pty v. Nine Network Australia Pty Ltd* [2009] HCA 14 at paras 45–8 [*IceTV*]; *Telstra Corporation Limited v. Phone Directories Company Pty Ltd* [2010] FCA 44.
79. *IceTV*, Ibid. at paras 49, 52–4.
80. See Ibid. at para 28: 'That facts are not protected is a crucial part of the balancing of competing policy considerations in copyright legislation. The information/expression dichotomy, in copyright law, is rooted in considerations of social utility. Copyright . . . does not confer a monopoly on facts or information because to do so would impede the reading public's access to and use of facts and information. Copyright is not given to reward work distinct from the production of a particular form of expression.' See also Ibid. at para. 131: 'The Act does not provide for any general doctrine of "misappropriation" and does not afford protection to skill and labour alone.'
81. Britain looks unlikely to go down this path, however: see *Football Dataco Ltd & Ors v. Brittens Pools Ltd & Ors* [2010] EWHC 841 (Ch) at [81]–[82] [*Football Dataco*]. Canadian courts applying *CCH* should have regard only to the skill and judgment involved in the expression of a work, and not all of the skill and judgment involved in the production of a compilation work.
82. In fact, 'there is no clear authoritative statement that the exercise of considerable labour is sufficient in itself to confer copyright protection, and that therefore the sweat of the brow doctrine is part of UK copyright law.' Mark J. Davison, *The Legal Protection of Databases* (Cambridge: Cambridge University Press, 2003) at 143.
83. *Ladbroke (Football) Ltd v. William Hill (Football) Ltd* [1964] 1 All E.R. 465 (HL) [*Ladbroke*], cited in Ibid. at 144 [emphasis added].
84. Ibid. at 273 [emphasis added].
85. [1959] 1 Ch 63 at 65–2, cited in Davison, note 82 above at 144 [emphasis added].
86. *G.A. Cramp & Sons Ltd v. Frank Smythson Ltd* [1944] A.C. 329 [*Cramp*]. *Cf. Kelly v. Morris*, note 73 above.
87. *Cramp*, Ibid. at 336: '[E]ven functional matter must be the product of principled construction of authorship ('taste or judgment'), to attract proprietary protection.'
88. Ibid., Lord Porter.
89. See e.g. *Designers Guild Ltd v. Russell Williams (Textiles) Ltd* [2001] 1 All E.R. 700: Lord Hoffman understood originality 'in the sense of the contribution of the author's skill and labour,' (Ibid. at para. 27); Lord Bingham explained that copyright vested in 'anyone who by his or her own skill and labour creates an original work' (Ibid. at para. 2). See also *Newspaper Licensing Agency Ltd v. Marks & Spencer plc* [2002] R.P.C. 4.
90. Directive 96/9/EC of the European Parliament and of the Council of 11 March 1996 on the Legal Protection of Databases [1996] O.J. L77/20, art. 3.1: '[D]atabases which, by reason of the selection or arrangement of their contents, constitute the author's own intellectual creation shall be protected as such by copyright.' *Cf.* ss 3 and 3A of the British Copyright, Designs and Patents Act 1988.
91. Laddie, Prescott and Vitoria, *The Modern Law of Copyright and Designs*, 3rd edn (London: Butterworths, 2000) §30.27; cited in *Football Dataco*, note 81 above at para. 85.
92. *Football Dataco*, Ibid.
93. Ibid. at paras 41–3.
94. *Cf.* Davison, note 82 above at 144: 'The consensus of opinion amongst academic writers is that the standard of originality under UK copyright law is either a sweat of the brow standard, or one very close to it in which sweat of the brow, coupled with a very small amount of creativity, will be sufficient.' In my opinion, the UK position is best described as coupling sweat of the brow with a small amount of skill and/or judgment.
95. Ibid. at 143.
96. Note 17 above.
97. See Tanya Aplin, 'When are Compilations Original? Telstra Corporation v. Desktop Marketing Systems Pty Ltd' (2001) 23:11 Eur. I.P. Rev. 543 at 546. Aplin cites in

support: *BBC v. Wireless League Gazette Publishing Co.* [1926] Ch. 433; *Purefoy Engineering Co. Ltd v. Sykes Boxall & Co. Ltd* (1955), 72 R.P.C. 89; *Kalamazoo (Aust) Pty Ltd v. Compact Business Systems Pty Ltd* (1984), 84 F.L.R. 101; *T.R. Flanagan Smash Repairs Pty Ltd v. Jones* (2000), 48 I.P.R. 19.

98. Davison, note 82 above at 14.
99. *CCH (SCC)*, note 25 above at para. 24.
100. Note 22 above.
101. Ibid. at para. 34, Weiler J.A.
102. Ibid. at para. 51.
103. *CCH (SCC)*, note 25 above at para. 23.
104. Ibid. This refers back to the Supreme Court's statement of copyright's purposes in *Théberge*, note 37 above at paras 30–31.
105. *CCH (SCC)*, note 25 above at para. 15.
106. Ibid at para. 23.
107. 'Justice O'Connor's concerns [in *Feist*] about the 'sweat of the brow' doctrine . . . also resonate in Canada. I would not, however, go as far as O'Connor J. in requiring that a work possess a minimal degree of creativity to be considered original.' Ibid at para. 22.
108. *CCH (SCC)*, note 25 above at para. 24.
109. See Thomas Dreier and Gunnar Karnell, 'Originality of the Copyright Work: A European Perspective' (1992) 39 J. Copyright Soc'y USA 289 at 290: '[N]ovelty has acquired a distinct meaning in intellectual property language. It may, therefore, not seem advisable to dilute it or give it a particular additional copyright meaning.'
110. Note 2 above at 1287–8. In support of the originality of identical but independent creations, the Court cited *Sheldon v. Metro-Goldwyn Pictures Corp.*, 81 F.2d 49 (2d Cir. 1936) at 54.
111. Drassinower, note 54 above at n. 57. See also Daniel J. Gervais, 'Canadian Copyright Law Post-*CCH*' (2004) 18 I.P.J. 131 at 139; Teresa Scassa, 'Recalibrating Copyright Law? A Comment on the Supreme Court of Canada's Decision in *CCH Canadian Limited et al. v. Law Society of Upper Canada*' (2004) 3 C.J.L.T. 89 at 90–91 [Scassa, 'Recalibrating Copyright Law?'].
112. Ryan Littrel, 'Toward a Stricter Originality Standard for Copyright Law' (2001) 43 B.C.L. Rev. 193 at 201: '[T]he author's personal contribution, rather than the work itself, is the dispositive criterion.' See also Dreier and Karnell, note 109 above at 290–91: 'What is not new from a strict point of view (absolute novelty) can be seen as subjectively new and thereby worthy of copyright, only if the person who brought the item into being did not know of any such earlier item'. The criteria for originality thus 'inhere in the person who creates the work.'
113. Pursuant to Art. 112(1) C.P.I., the Code of Intellectual Property protects the rights of authors in 'all works of the mind.' French jurisprudence requires that the author shows his or her personality in the work, which at a minimum involves some intellectually creative choice. See Daniel Gervais, *La Notion d'Oeuvre Dans La Convention de Berne et en Droit Comparé* (Genève, France: Librarie Droz, 1998) at 85–6.
114. See A. Lucas and A. Plaisant, 'France' in M.B. Nimmer and P.E. Geller (eds), *International Copyright Law and Practice* (New York: Matthew Bender, 1999) at 4, cited in Davison, note 82 above at 114. See also Elizabeth F. Judge and Daniel Gervais, 'Of Silos and Constellations: Comparing Notions of Originality in Copyright Law' (2009) 27 Cardozo Arts & Ent. L.J. 375 at 378–9.
115. Charles Taylor describes 'this new power of expressive self-articulation' and its role in the Romantic period and definitions of the modern self, in Taylor, note 8 above at 389–90.
116. See Ginsburg, 'Creation and Value', note 31 above at 1881–8, discussing personality, individuality and authorship; see also, Ginsburg, 'A Tale of Two Copyrights: Literary Property in Revolutionary France and America' (1991) 64 Tul. L. Rev. 991.
117. See Thomas Dreier, 'Balancing Proprietary and Public Domain Interests: Inside or

Outside of Proprietary Rights?' in Dreyfuss, Zimmerman and First (eds), *Expanding the Boundaries of Intellectual Property: Innovation Policy for the Knowledge Society* (New York: Oxford University Press, 2001) first page of essay at 298. For a detailed comparison of common law and continental perspectives, see Alain Strowel, 'Droit D'Auteur and Copyright: Between History and Nature' in Brad Sherman and Alain Strowel (eds), *Of Authors and Origins: Essays on Copyright Law* (Oxford: Clarendon Press, 1994) 235.

118. Alain Strowel, *Droit d'auteur et copyright – Divergences et convergences: étude de droit comparé* (Paris: L.G.D.J., 1993) at 19–20, cited in *Théberge*, note 37 above at para. 62.
119. Ibid. at para. 116, Gonthier J.
120. Pierre-Emmanuel Moyse, 'La nature du droit d'auteur: droit de propriété ou monopole?' (1998) 43 McGill L.J. 507 at 562, cited in *Théberge*, note 37 above at para. 116.
121. See e.g. James Boyle, *Shamans, Software and Spleens: Law and the Construction of the Information Society* (Cambridge: Harvard University Press, 1996); Litman, note 5 above; Peter Jaszi, 'Toward a Theory of Copyright: The Metamorphoses of "Authorship"' (1991) 1991 Duke L.J. 455; Peter Jaszi, 'On the Author Effect: Contemporary Copyright and Collective Creativity' (1991/92) 10 Cardozo Arts & Ent. L.J. 293; Martha Woodmansee and Peter Jaszi (eds), *The Construction of Authorship: Textual Appropriation in Law and Literature* (Durham: Duke University Press, 1994). *Cf.* Mark Lemley, 'Romantic Authorship and the Rhetoric of Property' (1997) 75 Tex. L. Rev. 873.
122. Pessach, note 48 above at 43.
123. Drassinower, note 54 above at 117–18.
124. This being the goal of Canada's Copyright Act according to the Supreme Court: *Théberge*, note 37 above at paras 30–31; *CCH (SCC)*, note 25 above at para. 10.
125. *Tele-Direct,* note 17 above at 31–32.
126. Freedman, note 11 above at 591.
127. *Cf. CCH (SCC)*, note 25 at paras 22, 24.
128. 945 F.2d 509 (2d Cir. 1991)
129. Note 22 above.
130. See e.g. *CCC Information Services Inc. v. Maclean Hunter Market Reports Inc.*, 44 F.3d 61 (2d Cir. 1994), cert. denied, 516 U.S. 817 (1995), finding copyright in a work documenting the resale value of different makes/models of cars. A parallel can be drawn with *Edutile Inc. v. Ass'n pour la Protection des Automobilistes*, note 22 above, in which the Canadian court applied the *Tele-Direct* creativity test and found copyright in a price guide for used cars.
131. *Feist*, note 2 above, quoting 1 M. Nimmer and D. Nimmer, *Copyright* §1.08[C][1].
132. See e.g. *Matthew Bender & Co. v. West Publishing Co.*, 158 F.3d 674 (2d Cir. 1998) at 677, cert. denied, S. Ct. 526 U.S. 1154 (1999), denying copyright in the pagination and editing of Westlaw's published court reports on the basis that choices on selection and arrangement were 'obvious, typical, and lacking even minimal creativity.' Similarly, the Supreme Court of Canada denied protection to edited judicial reasons in *CCH*, note 25 above at para. 35: 'Any skill and judgment that might be involved in making these minor changes and additions to the judicial reasons are too trivial to warrant copyright protection. . . . [They] are more properly characterized as a mere mechanical exercise.'
133. *Cf.* Gervais, 'Canadian Copyright Law Post-*CCH*', note 111 above at 139: 'the Supreme Court chose a "middle path" only in appearance. In fact, Canada has taken on a standard essentially identical to that of our American neighbours'. Gervais describes the 'skill and judgment' test as 'functionally indistinguishable from the modicum of creativity test explicated in *Feist*' (Ibid. at 167). See also, Scassa, 'Recalibrating Copyright Law?', note 111 above at 91: '[I]t is difficult to see how, in terms of practical effect, a non-trivial exercise of skill and judgment will amount to anything other than a "spark" of creativity.' *Cf.* Judge and Gervais, note 114 above at 406–07.

134. See Scassa, 'Recalibrating Copyright Law?', Ibid. at 91.
135. *Feist,* note 2 above at 1289 (quoting Ginsburg, 'Creation and Value', note 31 above at 1868); *CCH (SCC)*, note 25 above at para. 22.
136. *Feist,* note 2 above at 1296; *CCH (SCC)*, note 25 above at para. 16.
137. Gervais explains creativity in terms of creative choice: '[A] creative choice is one made by the author that is not dictated by the function of the work, the method or technique used, or by applicable standards or relevant "good practice". Conversely, purely arbitrary or insignificant selection is insufficient. A conscious, human choice must have been made, even though it may be irrational.' Gervais, 'Feist Goes Global', note 23 above at 976–7.
138. Indeed, a work may exhibit creativity but fall short of displaying skill and judgment. For example, the spontaneous scribbling of a young child might involve archetypal creativity while demonstrating little or none of the skill or judgment required by the *CCH* standard.
139. Drassinower, note 54 above at n. 57.
140. [1980] 10 D.L.R. (3d) 249.
141. U.S. Const. art. I, §8 reads: 'Congress shall have the power . . . to promote the Progress of Science and the useful Arts, by securing for limited Times to Authors and Inventors the exclusive right to their respective Writings and Discoveries.' No equivalent statement exists in Canadian law (which is not to say that no equivalent purpose exists).
142. *CCH (FCA),* note 24 above at paras 28, 52.
143. See e.g. *Delrina Corp. v. Triolet Systems Inc.*, (2002 O.J. No. 3729; leave to appeal denied [2002] S.C.C.A. No. 189); *cf. Computer Associates International, Inc. v. Altai, Inc.*, 982 F.2d 693 (2d Cir. 1992). See also *Robertson v. Thomson Corp.* [2006] 2 S.C.R. 363; *cf. NY Times Co. v. Tasini*, 533 U.S. 483 (2001). Even when Canadian courts effectively endorse a US approach, they often distinguish their reasoning and rename the US doctrine (so, for example, Canada has a 'weeding out' test instead of the equivalent US 'abstraction-filtration-comparison' test for determining infringement of computer programs).
144. *CCH (SCC)*, note 25 above at para. 22.
145. Judge and Gervais, note 114 above at 408.
146. See e.g. *Robertson*, note 22 above at para. 56: '[U]nlike . . . in the United States, a work is considered to be original . . .even if creativity is not present. According to the [Supreme] court, the creativity standard of originality in the United States is too high.'
147. As Pessach explains, note 48 above at 43: 'What was novel about the [*Feist*] decision was the conviction that the requirement of creativity was the correct and desired way to implement copyright's policy of encouragement, and thus achieve the optimal result for promoting the public interest.'
148. *Cf.* Ibid. at 19. See also David Vaver, 'Canada's Intellectual Property Framework: A Comparative Overview' (2004) 17 I.P.J. 125 at 142, describing the originality doctrine as 'really a proxy for answering the question: Has the author done enough to justify preventing the world from copying from his or her output for a century or more?'
149. Kathy Bowrey, 'On Clarifying the Role of Originality and fair Use in 19th Century UK Jurisprudence: Appreciating "the Humble Grey which Emerges as the result of Long Controversy"' in Lionel Bently, Giuseppina D'Agostino and Catherine Ng (eds), *The Common Law of Intellectual Property: Essays in Honour of Prof. David Vaver* (Oxford: Hart Publishing, 2010) 45; available at http://papers.ssrn.com/sol3/papers.cfm?abstract_id=1402444 (accessed 26 January 2011) [Bowrey, 'Clarifying the Role of Originality', cited to SSRN].
150. Ibid. at 16.
151. Ibid. at 14.
152. Ibid. at 16.
153. Joseph Scott Miller, 'Hoisting Originality' (2009) 31 Cardozo L. Rev. 451 at 456.
154. Ibid. at 486.

155. Roberta Rosenthal Kwall, 'Hoisting Originality: A Response' (2009) 20 DePaul J. Art Tech. & Intell. Prop. L. 1 at 8.
156. 09-cv-01123, U.S. District Court, Southern District of New York (Manhattan). Note that the case of *Rogers v. Koons*, 960 F.2d 301 (2d Cir), cert. denied, 113 S. Ct. 365 (1992), which was criticised in Chapter 2 above, could lend itself to a similar analysis.
157. Peter Schjeldahl, 'Hope and Glory: A Shepard Fairey moment' *The New Yorker* (23 February 2009).
158. Sampsung Xiaoxiang Shi and Brian Fitzgerald, 'A Relational Theory of Authorship' in Mark Perry and Brian Fitzgerald (eds), *Knowledge Policy for the 21st Century* (Toronto: Irwin Law, forthcoming), available at: http://papers.ssrn.com/sol3/papers.cfm?abstract_id=1285947 (accessed 26 January 2011) [cited to SSRN].
159. Gideon Parchomovsky and Alex Stein, 'Originality' (2009) 95 Virginia L. Rev. 1505.
160. Kwall, note 155 above at 4.
161. For example, a compiler who employs a practiced aptitude for gathering data, and decides what data to include, might be granted rights over his data selection. But someone making creative choices in producing a work could be denied copyright if those choices demonstrate no particular skill, aptitude or ability. Scassa, 'Recalibrating Copyright Law?', note 155 above at 91: 'The Canadian standard embraces a broad range of utilitarian works while raising the spectre of more subjective interpretations of copyright in the traditional categories of copyright works.'

PART III

Use, transformation and 'appropriation': exploring the limits of copyright

6. Fair dealing and the purposes of copyright protection

6.1 INTRODUCTION

As the preceding chapters have shown, copyright law and policy have suffered at the hands of a theoretical framework ill suited to copyright's subject matter and purpose. Forced into the box of possessive individualism, the author-figure has been misconstrued as the isolated originator of meaning; the work has been reduced to an object of property; and the copyright system itself has been miscast as an institution meant to guarantee the protection of authors' natural proprietary entitlements. I have argued that a theoretical shift – away from an author-oriented deontology and towards a public-oriented teleology – is necessary if copyright is to encourage active participation in the creation and exchange of intellectual expression. In Chapter 5, I considered what this might mean in the context of originality determinations. Drawing upon the *CCH* case, I argued that a focus on the public interest provides the impetus necessary to depart from author-based reasoning and, consequently, reins in the scope of protection that copyright affords. In Chapter 6, I want to extend this reasoning into a discussion about the rights and interests of users of copyrighted materials. Just as a rights-based account of copyright expands the scope of protection by lowering the originality threshold, it also does so by limiting exceptions to infringement and discounting the claims of users in relation to protected works.

The theories of dialogism and relational selfhood explored in Chapter 3 led me to conclude that a justifiable copyright system must be capable of recognising and valuing the derivative, collaborative and communicative nature of creativity. Part III of this book tackles the challenge of accommodating the public's use, transformation and reinterpretation of protected works within a copyright system premised on private exclusivity and control. I begin, in Chapter 6, with an examination of the fair dealing defence and its American equivalent, fair use. Chapter 7 will continue to explore the appropriate limits of the copyright owner's control, examining the relationship between copyright protection and freedom of expression. Through these chapters, I hope to show that a property rights-based model, which focuses on the individual author-owner and overlooks the dialogic nature of expression, is not equipped either to respond to the needs and interests of users or to reflect the importance of downstream, derivative uses of protected works for society.

6.2 INTRODUCING FAIR DEALING

The fair dealing defence (and its US equivalent, fair use) performs an integral function within the copyright system: it permits substantial uses of copyright-protected works, which would otherwise be infringing, in order to ensure that copyright does not defeat its own ends. By creating the necessary 'breathing space'[1] in the copyright system, the fair dealing defence acknowledges the collaborative and interactive nature of cultural creativity, recognising that copyright-protected works can be used, copied, transformed and shared in ways that further – as opposed to undermine – the purposes of the copyright system. If copyright is to be justified as a means to encourage the creation and exchange of intellectual works to the benefit of authors and society as a whole, then a suitable fair dealing defence is essential to that justification.

Unfortunately, the state of Canadian jurisprudence on fair dealing, much like that of the United Kingdom, has tended not to reflect the critical nature of the role that it plays. Rather, fair dealing was for many years all but redundant in the Canadian courts: rarely raised and cursorily rejected. In recent years, it has made more frequent appearances in judicial decisions, but without much more success. It is only with the appellate decisions issued in the case of *CCH Canadian Ltd v. Law Society of Upper Canada*[2] that we have begun to see a reversal in the misfortunes of fair dealing in Canada. In *CCH*, both the Federal Court of Appeal and the Supreme Court rejected the strict construction of fair dealing that had characterised judicial decision-making, and insisted upon the integral nature of fair dealing in copyright policy.[3]

Just as it did in Chapter 5, then, Canada provides an interesting context in which to examine the evolving role and interpretation of fair dealing, setting it against a shift in the larger theoretical model used to justify the copyright system. The Canadian jurisprudence before and after this shift reveals how the restrictive construction of fair dealing is the obvious result of an author-centred approach to copyright; a focus on the public as an intended beneficiary of the copyright system entails a more expansive interpretation of user rights and exceptions, situating them at the heart of the copyright system.

By way of introduction to fair dealing, this section goes on to briefly describe the historical origins of fair dealing. Section 3 surveys fair dealing jurisprudence in Canada, examining how the face of fair dealing has changed with the *CCH* case and the more general shift in Canadian copyright policy away from its traditional preoccupation with authors' rights. The optimism generated by this case[4] is tempered, however, by a concern with the statutory formation of the fair dealing provisions, which continues to reflect a vision of fair dealing as a narrow exception to the copyright rules.[5] As such, Section 4 makes out the argument that the rigid fair dealing provisions currently found in Canada's Copyright Act – which resemble those of Britain and Australia – should be replaced with an open-ended defence similar in form to the United States' fair use defence. It is acknowledged, however, that the move to an open-ended fair use defence cannot, in itself, guarantee the necessary space for downstream use in the digital age. As the US experience reveals, the kind of cultural engagement protected by fair use still requires both an overarching commitment to copyright's public purposes, and a safeguard against technical controls, which have the capacity to render user exceptions effectively redundant. I will argue that any legal protection afforded to technical protection measures must respect the rights of users and the limits of the copyright monopoly, or risk defeating the goals of the copyright system.

6.2.1 The Origins of Fair Dealing

While the first modern copyright law, the Statute of Anne (1710), contained no exceptions or defences of the type commonly found in modern copyright statutes, the judiciary quickly rose to the challenge of protecting other publishers and the public interest, accepting as a matter of principle that there are circumstances in which unauthorised reproduction of part of another's work can be justified.[6] The introduction and development of the fair use exception occurred in the British common law over the hundred years between 1740 and 1840, gradually culminating in 'a relatively cohesive set of principles'.[7] In 1740, Lord Chancellor Hardwicke discussed the possible defence in a copyright action of so-called 'abridgement' in the case of *Gyles v. Wilcox*. Lord Hardwicke LC opined that a work that would normally constitute an infringement of copyright could avoid liability on the basis that it was a 'real and fair abridgement' of prior work. He reasoned that 'the invention, learning, and judgment of the author is shewn' in such abridgements such that they are best regarded as 'new' works that 'in many cases are extremely useful.'[8]

In the 1752 case of *Tonson v. Walker*, Lord Chancellor Hardwicke was again faced with deciding whether a work constituted a fair abridgement or an infringing copy, or in his terms, 'whether the alterations make it a new work, or are intended evasively to colour a new edition.'[9] Because the original author had compiled 1500 notes for an edition of Milton's poems while the alleged infringement contained only 28 additional notes, Lord Hardwicke LJ concluded that, although '[a] fair abridgement would be entitled to protection, . . . this [was] a mere evasion.'[10] The subsequent cases of *Dodsley v. Kinnersley*[11] and *Macklin v. Richardson*[12] went some way towards establishing the relevance of use for the purpose of review in infringement determinations, as well as the relevance of the effect on the market for the original work. In *Dodsley* the court found that an extract of Samuel Johnson's work published in a magazine did not constitute an infringement under the copyright statute; previous publications of extracts had not affected the market for or value of the original, and so 'could not tend to prejudice the plaintiffs.'[13] In *Macklin*, it was held that a magazine's publication of the first act of a play was not an abridgement and would be of 'great injury' to the plaintiff.[14] As William Patry observes, this case implicitly provided the basis for 'the principle that a review may not supplant the market for the work itself.'[15]

In 1803, in the case of *Cary v. Kearsley*, Lord Ellenborough's judgment was the first to recognise the concept of fair use as distinguished from fair abridgement: as opposed to capturing the essence of the original work in a reduced form, the second author/fair user made 'use of another's labour for the promotion of science and the benefit of the public.'[16] Lord Ellenborough thus regarded the issue as 'whether what is so taken . . . from the plaintiff's book, was fairly done with the view of compiling a useful book for the benefit of the public, upon which there had been a totally new arrangement of such matter – or taken colourably, merely with a view to steal the copyright of the plaintiff.'[17] Ellenborough also indicated that, where a work was taken *animo furandi*, a plaintiff would be deprived of the fair use defence. Patry observes that this condition – which requires a finding of good faith and fair dealing through both a moral inquiry and an evaluation of creative effort – is very much alive in modern fair use litigation.[18]

By early in the nineteenth century, then, the fair use or fair dealing defence was already beginning to resemble its modern form. Indeed, the much-quoted explanation offered in the *Cary* case continues to provide the basis for recognition of fair use: '[W]hile I shall think myself bound to secure every man in the enjoyment of his copyright, one must not put manacles on science.'[19] Over the following decades, the doctrine and its requirements were gradually concretised by the courts.[20] The actual term 'fair use' in respect of extracting first appeared in the case of *Lewis v. Fullarton* in 1839. Lord Langdale rejected the defence, reasoning that the defendant had not made productive or creative use of the work, having expended 'no other labour . . . than in copying the Plaintiff's work.'[21] As such, the allegedly infringing work simply involved 'communication of *the same knowledge*'[22] as was contained in the original. Mere repetition of the plaintiff's work conferred no notable advantage upon the public, and it was apparently for this reason that Lord Langdale refused to find fair use.

In the United States, fair use similarly evolved as judge-made law based on the principles and practices that had emerged in the English courts. In the 1841 case of *Folsom v. Marsh,* Justice Story cited the English fair abridgment cases with approval and confirmed that 'a reviewer may fairly cite largely from the original work, if his design be really and truly to use the passages for the purposes of fair and reasonable criticism.'[23] Justice Story famously provided, in this case, the principles upon which fairness was to be judged:

> In short, we must often, in deciding questions of this sort, look to the nature and objects of the selections made, the quantity and value of the materials used, and the degree in which the use may prejudice the sale, and diminish the profits, or supersede the objects, of the original work.[24]

Although the initial development of a concept of fair use was somewhat piece-meal, and was carried out absent of any broad statement of rationale behind the concept, the early cases seem to support the suggestion that fair uses were permitted because they involved 'originality on the part of the . . . user as manifested in a new work that also promoted the progress of science and thereby benefited the public.'[25] While this might be construed in part as recognition of the effort expended in the creation of this cognisably 'new work', the value attributed to the second work was based on its perceived 'newness'. Newness was regarded as pertaining to public benefit by virtue of its contribution to knowledge and encouragement of learning.[26] As Kathy Bowrey concludes, '[w]ith fair use there was more involved than simply equating "originality" with the plaintiff's effort and protecting that contribution. A finding of "piracy" was reserved for the cases where there was no public interest being served by the defendant's taking.'[27]

The origins of the fair use defence therefore lie in precisely the kind of relational, contextual and public interest-oriented reasoning discussed at the close of Chapter 5 with regard to originality. By having regard to the relative contributions of both the plaintiff and defendant's works, as well as the extent to which each contribution advanced public learning and the spread of knowledge, courts were able to resolve copyright disputes in a way that avoided the kind of absolutism typical of a pure property rights-based approach; instead, the concepts of fair abridgment, fair use and legitimate taking permitted the nuanced application of copyright in a way that cohered with the recognised social goals of the copyright system.

6.2.2 The Restriction of Fair Dealing

As Robert Burrell has argued, the judiciary that was so active in developing the defence subsequently proved active in reining it in. The shift away from a principled fair use defence towards a restrictive fair dealing defence is often attributed to the codification of fair dealing in the UK law. The doctrine that had developed in the courts over almost two centuries made its first statutory appearance in the United Kingdom in section 2(1)(i) of the Copyright Act 1911,[28] which provided that 'any fair dealing with any work for the purposes of private study, research, criticism, review or newspaper summary' would not constitute an infringement of copyright. The introduction of limited purposes for which fair dealing could be claimed looks, in retrospect, to have restricted, or at least frozen, the doctrine as developed by the courts. The evidence tends to suggest, however, that this provision was intended to codify the existing law rather than to mark the start of a less flexible approach to copyright exceptions.[29]

Nevertheless, what followed was a gradual development of a more restrictive view of fair dealing as necessarily confined to the list of approved purposes which should themselves be narrowly construed.[30] As part of the same process, the fair dealing test came to be treated completely independently of the new substantial part test, such that courts would determine whether a use was substantial and therefore *prima facie* infringing before assessing the availability of a fair dealing defence.[31] This bifurcated approach had the effect of reducing fair dealing to a minimal carve-out from the extensive rights of the copyright owner, such that any minimally substantial use was regarded as an incursion onto the property rights of the owner, which could be excused only in a limited number of specific circumstances.

Burrell suggests that this gradual restriction of fair dealing by the courts should undermine the common perception of the judiciary as the active guardian of the public interest in copyright law; indeed, he argues, the original development of fair dealing was little more than a necessary limit on the massive expansion of copyright effected by the judiciary since the enactment of the Statute of Anne.[32] Viewed from this perspective, 'subsequent cases which narrowed the fair abridgement/fair use principle look much less like an attempt to step back from an overly broad judicially created exception and much more like a further extension of owners' rights.'[33] However we explain this apparent shift in judicial attitudes towards fair dealing, it seems clear that, as the perception of copyright as an object of property grew throughout the latter part of the nineteenth and much of the twentieth century, the fair use doctrine found itself on increasingly uncertain footing. The resultant fair dealing defence thus came to reflect little more than 'a reluctant but necessary concession to users.'[34]

As Burrell explains, there are two different approaches that can be taken to user exceptions in copyright legislation: 'The first approach is to provide a small number of generally worded exceptions . . . The second approach is to provide for a larger number of much more specific exceptions encompassing carefully defined activities'.[35] The Copyright Act 1911 is arguably the origin of the latter approach and, because it was imperial legislation, this approach to copyright exceptions is now found in various forms across the Commonwealth, from Canada, Australia and India to Ireland, New Zealand and Singapore.[36] In contrast, the trajectory of fair use in the United States has remained closely aligned with the first approach. As we will see in the course of this chapter, the divergence between the first and second approach to user exceptions in copyright law has a significant impact on the capacity of copyright to advance the public purposes that justify its existence.

6.2.3 Fair Dealing v. Fair Use: Contrasting Concepts

The scope and application of the fair use principles drawn from British jurisprudence continued to develop in the US courts throughout much of the twentieth century without being restricted to specific purposes cemented in legislation. This large body of evolving and sometimes contradictory case law led one court to describe the issue of fair use as 'the most troublesome in the whole law of copyright.'[37] By the 1960s, however, the purpose and role of fair use came to be understood in the context of the overall purposes of the US copyright system. In *Rosemont Enterprises Inc. v. Random House*, the court explained that the 'fundamental justification for the [fair use] privilege lies in the constitutional purpose in granting copyright protection "to promote the progress of science and the useful arts." '[38] From a policy perspective, this purposive rationale for fair use avoids its marginalisation as a limited exception by acknowledging the role that it plays in the furtherance of copyright's public goals.[39]

When fair use was eventually codified in the United States, in section 107 of the Copyright Act of 1976,[40] its statutory form was explicitly intended neither to modify nor to crystallise the common law doctrine as it had developed in the jurisprudence.[41] Rather than restricting fair use to certain specified purposes, as the British 1911 Act had done, the defence was left open-ended in its potential applicability, and the factors identified for consideration in assessing the fairness of a use essentially mirrored those articulated by Justice Story in 1941.[42] Section 107 thus reflected a particular understanding of the fair use doctrine as 'an equitable rule of reason', such that 'no generally applicable definition is possible, and each case raising the question must be decided on its own facts'.[43] The result has been a fair use defence in US law that more closely reflects the origins and purposes of the fair use defence as originally conceived in the eighteenth century jurisprudence: that is, as a way to safeguard, on a case-by-case basis, the public interest that the copyright system is expected to serve.

Perhaps more important than the specific statutory formulation of the defence, however, is the perceived function of fair dealing that its statutory form both embodies and perpetuates. In the United States, the application of fair use is facilitated by its connection to the constitutionally prescribed and widely acknowledged public purposes of copyright; where fair use is a right reserved by the public in return for the grant of copyright protection, 'it is very difficult to justify the grant and enforcement of one without the protection of the other'.[44] In the United Kingdom and Canada, fair dealing has long been at the mercy of a copyright system whose justifications have been framed in terms of the author's entitlement. In this context, the way in which fair dealing serves the public purposes of the system is easily obscured beneath the mass of individual property rights and economic interests that define the system. Where permitted uses are viewed as an exception to the property rights of the entitled author-owner, they are 'grudgingly given and therefore easy to remove.'[45]

Fair dealing is thus aptly described as 'the battleground state of copyright politics'.[46] If we understand copyright norms to be concerned primarily with the rights of authors and owners, allowing otherwise infringing uses without requiring permission or compensation might seem incompatible with – or at least undesirable in light of – this normative foundation. It accordingly makes sense, from this perspective, to have a narrow fair dealing provision subject to restrictive interpretation and rarely applied.

However, if we recognise that public interest resides at the heart of copyright law, fair dealing occupies a comfortable position in a larger picture; it protects the public interest and thereby furthers copyright's goals. In particular, it creates space for the kind of dialogic interchange of ideas that I have identified as central to the purposes of copyright by allowing for the generation of new meaning out of pre-existing texts. This implies that fair dealing is not merely an exception to copyright:[47] it does not derogate from copyright norms but confirms them. Reconceptualising fair dealing in this way creates room for a more expansive defence, which in turn allows the copyright system to advance the public interest in the creation and exchange of meaning, and not simply to guard the rights-bearing author against every unauthorised use.

6.3 FAIR DEALING IN CANADIAN COPYRIGHT LAW

6.3.1 The Fair Dealing Provisions in Context

Canada's first Copyright Act of 1921 provided, in the same terms as Britain's 1911 Act, that any fair dealing for the purposes of private study, research, criticism, review, or newspaper summary would not constitute an infringement of copyright.[48] This formulation of the fair dealing defence, which was repeated in Canada's 1970 Copyright Act,[49] was the subject of review in a 1984 Canadian White Paper. The White Paper proposed that a new Act should 'provide both a definition of fair dealing (to be termed 'fair use') and a prioritised list of factors to be considered in determining whether a particular use of a work is a "fair use".'[50] The proposal thus drew guidance from the US fair use provisions enacted in 1976.

The Sub-Committee on the Revision of Copyright[51] subsequently advised against the proposed fair use model. It rejected the proposed list of relevant factors for consideration in fairness determinations, citing the need for flexibility; at the same time, it retained the list of enumerated purposes that could qualify as fair dealing in the name of certainty. Because fairness is moot in the absence of a permitted purpose, the desire for certainty triumphed over the perceived benefits of flexibility. The sub-committee emphasised the success of the existing Anglo-Canadian approach as evidenced by the paucity of litigation in Canada, particularly when contrasted against the substantial fair use litigation in the United States. It would have been more appropriate to regard the rarity of fair dealing cases in the Canadian courts as indicative of the doctrine's impotence rather than its success – the predictable result of a restrictive defence, ill-equipped to ameliorate the position of users or restrain the demands of owners.

Canada's fair dealing provisions thus continue to limit fair dealing with a copyrighted work to the purposes of research or private study, criticism or review or news reporting.[52] As such, they do not provide a general, open-ended defence for any dealing that can be regarded as 'fair'; the fairness of a particular dealing is relevant to infringement proceedings only if it was undertaken for at least one of these specific purposes.[53] In addition, where the dealing was for any purpose other than research or private study, the defence can succeed only if there has been sufficient acknowledgement of the source of the copied work.[54] There are, then, three hurdles to be met by a defendant who claims to have dealt fairly with a work: first, the purpose must be one of those listed in the Act; second, the dealing must be fair; and finally, sufficient acknowledgement must have been given where required by the Act. Failure to overcome any one of these hurdles causes the defence to fail.

Against this background, the following statement, made by Justice Laddie with reference to British copyright law, should resonate with Canadians:

> Rigidity is the rule. It is as if every tiny exception to the grasp of copyright monopoly has had to be fought hard for, prized out of the unwilling hand of the legislature and, once, conceded, defined precisely and confined within high and immutable walls. . . . [T]he drafting of the legislation bears all the hallmarks of a complacent certainty that wider copyright protection is morally and economically justified.[55]

Three recent copyright reform bills in Canada have only underscored the apparent intractability of this restrictive approach to fair dealing.[56] The *Report on the Provisions and Operation of the Copyright Act*, released in May 2002, raised the possibility of amending sections 29 and 29.1 of the Act 'to expand the scope of fair dealing to ensure that it does not exclude activities that are socially beneficial and that cause little prejudice to rights holders' ability to exploit their works and other subject matter.'[57] But rather than significant reform to fair dealing, two subsequent bills contained piecemeal amendments that would have added only specific and narrowly drawn exemptions. The most recent bill sought to add limited specified purposes to the list of fair dealing purposes rather than opening the list up to resemble the US approach. As things stand, Canada's fair dealing defence remains far removed from its US equivalent. In its present form, the fair dealing defence remains 'statutorily restrictive and not easily capable of a remedial, flexible, or evolutionary interpretation.'[58]

6.3.2 Judicial Treatment of Fair Dealing

For a long time, the Canadian approach to fair dealing was one of single-minded reliance upon specific rules, together with a distinct unwillingness to consider the purpose of fair dealing within the larger policy aims of copyright law. The result was a lack of principled discussion about the defence and a wide refusal to entertain it. This effectively eviscerated fair dealing;[59] it was bound too tightly to the strict statutory language and encumbered with an apparent, if unarticulated, sense that use of another's work without permission was *de facto* unfair.

The tendency amongst Canadian courts was to reject the fair dealing defence by invoking (and often creating) a bright-line mechanical rule that would preclude fair dealing on the facts of the case. The use of mechanical rules is suggestive of a general judicial unease, both with the flexibility inherent in the concept of fairness, and with the notion that someone might use another's work without permission. By automatically excluding a particular use from the protective sphere of fair dealing, a court can avoid analysing the interests at stake or inquiring into the purposes of the copyright system. So, for example, in the case of *Zamacois v. Douville*, fair dealing was denied because 'a critic cannot, without being guilty of infringement, reproduce in full, without the author's permission, the work which he criticizes.'[60] In *The Queen v. James Lorimer*, the defendant's abridgement of a government report failed to benefit from fair dealing because the defence was thought to require 'some dealing with the work other than simply condensing it into an abridged version.'[61] In *B.W. International v. Thomson Canada, Ltd*, it was held that the publication of a leaked work could not be fair dealing.[62]

Other courts used similarly bright-line rules to exclude uses from the narrow purposes of the Act, thereby rendering fairness moot. In *Hager v. ECW Press Ltd*, a biography was held not to be a work of 'research', because 'the use contemplated by private study and research is not one in which the copied work is communicated to the public.'[63] In *Boudreau v. Lin*, a University's copying and sale of course materials was found not be to for the purposes of 'private study' because the materials were distributed to all members of a class.[64] But perhaps the most striking example of the restrictive interpretation of enumerated purposes is found in *Cie Générale des Etablissement Michelin-Michelin & Cie. v. C.A.W. –Canada*,[65] which held that the defendants' parody of a corporate logo could not be included within the category of 'criticism.'[66]

It would not have required much imagination or judicial creativity to bring parody within the fair dealing provisions as a species of criticism,[67] yet one can understand how it came to be excluded from Canada's narrowly drawn defence. Justice Teitelbaum observed that, in contrast to the US position, the exceptions to acts of copyright infringement are 'exhaustively listed as a closed set', and inferred from this that '[t]hey should be restrictively interpreted as exceptions'. Parody was thought to require a new exception because it did not expressly appear in the closed set of permitted purposes.[68]

As a result of this extremely restrictive approach to fair dealing purposes, the best protection for parodists in Canada is simply to avoid substantial similarity to the original work.[69] However, the transformative value of parody and the power that it wields as a means of social critique make a strong case for its inclusion in the fair dealing defence.[70] The precarious situation of parody in Canadian copyright law – particularly compared to the room accorded to such uses in the US regime – thus exemplifies the shortcomings of a closed-purpose approach, and underscores the general inadequacy of Canada's current fair dealing defence to advance the public purposes of copyright.

6.3.3 *CCH* and the Transformation of Fair Dealing in Canada

This brings us to the case of *CCH Canadian Ltd v. Law Society of Upper Canada*, and the photocopying service offered by the Great Library to its patrons. The defendant argued that the purpose of the photocopy service was 'research' within the meaning of section 29 of the Act. The plaintiff responded that the relevant purpose under the Act is that of the individual or organisation dealing with the work, and not the persons to whom the copies are ultimately communicated. At first instance, Justice Gibson agreed:

> The copying by the defendant in the course of its custom photocopy service was not for a purpose within the ambit of fair dealing notwithstanding that the ultimate use by the requester of the photocopying might itself be within the ambit of fair dealing. . . . I am satisfied that the fair dealing exception should be strictly construed.[71]

This judgment was characteristic of the narrow confines within which the Canadian judiciary had drawn the fair dealing defence,[72] and underscored the potential for a restrictive construction of enumerated purposes to essentially foreclose larger considerations of fairness or public policy. Fortunately, when this ruling was appealed to the Court of Appeal, and subsequently the Supreme Court, we began to see a long overdue change in the fortunes of fair dealing.

The real breakthrough in the *CCH* decision came with the Court of Appeal's refusal to subject the fair dealing provisions to the traditionally narrow interpretation dominant in Canadian courts. According to Justice Linden:

> The Trial Judge erred in law when he stated that exceptions to infringement must be "strictly construed." There is no basis in law or in policy for such an approach. An overly restrictive interpretation of the exemptions contained in the Act would be inconsistent with the mandate of copyright law to harmonise owners' rights with legitimate public interests.[73]

Having welcomed the possibility of a more generous interpretation of section 29, the Federal Court of Appeal was able to engage in a principled discussion of the defence. Rather than casting fair dealing as a limited derogation from the norms of copyright law, Justice Linden acknowledged that 'user rights are not just loopholes' and are therefore deserving of a 'fair and balanced reading.'[74] Thus characterised, fair dealing is not an excuse for copyright infringement – a common perspective that buttresses calls for its limited application. If a person is dealing fairly within the meaning of the Act, there is no infringing activity in need of excuse.[75]

With a revised outlook on the nature and role of fair dealing, the majority rejected Justice Gibson's position that merely facilitating research was not research *per se*. Because the actions of the plaintiff were undertaken solely in response to its patrons' requests, it was permitted to adopt their purposes as its own.[76] The question of fairness also benefited from a more nuanced, less rigid, approach than commonly found in the Canadian jurisprudence. Rather than an *ad hoc* determination of fairness ostensibly derived from the perceived moral equities of the case, the Court of Appeal provided a principled survey of the factors to be considered, namely: the purpose, character and amount of the dealing, available alternatives to the dealing, the nature of the work, and the likely effect of the dealing on the market for the original. In large part, these factors mirrored those enumerated in the US fair use provision.[77] Rather than imposing the kind of mechanical rules typical of Canadian decisions, the court stressed that the 'elements of fairness are malleable' and 'none of the factors are [*sic.*] conclusive or binding.'[78] However, because the fairness of each potentially infringing activity conducted on behalf of patrons would have to be considered individually, the Court declared itself unable to hold that the Library's activities amounted to fair dealing across the board.

On appeal, the Supreme Court agreed that fair dealing is central – not exceptional – to the copyright scheme. Chief Justice McLachlin opined that 'the fair dealing exception is perhaps more properly understood as an integral part of the Copyright Act than simply a defence. Any act falling within the fair dealing exception will not be an infringement of copyright.'[79] Put otherwise, fair dealing does not merely excuse infringement, but rather *defines* it; the owner's rights end where the user's rights begin. The Court also praised Justice Linden's list of factors as a 'useful analytical framework to govern determinations of fairness in future cases.'[80] In applying the doctrine, however, the Supreme Court went further: relying on an expansive reading of section 29, the Court held the practices of the Great Library constituted fair dealing.[81] The Court insisted upon 'a large and liberal interpretation [of 'research'] in order to ensure that users' rights are not unduly constrained.'[82] Whereas the Court of Appeal had speculated upon the fairness of every individual, potentially infringing act, the Supreme Court chose instead to approach the issue with a focus upon the defendant's general practices and policies,[83] which it found to be 'research-based and fair'.[84]

The Supreme Court's broad and instrumental interpretation of the fair dealing provisions, informed by a sense of fair dealing's purpose within the copyright system, thereby permitted a non-profit institution to continue to facilitate research in the legal community. In spite of the restrictive statutory language that had impeded the defence at the Trial Division, and complicated the issue before the Court of Appeal, this is a perfect example of a socially useful activity that fair dealing ought to protect. Thanks to the kind of principled reasoning overwhelmingly absent from earlier fair dealing cases, it was finally able to do so.

6.3.4 Fair Dealing and the Purposes of Copyright

It was the reconceptualisation of fair dealing as integral, not exceptional, which paved the way for the Supreme Court's *CCH* ruling. It is important to recognise that this shift in the rationalisation of fair dealing did not find support in the fair dealing provisions, but occurred in spite of them. Rather, the changing face of fair dealing in Canada is the result of the larger theoretical shift that occurred in Canadian copyright policy, and which was described in Chapter 5: a shift away from the author's rights and towards the public interest.

As I have suggested, the common claim that fair dealing should be subject to strict construction – a claim typical of judicial pronouncements on fair dealing prior to *CCH* – appears to flow from a conviction that fair dealing is exceptional because antithetical to the normative presupposition of the copyright system: namely, that the author should have exclusive control over the use of her work. The role attributed to fair dealing thus reflects wider assumptions about the nature of copyright. Prior to *CCH*, courts would apply fair dealing by invoking a sense of right or wrong in relation to actions of the parties before them, but would not examine the degree to which the works before them contributed to the underlying goals of copyright.[85] Even in the absence of any explicit connection between fair dealing and copyright policy, one can detect, in these cases, a clear correspondence between owner-oriented justifications of copyright law and plaintiff-friendly interpretations of fair dealing. In other words, that sense of right or wrong was informed by a commitment to the primacy of the author's right.

By way of example, let us return briefly to the *Michelin* decision. In *obiter*, Justice Teitelbaum had cause to define what he considered to be the objectives of copyright law as '[t]he protection of authors and ensuring that they are recompensed for their creative energies and works'.[86] With the goal of copyright being to 'protect the interests of authors and copyright holders',[87] and no mention being made of users or the public at large, it is easy to understand why the court had so little inclination to apply fair dealing generously. This version of copyright theory is typified and compounded by the characterisation of copyright as a private property right like any other.[88] The combined result is a copyright holder cast as a worthy property owner; a Copyright Act rationalised as protection for copyright owners; and a defendant trade union cast as unlawful trespasser. Viewed against this backdrop, a successful fair dealing defence would seem to privilege the wrongful party and undermine the owner-oriented objectives of the Act: hence the extremely limited interpretation it receives.

Compare this to the policy framework employed in the US case of *Campbell v. Acuff-Rose Music Inc.*,[89] in which a rap parody of the Roy Orbison classic, 'Pretty Woman', was held to be fair use. The reasoning of the US Supreme Court flowed from its initial definition of copyright's purpose as the promotion of 'the Progress of Science and useful Arts.'[90] It recognised as inherent to this purpose a tension between protecting copyrighted materials and allowing others to build upon them. Against this background, the purpose and importance of the fair use doctrine was clear: '[it] permits and requires courts to avoid rigid application of the copyright statute when, on occasion, it would stifle the very creativity which that law is designed to foster.'[91] From this perspective, the defendant who benefits from fair use is not a lucky trespasser but a deserving creator in his own right, and one whose creative activities further the purposes for which copyright exists: hence the Court's generous consideration of fair use.[92]

Similarly, the divergent justifications offered for copyright can explain why the Trial Division and the Supreme Court reached opposite conclusions in the *CCH* case. As I explained in Chapter 5, Justice Gibson, whose restrictive interpretation of 'research' ruled out fair dealing, believed the object and purpose of the Copyright Act to be 'benefiting authors'.[93] This was consistent with the Supreme Court's position in *Bishop v. Stevens* that the 'single object' of the Copyright Act was 'the benefit of authors of all kinds'.[94] Notably, the Supreme Court in that case insisted upon a narrow reading of the exceptions available to users in the Act.[95] Similarly, Justice Gibson's restrictive interpretation of fair dealing corresponds to the identification of the sole intended beneficiary of the copyright system as the rights-bearing author.

In contrast, the Court of Appeal, which arrived at a much broader interpretation of fair dealing, acknowledged that copyright's purpose was also to 'encourage the disclosure of works *for the benefit of society at large*.'[96] Of course, this was in line with the notion of a balance between authors' rights and the public interest articulated by the Supreme Court in its *Théberge* decision.[97] In *CCH*, the Court of Appeal's more expansive interpretation of fair dealing thus corresponds to the recognition of the public interest as central to copyright policy.

The resurrection of public interest played a similarly pivotal role in the

Supreme Court's ruling in *CCH*. Affirming its articulation of copyright's goals in *Théberge*, the Court's analysis built upon the notion of a copyright balance. Its refusal to interpret the fair dealing purposes restrictively was declared necessary '[i]n order to maintain the proper balance between the rights of a copyright owner and users' interests', and 'to ensure that users' rights are not unduly constrained.'[98] The Court's focus upon the user of copyrighted material was thus a facet of its new concern with the public purposes of the Copyright Act.

The disparity between the rulings in *Michelin* and *Acuff-Rose*, as well as the trial and appellate rulings in *CCH*, underscores the connection between competing justifications for the copyright system and competing approaches to the fair dealing exceptions. An owner-oriented rationalisation of the copyright system goes hand in hand with a restrictive construction of defences to copyright infringement, while a public policy-oriented approach that embraces the public interest will support more expansive exceptions. The Supreme Court of Canada has held that there is no justification in law or policy for a preoccupation with the rights of the copyright holder to the detriment of the public. Following the *CCH* decision, it should be clear that, rather than a marginal exception to the norms of Canadian copyright law, the fair dealing defence is an instantiation of the public-author balance; one that is necessary to support the normative claims so often made on behalf of the system.

6.3.5 The Persistent Limits of Fair Dealing in Canada

The inclusion of the public as a primary beneficiary of the copyright system, and the broad reading of fair dealing that this entails, reflects an evolving role for users in Canadian copyright policy. Perhaps the most striking manifestation of this evolution is the Supreme Court's adoption of the concept of 'users' rights.'[99] Drassinower explains: 'the defence of fair dealing . . . is to be understood and deployed not negatively, as a mere exception, but rather positively, as a user right integral to copyright law.'[100] The copyright holder's interest in excluding others from its work has always benefited from the label of 'right'; consequently, when owners' rights have appeared to conflict with users' interests, the former have tended to prevail. Now that the abstract concept of public interest has been concretised in the form of users' rights, perhaps its fate is not so bleak. When competing rights clash, the owner's copyright should no longer act as trump.

The term 'users' rights' is important primarily because it creates the potential for conflicts between owners and users to be fought on equal footing,[101] and lends legitimacy to the demands of users who have typically been characterised as opportunists, free riders and scoundrels.[102] Users claiming the freedom to deal fairly with copyrighted works can now be seen to be demanding recognition of their own rights, and not simply seeking to violate or limit the rights of others. Furthermore, it is no longer defensible to equate fair dealing with 'fair stealing';[103] it is not stealing to use a thing one has the right to use. The hope is that the concept of users' rights will pave the way to a more balanced approach to fair dealing by ensuring that the focus is not solely on the rights that the copyright owner is prevented from enjoying.

For the purposes of Section 5 below, however, it is also important to stress the positive nature of a 'user right', in contrast to the negative nature of mere defences, justifications, exemptions or even privileges. A basic Hohfeldian analysis[104] reveals that, when conceptualised as a privilege, fair dealing establishes only the liberty or freedom to act: the owner has no right to prevent the privileged activity, and the user owes no duty to refrain from the activity. But conceptualised as a right, fair dealing establishes a corresponding *duty* on behalf of the owner to honour the user's right: in this analysis, the user has a positive claim-right against the copyright owner to be permitted to deal fairly with the work. Where fair dealing is recognised as a 'user right', it can be argued that copyright owners have a correlative obligation to permit users' fair dealings with their works.

It might appear, then, that the recognition of 'users' 'rights' has the capacity to radically redress the imbalance that we have seen in Canadian courts' consideration of copyright defences. Indeed, the fair dealing decisions at the Court of Appeal and Supreme Court in *CCH* – particularly when contrasted against the Trial Division ruling – might be thought to illustrate the strength of the 'users' rights' concept. However, while it is possible that the rights-based language could be harnessed and employed to expand protection for certain uses, there is no reason why it should be capable of accomplishing such a dramatic turnabout in Canadian copyright jurisprudence. Even if the owner has lost his trump card, clashing rights still require resolution, and there is nothing about the label of 'right' alone that determines the result.

Moreover, the simple proposition that fair dealing is a user's right does not demand that the scope of fair dealing be widened. If a user's activity does not fit within the limits of the fair dealing defence, as it is currently defined by the Act, then the user simply has no right to use. A court that is not inclined to recognise a user's right need only hold that the use does not meet all three of the hurdles established by our fair dealing provisions and the whole concept of users' rights is moot. The user only has a right to deal fairly within the present confines of the Act.

Claims to rights, whether by owners or users, have a tendency to obfuscate the real issues underlying policy debates. We cannot simply rely upon the language of users' rights to further users' interests; if we want to achieve substantive change, we will have to embrace the spirit of users' rights and then reconsider the scope of the fair dealing definition in light of the public interest that it reflects. The argument must be made that the spirit of users' rights is undermined by a fair dealing definition restricted to specific purposes and subject to additional limitations. After all, it is the definition of fair dealing that will determine if the user is exercising a right or infringing one.

Canadian jurisprudence reveals three distinct but related factors that have contributed to the limited reach of fair dealing in Canada: the rigidity of the fair dealing provisions in the Copyright Act; the judicial tendency to interpret these provisions restrictively; and the courts' general preoccupation with the rights of the copyright holder. In the wake of *CCH*, courts are called upon to give fair dealing a large and liberal interpretation, and to accord equal consideration to the rights of the user. The narrowly constructed fair dealing provisions, however, remain a significant obstacle to the Supreme Court's vision of fair dealing as an integral part of the copyright system, and as a means by which to further that system's goals.

Generally, a restrictive approach to the application of copyright defences is found in jurisdictions where fair dealing provisions are narrowly drawn. We need only look to the history of fair dealing for evidence of this connection, but a glance at the British or Australian jurisprudence supports the same conclusion.[105] Indeed, the link between narrowly drafted provisions and their narrow interpretation seems rather intuitive, based as it is upon simple rules of statutory interpretation: the more numerous and specific the exceptions are, the less likely it seems that Parliament intended their broad application or their extension to unspecified activities.

In *CCH*, the Supreme Court emphasised the need for a broad interpretation of fair dealing if it is to fulfil its role in the furtherance of copyright policy. But there is a tension inherent in giving a broad interpretation to the fair dealing defence when the provisions themselves are so narrowly drawn. The US fair use provision was evidently drafted to be broad, flexible and open to interpretation on a case-by-case basis, thereby establishing an active role for courts in shaping copyright law in the face of new challenges. Exhaustive fair dealing provisions, in contrast, lend themselves more readily to strict application, and result in a judicial tendency to look to Parliament for explicit guidance whenever new challenges arise.[106] Whereas the US concept of fair use encourages courts to engage in a policy-driven balancing act between the competing interests at stake, the Canadian provision discourages purposive interpretation. The onus remains upon Parliament to continuously develop new exceptions in the face of new challenges; the perceived role of the courts is still to assess whether the case at hand meets the specific demands of the fair dealing defence regardless of how that use relates to the larger goals of copyright of the copyright system.

While *CCH* represents a dramatic step forward for fair dealing in Canada, the wording of the Act dilutes its potential impact. Lower courts reluctant to welcome the new role for fair dealing and the limits it places upon owners' rights will continue to have an easy route by which to refuse the defence. Even courts that embrace the notion of a copyright balance, interpret the provisions broadly, and determine fairness even-handedly, may find themselves unable to accept the defence because of the language of the Act. No matter how large and liberal the interpretation of a defendant's purposes, not all fair dealings will be subsumable into the specified purposes: there is a limit to how far a 'users' rights' approach can stretch the finite meanings of words like 'research', 'private study', 'criticism', 'review' and 'news reporting.'

Even after *CCH*, it seems likely that American fair use can embrace a myriad of uses that simply will not fit within the confines of sections 29, 29.1 and 29.2 – a fact which is particularly obvious in the context of new technologies. Take, for example, the activity of 'time-shifting', where protected materials are recorded for the purpose of enjoying them at a later time. The US Supreme Court has held that the private use of video recorders to time-shift content for later viewing is a lawful fair use of copyrighted works.[107] It seems likely that a similar conclusion would be reached in the context of 'space-shifting', where protected materials are recorded onto a different device or in an alternative format.[108] In Canada, it has been held that 'as interesting as the time-shifting concept may be, this does not seem to be a realistic exception to the clear language contained in our legislation.'[109] Space-shifting, outside of the private copying exemption,[110] would seem destined for the same fate.

Sunny Handa has suggested that simply browsing the Internet may also fail to meet the hurdles of Canadian fair dealing because casual internet users are unlikely to be engaged in private study, research, criticism, review or news reporting.[111] Canadian courts concerned about the implications of finding fair dealing in an electronic context might be tempted to conclude that 'if the legislature had meant to exempt browsing under fair dealing it would have done so explicitly.'[112] Meanwhile, fair browsing could easily fall within the America's fair use defence.[113] Handa also doubts the ability of Canadian fair dealing to extend to the reverse engineering of computer programs.[114] While some such uses may qualify as research or private study, courts faced with reverse engineering (especially for competitive purposes) are more likely to reason that 'if reverse engineering was to be permitted under fair dealing, it would have been specifically included as one of the listed purposes.'[115] Meanwhile, reverse engineering, if done fairly, is permissible under the American fair use doctrine.[116]

Time-shifting, space-shifting, Internet browsing and reverse engineering are only a few examples of areas where new technologies are upsetting copyright's delicate balancing act. There are many other examples – making RAM copies, caching content, deep-linking, to name a few – that will continue to present challenges for copyright law, while new examples will undoubtedly emerge as digital technologies evolve. In the absence of a flexible defence to infringement, many of these new but everyday activities will prove to be unlawful, diminishing the perceived legitimacy of the copyright system. These new technologies also facilitate transformative practices such as the creation of 'mash-ups', 'fan fiction', 'machinima' and digital sampling, all of which may be excluded from fair dealing if they fail to fit the definition of 'criticism or review.'[117] Such uses frequently reflect the kind of creative engagement or dialogic response that copyright should encourage. Where such uses fail to fit within the enumerated purposes of the fair dealing provisions, however, they are beyond the reach of Canada's fair dealing defence; the power to achieve the appropriate balance between owners' and users' interests in this modern digital environment is therefore beyond the reach of Canada's courts.

6.4 THE FUTURE OF FAIR DEALING

6.4.1 Legislative Reform: From Fair Dealing to Fair Use?

Rigid fair dealing provisions have the potential to obstruct copyright's purposes. Rather than struggling to fit uses within restrictive categories, the central concern of any fair dealing inquiry should be 'to see . . . whether the new work merely "supersede[s] the objects" of the original creation . . . or instead adds something new, with a further purpose or different character, altering the first with new expression, meaning, or message.'[118] Copyright law, with the help of fair dealing, should aim to encourage the creation of new expressions, meanings and messages, even if this means permitting the use of protected expression. As described in Chapter 2, it is in the nature of expression and cultural development that the new builds upon the old.[119] In this postmodern age, where appropriation, adaptation and reinterpretation of existing texts is an established mode of cultural meaning-making (and the notion of true creation *ex nihilo* should be dismissed as a relic of the romantic age), downstream uses of protected works frequently reflect the kind of authorial creativity that copyright should encourage – but they typically fall outside the limited purposes of fair dealing. This only underscores the inherent weakness of a purpose-specific fair dealing defence tasked with preserving the appropriate balance between owners and users.[120]

In addition to requiring an enumerated purpose, restrictive fair dealing provisions also require the acknowledgement of the source and author of the protected work, without which dealings for the purposes of criticism, review or news reporting cannot benefit from the defence, no matter how fair, how necessary or how integral to copyright's purposes. This final hurdle restricts the power of fair dealing to perform the role given to it by the Supreme Court in *CCH*. If the *Michelin* case were to be decided today, a court applying the lessons of *CCH* could find that the dealing is indeed 'criticism' that satisfies the requirements of fairness, but it may nonetheless reject a fair dealing defence in the absence of an explicit acknowledgement of source. Again, this suggests a disconnect between the integral nature of fair dealing to copyright's purposes, and the fair dealing provisions in their current form.

The narrowly drafted fair dealing provisions in the Act thus present a challenging interpretative task for Canadian courts. Not only are these provisions an obstacle and a limit to the evolution of fair dealing, but they encapsulate a vision of fair dealing – and an understanding of the purposes of copyright law – that is no longer justifiable: fair dealing should not be narrowly defined if it is not a marginal exception to the general norms of copyright; and it should not privilege the owner over the user if copyright is equally concerned with the rights of both. In light of the balance articulated in *CCH*, we need 'to expand the scope of fair dealing to ensure that it does not exclude activities that are socially beneficial and that cause little prejudice to rights holders' ability to exploit their works'.[121]

Simply put, the adoption an open-ended fair dealing provision based upon the US fair use model is a necessary step towards ensuring that socially beneficial uses are not excluded. In the words of Britain's Whitford Committee: 'Any sort of work is likely to be of public interest, and the freedom to comment, criticise, to discuss and to debate, ought not, in principle, to be restricted to particular forms ("criticism or review" or "reporting current event").'[122] A flexible fair use model permits courts to address new challenges in a principled manner, guided by the policy concerns underlying the law. A purpose-specific model guarantees that Parliament is always playing catch-up, with socially beneficial uses stifled along the way.

The proposal to move from a narrow fair dealing to a broad fair use defence has been considered from time to time in various jurisdictions. Britain's Whitford Committee Report recommended the adoption of a general fair use defence in 1977, as did Canada's 1984 White Paper. Of course, both proposals were subsequently rejected. More recently, Britain's Gowers Review of Intellectual Property canvassed the benefits of US-style fair use, pointing to the economic value of many 'fair uses' and their capacity to 'spur on innovation'.[123] Ultimately, the review made a number of recommendations to expand the scope of user exceptions in the UK law, including the introduction of a defence for 'caricature, parody or pastiche',[124] and a push towards a defence for 'transformative use'.[125] While the review seemed almost entirely positive about the nature and potential of US fair use, its recommendations were clearly constrained by the limits imposed on UK lawmakers by the European Information Society Directive,[126] which takes a restrictive approach to permitted uses typical of the continental system and its prioritisation of the *droit d'auteur*.

In May 2005, the Australian government released an Issues Paper that raised the question of whether Australia ought to adopt a US-style 'fair use' defence to copyright infringement by consolidating its fair dealing provisions into a single open-ended exception.[127] It was noted that, amongst other benefits, '[t]he flexibility of the fair use exception has allowed the courts to play an active role in adapting United States copyright law to major changes in technology.'[128] It was ultimately decided, however, that the US model would cause 'confusion and uncertainty' if introduced in Australia, which should instead retain its system of specific exceptions. Some new exceptions were added to address particular concerns that had been raised in the reform process: most notably for our purposes, the Australian Copyright Act now includes a defence for fair dealings with protected works for the purposes of 'parody or satire'.[129]

In Canada, the most recent attempt to amend the Copyright Act, Bill C-32 (which, in March 2011, died on the order table like its two predecessors), was accompanied by claims that this reform legislation would offer 'a fair, balanced, and common-sense approach, respecting both the rights of creators and the interests of consumers in a modern marketplace.'[130] In particular, with respect to users and consumers, it was claimed that the bill would 'legitimiz[e] Canadians' everyday activities'[131] through the inclusion of several new exceptions from which users may benefit. Perhaps most notably, additional purposes were to be added to the fair dealing defence by expanding section 29 of the Act to include 'fair dealing for the purpose of research, private study, education, parody or satire'.[132]

The inclusion of parody and satire as enumerated fair dealing purposes would overcome many of the doubts and concerns that have persisted as a result of the *Michelin* ruling even after the *CCH* case. Notably, the fact that the categories in section 29 are not subject to an acknowledgement requirement (in contrast to dealings for the purpose of criticism) would further secure the position of parody as a potentially permitted use. Moreover, by including 'satire' specifically, as the revised Australian Act has done, the bill wisely avoided the artificial and problematic distinction between parody and satire that has arisen in the US context.[133] This distinction (between parodic works that specifically target the original and satirical works that use protected material to comment on other facets of society) is difficult for even literary theorists to maintain or apply.[134] It is also difficult to justify from a policy perspective; excluding satire from the realm of fair use silences a powerful and socially valuable form of critical expression for which permission is unlikely to be granted by the copyright owner.[135] The explicit inclusion of both parody and satire within Canada's fair dealing provisions would be a welcome amendment to the Act, advancing the goals of copyright law by making space for transformative downstream uses of protected material.

The addition of 'education' as a free-standing purpose is also potentially significant to the extent that it overcomes the possible limitations that may have been found to inhere in the definition of 'private study.' While the latter category left open contentious questions about the applicability of fair dealing to copies made for study purposes in the context of *classes* of students,[136] the inclusion of 'education' as a permitted purpose would undermine the validity of such tenuous but crucial distinctions. Copies made for educational or instructional purposes would be able to clear the first hurdle of the fair dealing inquiry, and the application of the defence would turn, then, on the fairness of the use that is made in light of all the relevant circumstances.

Also welcome was a proposed exception for 'non-commercial user-generated content',[137] which was intended to permit the use of legitimately acquired material in the creation of new works, as well as their use and dissemination, provided that the user's purposes are not commercial in nature, that the source is mentioned where reasonable, and that the new work has no 'substantial adverse effect' on the exploitation of the original. The government's fact sheet offered as examples 'making a home video of a friend or family member dancing to a popular song and posting it online, or creating a "mash-up" of video clips'.[138] As I have argued, in our digital environment, facilitated by new technologies and their accessibility, the transformative use of cultural content – mixing, mashing, (re) making and disseminating – is increasingly fundamental to the processes of cultural engagement and democratic participation. The creation of this exception would go some distance towards acknowledging and making space for the new reality. Of course, the user's rights in this version would remain subject to the commercial and attribution interests of the owner of the original content, such that the owner's rights essentially take priority. Nonetheless, this could be an important addition to the exceptions offered by the Act, both from a practical perspective (legalising common, non-commercial creative practices), and from a policy perspective (limiting owners' legal claims where the full enforcement of their rights would unduly restrain creative play and upset the copyright balance).

I also raised, in the preceding section, concerns about legal limits on common space-shifting and format-shifting practices. Bill C-32 proposed to address these concerns by creating specific exceptions for 'reproduction for private purposes'[139] and for 'fixing signals and recording programs for later listening or viewing',[140] as well as for the making of 'backup copies' of lawfully owned or licensed copies of protected works.[141] Each of these proposed exceptions was subject to a fairly extensive list of limitations, however, which were said '[t]o ensure that the legitimate interests of rights-holders are respected'.[142] Thus, for example, a person recording a programme for later viewing could benefit from the exception only if 'the individual keeps the recording no longer than is reasonably necessary in order to listen to or view the program at a more convenient time.'[143] A person reproducing a work for private purposes could benefit from an exception only if that copy or reproduction is destroyed before giving away or selling the original.[144] Perhaps most importantly, however, all three defences were to be unavailable where the user circumvented a technological protection measure [TPM] in order to perform the permitted action.

I will return to consider more fully the interaction of exceptions and TPM protection in the following section. Before I do so, however, I would like to emphasise the shortcomings of the proposed revisions to the fair dealing provisions and consumer exceptions even in their own right. For one thing, the additional permitted fair dealing purposes would not give much, if anything, more than that to which users would be entitled under the existing provisions. Educational uses are readily assumable within the category of 'research or private study' if these terms are given a suitably liberal reading. Parody and satire can be easily brought within the category of 'criticism', broadly interpreted. The explicit inclusion of these purposes would certainly be preferable to relying upon an appropriate interpretation of existing categories by the courts, but would be properly understood as an affirmation of the state of current fair dealing doctrine post-*CCH*, and not the creation of 'new' exceptions as some would have it portrayed.

Proposed exceptions for user-generated content, back-up copies, copies for personal use and for later listening and viewing could more properly be characterised as 'new', excluded as they likely are from the limited fair dealing purposes. However, from a common sense user perspective, it seems reasonably obvious that such activities should not have been regarded as infringing in the first instance; few people unfamiliar with copyright law would have imagined that they were breaking the law when they shot or shared a home video of their toddler dancing to a Beyoncé hit, or recorded a TV show to watch when the kids were in bed. Under a US fair use model, many of these uses could be presumed (or have been held)[145] to fall within the fair use defence, highlighting the inherent flexibility and trans-temporality of the American approach. What we saw in the Canadian copyright reform proposal was a piecemeal expansion of the narrowly constructed exceptions that already exist in the Copyright Act; what we need instead is a broad, principled and purposive approach to user rights that is capable of evolving and expanding to embrace new and common practices as they arise. As Murray and Trosow warn, '[a]ugmenting the list of categories might be part of a clarification of fair dealing. But adding categories alone would be unlikely to create laws flexible enough to address the range of appropriate and fair uses'.[146]

Rather than perpetuating the restrictive approach to user exceptions that has been part of Anglo-Canadian copyright law since the early twentieth century, the fair dealing provisions should be revised to expressly include the purposes enumerated in the Act and those proposed in Bill C-32 as *examples* of the kind of uses that may be considered fair, but without restricting the defence to those purposes exclusively. It should also provide a non-exhaustive list of factors to be considered in determining the fairness of a use, incorporating the factors set out by the Court of Appeal and endorsed by the Supreme Court in *CCH*.[147] The current acknowledgement requirement should either be removed or relegated to a consideration in fairness determinations; there is no place for such mechanical rules in a flexible fair use model.[148] Finally, in order to ensure adequate space for parody, satire and other transformative uses that could be regarded as prejudicial to the honour or reputation of the original author, fair dealing should be available as a defence to both economic and moral rights infringement claims.

The Supreme Court in *CCH* established a vision of fair dealing that differed from anything previously seen in the Canadian courts. As the case progressed from Trial Division to the highest court in the land, fair dealing was transformed from a limited exception to an integral part of the copyright system; from a controversial privilege to a recognised right; from an anomaly in an owner-oriented system to an instantiation of the public-owner balance. Taking its lead from the Supreme Court, the Canadian legislature should acknowledge the centrality of fair dealing in Canadian copyright policy, and the need for a broad defence to ensure that users' interests are not undermined. This should translate into a proposal for an open-ended fair dealing defence, amenable to principled and purposive interpretation, and flexible enough to withstand the test of time.

The goal should be to achieve, through statutory revision, a fair dealing defence that is capable of principled application, guided by the purposes that underlie the copyright system, and responsive to the ever changing nature of cultural creativity and exchange in the (post)modern, digital environment. Even with the improvements to fair dealing and other user exceptions found in the revised Australian law, and currently proposed in the UK and Canada, defences to infringement will remain 'statutorily restrictive and not easily capable of a remedial, flexible, or evolutionary interpretation.'[149] The more numerous and specific the exceptions are, the less conducive they are to broad interpretation. The limited purposes and specific exemptions approach to user rights reflects a vision of fair dealing as an exceptional derogation from the general copyright norm of exclusive control. This vision is at odds with the goals of the copyright system and is therefore an obstacle to their attainment.

6.4.2 The Limits of Fair Use

I suggested, in the preceding section, that the adoption of an open-ended fair dealing provision based upon the US fair use model is a necessary step towards ensuring that socially beneficial uses of protected works are not silenced by copyright law. I did not, however, suggest that the move from fair dealing to fair use would, in itself, be sufficient to safeguard such uses from overly expansive copyright protection. A flexible fair use defence makes possible a purposive, context-specific application of copyright that reflects the social goals that justify the system; it does not guarantee it. As Burrell reminds us, the restrictive judicial application of fair dealing gives us good reason 'to doubt the assumption that all that has prevented judges from adequately safeguarding user interests is an absence of appropriate legislative tools.'[150] There is, then, no real basis on which to suppose that the judiciary, armed with a flexible fair use defence, would embrace it as a means to limit the exclusive control of copyright owners or further the public interest. The introduction of such a defence should not, therefore, be viewed as a panacea; what is really needed is a continuation and development of the kind of attitudinal shift that is discernable in recent Canadian Supreme Court jurisprudence. Courts, commentators and policy makers have to view user exceptions as integral to the copyright system, which in turn requires that they view the public interest as central to copyright's justificatory framework. The US experience reveals the weight of this warning, first through the limits that have been placed on fair use by US courts to constrain its application, and second, through the effective evisceration of fair use in the face of technical control, as supported by the Digital Millennium Copyright Act 1998.[151]

6.4.2.1 Judicial constraints on fair use

I have argued that Article 107 of the US Copyright Act provides a suitable statutory framework for the kind of inquiry that the fair use doctrine necessitates, permitting a principled evaluation of the particular use in the light of the intent behind the fair use doctrine and the public policy goals of copyright law. The American fair use defence has the potential to function as part of the internal dynamic of the copyright system, maintaining the integrity of the system's incentive structure while recognising and preserving the social value of certain uses of protected works. This potential, however, has not been consistently realised. Notwithstanding the intended flexibility of the statutory language, courts have searched for rigid rules to guide its application.[152] Perhaps to simplify their task or, more likely, to protect the party who is perceived to have been wronged, US courts have actively sought to establish bright line mechanical rules to facilitate fairness determinations. As de Zwart observes, 'most recent decisions have seen courts apply the four limbs of section 107 in a rigid step-by-step fashion [with] no assessment of the overall fairness of the use.' Each factor is considered and the outcome determined 'according to whether a majority of factors favour the plaintiff or defendant.'[153]

The 1984 Supreme Court case of *Sony Corp. of America v. Universal City Studios Inc.*, which concerned the use of the Betamax video tape recorder for the purpose of domestic 'time-shifting' of television programmes, was largely responsible for triggering this judicial distortion of fair use.[154] It signaled the start of a long period in which US courts assessed the fairness of a use almost entirely in light of its capacity to compete with the original work. In assessing the 'purpose and character' of the use, the court stated that 'every commercial use of copyrighted material is presumptively an unfair exploitation of the monopoly privilege that belongs to the owner of copyright.'[155] The *Sony* case also appeared to create a presumption with regard to the fourth statutory factor, 'the effect of the use on the potential market.' Analysing this factor, the court stated: 'What is necessary is a showing . . . that some meaningful likelihood of future harm exists. If the intended use is for commercial gain, that likelihood may be presumed.'[156]

The damage arising from these statements is perhaps less attributable to the *Sony* court itself (which rejected a finding of infringement on the basis of the non-commercial nature of private home recording) than to the courts who subsequently employed these presumptions as a quick fix in fair use cases.[157] Nonetheless, the Supreme Court's apparent reformulation of fair use in *Sony* limited the doctrine's applicability in connection with commercial uses, thereby seriously restricting the flexibility that was intended to be the defining feature of section 107, and tilting the doctrine in favour of copyright owners.

The opinion delivered by the Supreme Court in *Harper & Row Publishers Inc. v. Nation Enterprises*[158] was 'the final step toward establishing a strong presumption against, and a broad definition of, "commercial use" in the fair use context.'[159] The Court endorsed *Sony*'s emphasis upon the commercial nature of the appropriating work and went on to say that: 'The crux of the profit/nonprofit distinction is not whether the sole motive is monetary gain but whether the user stands to profit from exploitation of the copyrighted material without paying the customary price.'[160] The court thus rejected an interpretation of 'commercial purpose' that involved analysis of the public benefit in the secondary work.[161] It also confirmed that 'undoubtedly the single most important element of fair use' is the effect of the defendant's work on the potential market for the original. In doing so, the court seemingly endorsed the notion that fair use is appropriate only in cases where there is 'market failure' that precludes an efficient market transaction, or where the customary fee for use approaches zero.[162]

The importance of these Supreme Court cases has since been minimised by the seminal *Acuff-Rose* decision, which stressed that, rather than prioritising any particular factor in fairness determinations, 'all factors are to be explored, and the results weighed together, in light of the purposes of copyright.'[163] However, the *Sony* and *Harper & Row* decisions reveal a danger inherent in the US formulation of fair use, which should not be overlooked. These and other cases suggest a judicial tendency to establish rigid rules, evolved from in-built biases or assumptions, in the face of a broad provision conferring a general discretion. In the US context, this has resulted in an overemphasis on competition, commercial considerations and owners' economic interests, such that market harm generally dooms a fair use claim.[164] This focus reflects the dominance of economic utilitarianism in US copyright discourse, which often tends towards a conception of copyright as fundamentally concerned with the economic interests of the author-owner. In spite of the explicit instrumentalism of the US system and its constitutionalised social purpose, where protection of owners' interests is too readily assumed to further the public interest, copyright begins to look like an end in itself rather than a means to an end. Ultimately, the elevation of commercial concerns returns us to an owner-oriented vision of copyright that obstructs the application of fair use.

Moreover, it is a short step from the prioritisation of owners' economic interests to a preoccupation with property *per se*. Notably, in *Harper*

& Row, Justice O'Connor explained in distinctly Lockean terms that '[t]he rights conferred by copyright are designed to assure contributors to the store of knowledge a fair return for their labours.'[165] In the case of *Iowa State University Research Foundation Inc v. American Broadcasting Companies Inc.*, the court emphasised that '[t]he fair use doctrine is not a license for corporate *theft*, empowering a court to ignore a copyright wherever it determines the underlying work contains material of possible public importance.'[166] As Waldron explains, '[t]he idea seems to be that all use of an author's work by another without his permission is putatively dishonest and larcenous, and that "fair use" represents a strictly limited departure from that background prohibition on stealing.'[167]

The expressly instrumental foundations of US copyright law have not proved immutable in the face of popular misconceptions regarding the nature of intellectual property as a moral or natural entitlement. Such misconceptions remain capable of guiding the American courts' fair use analyses, strengthening the claims of copyright owners at the expense of users and society. A persistent preoccupation with owners' rights would similarly limit and obstruct the operation of a broad statutory fair use defence in Canada and elsewhere.

6.4.2.2 The digital threat to fair use

While we debate the definitional boundaries of fair dealing, however, an even larger problem looms: technological protection measures [TPMs], also known as 'digital locks', threaten to undermine the significance of fair dealing and other exceptions by making them ineffectual in the face of technical controls. A TPM is 'a technological method intended to promote the authorized use of digital works.' As Kerr, Maurushat and Tacit explain, '[t]his is accomplished by controlling access to such works or various uses of such works, including copying, distribution, performance and display. TPMs can operate as "virtual fences" around digitized content, whether or not the content enjoys copyright protection.'[168] Where TPMs control access, they operates as a 'virtual lock' that excludes outsiders from the digital content; use-control TPMs restrict the uses that can be made of that content even once accessed – most commonly, although not necessarily, preventing the making of copies.

The overarching problem associated with the widespread use of TPMs in the distribution of digital content is simple enough to state: TPMs do not – and generally cannot – distinguish between lawful and unlawful uses and users. There is no necessary (and, typically, no practical) correlation between the limits imposed on would-be users by TPMs and the rights granted to copyright owners under the law. Acts permitted in relation to owned content – users' rights to research, study, criticise, transform, even read and listen – can be prevented by the use of technical controls. The effect of a TPM is thus to prevent the kinds of activities that should be protected from private owner interests, and which are central to advancing the purposes of copyright.

It may be argued that TPM-free versions of protected works will typically be available for anyone who wishes to deal fairly, but it is not satisfactory to restrict fair dealings to technologically inferior versions of copyright works.[169] Beneficiaries of copyright exceptions, like right holders, should be able to enjoy the opportunities presented by digital technologies, and should be free to engage with cultural resources in the technological environment in which they are situated. Moreover, the analogue equivalent is likely an endangered species. In our networked society, our culture is digitised; our information, news, research and educational resources and entertainment all come to us in digital packets. Increasingly, the way in which consumers access, use and consume digital content *is* the way in which we, as citizens, explore, experience and engage with our cultural environment. When it comes to technical and legal controls over intellectual works, then, the ability to actively and meaningfully participate in our culture is at stake.

Albeit that digital technologies promise to advance the overarching aims of copyright policy, they threaten to undermine the vision of copyright as a system that ensures exclusive control over intellectual products. By providing a practical means to ensure excludability and control, TPMs are viewed by many as the key to ensuring a viable market for digital products and services in the online environment. While owners develop and employ TPMs to protect content, however, users develop new technologies to circumvent them, resulting in a technical 'arms race' that is destined never to be won. Turning to the law, demands are made for more regulation to support owners' efforts to maintain control in the face of the 'internet threat.' Technical controls enable owners to side-step some of the costs and practicalities associated with the assertion of legal rights (providing an effective second layer of protection), but it does not naturally follow that legal rights should be expanded to protect the application of TPMs (thereby effectively establishing a third layer of protection). If anything, one may think that the availability of these technical controls threatens the copyright balance, such that the law should step in to regulate their use.

Although it requires a logical leap to offer protection to TPMs through the copyright system, it is a leap that has been taken at the international level, and consequently, by domestic legislatures around the world. This development traces back to a 1995 US government White Paper, which recommended legislation to outlaw technologies having the primary purpose or effect of bypassing TPMs as a way 'to assist copyright owners in the protection of their works'.[170] While the White Paper recommendations stalled in the face of domestic opposition,[171] a draft treaty mirroring its proposals was distributed amongst members of the WIPO for consideration at the international diplomatic conference in Geneva in 1996.

WIPO negotiations culminated in the WIPO Copyright Treaty (WCT) and the WIPO Performances and Phonograms Treaty (WPPT),[172] which include key provisions introducing new protection against the circumvention of TPMs.[173] Article 11 of the WCT (mirrored by Article 18 of the WPPT) provides:

> Contracting Parties shall provide adequate legal protection and effective legal remedies against the circumvention of effective technological measures that are used by authors in connection with the exercise of their rights under this Treaty or the Berne Convention and that restrict acts, in respect of their works, which are not authorised by the authors concerned or permitted by law.

The final text of the anti-circumvention provisions diverged significantly from the original US proposal, reflecting an international compromise that leaves member states with significant latitude in terms of domestic implementation. First, the Treaty requires only 'adequate' legal protection and 'effective' legal remedies, leaving domestic legislatures to determine the meaning of these subjective standards.[174] Furthermore, 'the only TPMs subject to legal protection against circumvention are those that: (a) are effective; (b) are used by authors to exercise copyrights; and (c) restrict acts not authorized by authors or permitted by law.'[175] Most important for our purposes are restrictions (b) and (c), which, taken together, appear to mean that member states are obliged to provide protection only in respect of TPMs that are used by authors in connection with the exercise of their copyright – and only to the extent that a TPM is used to restrict unauthorised acts that the law does not permit in relation to their protected works. Simply put, the protection afforded to TPMs under the treaties appears to coincide with the scope of copyright proper; the treaties are concerned specifically with circumvention activities that facilitate copyright infringements. According to this reading of Article 11, circumvention of TPMs for lawfully permitted purposes such as fair dealing are beyond the scope of the protection that the Treaty requires.[176]

With the WIPO Internet Treaties, TPM protection became part of an international strategy for tackling the challenges to copyright law presented by digital technologies. The United States, United Kingdom and Australia have all implemented anti-circumvention laws into their domestic legislation. As a signatory to the WIPO Copyright Treaties, Canada is now faced with the prospect of ratifying the treaties and bringing its laws into compliance with them. As such, the discussion of fair dealing reform would not be complete without considering the impact of TPM protection on the capacity of fair dealing to confine copyright control within appropriate limits.

Having hailed the US approach to fair use as a model for others to follow, it should now be stressed that the US DMCA offers what is perhaps the weakest approach amongst member states to safeguarding traditional user privileges in the face of TPM protection. The controversial anti-circumvention provisions in this Act offer a level of protection significantly beyond that required by the WIPO treaties. The DMCA prohibits the circumvention of TPMs that control access to a protected work (regardless of whether such access results in copyright infringement),[177] and forbids the manufacture, distribution and importation of circumvention tools (including tools that circumvent both 'access-control' and 'use-control' measures).[178] Because anti-circumvention protection does not attach to use-control measures, it has been suggested that fair use is not *per se* affected. Indeed, §1201(c)(1) explicitly states that, '[n]othing in this section shall affect rights, remedies, limitations, or defenses to copyright infringement, including fair use, in this title.' Of course, the reality is that access to a work is a prerequisite of fair use, and access to a circumvention tool may be a prerequisite of access to a TPM-protected work. The combined effect of the access-control circumvention prohibition and circumvention device prohibitions is the practical restriction of otherwise lawful fair use activities in relation to TPM-protected content.

The DMCA anti-circumvention rules are subject to a set of seven narrow and hard-fought exceptions that shield circumvention activities from liability in specific circumstances, including, for example: non-profit libraries making acquisition decisions[179]; governmental actors conducting national security activities;[180] and encryption researchers identifying vulnerabilities in encryption technologies.[181] Litman has rightly accused these exceptions of being 'cast in prose so crabbed and so encumbered with conditions as to be of little use to anyone who doesn't have a copyright lawyer around to explain which hoops to jump through.'[182]

In addition to the specified exemptions, the DMCA authorises the Librarian of Congress, in consultation with the Register of Copyright, to assess the impact of the circumvention ban on traditional fair use practices and, if necessary, to issue rules exempting certain users of certain categories of works from the ban.[183] Each round of this triennial rulemaking proceeding yields a minimal number of temporary exemptions for narrowly defined classes of works.[184] However, such exemptions are not permitted to extend to the prohibition on circumvention technologies (device controls), with the consequence that, '[a]s a practical matter,

. . . any exemptions ultimately declared will have very limited utility; self-evidently, most users will be unable to exercise their circumvention rights unless they are provided with the tools to do so.'[185] Moreover, by granting such power to an administrative agency, this procedure has the clear and apparently intended effect of reducing the role of the courts and the relevance of fair use in the digital age.[186] The prospective creation of exemptions based on 'classes of works' turns on its head the traditionally purposive, use-based and post hoc application of fair use by the courts.[187] Indeed, the clear impoverishment of fair use effectuated by the DMCA led David Nimmer to suggest that the Act was 'a conscious contraction of user rights'.[188]

Since the enactment of the DMCA, a number of incidents and cases have revealed that this apparent threat to fair use activities is more than hypothetical.[189] Perhaps most notable is the case of *Universal City Studios v. Remeirdes*,[190] which concerned a software program, DeCSS, posted online by the defendant, which could be used to crack the Content Scramble System [CSS] on commericial DVDs, allowing users to copy and manipulate a DVD's content. In an *amicus* brief, Professors Benkler and Lessig described CSS as 'a device that makes fair and otherwise privileged uses of digitized materials practically impossible'.[191] The defendant challenged the constitutionality of the DMCA, arguing *inter alia* that it unduly obstructs the 'fair use' of copyright materials. The US District Court held that fair use was not a defence to violations of the DMCA and issued injunctions. Upholding this decision, the US Court of Appeals dismissed the appellant's constitutional claim as 'extravagant.'[192] The appellant was not personally engaged in any fair use of copyright materials, and the court was unimpressed by the argument that the devices were necessary for others to make fair uses of CSS protected content. Indeed, the Court was not persuaded that CSS prevents fair uses, not least because '[f]air use has never been held to be a guarantee of access to copyrighted material in order to copy it by the fair user's preferred technique or in the format of the original.'[193]

The narrow, piecemeal approach to protecting user exceptions under the DMCA is reminiscent of the restrictive approach to fair dealing that I have criticised. The breathing space offered by a flexible fair use defence is at risk of suffocation in the digital realm. As Samuelson explains, what drove the debate that led to the enactment of the DMCA was 'high rhetoric, exaggerated claims, and power politics from representatives of certain established but frightened copyright industries.'[194] Amidst such politics and rhetoric, the social goals of the copyright system were seemingly lost from sight.

Unfortunately, the DMCA led the way for other jurisdictions implementing the WIPO Internet Treaties, either because it provided a defining example to follow, or (as was the case for Australia) because it was effectively imposed through bilateral trade negotiations.[195] In Europe, the Copyright Directive of 2001 requires member states to enact broad anti-circumvention prohibitions against all acts of circumvention and the trafficking of circumvention devices and services, thereby far exceeding the scope of TPM protection demanded by the WIPO treaties.[196] In Canada, the most recent reform proposals essentially mirror the stringent anti-circumvention provisions found in the DMCA, failing to reflect the lessons readily drawn from the experiences of the United States and Europe: Bill C-32 sought to establish broad anti-circumvention rights covering devices and services, access- and use-control measures, and to do so without tying these rights to copyright infringement; it set out numerous complex exceptions with no general 'fair circumvention' exception; it neglected even to offer lip-service to the preservation of fair dealing rights comparable to statements found in Article 6(4) of the EU Directive[197] or section 1201(c) of the DMCA; it offloaded the responsibility for carving out any more exceptions on the Governor in Council; and it established no positive obligations for content providers, leaving any such obligations to be created through regulation, and only in respect of any new exceptions made under this regulatory power. It is also significant that many of the 'new' user exceptions that were included in the Bill – which were much lauded as exemplifying the government's commitment to a fair balance between owners and users – were made subject to non-circumvention provisos. This limitation on the application of the new user exceptions would render them redundant in the face of TPMs, thereby privileging owners' use of technical controls over the public policy goals that the exceptions were ostensibly designed to serve.

As we have seen, fair use and fair dealing should be understood as integral to the copyright system and its purposes. The legal protection of TPMs in a manner that fails to guard the contours of fair use from technological encroachment therefore denies users the ability to exercise their rights, tipping the copyright balance away from users and the public interest and thereby undermining the social goals of the copyright system. In 2007, US commentators Jerome Reichman, Graeme Dinwoodie and Pamela Samuelson coined the term 'prescriptive parallelism' to 'convey the notion that the traditional copyright balance of rights and exceptions should be preserved in the digital environment.'[198] The principle captures the general normative position that 'a technological adaptation, namely, the application of TPMs, should not alter the balance that existed under default rules of copyright law with respect to the enjoyment of exceptions and limitations.'[199]

Admittedly, a commitment to the principle of prescriptive parallelism presents at least as many questions as answers. How can copyright's complicated balancing act be performed in any meaningful way when the technological environment is increasingly one of absolutes – absolute freedom versus absolute control? More fundamentally, how can the law perform its role as the guardian of this metaphorical balance when its prescriptions are increasingly extraneous to the actions and actors that it purports to influence? Nonetheless, in the context of digital copyright reform, the principle could prove exceptionally useful: it offers a jumping-off point (a normative claim); it provides a sense of direction (a guidepost by which to chart progress); and it establishes an ideal (a goal against which to measure purported success). It is also difficult to refute, unless one is willing to openly take issue with the foundational principles that underlie our existing institutional structures. In this sense, the principle wields some political clout. It may be that genuine prescriptive parallelism is an unattainable aspiration, but to admit as much is not to undermine its normative significance; it is a goal at which we should aim, and one that we should be determined to achieve to the greatest extent possible.

If we accept that, as a matter of substantive principle, 'the application of TPMs should not alter the balance of rights between copyright owners and users', then it ought to follow that 'all uses privileged under traditional copyright principles should continue to be privileged in an era of digital rights management'.[200] This assertion is consistent with (and arguably mandated by) the recognition of exceptions to authors' rights as central to the copyright scheme. It follows that, if the principle of prescriptive parallelism is to be respected in the face of TPM protections, the protection afforded to TPMs must be as carefully circumscribed as the copyright interest itself.

Ideally, there would be no additional layer of protection afforded to TPMs: the capacity to control that TPMs afford is already a sufficient benefit that content owners can enjoy. If TPMs are to receive legal protection, that protection should be closely aligned with the existing rights of copyright owners, essentially reinforcing copyright proper by limiting unlawful circumvention to acts undertaken for purposes of copyright infringement.[201] Consistent with this approach, protection should be afforded only to use-control TPMs; copyright does not grant to owners exclusive control over access to protected works, and anti-circumvention provisions ought not to do so indirectly. Measures that control access to works for non-infringing purposes should not receive protection.[202] Furthermore, anti-circumvention provisions should not prohibit services and devices that are necessary in order for users to be able to make lawful uses of protected works. At the very least, any such prohibitions should be expressly limited to cases where the provider knows that the service or device will be, or is likely to be, used to infringe copyright.[203] An exception must then be carved out to allow for the provision of circumvention devices to persons lawfully offering circumvention services to facilitate lawful uses.[204] Finally, user exceptions should continue to apply notwithstanding any circumvention undertaken for the purposes of carrying out a permitted act; indeed, any anti-circumvention provisions should expressly operate 'without prejudice' to user exceptions.[205]

In order to ensure that fair dealings and other permitted acts are not only lawful on the books but also possible in practice, digital copyright laws should establish positive obligations for rightholders to facilitate fair and lawful dealings with TPM-protected works.[206] This could take the form of a basic requirement in the Act – similar to that found in the German law[207] – that owners make available the means by which lawful acts may be carried out in relation to TPM-protected works. Ideally, this would involve more than a bald statement of obligation, but would in fact include some easy and effective mechanism by which users could exercise their rights.[208]

Locked out fair users could, for example, be empowered to initiate a legal action, to instigate formal arbitration or mediation proceedings, or to follow a new administrative procedure by which a request or complaint could be lodged. It would be preferable, however, to establish a route that is less onerous and costly, and therefore less likely to prove prohibitive. This may require the identification of an intermediary body or bodies to facilitate fair dealings and permitted acts by providing TPM-free copies, circumvention services or 'digital keys' on request.[209] This role could be performed by existing institutions (public libraries, archives, educational institutions) or by existing or newly created administrative bodies. With an appropriate declaration of lawful purpose, user identification and/or traceable copies or keys, the appropriate intermediary or 'qualified person' could ensure that fair dealing practices are both practical and possible, while allowing a copyright owner to protect his or her copyright interest in the work.[210]

The development of an adequate lawful use infrastructure in response to the proliferation of technical controls is, admittedly, a complicated and potentially resource-heavy proposition. It is also difficult to conceive of a lawful use mechanism that does not have a chilling effect on fair dealing practices by increasing user transaction cost and inhibiting spontaneous uses. Some effort must be made, however, to maintain user rights in the face of digital locks and so to safeguard the copyright balance. At the very least, then, users seeking to make lawful use of protected works (and the third parties who assist them) should be shielded from liability;

preferably, owners seeking to benefit from technical controls should be obligated by law to make available the means necessary for such users to carry out lawful acts; ideally, users will have an affordable and accessible mechanism 'by which to vindicate their rights and to secure the certainty required to engage in creative activity privileged under traditional copyright principles.'[211]

6.5 CONCLUSIONS: CHANGING THE FATE OF FAIR DEALING

In this chapter, I have argued that the fair dealing defence, which has long been marginalised as an exceptional derogation from copyright norms, is in fact vital to the copyright system and its capacity to further the social goals that justify its existence. We have seen that, over time and across jurisdictions, the fate of fair dealing has ebbed and flowed in response to the theoretical frameworks and discourses that have been brought to bear on copyright in general. Thus, where copyright has been regarded as a matter of natural entitlement or private property, fair dealing has been viewed as 'lawful trespass' or 'fair stealing', with the effect that its application has been restricted in favour of the copyright owner's absolute control. Where copyright has been regarded in light of the public purposes that it is intended to serve, however, fair dealing has been recognised as an essential limitation upon owners' control that is necessary in order to prevent copyright from defeating its own ends. The Canadian context brought this distinction into sharp relief. The shift in Canadian copyright policy effectuated by the Supreme Court of Canada in its *Théberge* decision – the shift from a primary focus on authors' rights to the recognition of a balance between authors' rights and the public interest – entailed, in *CCH*, a dramatic shift in the interpretation and application of Canada's fair dealing provisions. Fair dealing was, for the first time, characterised as a 'user right' that is 'integral' to the copyright system and which ought not to be strictly construed.

Unfortunately, this shift in the nature and role of fair dealing cannot be fully realised in the context of restrictive fair dealing provisions that limit the defence to specified purposes. As such, I have advocated for legislative reform that would see narrow fair dealing provisions replaced with an open-ended fair use defence similar to that found in US copyright law. In contrast to fair dealing, fair use allows for a flexible, contextualised application of the defence that can limit the control afforded to copyright owners in response to the particularities of a case as well as the changing technological contexts in which uses occur. At the same time, I have insisted that the creation of a broad fair-use defence is not a panacea to copyright's problems. As the US experience reveals, fair use, like fair dealing, is at the mercy of an owner-oriented understanding of copyright. Recognition of the public purposes of copyright and the role that fair use plays in furthering these purposes remains the most important factor in improving the fate of fair use in the courts.

Finally, I have warned that the future of both fair use and fair dealing is bleak in the face of technological controls and their over-protection. Without a commitment to the principle of prescriptive parallelism – a determination to ensure that permitted uses of copyright works in the analogue world remain both permitted and possible in the digital world – there is a risk that fair use and copyright exceptions, however defined, will become redundant in the face of technical control. Notably, this means that additional user exceptions or the introduction of a broad fair use defence should not be regarded as an adequate counter-balance to the imposition of expansive TPM protections. Anti-circumvention laws have to be more carefully tailored, and permitted uses actively facilitated, if copyright law is to be able to further its public goals in the digital environment. If copyright is justified in light of its capacity to serve these public goals, the failure to protect fair dealing from its fate casts doubt upon the legitimacy of the copyright system as a whole.

NOTES

1. In the famous US Supreme Court decision of *Campbell v. Acuff-Rose Music Inc.*, 510 U.S. 569 at para. 579, 114 S. Ct. 1164 (1994) [*Acuff-Rose* cited to U.S.], Souter J. referred to the 'fair use doctrine's guarantee of breathing space within the confines of copyright.' The need for breathing space flows from 'the need simultaneously to protect copyrighted material and to allow others to build upon it.' Ibid. at para. 575.
2. 2002 FCA 187 [2002] 4 F.C. 213, 212 D.L.R. (4th) 385 [*CCH (FCA)* cited to F.C.]; 2004 SCC 13, [2004] 1 S.C.R. 339, 30 C.P.R. (4th) 1 [*CCH (SCC)* cited to S.C.R.].
3. See *CCH (FCA)*, Ibid. at para. 126; *CCH (SCC)*, Ibid. at para. 48.
4. See e.g. Teresa Scassa, 'Recalibrating Copyright Law? A Comment on the Supreme Court of Canada's Decision in *CCH Canadian Limited et al. v. Law Society of Upper Canada*' (2004) 3 Can. J.L. & Tech. 89 at 80:

   > 'The unanimous Court in *CCH Canadian* makes it clear that *Théberge* was not an isolated case; . . . the Court seems poised to take an interpretive approach that places limits on the scope of the rights of owners of copyright. . . . The decision . . . signals an open and expansive approach to interpreting the fair dealing defences. The impact of *CCH* Canadian is likely to be far-ranging.'

5. As Scassa notes, Ibid.: 'The approach that the courts may take to interpreting fair dealing remains substantially constrained by the wording of the legislation'.
6. Robert Burrell, 'Reining in Copyright Law: Is Fair Use the Answer?' (2001) 4 I.P.Q. 361 at 366; citing William F. Patry, *The Fair Use Privilege in Copyright Law*, 2nd edn (Washington DC: Bureau of National Affairs, 1995) at 3.

7. Patry, Ibid. at 3.
8. 2 Atk. 141 at 143 (1740). Quoted in Patry, *The Fair Use Privilege*, note 6 above at 6.
9. 3 Swans. (App.) 672 at 667 (1752).
10. Ibid. at 680.
11. Amb. 403 (1761) (No. 212) [*Dodsley*].
12. Amb. 694 (1770) (No.341) [*Macklin*].
13. *Dodsley*, note 11 above at 405–06.
14. *Macklin*, note 12 above at 696.
15. Patry, note 6 above at 9.
16. 4 Esp. 168 (1803) at 170. See also *Patry*, note 6 at 17.
17. Ibid. at 171.
18. Patry, note 6 above at 11. In support of this observation, Patry cites *inter alia* the decision of the Second Circuit in *Iowa State University Research Foundation Inc. v. B.C.*, 621 F. 2d 57, 62 (1980).
19. 4 Esp. 168 (1803) at 171.
20. The applicability of the defence with respect to the right to extract for the purposes of criticism was determined in the cases of *Whittingham v. Wooler*, 2 Swans. 428 (1817), and *Bell v. Whitehead* (8 L.J. (N.S.) Ch.141 (1839). Questions as to the quantity allowed to be taken within the scope of the defence were approached by the court in *Wilkins v. Aitkin*, 17 Ves. (Ch.) 422 (1810), *Mawman v. Tegg*, 2 Russ. Ch. 385 (1826) at 393, and *Bramwell v. Halcomb*, 3 My. & Cr. (Ch.) 737 (1836). For a full overview of these cases, see Patry, *The Fair Use Privilege,* note 6 above at 12–16.
21. 2 Beav. 6 (1839) at 9.
22. Ibid. at 98 [emphasis added].
23. 9 F. Cas. 342 (C.C.D. Mass. 1841) (No. 4, 901) at 344.
24. Ibid. at 348.
25. Patry, note 6 above at 17.
26. See also *Scott v. Stanford* [1867] L.R. Vol 3 718; *Mawman v. Tegg* [1826] 2 Russ 385; *Martin v. Wright* 58 Eng. Rep. 605 (Ch. 1833); *D'Alamaine v. Boosey* 160 Ex. Rep. 117 (Ex. 1835).
27. Kathy Bowrey, 'On Clarifying the Role of Originality and fair Use in 19th Century UK Jurisprudence: Appreciating "the Humble Grey which Emerges as the result of Long Controversy"' in Lionel Bently, Giuseppina D'Agostino and Catherine Ng (eds), *The Common Law of Intellectual Property: Essays in Honour of Prof. David Vaver* (Oxford: Hart Publishing, 2010) 45.
28. 1 & 2 Geo. 5, c. 46, *An Act to Amend and Consolidate the Law Relating to Copyright*.
29. Burrell, note 6 above at 368.
30. See e.g. *Hawkes & Son (London) Ltd v. Paramount Film Service Ltd* [1934] Ch. 593 [*Hawkes & Son*] in which the term 'newspaper summary' was held not to extend to a newsreel. See also, *British Oxygen v. Liquid Air* [1925] 1 Ch. 383, holding that fair dealing could not justify copying from an unpublished work.
31. See *Hawkes & Son*, Ibid. at 602: Lord Hamworth M.R. assessed substantial taking by asking whether the part taken 'is so slender that it would be impossible to recognise it.' The 'recognisability' test essentially reduces the substantial part inquiry to 'little more that a de minimus threshold.' See also *Johnstone v. Bernard Jones Publication* [1938] 1 Ch. 599.
32. Burrell, note 6 above at 367–73
33. Ibid. at 367.
34. Melissa de Zwart, 'A Historical Analysis of the Birth of Fair Dealing and Fair Use: Lessons for the Digital Age' (2007) 1 I.P.Q. 60 at 90.
35. Burrell, note 6 above at 361.
36. Ibid. at 362 and accompanying notes.
37. *Dellar v. Samuel Goldwyn*, 104 F.2d 661 (1939) (2nd Cir.) at 662.
38. 366 F.2d 303 (1966) (2nd Cir.) at 307; cited in de Zwart, note 34 above at 88.
39. See e.g. *Berlin v. EC publications, Inc.* 329 F.2d 541 (1964) at 544: 'Courts . . . must

occasionally subordinate the copyright holder's interest in maximum financial return to the greater public interest in the development of art, science and industry.' (Cited in de Zwart, note 34 above at 88.)

40. *An Act for the general revision of the Copyright Law, title 17 of the United States Code, and for other purposes*, Pub. L. 94-553 (19 October 1976).
41. See House Report no. 94–1476: 'Beyond a very broad statutory explanation of what fair use is and some of the criteria applicable to it, the courts must be free to adapt the doctrine to particular situations on a case-by-case basis. Section 107 is intended to restate the present judicial doctrine of fair use, not to change, narrow, or enlarge it in any way.'
42. 17 U.S.C. §107 (1976) provides: 'The fair use of a copyright work . . ., for purposes *such as* criticism, comment, news reporting, teaching . . ., scholarship, or research, is not an infringement of copyright' [emphasis added]. Factors to be considered to determining whether a particular use is a fair use include: '(1) the purpose and character of the use, including whether such use is of a commercial nature or is for non-profit educational purposes; (2) the nature of the copyrighted work; (3) the amount and substantiality of the portion used in relation to the copyrighted work as a whole; and (4) the effect of the use upon the potential market for or value of the copyrighted work.'
43. House Report no. 94–1476. See also Leon Seltzer, *Exemptions and Fair Use in Copyright: The Exclusive Rights Tensions in the 1976 Copyright Act* (Cambridge, Mass: Harvard University Press, 1977) at 19–20.
44. de Zwart, note 34 above at 60.
45. Ibid.
46. Michael J. Madison, 'Rewriting Fair Use and the Future of Copyright Reform' (2005) 23 Cardozo Arts & Ent. L.J. 391 at 393.
47. See *CCH (SCC)*, note 2 above at para. 48: '[T]he fair dealing exception is perhaps more properly understood as an integral part of the *Copyright Act* than simply a defence.'
48. The Canadian Copyright Act 1921, c. 24, s. 16(1)(i); *cf. An Act to Amend and Consolidate the Law Relating to Copyright*, 1 & 2 Geo. V, c. 46, s. 2(1)(i).
49. 11–12 Geo. V. c. 24, s. 17(2), declared as lawful '(a) Any fair dealing with any work for the purposes of private study, research, criticism, review or newspaper study.'
50. Francis Fox and Judy Erola, *From Gutenberg to Telidon: A White Paper on Copyright* (Ottawa: Consumer & Corporate Affairs Canada, 1984) at 39–40. Barry Torno also recommended this revision in his report, *Fair Dealing: The Need For Conceptual Clarity on the Road to Copyright Revision* (Ottawa: Corporate Revision Studies, Consumer & Corporate Affairs Canada, 1981).
51. Canada, Standing Committee on Communication and Culture, *A Charter of Rights for Creators* (Ottawa: Minister of Supply and Services, 1985) at 63–6.
52. Copyright Act, R.S.C. 1985, c. C-42, ss. 29–29.2.
53. In *CCH (FCA)*, note 2 above at para. 127, Linden J. explained the significance of the closed list of purposes in the Act: 'If the purpose of the dealing is not one that is expressly mentioned in the Act, this Court is powerless to apply the fair dealing exemptions.'
54. Copyright Act, note 52 above . Both ss. 29.1 and 29.2 contain the caveat:

    '. . . if the following are mentioned:
    (a) the source: and
    (b) if given in the source, the name of the
        (i) author, in the case of a work . . .'

55. Justice Laddie, 'Copyright: Over-Strength, Over-Regulated, Over-Rated' [1996] 18(5) E.I.P.R. 253 at 259.
56. Bill C-60, *An Act to Amend the Copyright Act*, first reading 20 June 2005; Bill C-61, *An Act to Amend the Copyright Act*, first reading 12 June 2008; Bill C-32, *Copyright*

Modernization Act, *An Act to Amend the Copyright Act*, first reading 2 June 2010. A further example is the withdrawal of Bill C-316, *An Act to Amend the Copyright Act*, 1990, which attempted to move towards a US-style 'fair use' concept.

57. Industry Canada, *Supporting Culture and Innovation: Report on the Provisions and Operation of the* Copyright Act (Ottawa: Intellectual Property Policy Directorate, 2002), online: Government of Canada http://strategis.ic.gc.ca/epic/internet/incrp-prda.nsf/en/rp00873e.html#B2_8 (accessed 26 January 2011) at B.2.8 [Industry Canada, 2002].
58. Howard Knopf, 'Limits on the Nature and Scope of Copyright', in Gordon F. Henderson (ed.), *Copyright and Confidential Information Law of Canada* (Scarborough: Carswell, 1994) at 257.
59. *Cf.* David Fewer, 'Constitutionalizing Copyright: Freedom of Expression and the Limits of Copyright in Canada' (1997) 55 U.T. Fac. L. Rev. 175 at 207 [Fewer, 'Constitutionalizing'].
60. (1943), 2 C.P.R. 270 at 302, 2 D.L.R. 257. *Cf. Allen v. Toronto Star* (1997), 78 C.P.R. (3d) 115, 152 D.L.R. (4th) 518 [*Allen* cited to C.P.R.].
61. [1984] 1 F.C. 1065, 77 C.P.R. (2d) 262 at 269 [*Lorimer* cited to C.P.R.]
62. (1996), 137 D.L.R. (4th) 398, 68 C.P.R. (3d) 289. This is in line with the British case, *Beloff v. Pressdram Ltd* [1973] 1 All E.R. 241 (Ch.), and the Australian case of *Australia v. John Fairfax & Sons Ltd* (1980), 147 C.L.R. 39.
63. (1998), 85 C.P.R. (3d) 289 at para 55.
64. (1997), 150 D.L.R. (4th) 324 at 335, 75 C.P.R. (3d) 1: 'The material was distributed to all the members of the class of students. This does not qualify as "private study."' This decision was in line with the British case of *Sillitoe v. McGraw-Hill Book Co.* [1983] F.S.R. 545 (Ch.D).
65. (1996), [1997] 2 F.C. 306, 71 C.P.R. (3d) 348 (T.D.) [*Michelin* cited to C.P.R.]
66. Ibid. at 381.
67. See James Zegers, 'Parody and Fair Use in Canada After *Campbell v. Acuff-Rose*' (1994–95) 11 C.I.P.R. 205.
68. *Michelin*, note 65 above at 379. '[E]xceptions to copyright infringement should be strictly interpreted. I am not prepared to read in parody as a form of criticism and thus create a new exception.' The court also held that the implicit acknowledgement of source was insufficient (Ibid. at 382–4), and the parody was unfair because it held the plaintiff's work up to ridicule (Ibid. at 384). *Cf. Productions Avanti Ciné-Vidéo Inc. v. Favreau* (1999) 1 C.P.R. (4th) 129, 177 D.L.R. (4th) 568, suggesting that 'true parody' could be fair dealing where all the requirements of the Act are met.
69. If the parodist does not take a substantial part of the original, there will be no *prima facie* infringement; but the nature of parody requires that the original work is apparent to the audience.
70. *Cf. Acuff-Rose*, note 1 above at 579, Souter J.: '[T]he goal of copyright . . . is generally furthered by the creation of transformative works. Such works thus lie at the heart of the fair use doctrine's guarantee of breathing space within the confines of copyright.'
71. (1999), [2000] 2 F.C. 451, 179 D.L.R. (4th) 609, 2 C.P.R. (4th) 129 (T.D.) at para. 175 [*CCH* (TD)].
72. One exception to this rule is *Allen*, note 60 above. The reproduction of a photograph was found to be fair dealing for the purposes of news reporting. Because the entire work was copied, the lower court had declared fair dealing to be 'an interesting issue which . . . has no application to the case at bar.' (1995), 63 C.P.R. (3d) 517 at 525.
73. *CCH (FCA)*, note 2 above at para. 126.
74. Ibid., quoting David Vaver, *Copyright Law* (Toronto: Irwin Law, 2000) at 171.
75. 'Simply put, any act falling within the fair dealing provisions is not an infringement of copyright.' *CCH (FCA)*, note 2 above at para. 126. See Copyright Act, note 52 above, s. 3(1). See also Lloyd L. Weinreb, 'Fair Use' (1999) 67 Fordham L. Rev. 1291 at 1292–3, describing the distinction between non-infringing and excused infringement as an 'analytic nicety' that is 'not without significance.'

76. *CCH (FCA)*, note 2 above at paras 143: 'In essence the Law Society can vicariously claim an individual end user's fair dealing exemption, and step into the shoes of its patron.'
77. Ibid. at para. 150. Only the availability of alternatives to the dealing is not an enumerated factor in the US law. See note 42 above.
78. Ibid.
79. *CCH* (SCC) note 2 above at paras 48–9.
80. Ibid. at para. 53.
81. Ibid. at para. 73.
82. Ibid. at para. 51. Also at para. 54: '[A]llowable purposes should not be given a restrictive interpretation or this could result in the undue restriction of users' rights.'
83. Ibid. at para. 63.: '"Dealing" connotes not individual acts, but a practice or system.'
84. Ibid. at para. 73. The Library's 'Access to the Law' Policy put in place reasonable safeguards to ensure that materials requested were being used for the purposes of research or private study.
85. *Cf.* Fewer, 'Constitutionalizing', note 59 above at para. 62.
86. *Michelin*, note 65 above at para. 115.
87. Ibid. at para. 111.
88. Ibid. at para. 103: '[J]ust because the [copy]right is intangible, it should not be any less worthy of protection as a full property right.'
89. Note 1 above.
90. Ibid. at 575, citing U.S. Const., art I, §8, cl. 8.
91. *Acuff-Rose*, note 2 above at 577.
92. The transformative value of the defendant's work, the social benefit of humorous criticism, the need to conjure up the original work, and the limited market consequences of the use were identified as supporting fair use.
93. *CCH (TD)*, note 71 above at para. 116.
94. [1990] 2 S.C.R. 467 at 478–9, 72 D.L.R. (4th) 97, McLachlin J. (as she then was). [*Bishop* cited to S.C.R.] citing Maugham J., in *Performing Right Society, Ltd v. Hammond's Bradford Brewery Co.* [1934] 1 Ch. 121 at 127.
95. *Bishop*, Ibid. at 480–81, McLachlin J.: 'an implied exception . . . is all the more unlikely . . . in light of the detailed and explicit exception's in [the Act].' Cited in *Michelin*, note 65 above at 381.
96. *CCH (FCA)*, note 2 above at para. 23 [emphasis added].
97. *Théberge v. Galerie d'Art du Petit Champlain Inc.* 2002 SCC 34, [2002] 2 S.C.R. 336, 210 D.L.R. (4th) 385 at para. 30 [*Théberge* cited to S.C.R.] at para. 31, describing copyright's purpose as 'a balance between promoting the public interest in the encouragement and dissemination of works of the arts and intellect and obtaining a just reward for the creator.'
98. *CCH (SCC)*, note 2 above at paras 48, 51.
99. *CCH (FCA)*, note 2 above at para. 126; *CCH (SCC)*, note 2 above at para. 12.
100. Abraham Drassinower, 'Taking User Rights Seriously', in M. Geist (ed.), *In the Public Interest: The Future of Canadian Copyright Law* (Toronto: Irwin Law, 2005), 462–79 at 67.
101. Daniel J. Gervais, 'Canadian Copyright Law Post-*CCH*' (2004) 18 I.P.J. 131 at 156: 'When reading *CCH*, one is drawn to the conclusion that the court weighted the author's exclusive rights and the users' "right" to use the works on level plates of the proverbial scale.'
102. See e.g. *Michelin*, note 65 above at para. 75: 'To accept the Defendants' submissions on parody [as fair dealing] would be akin to making the parody label the last refuge of the scoundrel.'
103. See e.g. Jeremy Phillips, 'Fair Stealing and the Teddy Bears' Picnic' (1999) 10 Ent. L. Rev. 57 at 57–60.
104. W.N. Hohfeld, *Fundamental Legal Conceptions as Applied in Judicial Reasoning*

(New Haven, CT: Yale University Press, 1946). See also Wendy J. Gordon, 'An Inquiry into the Merits of Copyright: The Challenges of Consistency, Consent, and Encouragement Theory' (1989) 41 Stan. L. Rev. 1343.

105. See e.g. *Hyde Park Residence Ltd v. Yelland* [2001] Ch. 143, [2000] E.C.D.R. 275; *Newspaper Licensing Agency Ltd v. Marks and Spencer plc* [2001] Ch. 257 (CA), [2000] All E.R. 239; *Ashdown v. Telegraph Group Ltd* [2002] QB 546; *de Garis v. Neville Jeffress Pidler Pty. Ltd* (1991), 20 I.P.R. 605; *Nine Network Australia Pty Ltd v. Australian Broadcasting Corporation* (1999), 48 I.P.R. 333; *TCN Channel Nine Pty Ltd v. Network Ten Pty Ltd* (2002), 118 FCR 417.
106. See e.g. *Michelin*, note 65 above at 381: including parody within 'criticism' would be 'creating a new exception to the copyright infringement, a step that only Parliament would have the jurisdiction to do.'
107. *Sony Corporation v. Universal City Studios*, 464 U.S. 417 (1984).
108. See *RIAA v. Diamond Multimedia*, 180 F. 3d 1072 at 1079 (9th Circ. 1999): 'Rio [a portable MP3 player] merely makes copies in order to render portable, or "space-shift," those files that already reside on a user's hard drive. Such copying is a paradigmatic noncommercial personal use.'
109. *Tom Hopkins International Inc. v. Wall & Redekop Realty Ltd* (1984), 1 C.P.R. (3d) 348 at 352–3.
110. See Copyright Act, note 52 above, s. 80(1), which creates an exception to infringement for the audio-recording of musical works made for private use, subject to certain limitations.
111. Sunny Handa, *Copyright Law in Canada* (Markham, Ont.: Butterworths, 2002) at 294 [Handa, *Copyright*]. See also Lisa Anne Katz Jones, 'Is Viewing a Web Page Copyright Infringement?' (1998) 4 Appeal 60 at 62–3; Industry Canada's Information Highway Advisory Council report, *Copyright and the Information Highway: Final Report of the Copyright Sub-Committee* Ottawa: publisher, March 1995) at 11: '[A]ny act of [digitally] accessing a work constitutes a reproduction, [and] as such, . . . is subject to the right of reproduction.'
112. Handa, *Copyright*, Ibid.
113. See *Religious Technology Center v. Netcom On-Line Communication Services, Inc.*, 907 F. Supp. 1361 (N.D. Cal. 1995).
114. Handa, *Copyright*, note 111 above at 297–8. See also Sunny Handa, 'Reverse Engineering of Computer Programs under Canadian Copyright Law' (1995) 40 McGill L.J. 621.
115. Handa, *Copyright*, Ibid. at 297.
116. See *Sega Enterprises Ltd v. Accolade Inc.*, 24 U.S.P.Q.2d 1561, 977 F.2d 1510 (9th Cir. 1992); *Atari Games Corp. v. Nintendo of America Inc.*, 975 F.2d 832 (Fed. Cir. 1992).
117. See e.g. Rebecca Tushnet, 'Payment in Credit: Copyright Law and Subcultural Creativity' (2007) 70 Law & Contemp. Prob. 135; Graham Reynolds 'All the Game's a Stage: Machinima and Copyright in Canada' (forthcoming 2010) *Journal of World Intellectual Property*.
118. *Acuff-Rose*, note 1 above at 579, Souter J.
119. Alan L. Durham, 'Copyright and Information Theory: Toward an Alternative Model of Authorship' (2004) B.Y.U.L. Rev. 69 at 94.
120. Notably, such uses have not always received a favourable outcome even in the United States. See e.g. *Rogers v. Koons*, 960 F.2d 301 (2d Cir), cert. denied 113 S. Ct. 365 (1992); *Bridgeport Music Inc. v. Dimension Films*, 383 F.3d 390 (6th Cir. 2004).
121. Industry Canada, 2002, note 57 above.
122. Sir John Whitford, *Copyright and Designs Law: Report of the Committee to Consider the Law on Copyright and Designs,* (London: HMSO) (Cmnd 6732, 1977) at para. 676 [*Whitford Report*].
123. Andrew Gowers, *Gowers Review of Intellectual Property* (2006) (HM Treasury), ss. 4.69, 4.70, 4.85.

124. Ibid. at s. 4.90.
125. Ibid. at s. 4.88: 'At present it would not be possible to create a copyright exception for transformative use. . . . However, the Review recommends that the Government seeks to amend the Information Society Directive to permit an exception along such lines to be adopted in the UK.'
126. Directive 2001/29/EC of the European Parliament and of the Council of 22 June 2001 on the harmonisation of certain aspects of copyright and related rights in the information society [2001] O.J. L167/10, 12, Art. 5[Copyright Directive].
127. Government of Australia, 'Fair Use and Other Copyright Exceptions: An examination of fair use, fair dealing and other exceptions in the Digital Age' (Issues Paper, 2005).
128. Ibid. at para. 7.12.
129. Copyright Act 1968, ss. 41A, 103AA, introduced by the Copyright Amendment Act 2006, no. 158. See also Melissa De Zwart 'The Copyright Amendment Act 2006: the new copyright exceptions' (2007) 25 *Copyright Reporter* 4; Nicolas Suzor 'Where the bloody hell does parody fit in Australian copyright law?' (2008) 13 *Media & Arts Law Review* 218.
130. Balanced Copyright, News Release, 'Government of Canada Introduces Proposals to Modernize the *Copyright Act*', 2 June 2010, available at: http://www.ic.gc.ca/eic/site/crp-prda.nsf/eng/h_rp01149.html (accessed 26 January 2011).
131. Balanced Copyright, *Copyright Modernization Act – Backgrounder*, available at: http://www.ic.gc.ca/eic/site/crp-prda.nsf/eng/h_rp01151.html (accessed 26 January 2011).
132. Bill C-32, note 56 above, s. 21.
133. This distinction emerged from *Acuff-Rose*, note 1 above at 580–1. The Ninth Circuit, in particular, has maintained a strict distinction between parody and satire. See e.g. *Dr. Seuss Enterprises v. Penguin Books USA*, 109 F.3d 1394 (9th Cir. 1997).
134. *Cf.* E Gredley and S. Maniatis, 'Parody: A Fatal Attraction? Part 1: The Nature of Parody and its Treatment in Copyright' [1997] 7 EIPR 339 at 343., arguing that the parody/satire distinction requires courts 'to devise near impossible distinctions between satiric parodies and parodic satires.'
135. See Suzor, note 142 above at 238–43 and Daniel Austin Green 'Gulliver's Trials: A Modest Proposal to Excuse and Justify Satire' (2006) 11 Chapman L. Rev. 283.
136. See e.g. *Boudreau v. Lin* (1997) 150 D.L.R. (4th) 324, 75 C.P.R. (3d) 1.
137. Bill C-32, note 56 above, s. 29.21.
138. Balanced Copyright, '*What the New* Copyright Modernization Act *Means for Consumers*', available at: http://www.ic.gc.ca/eic/site/crp-prda.nsf/eng/rp01186.html (accessed 26 January 2011).
139. Bill C-32, note 56 above, s. 29.22.
140. Ibid., s. 29.23.
141. Ibid., s. 29.24.
142. Balanced Copyright, note 138 above.
143. Bill C-32, note 56 above, s. 29.23(d).
144. Ibid., s. 29.22(4). A similar condition exists for reproductions made for back-up purposes: s. 29.24(3).
145. *Sony* note 107 above.
146. L.J. Murray and S.E.Trosow, *Canadian Copyright: A Citizen's Guide* (Toronto: Between the Lines Press, 2007).
147. *CCH (SCC)*, note 2 above at paras 53–60.
148. Murray and Trosow, note 146 above at 204, have proposed the following revision along the same lines:

> '29 (1) Fair dealing for purposes such as research, private study, [education, parody, satire] criticism, review or news reporting does not infringe copyright.

(2) In determining whether the use made in any particular case is fair dealing, the factors to be considered shall include –
(a) the purpose of the dealing,
(b) the character of the dealing,
(c) the amount of the dealing,
(d) the nature of the work or other subject matter,
(e) available alternatives to the dealing,
(f) the effect of the dealing on the work or other subject matter,
(g) the extent to which attribution was made where reasonable in the circumstances.'

149. Knopf, note 58 above at 257.
150. Burrell, note 6 above at 373.
151. Pub. L. No. 105-304, 112 Stat. 2860 (1998).
152. William F. Patry and Shira Perlmutter, 'Fair Use Misconstrued: Profit, Presumptions, and Parody' (1993) 11 Cardozo Arts & Ent. L.J. 667 at 670.
153. Melissa De Zwart 'Fair Use? Fair Dealing?' (2006) 24 Copyright Reporter 20 at 23 [de Zwart, 'Fair Use'].
154. *Sony,* note 120 above.
155. Ibid. at 451. Also, at 449, the court stated that '[I]f the Betamax were used to make copies for a commercial or profit-making purpose, such use would presumptively be unfair'.
156. Ibid. at 451.
157. See e.g. *Financial Info. Inc. v. Moody's Investors Serv. Inc.* 751 F. 2d 501 (2nd Cir. 1984) at 509: '*Sony* requires that we recognize a presumption of unfair use by Moody's arising from its commercial use of the copyrighted material'. See also *West Publishing Co. v. Mead Data Cent., Inc.* 616 F. Supp. 1571 (D. Minn., 1985), *aff'd* 799 F.2d 1219 (8th Cir. 1986); *Radji v. Khakbaz* 607 F. Supp. 1296 at 1302 (D.D.C. 1985); *Hutchinson Tel. Co. v. Fronteer Directory Co.*, 640 F. Supp. 386 (1986) at 390; *Paramount Pictures Corp. v. Labus* 16 U.S.P.Q. 2d 1142 (1990).
158. *Harper & Row v. Nation Enterprises*, 471 U.S. 539 (1984) [*Harper & Row*]. This famous case involved the unauthorised publication of excerpts from the pre-publication manuscript copy of President Ford's memoirs.
159. Gary L. Francione, *Facing the Nation: The Standards for Copyright, Infringement, and Fair Use of Factual Works*, 134 U. Pa. L. Rev. 519 (1986), at 549. Francione criticises the *Harper & Row* court for having 'placed the cure-all of fair use in a very small bottle.' Ibid. at 522.
160. *Harper & Row*, note 158 above at 562.
161. See e.g. *Rosemont Enterprises v. Random House, Inc.*, 366 F.2d 303 (2nd Cir.), cert. denied, 385 U.S. 1009 (1967) which relegated commercial motive to practical irrelevance as long as the use was in the public interest. See also *Time Inc. v. Bernard Geis Assocs.*, 293 F. Supp. 130, at 146: 'hope by a defendant for commercial gain is not a significant factor in this circuit.'
162. de Zwart, 'Fair Use' note 163 above at 24–5, noting the Court's citation with approval of Wendy Gordon, 'Fair Use as Market Failure: A Structural and Economic Analysis of the Betamax Case and its Predecessors' (1982) 82 Colum. L. Rev. 1600.
163. 114 S.Ct. 1164 (1994). See also *American Geophysical Union v. Texaco, Inc.* 60 F.3d 913 (2nd Cir. 1994) at para. 64.
164. See Neil Netanel, *Copyright's Paradox* (Oxford University Press, Inc., New York: 2008) at 64, complaining that 'Since *Harper & Row*, the Blackstonian property-centred view of fair use has steadily gained ground.'
165. 471 U.S. 539 (1985), at 546.
166. 621 F.2d 57 (2d Cir.1980) at 61.
167. Jeremy Waldron, 'From Authors to Copiers: Individual Rights and Social Values in Intellectual Property', 68 Chic-Kent L. Rev. 841 (1993) at 860.

168. Ian R. Kerr, A. Maurushat and C.S. Tacit, 'Technical Protection Measures: Tilting at Copyright's Windmill' (2002–03) 34(1) Ottawa L. Rev. 7 at 13.
169. Stefan Bechtold, 'Digital Rights Management in the United States and Europe' (2004) 52 Am. J. Comp. L. 323 at 363.
170. White Paper: Intellectual Property and the National Information Infrastructure (1995) *The Report of the Working Group on Intellectual Property Rights* [online] at 231, available at: http://www.uspto.gov/web/offices/com/doc/ipnii/ipnii.pdf (accessed 26 January 2011).
171. See Jessica Litman, *Digital Copyright* (New York: Prometheus Books, 2001) at 122–9.
172. WIPO treaties (1996), available at: http://www.wipo.int/treaties/en/ip/wct/trtdocs_wo033.html and http://www.wipo.int/treaties/en/ip/wppt/trtdocs_wo034.html (both accessed 13 January 2011).
173. For a detailed account, see Pamela Samuelson, 'The U.S. Digital Agenda at WIPO' (1997) 37 Va. J. Int'l. L. 369. With regard to the regulation of circumvention technologies specifically, see Litman, note 171 above at 129–33.
174. See Pamela Samuelson, 'Regulating Technologies to Protect Copyrighted Works' (1996) 39 Communications of the ACM 17, arguing that existing US law would have satisfied Article 11 obligations.
175. Kerr *et al.*, note 168 above at 34; citing K. Koelman and N. Helberger, 'Protection of Technological Measures', in P. Bernt Hugenholtz (ed.), *Copyright and Electronic Commerce: Legal Aspects of Electronic Copyright Management* (The Hague: Kluwer Law International, 2000) at 171.
176. This interpretation of the text of Article 11 is not without its critics. See Kerr *et al.*, note 168 above at 36.
177. DMCA, §1201(a)(1)(A).
178. DMCA, §1201(a)(2) and §1201(b). §1201(a)(2) prohibits trafficking in devices that circumvent access controls; §1201(b) prohibits trafficking in circumvention devices designed or produced to circumvent TPMs that protect the exclusive rights of copyright holders.
179. DMCA, §1201(d).
180. DMCA, §1201(e)
181. DMCA, §1201(g). The list also includes: circumvention to achieve interoperability of computer programs (§1201(f)); to prevent minors from accessing material on the Internet (§1201(h)); when either the technical measure or the work collect or disseminate personally identifying information about the user's online activities (§1201(i)); to test the security of a computer, computer system, or network (§1201(j)).
182. Litman, *Digital Copyright*, note 171 above at 31.
183. DMCA, §1201 (a)(1)(B)-(D)
184. Current exemptions from circumvention prohibitions can be found online at: http://www.copyright.gov/1201/ (accessed 26 January 2011).
185. Daniel L. Burk and Julie E. Cohen, 'Fair Use Infrastructure for Rights Management Systems' (2001) 15 Harv. J.L. & Tech. 41at 49–50.
186. See B.D. Herman and O.H. Gandy, Jr., 'Catch 1201: A Legislative History and Content Analysis of the DMCA Exemption Proceedings' (2006) 24 Cardozo Arts & Ent. L.J. 121 at 188, criticising the scheme for 'taking the responsibility for ensuring fair use away from the courts and giving it to an obscure, relatively toothless rulemaking process,' and 'leaving wider fair use concerns without a venue'.
187. Ibid. at 143–4.
188. D. Nimmer, 'A Riff on Fair Use in the Digital Millennium Copyright Act' (2000) 148 U. Pa. L. Rev. 673 at 675, cited in Herman and Gandy Jr., note 186 above at 187.
189. For a number of illustrative examples of restrictions imposed by the DMCA, see Kerr *et al.*, note 168 above at 69–74. A full list of DMCA cases that have presented fair use, free speech and privacy concerns can be found online at: http://www.eff.org/issues/dmca (accessed 13 January 2011).

190. 111 F. Supp. 2d 294 (SDNY 2000).
191. Yochai Benkler and Lawrence Lessig (2001) 'Profs. Benkler and Lessig Amici Brief in "MPAA v. 2600" Case' (2001), available at: http://w2.eff.org/IP/Video/MPAA_DVD_cases/20010126_ny_2profs_amicus.html (accessed 26 January 2011).
192. *Sub. nom. Universal City Studios Inc. v. Eric Corley*, 273 F.3d 429 (2nd Cir. 2001) (*Corley*).
193. Ibid. at 429.
194. Pamela Samuelson, 'Intellectual Property and the Digital Economy: Why the Anti-Circumvention Regulations Need to be Revised' (1999) 14 *Berkeley Technology Law Journal* 519 at 533.
195. In its original enactment of anti-circumvention laws, Australia included a novel mechanism by which lawful users could obtain circumvention devices or services from 'qualified persons' to enable or facilitate permitted uses: Copyright Amendment (Digital Agenda) Act 2000 No. 110, 2000 (Cth), s 116A(3). Following the coming into force of the Australia-United States Free Trade Agreement 2005, Australia has enacted revised anti-circumvention provisions that more closely align with those of the DMCA. Revised Copyright Act 1968, available at: http://www.austlii.edu.au/au/legis/cth/consol_act/ca1968133.txt (accessed 26 January 2011). See also K.Weatherall, 'Locked In: Australia Gets a Bad Intellectual Property Deal' (2004–05) 20 *Policy: a journal of public policy and ideas* 18.
196. Copyright Directive, note 126 above, art. 6. In accordance with Art. 6(3), the protection encompasses the act of circumvention and trafficking in devices and services both in relation to copyright control measures and access control measures.
197. Ibid. Art. 6(4) states: 'in the absence of voluntary measures taken by right holders . . . Member States shall take appropriate measures to ensure that right holders make available to the beneficiary of an exception or limitation provided for in national law . . . the means of benefiting from that exception or limitation.' Although this article is laudable for the positive dimension that it attributes to copyright exceptions, its textual and practical limitations have caused it to be described as a 'toothless tiger' (Bechtold, 2004, note 169 above at 379).
198. J.H. Reichman, G.B. Dinwoodie and P. Samuelson, 'A Reverse Notice and Takedown Regime to Enable Public Interest Uses of Technically Protected Copyrighted Works' (2007) 22 Berkeley Tech. L.J. 981.
199. Ibid. at 1041–2.
200. Reichman *et al.*, note 198 above at 1045.
201. Bill C-60, note 56 above, s. 34.02.
202. See New Zealand's Copyright Act 1994 No. 143 (as amended by the Copyright (New Technologies) Amendment Act 2008 (NZ)), s. 226(b): 'For the avoidance of doubt, [TPM] does not include a process, treatment, mechanism, device, or system to the extent that, in the normal course of operation, it only controls any access to a work for non-infringing purposes.'
203. *Cf.* Ibid. s. 226A(2).
204. New Zealand's system allows people wishing to carry out permitted acts in relation to TPM-protected works to seek assistance from 'qualified persons' who can lawfully provide circumvention services and can lawfully be supplied with circumvention devices. Ibid., ss 226D and 226E.
205. *Cf.* Ibid. at s. 226D: anti-circumvention rights 'do not prevent or restrict the exercise of a permitted act'. The Indian Copyright (Amendment) Bill, 2010, s. 65A(2)(a), similarly states that nothing in its anti-circumvention provision 'shall prevent any person from doing anything referred to therein for a purpose not expressly prohibited by this Act.'
206. *Cf.* Kerr *et al.*, note 168 above at 78, proposing a 'positive obligation to provide access-to-a-work when persons or institutions fall within an exception or limitation set out in the Copyright Act.'
207. Section 95b(1) of the German Copyright Act (Urheberrechtsgesetz, UrhG), added by the Law for the Regulation of Copyright in the Information Society 2003, requires

rightholders to provide necessary means for users to benefit from recognised exemptions. See Wencke Baesler, 'Technological Protection Measures in the United States, the European Union and Germany – How Much Fair Use Do We Need in the "Digital World"?' (2003) 8 Va. J.L. & Tech. 13 at 20–22.

208. See Reichman *et al.*, note 198 above at 985, suggesting a 'reverse notice-and-take-down': 'users would be able to give copyright owners notice of their desire to make public interest uses of technically protected copyrighted works, and right holders would have the responsibility to take down the TPMs or otherwise enable these lawful uses.'

209. I have discussed in detail elsewhere various possible models and roles for such an intermediary. See Carys Craig, 'Digital Locks and the Fate of Fair Dealing: In Pursuit of 'Prescriptive Parallelism'" (2010) 13:4 *Journal of World Intellectual Property* 503. See also Burk and Cohen, note 185 above; Paul Ganley, 'Digital Copyright and the New Creative Dynamics' (2004) 12 Int'l J. L. & I.T. 282; Reichman *et al.*, note 198 above.

210. It should be noted that a system that requires users to identify themselves and their intended activities in order to benefit from exceptions inevitably raises privacy concerns that would have to be overcome (Burk and Cohen, note 185 above at 63–5).

211. Reichman *et al.*, note 198 above at 1045.

7. Dissolving the conflict between copyright and freedom of expression

7.1 INTRODUCTION

This chapter is concerned with the relationship between freedom of expression and copyright law, and more fundamentally, with what this relationship – its conflicts, tensions and purported resolutions – can reveal to us about the nature of the copyright interest. Freedom of expression protects an individual's right to express herself without limitations imposed upon the content of her speech, while copyright law prevents an individual from expressing herself through another's copyrightable expression. This apparent inconsonance led Melville Nimmer to ask:

> Is not [the Copyright Act] precisely a "law" . . . which abridges the "freedom of speech" and "of the press" in that it punishes expressions by speech and press when such expression consists of the unauthorised use of material protected by copyright?[1]

With this question in mind, it would not seem far-fetched to suggest that an absolutist conception of the right of free expression could render the Copyright Act unconstitutional. But then, as Nimmer reminds us, the 'reconciliation of the irreconcilable, the merger of antitheses . . . are the great problems of the law.'[2] As we have seen, when irreconcilable assertions are embodied in competing individual rights, reconciliation tends to be proffered in the language of 'balance', 'compromise' or 'trump'. These words embody the analytic tools by which the interface between copyright protection and the right of freedom expression has typically been shaped and defined (to the extent that it has been acknowledged at all). In the discussion that follows, I hope to show that these tools are inadequate for the task.

Having locked potentially antagonistic rights into 'logic-tight compartments',[3] courts and lawmakers have been surprisingly successful at maintaining the separation of freedom of expression considerations and copyright law. Indeed, in the famous US case of *Eldred v. Ashcroft*, one lower court decision went so far as to declare that 'copyrights are categorically immune from challenges under the First Amendment.'[4] Given the nature of the copyright interest, however, there are necessarily moments where both copyright and the right of free expression are irrefutably at play, and apparently in conflict. In such instances, this neatly compartmentalised understanding leads to an overly simplistic resolution: one concern is temporarily given more weight than the other (balance), substantively diluted (compromise), or forced to give way completely (trump). The characterisation of copyright as a species of private-property entitlement tends to afford it moral and legal primacy. This ensures that free expression concerns typically give way to private copyright control, and, I will argue, thereby shifts copyright law further from the justificatory foundations upon which it stands.

My purpose here is to show that the characterisation of copyright and freedom of expression as individual rights vested in the liberal subject undermines the importance of both sets of interests, and ultimately restricts the communicative activity that both copyright and freedom of expression are intended to further. The social values that lie at the core of the copyright system are the same values affirmed by our belief in the guarantee of freedom of expression: the value that we attach to communication, to interaction between members of society, and to participation in a social dialogue. The key to understanding the relationship between freedom of expression and copyright is to see them both in light of their mutual goal: the goal of maximising cultural flows and channels of communication between members of society. Therefore, copyright must embrace the values of freedom of expression in order to ensure its effectiveness and its legitimacy. Premised upon this assertion, my argument will be that a vision of copyright as a private, proprietary entitlement capable of trumping free-expression interests disrupts the internal coherence of the copyright system and its justificatory principles.

Without a shift in the dominant conception of copyright, the system is indeed irreconcilable with the right of free expression, both as a legal abstraction and as a practical matter; but when copyright is conceptualised in relational terms, the system shares and (at least potentially) furthers the values that underlie the guarantee of freedom of expression. Rather than purporting to reconcile the irreconcilable, then, copyright policy should concern itself with fostering the human, creative capacities that it is intended to encourage. The clash between copyright owners' rights to control expression and citizens' rights to express themselves cannot be adequately resolved. By focusing on relationships and values rather than individuals and rights, however, the conflict between free speech and copyright quickly dissolves.

The Canadian context again offers an illuminating example from which larger lessons can be learned. In Section 2, I describe the conflict that exists at the level of individual rights between freedom of expression, which in

Canada is guaranteed by section 2(b) of the Canadian Charter of Rights and Freedoms,[5] and the rights granted to authors of original works pursuant to the Copyright Act.[6] The discussion provides an overview of the way in which the Canadian courts have defined freedom of expression and have approached its relationship to intellectual property. In Section 3, I examine the approach taken in the case of *Cie Générale des Etablissements Michelin-Michelin & Cie v. C.A.W.-Canada*,[7] where the court relied upon analogy with physical property and private property rights to dismiss the constitutional challenge. I also critically examine the approach taken by recent British and US courts that have similarly struggled to acknowledge and resolve this tension between speech and copyright. In Section 4, I examine the principles of freedom of expression in terms of communication and community, and make the argument that the social values informing freedom of expression are the same as those embodied by the copyright system. Section 5 concludes that, if we are to justify copyright in terms of the encouragement of authorship, the rights granted to authors under that system cannot be characterised as individual private property entitlements, but must instead be viewed through a relational lens and justified in terms of the public goals that they advance.

7.2 THE CONFLICT: COPYRIGHT V. FREEDOM OF EXPRESSION IN CANADA

At their most basic level, copyright laws allow individuals to call upon the state to prevent someone from speaking or expressing themselves in a particular way. By giving the copyright holder a monopoly over the use of the copyrighted work, copyright law creates private interests ostensibly hostile to the freedom of expression interests of other members of the public. On the one hand, individual A has the right to express herself freely, while on the other, individual B has the right to prevent A from copying expression substantially similar to B's copyrighted expression. Section 2(b) of the Canadian Charter of Rights and Freedoms constitutionally guarantees freedom of expression, while the Copyright Act creates an exclusionary interest over the expression of an idea fixed in a tangible form. Put in this way, the question is not whether the Copyright Act is constitutionally questionable, but rather, how can it be anything but? Sunny Handa has explained the freedom of expression challenge for copyright law:

> One would think that the place of copyright in the context of freedom of expression would be a precarious one. After all, copyright broadly targets expression and provides that exclusive rights of expression be given to creators. Once a work is created, one cannot repeat it without paying some royalty. In fact, the

> right to repeat it need not be given; it may be withheld whereupon one may not repeat the expression. Framed in this way, copyright laws appear to offend freedom of expression rules. Yet no real challenges have been brought.[8]

No doubt there are many reasons for the paucity of constitutional scrutiny of the Copyright Act – not least, the economic and political strength of those who favour expansive copyright protection, together with the intuitive appeal of basic copyright doctrine and its accompanying rhetoric. Or perhaps the real problem is simply that the application of copyright law proves complex enough without the 'superimposition' of free speech principles.[9] Another contributing factor, however, has been the largely unchallenged assumption amongst policy makers and commentators alike that the copyright system sufficiently respects freedom of expression values by virtue of internal mechanisms such as the originality requirement, the idea–expression dichotomy and the fair dealing defence.[10] The invocation of the idea–expression dichotomy largely misses the point; the right of free expression surely encompasses the right to use others' expression and not merely the right to express ideas anew. As for the originality and fair dealing doctrines, we have already seen that these limiting doctrines neither clearly nor adequately circumscribe the copyright interest. While copyright protection continues to expand, facilitated by a proprietary, owner-oriented vision of copyright's purposes, the internal doctrinal safeguards that could ensure its coherence with free speech principles are simply not up to the task.[11] Certainly, their mere existence does not obviate the need for constitutional scrutiny.

Whatever explanations are available, legislative and judicial complacency about the constitutionality of copyright regulation cannot be explained on the basis that copyright protection does not touch upon matters of fundamental constitutional significance, for it is overwhelmingly clear that it must: copyright deals exclusively with the manipulation of expression.[12] As Neil Netanel explains:

> [I]t is a mistake to view copyright as just another property right. Unlike most property rights, copyright law is fundamentally an instrument of media and communication policy and an integral part of our system of free expression. Copyright's fabric of incentives and restraints, exclusive entitlements and statutory licenses, capacious rights and exceptions to those rights, does far more than allocate private interests and regulate trade. It fundamentally benefits and burdens speech.[13]

7.2.1 The Freedom of Expression Guarantee

Section 2(b) of the Charter guarantees to everyone the 'freedom of thought, belief, opinion and expression, including freedom of the press and other media of communication.'[14] Legal scholarship and jurisprudence almost invariably invoke three broad justifications for free expression principles. Perhaps the most prevalent justification recognises the right of free expression of opinion and of criticism as 'essential to the working of a parliamentary democracy such as ours.'[15] The most renowned advocate of this 'democratic' interpretation of free speech principles was Alexander Meiklejohn,[16] who argued that the right to free speech followed by deduction from the notion of democratic self-government: the legitimacy of democratic institutions derives from their nature as representative of the interests of the political citizenry, and so it is axiomatic that people have had the opportunity to formulate and express their views to those who purport to represent them.[17] A second explanation often given for the freedom of expression is the search for truth, for 'steadily advancing enlightenment, for which the widest range of controversy is the *sine qua non*'[18]; as John Stuart Mill argued, the freedom can be understood in a utilitarian sense as the key to the unrestricted exchange of ideas from which the truth is most likely to emerge.[19] A third rationale frequently posited for the guarantee of freedom of expression is its role as a means of achieving personal fulfilment. This approach makes free speech the end in itself, allowing individuals to achieve their full potential without government interference in the individual's development of his own personality and integrity. In essence, this justification is grounded in the liberal notion of autonomy, which makes freedom of speech a requirement of state neutrality. This argument from autonomy, put in Rawlsian terms, posits freedom of speech as a 'primary good': whatever else one wants, it is rational to want freedom of speech because it is part of a framework that enables individuals to pursue whatever is their conception of the 'good life'.[20]

The significance of how we choose to understand and rationalise our commitment to freedom of expression will become apparent in the course of the discussion that follows. For the moment, it will suffice to note that the Supreme Court of Canada has seemingly endorsed all three reasons for protecting freedom of expression. In *Irwin Toy v. Quebec*,[21] the Court attempted to explicate the constitutional guarantee of freedom of expression on the following bases: '(1) seeking and attaining the truth is an inherently good activity; (2) participation in social and political decision-making is to be fostered and encouraged; and (3) the diversity in forms of individual self-fulfilment and human flourishing ought to be cultivated'.[22]

As Peter Hogg has noted, 'the acceptance of all three reasons as the basis for the right to freedom of expression entails a very broad definition of the right.'[23] Having indicated the centrality of the role of free expression in our liberal democracy, the *Irwin Toy* court broadly defined the coverage of the freedom, stating: 'if the activity conveys or attempts to convey a meaning, it has expressive content and *prima facie* falls within the scope of the guarantee.'[24] It would seem that very little human activity could be excluded from this expansive definition. Clearly, purely physical action which does not and is not intended to convey meaning is excluded,[25] but it is equally clear that all forms of art – novels, films, paintings, dance, music and so on – are sufficiently communicative to fall within the broad scope of the section 2(b) guarantee.[26] It hardly need be said that these communicative forms of artistic expression, embraced as protected speech under section 2(b) of the Charter, constitute precisely the kind of 'literary, dramatic, musical and artistic work' contemplated by section 5(1) of the Copyright Act as the subject-matter of copyright protection.

In contrast to the US guarantee of free speech contained in the First Amendment, the Charter maintains a distinction between questions that go to the scope of the freedom of expression guarantee and questions concerning the grounds upon which the freedom can be limited. Freedom of expression is set out in section 2(b), while section 1 recognises that legitimate factors can justify placing limits upon the freedom in certain circumstances. Something that would *prima facie* constitute a violation of freedom of expression can therefore be declared constitutional under section 1 if it falls within 'such reasonable limits prescribed by law as can be demonstrably justified in a free and democratic society.'[27] In order to be constitutionally valid, then, a law limiting the broad protection afforded to speech interests under section 2(b) must meet the section 1 standard. The cumulative standards of reasonableness and demonstrable justification were examined by the Supreme Court in *R. v. Oakes*,[28] which articulated four criteria to be satisfied in order for a limitation on a Charter right to qualify as a reasonable limit under section 1: the law must pursue an objective sufficiently important to justify limiting the right; it must be rationally connected to the objective; it must impair the right no more than is necessary to accomplish the objective; and it must not have a disproportionately severe effect on the persons to whom it applies.[29] For our purposes it is perhaps worth noting that nearly all of the section 1 cases considered thus far have turned upon the answer to the third inquiry: not whether the law limits the right, but whether it does so more than is necessary to achieve its purpose.[30]

7.2.2 Section 2(b) Challenges to Intellectual Property

Given the expansive interpretation of the section 2(b) guarantee, and the broad, deep-rooted principles upon which it has been rationalised by the

Canadian courts, it seems rather incredible that copyright – a direct limitation upon expressive or communicative activity – has succeeded in almost wholly avoiding constitutional challenge. Even more remarkable is that the courts have never found it necessary to rely upon a section 1 analysis to justify the limits that the Copyright Act imposes upon communicative activity. Charter jurisprudence suggests that almost any impugned statute would *prima facie* be found to violate the section 2(b) guarantee, and so almost invariably require justification under section 1 as a reasonable limitation upon free expression. However, constitutional challenges to the Copyright Act have either been dismissed out of hand or have faltered at the first stage of analysis in section 2(b).

As exemplified by the *Michelin* case, discussed in Section 3 below, this failure to satisfactorily consider copyright in the light of freedom of expression values can be traced back to a broader failure to appreciate the nature and the purpose of copyright. In my opinion, the court's mischaracterisation of copyright's nature and purpose in the *Michelin* case can account for the weak application of section 2(b) and, in *obiter*, section 1. The court's myopic focus upon proprietary principles and the rights-bearer's interests in the face of significant freedom of expression concerns is testament indeed to 'the mesmeric effect that the notion of copyright as property has.'[31]

Freedom of expression has only been raised in a small number of copyright cases in Canada and, as I have suggested, to little avail. Before tackling the *Michelin* case, the case of *R v. James Lorimer*[32] provides a helpful backdrop. In *Lorimer*, a defendant had distributed an affordable abridgement of a government report on Canada's oil monopoly. By holding for the plaintiff, the court permitted the government to use Crown copyright as a tool to control the dissemination of an investigative report, and, in effect, the ideas and information contained within that report. The ease with which the Federal Court of Appeal dismissed the defendant's freedom of expression claim is indicative of the nonchalance with which the courts have greeted the 'encroachment' of fundamental democratic ideals and social values into the copyright context. The court explained the failure of the defendant's Charter challenge in the following terms: '[S]o little of its own thought, belief, opinion and expression is contained in the respondent's infringing work that it is properly to be regarded as entirely an appropriation of the thought, belief, opinion and expression of the author of the infringed work.'[33]

This statement of the court seems flawed for two reasons. First, the court perceives no problem in characterising the defendant's action as the 'appropriation' of the author's *thought, belief, or opinion*. The court's use of the language of appropriation – the language of ownership – with reference to things that are by their nature uncopyrightable and unownable, is telling in itself, suggesting that the notion of property was exercising its mesmerising powers, influencing the court's opinion on the matter of who has the right to speak, and what they have the right to say. Put another way, the court's language, already imbued with a moralistic tone, seems to reify and extend the proprietary concept employed by the statutory copyright scheme, causing the court to judge the defendant's communicative act in light of its nature as an appropriative act, even if beyond the scope of the copyright system. When we talk of appropriating something that belongs to another person, this characterisation is not value-neutral: it is necessarily informed by the moral nuances of entitlement. And this is in regard to subject matter – thoughts and opinions – incapable of ownership, and necessarily free from such proprietary claims in the name of freedom of expression.[34]

The second cause of concern is perhaps even more acute for the purposes of my argument here. In the quoted passage, the court minimises the importance of the defendant's expressive activity on the basis that it involved 'so little of its own thought, belief, opinion and expression', thereby attributing legal significance to the fact that the defendant's communicative act involved someone else's expression.[35] There is no justification for this in terms of free expression principles. That the expression originates with the speaker is simply not a requirement of an attempt to convey meaning before it can fall within the freedom of expression guarantee. If a person protesting against the cruel treatment of laboratory animals distributes a pamphlet containing a graphic photograph of a mistreated animal, there can be little doubt that she is attempting to convey meaning through this act, whether or not she took the photograph or owns the copyright therein. If someone writes 'War is Terrorism!' on multiple placards and hands them out to protesters in a crowd, each protestor is expressing his- or herself by carrying the placard that he or she was given. The expression is not *theirs* in the copyright sense of having originated from them as authors, but by demonstrating their support of that message, the protesters are undoubtedly engaged in acts of self-expression.

It is not hard to identify the root of the court's apparent confusion: it imported ownership values derived from copyright into what should have been an examination of the defendant's communicative activity. Whether the expression originated with James Lorimer or was 'his', whatever that may mean, is not a relevant consideration in the freedom of expression inquiry. Section 2(b) of the Charter does not guarantee to everyone the freedom of only *original* expression, and the right to free expression is not limited in constitutional jurisprudence by anything akin to the standards of copyrightability. What we can detect here is the entirely inappropriate transportation of the values that pervade copyright dogma, and the ownership tropes that accompany it, into the realm of free expression.

The judgment in *Lorimer* supports the contention that judicial consideration of freedom of expression in Canadian copyright jurisprudence has been flawed by the subterranean presence of copyright morality lying beneath the constitutional inquiry. This copyright morality ensures that private proprietary interests of copyright owners are accorded primacy over other kinds of social interests without sufficient appreciation of the broader legal, social and political context within which the rights are asserted. It seems to me that the well-established principle of freedom of expression begins to look twisted and misshapen in the copyright context. Perhaps this is the inevitable consequence of the fact that, when copyright is reduced to a private property entitlement that inheres in an individual rightholder, the plaintiff's copyright and the defendant's freedom of expression are indeed competing and contradictory interests. The strained reasoning that comes through the cases is, therefore, the predictable result of a struggle to achieve reconciliation of competing individual claims to a right through balance or compromise or – more often and most ominously – through the power to trump.

One further case, concerned this time with trademark law, is also particularly illustrative of the strength of the proprietary vision of intellectual property rights and the effect that this vision can have on an analysis of freedom of expression. In *Source Perrier SA v. Fira-Less Marketing Co. Ltd*,[36] the defendant, who had marketed bottled water under the name 'Pierre, Eh', a reference to then Prime Minister Trudeau, argued that parody and satire ought to be recognised as deserving substantial freedom in accordance with constitutional prescription. The court, however, opined:

> [T]he most liberal interpretation of "freedom of expression" does not embrace the freedom to depreciate the goodwill of registered trade marks, nor does it afford licence to impair the business integrity of the owner of the marks merely to accommodate the creation of a spoof. It must be borne in mind that this application for an injunction does not originate from the targets of the parody . . . but from the owner of the trade marks.[37]

Because it was the *owner* of a trademark who requested an injunction – someone trying to protect a property interest as opposed to simply silencing criticism – the fact that an injunction would in fact silence the parodic expression was beyond the scope of section 2(b). Because the expression might depreciate the goodwill of a registered trademark, it was not free expression: even the most expansive definition of freedom of expression, we are told, could not possibly give the right to interfere with the intellectual property of the plaintiff. But notice, also, the moralism detectable in the court's description of the scenario: the 'business integrity of the owner' is juxtaposed with the defendant's 'mere creation of a spoof.' The court aggrandises the corporate owner of intellectual property, who is portrayed as respectable and upright, while thoroughly undermining the speech interests and communicative efforts of the defendant, which are portrayed as trivial and frivolous – elevating property and diminishing speech.

One commentator speculated that, following the court's broad interpretation of the section 2(b) guarantee in *Irwin Toy*, the attitude of the Canadian courts toward freedom of expression challenges to intellectual property law would have to change.[38] But this was not to be the case. In December of 1996, the case of *Cie Générale des Etablissements Michelin-Michelin & Cie v. C.A.W. -Canada*[39] was decided in a judgment that would all but close the door on freedom of expression challenges to the Copyright Act if followed and embraced by the Canadian courts. Judgment was issued only at the Federal Court Trial Division level, but the ruling has been an important one nonetheless, and remains 'the most explicit decision on the conflict between copyright protection and freedom of expression as guaranteed by the Charter'.[40] To date, it has been either followed or mentioned in over a dozen cases, including judgments by provincial superior courts,[41] the Federal Court of Appeal[42] and even by the Supreme Court of Canada.[43] It has never been distinguished or overruled, and as such, is apparently still good law in Canada. One may speculate as to whether the restrictive interpretation of 'criticism' found in the *Michelin* fair dealing inquiry remains good law in light of the Supreme Court's decision in *CCH*;[44] however, even after *CCH*, *Michelin* has been cited with approval in support of the proposition that 'parody is not an exception to copyright infringement.'[45] This being said, the purpose of the discussion that follows is not to provide a case commentary of the lower court decision, whatever its current or potential value as precedent. Rather, I want to use this troubling case to epitomise the obstacles that a proprietary notion of copyright erects in the way of copyright's goal of maximising expression and communication.

7.3 THE *MICHELIN* CASE: BIBENDUM SILENCES HIS CRITICS

7.3.1 The *Michelin* ruling

The defendants in this case were actively campaigning to become trade union representatives for the employees at the plaintiff's factory plants.

Their campaign involved the distribution of leaflets depicting 'Bibendum', the 'Michelin Man', which was the subject of trademark and copyright protection belonging to the plaintiffs. In the leaflets, a happy Bibendum was depicted stomping on the head of a small and unsuspecting worker standing beneath him.[46] Bibendum's unauthorised appearance on the campaign literature prompted CGEM Michelin to bring an action for infringement of copyrights and trademarks. The defendants mounted a constitutional defence to the copyright infringement claim, arguing that the leaflets depicting Bibendum constituted expression protected by section 2(b) of the Charter and as such, if the infringement provisions of the Copyright Act prevented them from using Bibendum in their advertising campaign, then the provisions amounted to an unconstitutional restriction upon their freedom of expression.[47]

It deserves to be stressed that in *Michelin*, unlike in the *Lorimer* case, the copyright owner was the targeted subject of the parodic ridicule. This point testifies to the censorial power provided by copyright's monopoly, which allows critics to be silenced in the name of protecting copyright interests. Where the copyright owner is the target of the parody's critique, it is likely that he or she will refuse to authorise or to license at any price. In such situations, copyright is an effective tool to quash critique. It seems clear that this should raise freedom of expression concerns; and given copyright's historical beginnings as a tool of censorship, a means of suppressing religious and political dissent,[48] copyright's power in this regard ought not to come as a surprise. What is surprising, rather, is the complacency with which courts today regard the silencing of critical speech through the tool of copyright, and blindly accept the chilling effects that accompany it as a matter of course.

The facts presented in this case implicate important democratic principles and concerns about meaningful participation in social decision-making. The labour dispute provides a compelling backdrop against which to view the defendants' defences to copyright infringement. But the court, having recognised the relevance of constitutional considerations,[49] was nonetheless content to dismiss the defendants' section 2(b) constitutional challenge on basis that 'the Defendants' right to freedom of expression was not restricted. The Charter does not confer the right to use private property – the Plaintiff's copyright – in the service of freedom of expression.'[50]

The court did not perceive a need to justify, by way of a section 1 balancing inquiry, the restriction imposed by the Copyright Act upon the defendant's expressive activity. Rather, the defendants' speech was excluded from the protective scope of section 2(b) altogether, notwithstanding the finding that their activity was an attempt to convey meaning and was indeed 'expressive'.[51] The court was able to remove the expression from the protective umbrella of section 2(b) on the basis that the use of copyright, which is the plaintiff's private property, was a prohibited *form* of expression, and so a 'special limitation' on the section 2(b) guarantee. In other words, where a person uses someone else's copyrighted speech to convey meaning, this is a 'special circumstance' that 'warrant[s] removing that expression from the protected sphere under the Charter.'[52] This conclusion follows directly from the depiction of the plaintiff's copyright as his 'private property.'

The court's interpretation of the scope of section 2(b) protection was based largely upon an appeal to the authority of *Committee for the Commonwealth of Canada v. Canada*,[53] and in particular, the judgement of then Chief Justice Lamer. In this Supreme Court case, which concerned the use of a publicly owned airport for the distribution of political pamphlets, six members of the panel found that it was appropriate to reject claims of access to government property for purposes of expressive activity as part of the section 2(b) analysis. It was agreed that section 2(b) was not sufficiently broad to encompass all claims of access, and three justices agreed that the appropriate standard for determining the threshold of a section 2(b) breach was the so-called 'compatibility' test.[54] On this view, articulated by Chief Justice Lamer, section 2(b) only protects access to government property if the 'form' of expression used by the individual is compatible with the principal function or intended purpose of the physical place.[55] In cases where a party asserts the right to use public property, the necessary balancing of the parties' interests defines the scope of the freedom itself, and so occurs before the Section 1 analysis. In *Michelin*, Justice Teitelbaum expanded this principle, concluding: 'a similar but stricter balancing of interests is to occur if the party . . . asserts the right to use *private* property.'[56] Justice Teitelbaum balanced the relevant interests thus:

> In the balance of interest and rights, if the defendants have no right to use the Plaintiff's "Bibendum", they have a multitude of other means for expressing their views. However, if the Plaintiff loses its right to control the use of its copyright, there is little left to the Plaintiff's right of private property.[57]

The court concluded, then, that the threshold for prohibiting forms of expression under section 2(b) was 'not so high that use of another's private property is a permissible form of expression.'[58] The Trade Union's use of *Michelin*'s corporate logo on their posters and leaflets was held to infringe the company's copyright and so amounted to a trespass upon their private property: an expressive act beyond the scope of their right of free expression.

The *Michelin* court went on to say that, even if the defendants' expression had not been excluded from section 2(b) protection and a *prima facie* violation had been found, the defendants' constitutional challenge would nonetheless have failed at the next stage of analysis, under the section 1 balancing clause. Justice Teitelbaum opined that the limitations imposed upon their freedom of expression by the Copyright Act would be 'reasonable limits prescribed by law . . . demonstrably justified in a free and democratic society.'[59] My focus here is the exclusion of copyrighted expression from the section 2(b) guarantee of freedom of expression, and not the extent to which copyright is a justifiable limitation of free expression within the meaning of section 1. However, I would suggest in passing that the Court's treatment of the section 1 analysis in *Michelin* was similarly distorted by its proprietary characterisation of copyright and its singular concern with the rights of the copyright owner.[60]

The Court's casual assertion that copyright law is undoubtedly capable of being saved by section 1 underscores the pervasiveness of author-oriented assumptions about the nature and purpose of the copyright interest. For example, the court premised its application of the *Oakes* test upon the assertion that the purpose of copyright was the 'protection of authors and ensuring that they are recompensed for their creative energies.'[61] Having identified the ultimate purpose of the Copyright Act as the protection of authors – and not, say, the public interest in encouraging the creation and dissemination of intellectual works – the court could hardly avoid the conclusion that enforcing the author's monopoly was a rational and efficient means by which to achieve that purpose.[62] Perhaps, post-*Théberge*, a Canadian court forced to consider the justifiability of the Copyright Act under section 1 of the Charter would have to actively engage with the question of whether the protection of the copyright interest is also a rationale and efficient way to 'promot[e] the public interest in the encouragement and dissemination of works of the arts and intellect (and, indeed, whether it minimally impairs free expression in pursuit of this goal).'[63]

7.3.2 The *Michelin* mistakes

Let us return now to examine in more detail the section 2(b) analysis of the *Michelin* court, which held that use of another's copyrighted material is not constitutionally protected expression because it involves use of a person's private property and so falls outside section 2(b)'s protective sphere. My purpose in this discussion is to illustrate the extent to which the judgement ultimately depended on an array of questionable assumptions about the nature of copyright.

First, the court in *Michelin* derived principles from an analysis of the law of real property and directly applied those principles to intellectual property. In the course of its judgment, the court continuously employed the physical analogue as an analytic tool, dismissing any argument that the analogy was problematic. While briefly acknowledging the conceptual distinction between tangible and intangible property, the court did not allow the distinction to disrupt the analogy, but instead asserted: 'just because the right is intangible, it should not be any less worthy of protection as a full property right.'[64] Far from appreciating the difference between intellectual and physical property, the court took pains to render this distinction meaningless, warning that recognition of the intangible nature of the plaintiff's property would actually distort the section 2(b) balancing inquiry, or, using Justice Teitelbaum's phraseology, would 'colour our perceptions'. In order to avoid being thus 'misguided', the court warned, we must 'guard against our instincts', which 'might lead us to undervalue the nature of the Plaintiff's copyright [as private property] and overestimate the breadth of the Defendants' freedom of expression.'[65]

This statement implicitly acknowledges that the court was effectively reigning in the scope of the defendant's free expression when it drew the boundaries of the plaintiff's property right. However, having confined its decision to the section 2(b) stage of inquiry, the court claimed simply to be recognising and enforcing an *a priori*, objectively defined private property right. Making the analogy between a copyright work and a tangible, owned object, reifies, and to some extent even physicalises, the subject matter of copyright, creating the impression that the court is merely applying the law to an objective reality, rather than constructing that reality (or simply discovering the plaintiff's right rather than determining its scope). In this way, by obviating the tangible–intangible divide, the court avoids the appearance of imposing limits on the defendants' expressive activity, and so avoids the need to invoke a justification that would take it into the realm of section 1.

It should be clear that the intangibility of copyright's subject matter is fundamental to understanding the nature and scope of the plaintiff's copyright interest. Consider the essential difference between ownership of a physical manuscript and ownership of copyright in the literary work: this is the axiomatic distinction between the book as corporeal artefact and the book as speech, as the author's discourse with the public, as *expression*.[66] Where the subject matter of copyright is properly understood as the latter, and not simply as analogous or equivalent to the former, the relevance of the distinction for the freedom of expression inquiry should be self-evident: the 'property' itself *is* expression. Viewed in this way, the difference between copyright's intangible subject matter and the tangible object of, say, land law, is fundamentally relevant to determining the limits of copyright in light of free expression values. Unlike the object of traditional property, the object of the copyright interest – the copyrightable work – is not a 'thing', but is itself 'speech'. Focusing on this distinction clarifies rather than 'colours' our perception, and our 'instincts' in this regard should be given more credit. If anything, the instincts we ought to beware of are those that lead us to reify the copyright interest and to objectify the expressive subject matter of copyright out of desire for conceptual ease and a familiar moral equation.

As I argued in Chapter 4, the use of the physical property analogy brings with it an unmistakably moralistic edge. The category employed generates an emotional response to the parties' activities, with the propertisation of the copyright holder's right polarising the parties, casting them in oppositional roles as owner and trespasser. The nature of copyright as a system that manipulates expressive activity is obscured: instead, it is recast in a conceptually neater role as a system for the protection of private individuals' rights against the world, with its primary purpose being the protection of copyright owners' property. Unfortunately this role misrecognises the nature of copyright and situates it, in relation to the freedom of expression ideal, in a position that ultimately threatens its internal coherence.

In addition to its misplaced reliance on the physical analogue, the court's property analysis can also be faulted for its concern with the private nature of the plaintiff's right. The *Michelin* court relied upon the *Commonwealth* case, and the 'balancing of interests' in that decision, to exclude the use of copyright from the scope of section 2(b), finding that 'a similar but stricter balancing of interests is to occur if the party . . . asserts the right to use *private* property.'[67] The defendants in *Michelin* argued that this characterisation of copyright as *private* property was inaccurate in light of copyright's nature as state-sanctioned property or, put another way, the fact that it depends upon a statutory grant. The Court seemingly regarded this argument as little more than a desperate strategy designed to skew the proper application of the *Commonwealth* precedent,[68] and proceeded to dismiss it out of hand:

> I have no hesitation in stating that I can find no merit in the Defendants' characterisation of the Plaintiff's copyright as a piece of quasi-public property. The fact that the Plaintiff's copyright is registered by a state-formulated system under the aegis of the Copyright Act in no way diminishes the private nature of the right.[69]

The defendants' argument should not have been so summarily dismissed. First, the reference to copyright's registration system largely misses the point. The copyright interest exists with or without registration; it is not its registration, but its very existence that depends upon the state-formulated system. In any event, the defendants' attempt to differentiate between copyright and other kinds of private property interests is certainly not groundless. While traditional property necessarily depends upon recognition and enforcement by the State, we should distinguish between a state-sanctioned and state-enforced property law system and a regulatory system such as copyright. It is not controversial to assert that copyright law is a statutory construct, and so a state creation, but as the following, frequently cited statement from the Supreme Court of Canada confirms, certain distinctions flow from this: '[C]opyright law is *neither tort law nor property law* in classification, but is statutory law. . . . Copyright legislation simply creates rights and obligations upon the terms and in the circumstances set out in the statute.'[70]

As with any other piece of legislation, the Copyright Act must respect Charter values and must not violate any of the rights accorded Constitutional protection by the Charter.[71] Because copyright is an interest conferred by government regulation, it follows that it can be subjected to Charter scrutiny and limited in the name of the rights enshrined in the Charter. According to Justice Teitelbaum's reading of the *Commonwealth* decision, Charter rights are limited by private property; the right to express oneself ends at the owner's fence. By treating copyright as simply another species of private property, the court goes one crucial step further, allowing a state-granted interest to restrict the Constitutional right of free expression: precisely the kind of result that ought to be prevented through judicial review.[72]

The mesmeric effect of the badge of 'property' seems to be at work once again. The court's position is that copyright is property, and by definition, property is not speech regulation.[73] Copyright remains in its logic-tight compartment. With this partition erected between copyright and speech, the appeal to constitutional speech values from within copyright's compartment is regarded as no more than the unjustifiable encroachment of one area of law into the exclusive domain of another. The enactment of laws creating liability for speech actions (hate speech or the production of pornography, for example) would clearly present constitutional problems in light of section 2(b), but according to the *Michelin* court, a law that creates liability for copyright infringement does not present a similar cause for concern. The operative assumption must be that liability for speech actions and liability for copyright infringement are 'really just apples and oranges'.[74]

In light of the limits that the Copyright Act imposes upon speech activity, the flaw in this position should be clear. By characterising copyright as private property pure and simple, the court obscures the nature of copyright as speech regulation, and then proceeds upon the unanalysed assumption that copyright as property is protected by property law in the same way as any other species of private property. By virtue of the private property category and the analogies that this category permits, the nature of copyright is distorted to fit assumptions regarding traditional private property entitlements.[75] L.R. Patterson explains the error inherent in this approach:

> [T]he importance of whether one views copyright law as protecting property or regulating trade is twofold. First, to view copyright as protecting property is to subject its regulatory aspects to proprietary concepts and thus to minimise, if not defeat, the goal of public access. Second, viewing copyright as protecting property implies that copyright is a unitary rather than complex concept . . . [which] is to ignore reality.[76]

Substantiating Patterson's warning, the Court's failure in *Michelin* to adequately consider the nature of copyright as a regulatory, 'state-formulated' system was not merely academic, but was in fact determinative of the constitutional analysis that ensued. Recognising the author's right as a simple creature of statute is critical to identifying the relevance and importance of constitutional norms at stake in the copyright realm. Where we locate the boundaries of freedom of expression will depend upon how we perceive the right of the copyright owner. When copyright is regarded as the flexible product of social choice, the private copyright interest cannot be permitted to operate as the *ad hoc* threshold to the public's guarantee of free expression, at least in the absence of a broad appeal to social policy objectives as justification.[77] If we see the copyright system as a state-created, regulatory tool that is intended to further the collective interest – but which imposes restrictions upon communicative activity in order to do so – it seems clear that the restrictions it imposes must be justifiable under section 1. Constitutional values should inform the scope of the exclusive control that a copyright holder is given under the Copyright Act, rather than be declared irrelevant simply because such exclusive control has been granted.

As such, there is strength to Patterson's critique, which portrays this private property approach as conceptually reductionistic and a disservice to copyright's goals. Copyright is not a unitary concept with clear and specific boundaries, but is rather a complex concept whose characteristics vary according to the type of work it protects, the uses it seeks to regulate, and to what end.[78] In *Michelin*, copyright was portrayed as a stable thing that was privately owned. By extrapolating principles from the 'private' and 'proprietary' nature of the plaintiff's copyright, the court ultimately avoided the public access issues at play, denied the relevance of the distinctions the defendants sought to draw, and succeeded in portraying speech interests as all but irrelevant to a body of law whose primary justification is the encouragement of creative expression.

Finally, the *Michelin* court's section 2(b) 'balancing' analysis placed undue reliance on the so-called form/content divide, which is simple enough to draw if one assumes that copyright is private property, but which becomes elusive when one acknowledges the true nature of the copyright interest. Pursuant to this divide between the 'form' of expression and its 'content', articulated in the *Irwin Toy* decision, acts attempting to convey meaning can be excluded from the protective sphere of section 2(b) on the basis of the form that the communication takes (throwing a punch, for example) without falling foul of the free speech principle that dictates content-neutrality.[79] However, there is an argument to be made that the form-content divide, which allowed the court to exclude the defendants' expression from section 2(b) based on its form (use of copyright protected material), is inapposite in the realm of copyright.

Copyright attaches to expression. It is therefore the nature of the expression that gives the protected work its form as such, and this form can only be defined in relation to the expression. This is part of what makes copyright a complex right, and one reason why copyright cannot be fitted squarely into categorical analogy. In *Keegstra*, the Supreme Court of Canada held that violent threats (as opposed to violent acts) could not be excluded from section 2(b) because, in order to ascertain that something was indeed a violent threat, it was necessary first to evaluate the content of the expression, thereby offending the content-neutrality principle.[80] The question of whether a work as a whole is subject to copyright, and if so, what elements of the work fall within the scope of the owner's interest, cannot be divorced from an inquiry into the nature and content of the expressive work. Even to find that there is copyright in a particular work is not to say that the intangible object of the copyrightable work is protected in its entirety: only the copyrightable elements of the copyrighted work are within the scope of the copyright owner's interest.[81] In order to ascertain whether something is an infringement of copyright, it is therefore necessary to evaluate the content of the expression, both in regard to establishing the copyrightability of the original expression taken, and in the determining whether the taking constitutes an infringement of the copyright at all.

First, if copyright is to attach to an expression, that expression must be determined to fit into at least one of the categories of 'literary, dramatic, musical or artistic' expression.[82] Then, as we saw in Chapter 5, the expression must be deemed to be 'original'; it must originate from the author, meaning that it must not be copied, consciously or unconsciously, and it must require more than a trivial amount of skill and judgement in its creation.[83] In order for the expression to be something to which copyright can attach, its content must be sufficiently specific or detailed; mere vague, general, or undeveloped ideas exist at a level of abstraction that place them on the uncopyrightable side of the idea–expression dichotomy.[84] The expression must be a copyrightable subject matter; it cannot, for example, merely state a fact, system, method or an abstract theorem, and it must contain more than stock characters, common literary efficiencies or *scènes à faires*.[85] Furthermore, according to the merger doctrine, if an examination of the content of the expression reveals that the idea expressed is only capable of being expressed in one or a limited number of ways, the expression will not attract copyright protection.[86] For the purpose of establishing that the use amounts to infringement of the owner's copyright, it is then necessary to ascertain that the substance of the defendant's expression bears an objective 'substantial similarity' to the plaintiff's expression[87] and that the defendant has taken a quantitatively and qualitatively 'substantial part' of the plaintiff's copyrighted material.[88] As we saw in Chapter 6, it is also necessary to establish whether the taking fits into the fair dealing exceptions, which will depend on, among other things, the nature of the protected work, the particular use that was made of it, and the purpose that the use was intended to achieve.[89]

In all aspects of this inquiry it seems clear that, before a court can determine that a defendant's expression has taken the *form* of a use of the plaintiff's property, the court must have regard to the *content* of the expression at issue. Whether an expression assumes a copyrightable form, and whether a particular use constitutes an infringement of copyrighted material, are both questions whose answers require reference to the expression's content. In fact, more than that, one might say that the content of the expression *is* its form, for to call something 'copyright' or 'copyright infringement' is to attribute certain characteristics to the *content* of that expression. As such, it should not be possible to assert the form/content divide to justify the exclusion of expression from the section 2(b) guarantee on the basis that it infringes another's copyright.

This discussion only underscores the criticism I have already launched against the court's reliance upon physical and private property concepts. By failing to consider copyright as a discrete area of law that is not amenable to simple categorisation and analogy across parallel categories, the court discounts the unique characteristics of copyright regulation, misrecognises the nature of copyright and disregards its public purposes. Copyright is concerned not with a parcel of land, but with a communicative act; it is not about individual entitlement, but is rather a creature of public policy; it is not an objectifiable thing, but is instead the metaphorical 'thingification' of expression. It is hardly surprising that, having denied copyright its essential nature and purpose, the court in *Michelin* arrived at a conclusion that undermines the fundamental rationale for the copyright system – it silenced the parodic, transformative and critical use of a minimally original corporate logo.

7.3.3 *Ashdown* and *Eldred* Compared

While the Canadian *Michelin* case offers a powerful example of the capacity for owner-oriented, property-based reasoning to obscure the free expression implications of the copyright system, it is worth mentioning that comparable examples of this tendency – and the general inadequacy of copyright to accommodate free speech values – can be found in both the United Kingdom and the United States.

In Britain, the relationship between copyright law and freedom of expression was relatively unexplored until the recent 2001 case of *Ashdown v. Telegraph Group Ltd.*[90] The case involved the publication of a previously unpublished minute written by Paddy Ashdown, the then leader of the Liberal Democrats, documenting a secret meeting with the Prime Minister. Following Ashdown's resignation, he planned to publish his memoirs and presented parts of his diaries, including the minute, to several publishers on a confidential basis. The defendant newspaper, *The Telegraph*, was given a copy of the minute without Ashdown's knowledge, and later published an article that contained several verbatim quotations. Ashdown brought proceedings for copyright infringement, while *The Telegraph* invoked the fair dealing defence, the public interest defence and the right to freedom of expression under the Human Rights Act 1998 [HRA] and Article 10 of the European Convention of Human Rights [ECHR].

With the enactment of the HRA, freedom of expression made its first explicit appearance in the British legal landscape with the normative status of 'human right', and the *Ashdown* case represents the first judicial attempt to address the potential conflict between this human right and the copyright regime. Lord Phillips M.R. explicitly acknowledged the conflict: '[C]opyright is antithetical to freedom of expression. It prevents all, save the owner of the copyright, from expressing information in the form of the literary work protected by the copyright.'[91] As Michael Birnhack observes, the court of first instance had been unwilling to entertain the idea of an external conflict between the two regimes, instead internalising the conflict within the copyright regime, deferring to the balance struck by the legislature in the copyright legislation.[92] The Court of Appeal, in contrast, recognised that the internal mechanisms of copyright may sometimes be insufficient to mitigate the conflict:

> [R]are circumstances can arise where the right of freedom of expression will come into conflict with the protection afforded by the Copyright Act, notwithstanding the express exceptions to be found in the Act. In these circumstances, we consider that the court is bound, insofar as it is able, to apply the Act in a manner that accommodates the right of freedom of expression. This will make it necessary for the court to look closely at the facts of individual cases (as indeed it must whenever a "fair dealing" defence is raised).[93]

This statement is important, first because it resists the assumption that copyright's internal limits ensure its compatibility with the right of free expression, and second, because it admits that the interpretation of copyright's doctrines should be guided by the HRA. Thus, for example, the court warned against applying inflexible tests to the assessment of fairness and stated that 'considerations of public interest are paramount.'[94] On the other hand, the Court of Appeal's interpretation of fair dealing and its application to the case at hand did little to confirm the significance of this statement. Indeed, as Birnhack claims, 'the court did not follow its own imperative of interpreting copyright law in light of the ECHR and freedom of expression.'[95] This case was found not to be one of those 'rare' ones in which the court should look beyond the copyright statute to freedom of expression principles; rather, the statutory fair dealing defence was considered perfectly adequate to resolve the dispute.[96]

Of particular note is the Court of Appeal's restrictive interpretation of fair dealing. While the court 'liberally' interpreted 'reporting current news' to include reporting events that had occurred two years previously, it refused to find that the purpose was for 'criticism or review' because 'the articles are not criticising or reviewing the minute; they are criticising or reviewing the actions of the Prime Minister and Mr Ashdown. It was not necessary for that purpose to copy the minute at all.'[97]

The court's analysis of the fairness of the dealing further perpetuated the narrow approach to fair dealing seen in earlier UK cases. For example, rather than examining the facts of the case in light of the free expression concerns implicated, the court placed significant emphasis on the fact that *The Telegraph*'s publication had 'destroyed' part of the (market) value of the memoirs, while the use of quotations by *The Telegraph* 'will have been of significant commercial value.'[98] Meanwhile, the broader purpose and effect of the publication as 'political speech' that conveyed information to the public went unheeded.[99]

In short, the *Ashdown* decision proved disappointing insofar as it failed to depart, in any meaningful way, from the traditionally restrictive application of fair dealing found in the British jurisprudence. Indeed, it was 'remarkably strict' in its consideration of fairness,[100] and focused 'exclusively on the actions and interests of the parties to the proceedings [without taking] account of the public interest in access to information protected under Article 10.'[101] Its emphasis on the commercial nature of the defendant's use evidences a preoccupation with unfair competition considerations beneath which freedom of expression principles appear to have faded from view. It is notable that the court began its analysis by identifying as pertinent the right to the protection of property and the peaceful enjoyment of possessions guaranteed by Article 1 of the ECHR's First Protocol, and then pointing to the explicit statement, in section 1(1) of the UK Copyright, Design and Patents Act 1988, that '[c]opyright is a property right'.[102] Birnhack notes that the intuition that copyright is property obscures the conflict between copyright and free expression.[103] As I have argued, when an inquiry into the legality of an unauthorised use begins with the premise that copyright is property like any other, that analysis is likely to conclude that the use is an unjustified encroachment onto that property. Ultimately, and unfortunately, the *Ashdown* case only confirms this assertion.

The most recent and authoritative statement on the interaction between copyright and the First Amendment in the United States is the Supreme Court's ruling in *Eldred v. Ashcroft*.[104] The case concerned a First Amendment challenge to the Copyright Term Extension Act of 1988, which extended copyright's term by 20 years, brought by archivists and publishers of public domain materials. The petitioners questioned the constitutional validity of the Act, arguing that it was a content-neutral speech regulation that did not advance important governmental interests; a retroactive term extension could not, after all, incentivise the creation of new works. As noted above, the lower courts in this case declared copyright to be categorically immune from First Amendment challenge, with the DC Circuit court explaining that 'the plaintiff's lack any cognizable first amendment right to exploit the copyrighted work of others.'[105] This decision, in substance and effect, closely aligned with the Canadian *Michelin* ruling.

At the Supreme Court, the plaintiff's free speech arguments fared only marginally better. The Court acknowledged that copyright was not immune from First Amendment challenge, but continued to regard copyright as largely beyond the scope of free speech concerns, with the majority insisting that '[t]he First Amendment securely protects the freedom to make – or decline to make – one's own speech; it bears less heavily when speakers assert the right to make other people's speeches.'[106] I have already criticised this argument as dependent on the unjustifiable importation of originality principles into free speech values. The Supreme Court also stated that, in light of the temporal proximity of the copyright clause and the First Amendment, 'in the Framers' view, copyright's limited monopolies are compatible with free speech principles.'[107] Apparently, this was considered a sufficient basis on which to assume such compatibility notwithstanding the remarkable expansion of these limited monopolies that has occurred since that time.[108] Without further examination of copyright's current scope or expanding term, the Court was able to conclude that copyright was an 'engine of free expression' with 'built-in First Amendment accommodations', [109] such that, in its traditional form, it is essentially, if not categorically, immune from any external constraints that the First Amendment may otherwise impose.[110]

As Netanel suggests, there is no sound basis for the Court's complacent certainty that copyright is compatible with free speech principles. Rather, 'the judicial immunization of traditional copyright from First Amendment scrutiny [which was largely perpetuated in *Eldred*] is a peculiar and pernicious anomaly.'[111] The anomalous treatment or privileged status of copyright in US constitutional jurisprudence implies an unwavering commitment to the premise that private control over expression ultimately encourages creativity and the dissemination of ideas. This mirrors a larger conviction that the protection of private property in a free marketplace will ultimately serve the interests of society as a whole. As I argued in Chapter 6 regarding the impoverishment of fair use, such reasoning allows the public purposes of copyright to be subsumed within the economic interests of the owner. Instead, as Netanel argues, courts should actively ensure, through their interpretation and application of copyright doctrine, that copyright in fact accommodates the principles of free speech.[112] Once again, however, this change in approach demands a fundamental shift in perspective along the lines that I have advocated. As Netanel explains: 'To remain cognizant of those principles requires . . . that copyright be understood and construed as a limited statutory requirement, not a Blackstonian property right.'[113]

7.4 UNDERSTANDING FREEDOM OF EXPRESSION

I have argued that the characterisation of copyright as a private property interest undermines the nature of copyrightable expression as a communicative act. In the discussion that follows, I briefly set out a view of freedom of expression that departs from the classical liberal vision of speech as an individual act, and instead values speech acts as communicative, relational and therefore formative of human society and individuality. With this constitutive theory of speech in mind, I refer back to the relational theory of copyright described in Chapter 3, which emphasises the maximisation of communicative activity between members of society. My aim in this chapter is to illuminate the essential congruity of these spheres of law once our vision shifts from the individual rights-bearer to the social/relational self. To the extent that we accept a justification of the copyright system based on society's interest in the production and dissemination of artistic, literary, musical and dramatic works, the coherence of the copyright system demands a departure from the individual rights-based analysis. In its place we need this community-based perspective, which is capable of recognising copyright's communicative function and the social values that it embodies. In setting out my understanding of the freedom of expression ideal, then, my purpose here is ultimately to show how this ideal is capable of embracing a copyright system built around public interest considerations and social goals, but not one premised upon concepts of private property and individual entitlement.

7.4.1 Expression as Communication

While free speech ostensibly protects only the right of the individual to speak and write, its obvious essence is the right of the public to hear and to read, the right to public access. The threat of censorship is directed not to the speech or writing of the individual, but to the dissemination of the speech or writing to the public. The individual's guaranteed right to speak and to write would be of little value either to the public or to the individual if this right did not include the right to be heard and to be read. The right of free speech, in other words, is not merely a public right; it is a right of the public.[114]

The 'expression' with which we are concerned in the constitutional inquiry, is expression intended to convey meaning, or to *communicate* a message from a speaker to an audience. As Gavin Anderson has explained, 'acts of expression are not singular but involve simultaneous and reciprocal acts of speaking and listening' – a view which belies the 'essentially linear' liberal account of expression that emphasises 'independent individual acts of speech' separately undertaken by either the speaker or the listener.[115] The common approach to freedom of expression is to frame it as a negative right vested in the individual and explained in terms of individual autonomy. However, this vision of free expression fails to account for precisely that which lends the greatest weight to the right: the communicative nature of the expressive act. Communication is a richer concept than simply the freedom to express oneself without external interference. The right to free speech is eviscerated if it does not account for the receipt of the message conveyed. The right to say whatever one chooses while alone and behind closed doors does not encapsulate the ideals of freedom of expression nor reflect its social and political importance. This is because the value of expression 'lies in creating the opportunity for individuals to engage in meaningful relationship of communication.'[116] To appreciate the significance of freedom of expression therefore requires appreciation of the nature and value of communicative activity. Expression is important because it communicates, and communication – the act of intentionally making and conveying a representation to someone[117] – assumes both a source and a recipient. This may appear self-evident, but the impact of this statement lies in the social nature of the expressive act that this perspective reveals.

In order to grasp the significance of communication as a human activity, it is necessary to transcend liberalism's concentration on the individual subject as the appropriate unit of analysis. Communication is an instance of social interaction that can be adequately understood only as essentially relational. Put another way, it can be said that expressive activity as encapsulated in the ideals of freedom of expression is an inherently social activity. An awareness of what it means for individuals to belong to a society is therefore essential to any satisfactory analysis of freedom of expression principles. The atomistic individual cannot be the instance through which expression is understood, for understanding the significance of freedom of expression means understanding that the individual is formed by the society in which she exists, and that the individual's interaction with others is in turn formative of that society.[118]

The key to understanding the value of communication is in recognising the relevance of 'public connectedness.' As C.B. Macpherson writes: 'Human society is the medium through which human capacities are developed. A society of some kind is a necessary condition of the development of human capacities.'[119] By understanding human society as constitutive of the individual, it is possible to see the importance of communication between members of society as crucial to the formation of the human self: '*speech* [is] the activity by which we gain a kind of explicit self-aware consciousness of things which as such is always related to an unreflective experience which precedes it and which it illuminates and hence transforms.'[120] As such, it should be clear that our ideological vision of the individual agent is critical to the normative version of free expression that we advance:

> First, following from the view that the world consists of socially constructed beings, [the constitutive theory of speech] sees speech and language as relational. . . . Second, . . . speech is not transparent but both shapes the world into which we are born and is the means whereby we can change the shape of that world ourselves.[121]

Bringing together these statements, from the ontological perspective of social constructionism flows a commitment to the public goods and values that express the interdependent aspects of human existence. What follows is a commitment to communication as a public good, which reveals the value that we place in speech as both an expression of our independent selves and an example of our innate inter-connectedness. Viewed in this way, our commitment to freedom of expression is not value-neutral, as Rawls's primary good theory might have us believe. As we saw in Chapter 3, the ostensible meta-ethics of liberalism have been widely criticised for their inability to capture and embrace the notion of the situated self. When the human subject is thus misrecognised, freedom of expression is explained in terms that purport to transcend notions of communal values or social good, but individualistic explanations are inadequate: the value that we attach to freedom of expression is grounded in the recognition that the good of the individual is bound together with the community, and that expression is the way in which we interact with others, participate in social goods and develop our human capacities.[122] Relationships of communication are foundational to the autonomous agency that classical liberalism assumes but misunderstands:[123] 'Communication is the way we interact with others and so participate in social goods such as knowledge, friendship and self-government. As well, through communication the human capacities we value such as thought and feeling are developed.'[124]

7.4.2 Communication and Community

When we ascribe rights, we are in effect ascribing a value to a particular human capacity and implicitly asserting that we should foster and nurture this capacity in ourselves and the other members of our society.[125] If a certain kind of society is required in order to foster these human activities and capacities, the value we place in them entails the normative conclusion that we ought to create the conditions necessary to obtain and sustain this kind of society.

At the root of the liberal explanation for free expression is the assumption that only a system protecting an individual's right to speak freely could 'comport with the premise of individual dignity and choice upon which our political system rests.'[126] This explanation reflects the 'dignitarian paradigm', which sees the role of free expression as the fundamental basis of human dignity, of individual autonomy. Also present in this explanation is the 'instrumental paradigm', which posits the individual's right to speak freely as fundamental to liberal democracy.[127] When we understand freedom of expression from the starting point of community, it is apparent that the dignitarian paradigm relies on a restrictive conception of personhood and autonomy.[128] However, upholding the autonomy of the speaker in itself relies upon a moral idea about an individual; implicit in the dignitarian paradigm is an appreciation of the value of expressive activity in the development of true personal autonomy. As Richard Moon explains: 'Freedom of expression is central to self-realization and autonomy because individual identity, thought, and feeling emerge in the social realm.'[129] Similarly, because the implications of the instrumental or democratic paradigm extend beyond political expression, this explanatory framework, which is premised upon representative government, implies a focus upon personal development and the capacity for choice, judgment and reflective dialogue. The capacity of choice is not a given, but a potential that has to be developed, and our society must be conducive to that development.[130] Freedom of expression therefore has an undeniable moral significance because, however it is characterised, the existence of the right *implies* the conception of the good that we attach to communication, open discussion and social intercourse.[131]

Both democracy and autonomy are concepts that presuppose values that our society shares: values that we attach to developed or acquired (as opposed to inherent or pre-social) human capacities. The concern motivating the principles of free expression is the need to encourage and protect social interaction. Its normative significance resides in its recognition of the interdependence of the human self in the realisation of human qualities. The value that we attach to freedom of expression is therefore grounded in the recognition that 'human autonomy/agency is deeply social in its creation and expression', and that 'human judgment, reason, feeling, and identity are realised in communicative interaction with friends, family, co-workers, and other members of the community.'[132] From the value we place in such human capacities, together with the reality of the individual's social embeddedness, can be seen the need to encourage communication, reflexive and deliberative dialogue within the community.

7.4.3 Drawing the Connection Between Free Expression and Copyright

The human self can only achieve the identity of autonomous agent in the context of a culture that encourages communication and interaction between its members. However, as Charles Taylor explains, the facets of culture necessary to provide this encouragement do not come into existence spontaneously:

> They are carried on in institutions which require stability and continuity and frequently also support from society as a whole – almost always the moral support of being commonly recognised as important but frequently also considerable material support. These bearers of our culture include museums, symphony orchestras, universities, laboratories, . . . newspapers, publishing houses, television stations, and so on.[133]

Producers and distributors of cultural and intellectual expressions make important contributions to social discourse. Free speech, which affirms the value we attach to communication and social interaction, must therefore embrace artistic and cultural expression: the subject matter of copyright. Taylor's statement enables us to see that, in order to create and maintain a society conducive to this form of communication, we will be required to create and maintain societal institutions that open the channels of such communication. Herein lies the explanation for the copyright system: as I have described it, copyright is an institution whose existence and maintenance encourages the kinds of communicative activity that lie at the heart of the rationale for freedom of expression, and so at the heart of a culture and society that aims to further the capacities of the human self that we most value.

As I have argued, the self is always-already situated in a cultural world and within a network of social relations. Language and literature, websites and social media platforms, music and art, dance and theatre, films and television programmes are all aspects of the cultural world in which we exist. The principle of freedom of expression, analysed in light of our society's cultural values, affirms our commitment to social interaction and communication between members of our society, and recognises that this expressive activity is fundamental to our own development and self-fulfilment. The copyright system should be regarded as one means by which we seek to ensure this cultural exchange. By providing the 'bearers of our culture' with sufficient support to ensure the creation and exchange of meaning, ideas and knowledge, the economic and other incentives that copyright offers are meant to encourage a participatory and interactive society, and to further the social goods that flow through public dialogue. This is the key to the reimagination of copyright described in Part I of this book. Copyright's purpose is to create opportunities for people to speak – developing relationships of communication between the author and the audience – and to fashion conditions that might cultivate a higher quality of expression. Its goal is therefore premised upon an appreciation of communication as relational, constitutive and vital to our personal and social development.

It should by now be clear that the ideal of communication underlying the right to free expression is the same as that which informs the right to copyright protection. The goal of maximising channels of communication lies at the heart of both, and only by recognising the value of communication as social interaction can we hope to provide a satisfactory rationale for either. It follows that both copyright and freedom of expression demand recognition of the relational self and the importance of cultural dialogue if they are to be fully understood and sufficiently valued. It is an understanding of the importance of cultural dialogue and social interaction – fundamentally grounded in recognition of the human self as inter-subjective and socially constituted – that causes us to guarantee the right of free expression, and that informs our development, design and maintenance of the institution of copyright.

7.5 CONCLUSIONS: ON THE NATURE OF COPYRIGHT AND COMMUNICATION

I have argued that the *Michelin* judgment radically misconstrued the nature and purpose of copyright law and, as a result, arrived at a flawed conclusion about the relationship between the Copyright Act and the guarantee of freedom of expression found in section 2(b) of the Canadian Charter of Rights and Freedoms. The root of the problem was the court's untenable analogy between copyright interests in original expression and the private property rights that attach to objects in the physical world. By invoking the private property analogue, the court was able to avoid the complexities that necessarily result from acknowledging the distinct nature and character of the copyright interest. A finding that the Copyright Act restricts speech (as opposed to protecting property) would have entailed a struggle to account for the democratic justifiability of the Copyright Act. Proprietary reasoning provided a simpler route towards disposition of the case. But when the court rejected all of the distinctions the defendants sought to draw between copyright and traditional private property rights, it did a great disservice not only to the defendants in the case, but also to the public, and so to the copyright system itself.

Even leaving aside the democratic norms of political and social representation at issue in this case, it is clear that the defendants' use of the plaintiff's copyrighted logo was a communicative act intended to convey meaning, and so an act that *prima facie* falls within the scope of the free expression right. Indeed, the *Michelin* court correctly conceded that this use constituted an expressive act. Furthermore, notwithstanding the use of a substantial part of the Bibendum character, the defendants' depiction of Bibendum contributed something to the public understanding, generating new meaning by recontextualising a powerful communicative symbol, expressing it anew and with a radically different message. In doing so, the defendants' use of the plaintiff's copyrighted logo furthered the public purpose of copyright protection in the creation and exchange of expressive works. The copyrighted logo was adopted and adapted to mount a social critique; this critique contributed to the cultural and political dialogue and diversification of ideas that lie at the heart of copyright's public purpose and the freedom of expression guarantee. The court should, therefore, have relied on a broad and contextual interpretation of fair dealing to find that the defendant's use of the protected work was non-infringing. By silencing the critique, the court silenced precisely the kind of interactive communication and dialogic response that copyright law is supposed to encourage. The fact that the court's conclusion was inconsistent with the principles and purposes of copyright protection underscores the deficiency of the interpretive metaphors employed by the court in reaching its conclusion.

Relying upon the premise that copyright is a form of private property, the court in *Michelin* concluded that copyrighted works cannot be used in the exercise of one's right to free expression regardless of the extent to which one's use is consistent with the purposes and principles embraced by section 2(b). I have argued that freedom of expression and copyright are both affirmations of the value our society places in relationships of communication. Based on that proposition, my argument is that the court's conclusion in itself reveals the flawed nature of its premise.

If characterising copyright as private property pits the copyright system against freedom of expression, then we should avoid this characterisation. Because the copyright system is concerned with maximising the flow of meaning through cultural communication, copyright's very coherence is dependent upon its congruence with the principles of freedom of expression. As such, conceptualising the copyright system as inherently in conflict with freedom of expression (such that it simply overrides free speech concerns) undermines copyright's own rationale and threatens its internal coherence. Of course, the intrinsic paradox of copyright has always been that it restricts participation in cultural and social dialogue in order to encourage cultural production and dissemination; in other words, it must limit communication in the name of encouraging communicative activities.[134] We are told (and many of us trust) that, in doing so, the system provides very real encouragement for the development and dissemination of ideas. However, when it limits communication in the name of individual rights, and chills expression rather than cultivating it, the copyright system simply restricts participation in cultural dialogue without providing the concomitant benefit that may justify this restriction. To conclude that copyright, in effect, *trumps* free expression is thus to deprive copyright of its justification, and to render incoherent a public interest based theory of copyright law.[135]

Interdependence is the central fact of social and cultural life and the precondition for true individual autonomy.[136] By recognising the interconnectedness of the self, our attention must turn away from liberal 'rights as limits', and towards a concern with structuring relationships within society, and creating and maintaining social institutions that make the development of certain values possible.[137] Understanding rights as the metaphorical embodiment of common values forces us to examine those values and to assess the kinds of relationships, institutions and concepts that will foster them. It has been my argument that both copyright and freedom of expression embody the values that we as a society attach to communication and discursive interaction between the members of our community. Such interaction is recognised as essential to the achievement of democracy and autonomy in any real sense. Both copyright and freedom of expression therefore represent our attempt to structure the relations between members of society – whether speakers, listeners, authors, audiences or users – in furtherance of our communication ideal.

The fact that copyright and freedom of expression are presently characterised as conflicting ideals only illustrates that, if we are to foster the communicative activities we value, we need to move beyond the individualistic assumptions that currently inform our understanding. We need to transcend the liberal project whose aim is always, ultimately, the reconciliation of individual competing rights, for this entirely fails to grasp the relevance and importance of these rights, and their fundamental congruity as embodiments of the same social values. By focusing instead upon the nature of communication as a community-based and relational act, it might be possible to attain a level of analysis wherein '[t]he human interactions to be governed are not seen primarily in terms of the clashing of rights and interests, but in terms of the way patterns of relationship can develop and sustain . . . an enriching collective life'.[138]

The *Michelin* approach to copyright and freedom of expression relies upon the notion of individual property rights as trumps to democratic outcomes. At best, this approach is wholly unhelpful when it comes to realising the social goals at issue; it obfuscates the interests at stake, closing down all debate about the values implicated and the policy objectives sought.[139] Ultimately, this means that claims to copyright as a private proprietary right are separated from, and defined in contradistinction to, the social purposes that underpin that right. When defined in opposition to the social purposes of free expression, copyright loses its coherence and hence its legitimacy. If the private property rights conferred in the name of copyright contradict the values underlying free expression, they also work against the values that underlie copyright: the copyright system then fails on its own terms. If copyright is to be justifiable as a legitimate limitation upon expression that furthers the public interest in the creation of intellectual products, then the characterisation of copyright as private property is an obstacle to that end.

The legitimacy of the copyright system is dependent upon the coincidence of the public interest in the maximum generation and exchange of knowledge with the interests of authors in the protection of copyright. Essentially, the copyright system must stand or fall as an institution that is able to maximise social communication and cultural interaction. As a legal and social institution, copyright plays a significant role in determining our access to and participation in cultural dialogue – increasingly so in a digital age in which technological advances continue to improve potential for free and unrestrained access and dissemination of works, as well as lowering the costs traditionally associated with the production of meaning. A system that establishes exclusive rights to control communicative expression is justifiable only to the extent that it increases opportunities for qualitative cultural production and exchange, ultimately furthering our communication ideals and so advancing the social good.

From this perspective, the copyright holder's interest and the social good are mutually dependent and so entirely compatible; they do not present conflicting ends requiring division, balance or compromise through the means of individual rights and in light of individualised goals. However, where the enforcement of a particular copyright interest in a certain context threatens to undermine the larger public interest in encouraging participation in cultural dialogue, it is the public interest that should decide the day: the copyright owner's rights find their justification in that public interest, and so they should not be enforced in spite of it.

It follows that the expansion of copyright should be confined by the principles of free expression, while courts should be willing to subject copyright law to constitutional scrutiny and should consistently apply copyright's doctrines with a view to those principles. Amongst other things, this would entail the kinds of doctrinal modifications that I have proposed in preceding chapters: a relational and contextual approach to originality and infringement determinations (as such determinations would have to be made with regard to the expressive value of the allegedly infringing work); an expansive and flexible approach to fair dealing determinations (as works that contribute new meaning or otherwise further the social values underlying free expression ought to be beyond the scope of the copyright owner's control); and a restrictive approach to the protection of technical controls (as anti-circumvention laws restrict access to public domain materials, information and ideas, as well as unduly limiting the uses that can be made of protected expression).[140] The much needed incorporation of free expression principles in the development and application of copyright law would thereby ensure that copyright furthers its own public purposes.

Part III of this book has explored the limits of copyright protection and the freedom of the public to use protected works as part of their own contribution to cultural dialogue. I have argued that an author-oriented approach to copyright policy, combined with a proprietary understanding of the copyright interest, extends the scope of copyright protection and undermines the importance of exceptions and limitations thereto. If we are to give due weight to copyright's limited nature, then we have to resist the possessive individualism that pervades traditional copyright theorising, and re-imagine the copyright model in relational terms. Only by giving sufficient consideration to the public interest that underlies copyright, and by recognising the social values that provide its foundation, can we appreciate the limited nature of the copyright interest, and the room it must leave for the ongoing generation and exchange of meaning.

NOTES

1. Melville Nimmer, 'Does Copyright Abridge the First Amendment Guarantees of Free Speech and Press?' (1970) 17 UCLA L. Rev. 1180 at 1181.
2. Jerome Frank, *Law and the Modern Mind* (New York: Coward-McCann, 1949) at 30, cited in Ibid. at 1180.
3. Frank, Ibid, cited in Nimmer, note 1 above at 1181: '[We] maintain, side by side as it were, beliefs which are inherently incompatible. . . . We seem to keep these antagonistic beliefs apart by putting them in "logic-tight compartments."' Nimmer goes on to note: 'Nowhere is this phenomenon better illustrated than in the . . . failure to perceive that views of copyright and the first amendment, held "side by side" may, in fact, be contradictory.'
4. *Eldred v. Reno*, 239 F.3d 372 (US Ct of Apps (D.C. Cir.), 2001) at 375 [*Eldred* (DC Cir.)]; rhrg denied, 255 F.3d 849 (D.C. Cir. 2001).
5. Part I of the Constitution Act 1982, being Sch. B to the Canada Act 1982 (UK) 1982, c.11 [*Charter*].
6. R.S.C. 1985, c.42 [Copyright Act]
7. (1996), 71 C.P.R. (3d) 348 (F.C.T.D.). [*Michelin*].
8. Sunny Handa, *Copyright Law in Canada,* (Markham, Ont.: Butterworths, 2002) at 95.
9. *Cf. In re Aimster Copyright Litig.* 334 F 3d 643 (7th Cir, 2003) at 656, Posner J.: 'Copyright law and the principles of equitable relief are quite complicated enough without the superimposition of First Amendment case law on them.'
10. This argument is addressed from a Canadian perspective by Ysolde Gendreau, 'Copyright and Freedom of Expression in Canada' in Paul Torremans (ed.), *Copyright and Human Rights* (Netherlands: Kluwer Law International, 2004) 21.
11. *Cf.* Neil Netanel *Copyright's Paradox* (Oxford University Press, Inc., New York: 2008) [Netanel, *Paradox*], making this argument in the US context.
12. This is the description of copyright employed by David Fewer in his discussion of 'the expression paradox,' in his article, 'Constitutionalizing Copyright: Freedom of Expression and the Limits of Copyright in Canada' (1997) 55 U. of T. Fac. of L. Rev. 175 at 177.
13. Netanel, *Paradox*, note 11 above at 37.
14. Note 5 above, s. 2(b).
15. *Switzman v. Elbing* [1957] S.C.R. 285 at 369, Rand J.
16. Alexander Meiklejohn, *Political Freedom: The Constitutional Powers of the People* (New York: Oxford University Press, 1965). See also, Alexander Meiklejohn, 'The First Amendment is an Absolute' (1961) Sup. Ct. Rev. 245 at 255–7.

17. Rand J. also articulated a powerful democratic interpretation of free expression principles in *Saumar v. The City of Quebec* [1953] 2 S.C.R. 299 at 330: '[G]overnment rest[s] ultimately on public opinion reached by discussion and the interplay of ideas. If that discussion is placed under licence, its basic condition is destroyed: the government as licensor becomes disjoined from the citizenry'.
18. Ibid.
19. See John Stuart Mill, *On Liberty* (Harmondsworth, UK: Penguin, 1982). In the case of *Red Lion Broadcasting Co. v. FCC*, 395 U.S. 367 (1969) at 390, the US Supreme Court rationalised free speech as the means by which to 'preserve an uninhibited marketplace of ideas in which truth will ultimately prevail'. This principle alone, however, cannot explain the protection accorded to fraudulent statements that only hinder the 'search for truth'; in *R. v. Lucas* [1998] 1 S.C.R. 439, the Supreme Court of Canada confirmed that deliberate falsehoods were protected by section 2(b) of the *Charter*.
20. See John Rawls, *A Theory of Justice* (Cambridge, MA: Belknap Press, 1971). For an interesting discussion of this and other manifestations of the argument from autonomy, see Richard Moon, 'The Scope of Freedom of Expression' (1985) 23 Osgoode Hall L.J. 331 at 340–46 [Moon, 'Freedom of Expression']. Moon asserts that a general right to free speech advances one conception of the good life and constrains others, favouring speech over silence, interaction over isolation. The protection of freedom of expression thus 'favours those conceptions of the good that involve communication, open discussion and social intercourse' (Ibid. at 344).
21. [1989] 1 S.C.R. 927 [*Irwin Toy*].
22. Ibid. at 976. See also, *RWDSU v. Dolphin Delivery* [1986] 2 S.C.R. 573 at 583–6; *R. v. Keegstra* [1990] 3 S.C.R. 697, 727–8 at 827–8 [*Keegstra*].
23. Peter Hogg, *Constitutional Law of Canada*, 4th edn, looseleaf (Scarborough, Ont.: Carswell, 1997) at 40–49.
24. Note 22 above at 968.
25. Moon argues, in 'Freedom of Expression', note 20 above at 351, that, although all acts may convey information and be 'expressive' of the actor's thoughts or feelings, not all acts are intended to communicate something; the *point* of an act meant to convey meaning, is communication, and so simply striking someone with a fist, the point of which is to injure or physically harm that person, is not an act intended to convey meaning protected under section 2(b).
26. Hogg, note 23 above at 40–49.
27. US Const. amend. I. [First Amendment]
28. [1986] 1 S.C.R. 103.
29. Ibid. at 138–39; Hogg, note 23 above at 35-16–35-17.
30. Hogg, Ibid., at 35-17.
31. L. Ray Patterson, 'Free Speech, Copyright and Fair Use' (1987) 40 Vand. L. Rev. 1 at 57 [Patterson, 'Free Speech']. Regarding the failure of the court in *Pacific and Southern Co. v. Duncan*, 744 F.2d 1490 (11th Cir. 1984) to accord any weight to the free speech issues, Patterson explains: 'the court's disregard for the copyright clause indicates the mesmeric effect that the notion of copyright as property has'.
32. *The Queen v. James Lorimer* (1984), 77 C.P.R. (2d) 262 (F.C.A.) [*Lorimer*].
33. Ibid. at 273.
34. It is widely agreed that, if copyright were to protect ideas and not merely their expression, the freedom of speech concerns surrounding copyright would be far greater. See e.g. Nimmer, note 1 above at 1189: 'If [copyright] did [protect an author's ideas *per se*], there would certainly be a serious encroachment upon first amendment values. The market place of ideas would be utterly bereft and the democratic dialogue largely stifled if the only ideas which might be discussed were those original with the speakers.' In finding that copyright law strikes an appropriate balance with the First Amendment, Nimmer notes: 'It is exposure to ideas, and not to their particular expression, that is vital if self-governing people are to make informed decisions.' Ibid. at 1191. But *cf.* Rebecca Tushnet, 'Copyright as a Model for Free Speech Law:

What Copyright Has in Common with Anti-Pornography Laws, Campaign Finance Reform, and Telecommunications Regulation' (2002) 42 Bost. Coll. L. Rev. 1 at 7–11 [Tushnet, 'Copyright as a Model'], arguing that the idea/expression dichotomy does not eliminate copyright's free speech problems; if anything the centrality of this problematic distinction makes copyright even less supportable.

35. The assumption was that the defendant's use of the copyrighted material demonstrated insufficient original thought to be labelled protected expression under section 2(b). A similar position was taken in the case of *Canadian Tire Corp. Ltd v. Retail Clerks Union, Local 1518 of the United Food and Commercial Workers Union* (1985), 7 C.P.R. (3d) 415 (FCTD).
36. (1983), 70 C.P.R. (2d) 61 (FCTD).
37. Ibid. at 67.
38. Fewer, note 12 above at 208: 'To date the Canadian courts have been dismissive of freedom of expression claims in the context of copyright infringement. . . . Under the *Irwin Toy* test, future Canadian courts may well be barred from treating those claims in such summary fashion.' Fewer was including in his critique: *Rotisseries St-Hubert Ltée v. Le Syndicat des Travailleurs (Euses) de la Rotisserie St-Hubert de Drummondville (C.S.N.)* (1986), 17 C.P.R. (3d) 461 (Qc. S. C.), where use of a corporate logo in a parody for the purpose of picketing was held to infringe copyright in the logo; *R. v. Ghnaim* (1988), 23 C.I.P.R. 102, where criminal infringement of copyright in pornographic tapes did not fall within the scope of section 2(b); *Ludlow Music Inc. v. Canint Corp. Ltd* (1967), 62 D.L.R. (2d) 200 (Ex. Ct.), where an injunction was issued to restrain the sale of a song parody; and *ATV Music Publishing v. Ro Radio Broadcasting* (1982), 65 C.P.R. (2d) 109 (Ont. H.C.), where a song parody was found to infringe copyright in the original work.
39. *Michelin,* note 7 above.
40. Gendreau, note 10 above at 33.
41. See, e.g. *Fraser Health Authority v. Hospital Employees' Union* (2003), 226 D.L.R. (4th) 563 (B.C.S.C.) at para. 49; *British Columbia Automobile Assn. v. Office and Professional Employees' International Union Local 378* (2001), 10 C.P.R. (4th) 423.
42. In *CCH Canadian Ltd v. The Law Society of Upper Canada* [2002] 4 F.C. 213, (2002) 212 D.L.R. (4th) 385 (C.A.) at pars 144 and 148, the Federal Court of Appeal cited *Michelin* with approval in the context of its fair dealing analysis.
43. In *Théberge v. Galerie d'Art du Petit Champlain, Inc.* [2002] S.C.J. No. 32 at pars 46, 73 and 142, the Supreme Court of Canada cited *Michelin* several times, approving its treatment of the 'reproduction of a substantial part' infringement issue.
44. *CCH Canadian Ltd v. Law Society of Upper Canada* [2004] 1 S.C.R. 339 [*CCH* (SCC)]. The Court insisted on 'a large and liberal interpretation [of "research"] in order to ensure that users' rights are not unduly constrained.' Ibid. at para. 51; discussed in Chapter 6 above.
45. *Canwest Mediaworks Publications Inc. v. Horizon Publications Ltd,* 2008 BCSC 1609 at para. 14.
46. The leaflet depicted the worker saying 'Bob, you better move before he squashes you.' The worker in imminent danger under Bibendum's boot is saying, 'Nah, I'm going to wait and see what happens.' Underneath, the bold print reads: 'Don't wait until it's too late! Because the job you save may be your own. Sign today for a better tomorrow.'
47. *Michelin,* note 7 above at para. 77.
48. See L. R. Patterson, *Copyright in Historical Perspective* (Nashville: Vanderbilt Press, 1968), c. 6 at 114–42.
49. The court acknowledged that 'the use of a copyright by a union to parody a company logo in the midst of an organizing campaign does raise certain constitutional issues.', note 7 above at para. 79. But note how the court limits the democratic value of the defendant's expression by reference to the boundaries of intellectual property: '[T]here was certainly a link between the Defendant's leaflets and brochures *that did not depict*

the Bibendum and the value of expression enhancing participation in social and political decision-making. However, one should not confuse the entirely socially acceptable and legitimate overarching goal of the defendants' unionization activity with their inappropriate and unprotected means of expression under paragraph 2(b).' Ibid. at para. 98 [emphasis added].

50. Ibid. at para. 79.
51. Ibid.: 'Even though the defendants' leaflets represent a substantial reproduction of the plaintiff's "Bibendum" copyright and are not "original works" for the purposes of section 3 of the Copyright Act, they are still examples of expression.'
52. The court was invoking the judgement of Linden J. in *Weisfeld v. Canada* [1995] 1 F.C. 68 (C.A.), which stated that, having determined that something is 'expression', the court must also determine whether there are any special circumstances that would remove that expression from the protected sphere. One possible circumstance is the particular form that the expression takes.
53. (1991), 77 D.L.R. (4th) 385 (S.C.C.) [*Committee for the Commonwealth*].
54. Lamer C.J.C., Sopinka and Cory JJ. supported the compatibility test; La Forest and Gonthier JJ. concurred with McLachlin J.'s 'definitional' approach, which also accepted the role of justificatory considerations as informing the scope of the freedom of expression guarantee. See B. Jamie Cameron, 'A Bumpy Landing: The Supreme Court of Canada and Access to Public Airports Under Section 2(b) of the Charter' (1991) 2 Med. and Comm. L. Rev. 91; Michael Kanter, 'Balancing Rights Under Section 2(b) of the Charter: Case Comment on *Committee for the Commonwealth of Canada v. Canada*' (1992) 17 Queen's L.J. 489.
55. *Committee for the Commonwealth*, note 53 above at 395. Cameron, Ibid. at 97–9, criticises Lamer C.J.'s standard as essentially importing an American interpretation of the First Amendment, which was designed to compensate for the lack of a limitations clause in the US Constitution, into section 2(b) of the Charter: any assessment of compatibility should be based on justificatory considerations properly reserved for the Charter's section 1 balancing clause.
56. *Michelin*, note 7 above at para. 106.
57. Ibid.
58. Ibid.
59. Ibid. at para. 109.
60. For a discussion of the potential justifiability of the Copyright Act under section 1 of the Charter, see Jane Bailey, 'Deflating the *Michelin* Man: Protecting Users' Rights in the Canadian Copyright Reform Process' in Michael Geist (ed.), *In the Public Interest: The Future of Canadian Copyright Law* (Toronto: Irwin Law, 2005) 125 [Bailey, 'Deflating the *Michelin* Man'] at 147–56. Bailey rightly concludes, at 156: 'the Act as currently structured cannot be assumed to be consistent with freedom of expression, and . . . the justifiability of the violation is by no means a foregone conclusion – particularly in the digital networked context.'
61. *Michelin*, note 7 above at para. 109.
62. Ibid. at para. 109: 'There is a definite and efficient link between the goal of protecting the interests of authors and copyright holders by granting them a monopoly on the right to use and reproduce their works and the ability to enforce those interests in an action for copyright infringement.' The court was also satisfied that the 'minimum impairment' element of the *Oakes* test would be satisfied as a result of the 'very well-tailored structure of the Copyright Act with its list of exceptions.' Ibid. at para. 111. As I argued in Chapter 6 (and as exemplified by *Michelin*), the restrictiveness of these statutory exceptions does not permit them to further the public purposes of the copyright system. The court acknowledged copyright's role as a means by which to further the diversity of ideas (Ibid. at para. 104), but therefore assumed that the use of another's copyright *de facto* subverts the value of the promotion of ideas: '[I]f copyright is not respected and protected, the creative energies of authors and artists in furthering the diversity of ideas will not be adequately compensated or recognized.' Ibid. at para. 98.

63. *Théberge*, note 43 above at para. 30.
64. *Michelin*, note 7 above at para. 103.
65. Ibid.
66. See Immanuel Kant, 'On the Wrongfulness of Unauthorized Publication of Books' in *Practical Philosophy*, trans. and ed. Mary J. Gregor (Cambridge: Cambridge University Press, 1996).
67. *Michelin*, note 7 above at para. 106.
68. See Ibid. at para. 96: 'The Defendants fought against the *usual characterisation of copyright as private property*' and 'sought to *diminish the "private" nature* of the Plaintiff's property rights.' Teitelbaum J. objected on the basis that, '[i]f one were to extend the Defendants' test of "state sanctioned private property" to its logical extreme, no one in Canada could properly say that his or her house was "private property" since houses are also registered under various province designed systems of land title!'
69. Ibid.
70. *Compo Co. Ltd v. Blue Crest Music et al.* (1979), 105 D.L.R. (3d) 249 at 251, Estey J.
71. See Bailey, 'Deflating the *Michelin* Man' note 60 above at 141: '[S]ince copyright exists in Canada only as a result of its statutory creation in the [Copyright] Act, the existence of any such property right is dependent upon the constitutional validity of the legislation purporting to grant it.'
72. See Ibid. at 141–2: 'The FCTD's analysis in *Michelin* subverts the principal of constitutional supremacy. . . . The decision presupposes an existing property right in copyright material against which incursions for purposes of exercising freedom of expression must be justified. . . . Thus, the *Michelin* conclusion that users must justify their expression *vis-à-vis* the copyright owner's intended use of the "property" mistakenly places the statutory property cart before the constitutional expression horse.'
73. *Cf.* James Boyle, 'The First Amendment and Cyberspace: The Clinton Years' (2000) 63 J.L. & Contemp. Problems 337 at 343: 'Property isn't speech regulation; it's definitional. Of course, Mr Sullivan said the same thing about libel law' (referring to *New York Times v. Sullivan*, 376 U.S. 254 (1964)). The *Sullivan* case offers an example of constitutional limits imposed on legal doctrines that attempt to regulate expression. Boyle queries the constitutional exceptionalism around intellectual property – why is its treatment is so anomalous? Ibid. at 345. The same question should be asked in Canada. In *R v. Lucas*, note 19 above, the Supreme Court of Canada held that the publication of defamatory libels was protected by section 2(b), although libel laws were held to be justifiable under section 1.
74. This phrase was used by Bruce Lehman, Commissioner of Patents, to dismiss free speech issues around the extension of copyright. Quoted in Jessica Litman, 'Reforming Information Law in Copyright's Image' (1997) 22 Dayton L. R. 587 at 588.
75. *Cf.* Mark A. Lemley, 'Property, Intellectual Property and Free-Riding' (2005) 83 Tex. L. Rev. 1031 at 1034–5: '"Intellectual property" is an appealing term for a variety of reasons . . . it promises a connection to the rich and venerable legal and academic tradition of property law. . . . As the term 'intellectual property' settles over the traditional legal disciplines of patents, copyrights, and trademarks . . . courts and scholars increasingly turn to the legal and economic literature of tangible property law to justify – or to modify – the rules of intellectual property.'
76. Patterson, 'Free Speech', note 31 above at 9.
77. *Cf.* Moon, 'Access to Public and Private Property Under Freedom of Expression' (1988) 20 Ottawa L. Rev. 339 at 344.
78. See L. Ray Patterson, 'Private Copyright and Public Communications: Free Speech Endangered' (1975) 28 Vand. L. Rev. 1161 at 1209 [Patterson, 'Private Copyright'], arguing that copyright should be treated as a series of rights to which a given work is subject, rather than a pure right of ownership in the work.
79. See *Irwin Toy*, note 21 above at 970: '[A] murderer or a rapist cannot invoke freedom

of expression in justification of the *form* of expression he has chosen.' *Cf. Keegstra*, note 22 above at 828: '[T]he *content* of a statement cannot deprive it of the protection accorded by section 2(b), no matter how offensive it may be.'

80. *Keegstra,* Ibid. at 732–3.
81. As Judge Learned Hand explained in *Nichols v. Universal Pictures Corp. et al.*, 45 F.2d 119 (2d Cir. 1930) at 122 [*Nichols*], when the playwright wrote her play, 'her copyright did not cover everything that might be drawn from her play; its content went to some extent into the public domain.' The divide between public domain and copyright-protected material is a divide *internal* to the protected work.
82. Copyright Act, note 6 above, s. 5(1). Whether or not something is 'literary' may, for example, depend upon whether it 'was intended to afford either information and instruction, or pleasure in the form of literary enjoyment': *Exxon Corp. v. Exxon Insurance Consultants Ltd* [1982] RPC 69 (C.A.). Whether a 'work of artistic craftsmanship' is protected may depend on whether it was intended to 'appeal to the aesthetic senses' (*Cuisenaire v. South West Imports Ltd* [1968] 1 Ex. C.R. 493 [*Cuisenaire*]) or if it the public gets pleasure from looking at it (*George Hensher Ltd v. Restawhile Upholstery (Lancs.) Ltd* [1975] R.P.C. 31 (H.L.)). Dramatic works may require 'some attempt at pretence or storyline or dramatic incident' (*Hutton v. Canadian Broadcasting Corp.* (1989), 29 C.P.R. (3d) 398 (Alta. Q.B.)), and they may be denied protection if they lack 'sufficient unity' (*Green v. Broadcasting Corp. of New Zealand* [1989] 2 All E.R. 1056 (P.C)) or predictability (*FWS Joint Sport Claimants v. Copyright Board* [1992] 1 F.C. 487 (C.A.)). Each of these qualifications involves an examination of the content – and not merely the form – of the work at issue.
83. Copyright Act, note 6 above, s. 5(1); *CCH (SCC)*, note 44 above at para. 16.
84. See e.g. *Nichols*, note 81 above; and in Canada, *Moreau v. St. Vincent* [1950] 3 D.L.R. 713 (Ex. Ct.).
85. The Supreme Court of Canada recently confirmed that copyright does not extend to facts: *CCH (SCC)*, note 44 above at para. 22. Regarding systems or methods of operation, see e.g. *Holinrake v. Truswell* [1894] 3 Ch. 420 (C.A.) (denying copyright in a sleeve-measuring chart) and *Cuisenaire*, note 82 above, (denying copyright to coloured rods for teaching mathematics). Stock characters and settings were denied copyright in *Preston v. 20th Century Fox* (1990) 33 C.P.R. (3d) 242 (FCTD).
86. See e.g. *Morrissey v. Procter & Gamble Co.* 379 F.2d 675 (1st Cir. 1967); and *Herbert Rosenthal Jewelry Corp. v. Kalpakian*, 446 F.2d 738 (9th Cir. 1971). The merger doctrine was recognised by the Ontario Court of Appeal as a 'natural corollary of the idea-expression dichotomy' in *Delrina Corp. (Carolian Systems) v. Triolet Systems Inc.* [2002] O.J. No. 3729; leave to appeal denied [2002] S.C.C.A. No. 189.
87. Substantial similarity does not require a simple or literal copy of the protected work, but may also include 'colourable imitation': *Boutin v. Bilodeau* (1994), 54 C.P.R. (3d) 160 (SCC); *Francis Day & Hunter Ltd and Another v. Bron and Another* [1963] 2 All E.R. 16 (C.A.).
88. Copyright Act, note 6 above, ss. 3(1), 27(1). Whether a substantial part of the work has been copied depends on the quality and quantity of the part taken in relation to the whole work, and in particular, whether a 'salient' or 'principal' features or an 'essential' part of the work has been copied: *King Features Syndicate Inc. v. O and M Kleeman Ltd* [1941] A.C. 417 (H.L.).
89. Copyright Act, note 6 above, ss 29–29.2. To determine whether copyright is infringed, courts must have regard to the purpose and manner in which the work was used; whether the use was for the purpose of private study or research, criticism or review, or news reporting; and whether the use was fair in light of the particular circumstances of the case. This determination involves an examination of the content of the work that has been taken, both in the context of the plaintiff's work and the defendant's work.
90. [2001] E.M.L.R. 44(CA) [*Ashdown* (CA)]
91. Ibid. at para. 30 (Lord Phillips M.R).

92. Michael D. Birnhack, 'Acknowledging the Conflict Between Copyright Law and Freedom of Expression under the Human Rights Act' (2003) 14 Ent. L.R. 24 at 32–3 [Birnhack, 'Acknowledging the Conflict']. See *Ashdown v. Telegraph Group Ltd* [2001] Ch. 685 at 694: 'I can see no reason why the court should travel outside the provisions of the CDPA and recognize on the facts of particular cases further or other exceptions to the restrictions on the exercise of the right to freedom of expression constituted by the CDPA'; See also Ibid. at 700: '[T]he Human Rights Act is not a reason for interpreting CDPA any differently.'
93. *Ashdown* (CA), note 90 above at para. 45.
94. Ibid. at para. 71. This reveals the potential significance of importing freedom of expression principles into doctrinal analyses such as that required by the fair dealing defence.
95. Birnhack, 'Acknowledging the Conflict' note 92 above at 33.
96. Jonathan Griffiths, 'Copyright Law After *Ashdown* – Time to Deal Fairly with the Public' (2002) 3 *Intellectual Property Quarterly* 240 at 247 [Griffiths, 'Ashdown'], citing *Ashdown* (CA), note 90 above at para. 66.
97. *Ashdown* (CA), Ibid. at para. 24.
98. Ibid. at para. 72.
99. See Birnhack, 'Acknowledging the Conflict', note 92 above at 33.
100. See Christina J. Angelopoulos 'Freedom of Expression and Copyright: The Double Balancing Act' (2008) 3 *Intellectual Property Quarterly* 328 at 343.
101. Griffiths, 'Ashdown', note 95 above at 256, quoted by Angelopoulos, Ibid.
102. *Ashdown* (CA), note 90 above at paras 25, 29.
103. Birnhack, 'Acknowledging the Conflict', note 92 above at 30.
104. 537 US 186 (2003) [*Eldred* (USSC)]
105. *Eldred* (DC Cir.), note 4 above at 376.
106. *Eldred* (USSC), note 104 above at 221, Ginsburg J.
107. Ibid. at 218.
108. See Netanel, *Paradox*, note 11 above.
109. *Eldred* (USSC), note 104 above at 219.
110. Ibid. at 221: '[W]hen, as in this case, Congress has not altered the traditional contours of copyright protection, further First Amendment scrutiny is unnecessary.'
111. Netanel, *Paradox*, note 11 above at 194.
112. The Supreme Court appears to have left room for this interpretative approach, stating: 'it is appropriate to construe copyright's internal safeguards to accommodate First Amendment concerns.' *Eldred* (USSC), note 104 above at 221, citing *United States v. X-Citement Video, Inc.*, 513 U.S. 64 (1994) at 78.
113. *Eldred* (USSC), Ibid. at 193.
114. Patterson, 'Private Copyright', note 78 above at 1204.
115. Gavin W. Anderson, 'Understanding Constitutional Speech: Two Theories of Expression' in Gavin W. Anderson (ed.), *Rights and Democracy: Essays in UK-Canadian Constitutionalism* (London: Blackstone Press, 1999) 49 at 58–9 [Anderson, 'Understanding'].
116. Ibid. at 59–60.
117. This is how 'communication' is described in Moon, 'Freedom of Expression', note 20 above at 348.
118. Viewed as such, the social character of free expression, and the social nature of communication more generally, are incompatible with the liberal conception of the self. As noted by Colin Farrelly, 'The Social Character of Freedom of Expression: A Critical Notice of R. Moon, *The Constitutional Protection of Freedom of Expression*' (2001) 14 Can. J.L. & Jur. 261 at para. 9, Moon's vision of the social character of free expression is therefore complemented by the communitarian critique of the liberal notion of the unencumbered self. See e.g. Michael Sandel, *Democracy's Discontent: America in Search of a Public Philosophy* (Cambridge, MA: Belknap Press of Harvard University Press, 1996).

119. C.B. Macpherson, *Democratic Theory: Essays in Retrieval* (Oxford: Clarendon Press, 1973) at 57; cited in Moon, 'Freedom of Expression', note 20 above at 346.
120. Charles Taylor, *Hegel and Modern Society* (Cambridge: Cambridge University Press, 1978) at 165 [Taylor, *Hegel*]; Moon, 'Freedom of Expression', note 20 above at 347–8.
121. Anderson, note 114 above at 60. This idea plugs into the notion of the dialogic power of utterance discussed in Chapter 3.
122. See Moon, 'Freedom of Expression', note 20 above at 348.
123. See Jennifer Nedelsky, 'Reconceiving Autonomy: Sources, Thoughts and Possibilities' (1989) 1 Yale J.L. & Fem. 7.
124. Moon, 'Freedom of Expression', note 20 above at 333.
125. Ibid. at 349. See also Nedelsky, 'Reconceiving Rights as Relationship' (1993) 1 Rev. Const. Stud. 1 [Nedelsky, 'Reconceiving Rights'].
126. *Cohen v. California*, 403 U.S. 15 (1971) at 24, cited in Leon E. Trakman, 'Transforming Free Speech: Rights and Responsibilities' (1995) 56 Ohio St. L.J. 899 at 903.
127. These terms are used and explained by Trakman, Ibid. at 903–10.
128. See Ibid. at 909. Moon also criticises the autonomy-based account for its assumption that 'rights, such as freedom of expression, are aspects of the autonomy that the individual retains when he or she enters the social world, and that should be insulated from the demands of collective welfare': in Moon, *The Constitutional Protection of Freedom of Expression*, (Toronto: University of Toronto Press, 2000) at 20–21 [Moon, *Constitutional Protection*].
129. Moon, Ibid. at 21. See also Moon, 'Freedom of Expression', note 20 above at 345–6, arguing that we can see the importance of freedom of expression for autonomy when we 'lift the concepts of autonomy and self-realization out of the individualist framework.'
130. Taylor, *Hegel*, note 119 above at 49.
131. Moon, 'Freedom of Expression', note 20 above at 344.
132. Moon, *Constitutional Protection*, note 128 above at 21. See also, Moon, 'Lifestyle Advertising and Classical Freedom of Expression Doctrine' (1991) 36 McGill L.J. 76 at 94.
133. Taylor, *Hegel*, note 119 above at 56.
134. See, e.g., Neil Weinstock Netanel, 'Copyright and a Democratic Civil Society' (1996) 106 Yale L.J. 283 at 293: 'While copyright may provide a necessary incentive, it does so at the cost of burdening whatever uses of copyrighted expression fall within the scope of the owner's copyright.' As such, '[c]opyright law's perennial dilemma is to determine where exclusive rights should end and unrestrained public access should begin.' Ibid. at 283. A comparison can be made between copyright law and other laws such as pornography and hate speech regulation, which appear on their face to limit expression but which ultimately function to enhance relations of communication. For an interesting discussion along these lines, see Tushnet, 'Copyright as a Model', note 34 above.
135. *Cf.* Laura S. Underkuffler, *The Idea of Property: Its Meaning and Power* (Oxford: Oxford University Press, 2003) at 75: 'Claimed rights *will (and should) not have presumptive power* over competing public interests when the core values that underlie the claimed right and the core values that underlie the competing public interest are *the same in kind*' [emphasis in original]. She cites the regulation of pornography as an example of a limit upon free speech in the name of free speech values (Ibid. at 78).
136. See Nedelsky, 'Reconceiving Rights', note 125 above at 8.
137. See Ibid. at 9–10.
138. Ibid. at 8.
139. Invocating individual rights shuts down this kind of discussion because the rights are formulated as 'reified images that dispel rather than invite inquiry.' Ibid. at 16.
140. *Cf.* Netanel, *Paradox*, note 11 above at 67–70, criticising the unduly speech-burdening scope of anti-circumvention laws in the Digital Millennium Copyright Act of 1998, and suggesting that they should not survive constitutional scrutiny even post-*Eldred*.

8. Final conclusions

> There is more than a verbal tie between the words common, community, and communication. Men live in a community in virtue of the things which they have in common; and communication is the way in which they come to possess things in common. What they must have in common . . . are aims, beliefs, aspirations, knowledge – a common understanding. . . . Such things cannot be passed physically from one to another like bricks; they cannot be shared as persons would share a pie by dividing it into physical pieces.[1]

This book has inquired into the connection between the concepts of community, communication, culture and copyright. Authors, users, owners, infringers, audiences and every member of the public are always-already situated selves, constituted by – and constituting themselves in relation to – the communities in which they exist, and the texts and discourses that they encounter. Communication (the construction, apprehension and utilisation of symbolic forms)[2] is fundamental to the social processes involved in developing and shaping communities and identities: it is through the interactive process of communication that we develop our relations with others, and our own identities in relation to the world. The concept of culture[3] describes the domain in which our realities are created, maintained and transformed through collective conversation.[4] The literary, dramatic, artistic and musical expressions that make up the subject matter of copyright law are central to this ongoing dialogic process.[5]

Copyright is therefore intrinsically linked to the communicative practices of our communities, and so intricately tied to the development of our society and ourselves. John Carey captures the significance of intellectual expression when he explains: '[T]he site where artists paint, writers write, speakers speak, filmmakers film, broadcasters broadcast is simultaneously the site of social conflict . . . over the simultaneous co-determination of ideas, technique, and social relations.'[6] Copyright law regulates our participation in the conversation of culture by granting exclusionary powers over the books, films, programmes, newspapers, songs, paintings and other texts wherein this conflict is waged. In Carey's terms, 'some get to speak and some to listen, some to write and some to read, some to film and some to view.'[7]

Communication and culture are fundamentally interactive and not unidirectional. Recognising the power that copyright wields in the regulation of communication thus presents a challenge for copyright theorists. As Rosemary Coombe explains:

> If, as human selves in human communities, we are constituted by and constitute ourselves with shared cultural symbols, then it is important that legal theorists consider the nature of the cultural symbols "we" "share" in consumer societies and the recognition the law affords them.[8]

Any thesis that purports to justify the copyright system must first acknowledge the truly constitutive role of intellectual works as symbolic forms that are shared in an ongoing social and dialogic process. It must then be able to justify the power that copyright gives over such works, and the suppression of other communicative activities that it necessarily entails. In this book, I have acknowledged the potential for a justification of copyright law even in these terms. However, I have insisted that the justifiability of copyright depends upon its re-imagination and, ultimately, its capacity to facilitate the generation and exchange of intellectual expression such that nobody is denied the right to speak as well as to listen, to respond as well as to receive.

The re-imagination of copyright limits its protective sphere in the name of improving relations of communication between equal participants in the cultural conversation. The first step is to depart from the pervasive individualism that has obstructed our ability to see the social nature and value of expressive activities, and has caused us to misunderstand the processes of authorship and creativity. The next step is to leave behind the proprietary framework into which we have squeezed these activities and processes, as well as the conceptual 'physicalisation' to which we have subjected the expressive work. The knowledge, message or 'drive to meaning' manifested in an intellectual work is not passed from one individual to another like a brick. The culture, information and meaning generated through intellectual creativity cannot be divided among owners like so many pieces of a pie. The final step is to actively reduce the scope of copyright protection by limiting the kind of works to which it attaches, the level of protection is accords, and the variety of downstream uses that it prevents. Re-imagined in these terms, and restrained in this way, the copyright system can be justified as a cultural policy tool, designed to further the social good by maximising discursive engagement in a collective conversation, and thereby encouraging improved relations of communication between members of society. But when the private rights that copyright grants extend too far and unduly limit the expressive activities of non-owners, the justification crumbles and the copyright system fails on its own terms.

The good news for lawmakers is that this re-imagination, however radical it may appear, is easily within their grasp. The simple acknowledgement that there is no natural, trans-temporal or apolitical truth behind the constructs of modern copyright provides the freedom to shape and define these constructs in ways that will further the social policy goals regularly invoked to justify the system. As Marilyn Randall reminds us:

> At law, the notions of authorship, of originality and of intellectual property are statutory creations and not natural entities tending towards an ideal state . . .. It suffices that the law decree otherwise for the definitions of author, owner, and property to change. But in what direction, and by the force of what necessity?[9]

This is a critical reminder in an area of law where rights are so often portrayed as incontrovertible, inevitable and universal. Mark Rose has warned us that it is a mistake to believe in copyright and its concepts as 'ancient and eternal.'[10] If we discard notions of natural entitlement and resist the tendency to reify property constructs, we can change the shape of copyright in the name of the public interest. Through the process that I have described as 're-imagination', we can effect this change from the inside out, employing the concepts, discourses and social values that already adhere in the copyright construct.

Throughout this book, the Canadian context – and, in particular, the Supreme Court of Canada's rulings in *Théberge* and *CCH*[11] – has been employed as an example of how a change in the theoretical lens through which copyright is viewed can effect a substantive shift in the interpretation and application of copyright doctrine, limiting the works to which copyright attaches and the restrictions that it imposes on users and the public. The *Théberge* case offered a new sense of the public goals that underpin the copyright system in Canada, while *CCH* generated a renewed awareness of their relevance in directly shaping copyright norms. With its apparent departure from the patterns and constraints of traditional copyright rhetoric, and its willingness to part ways with the established approaches of courts in its own and other jurisdictions, the Supreme Court paved the way for the stakeholders of Canadian copyright law to begin the process of reshaping copyright policy to advance the public interest in the encouragement and dissemination of works of the arts and intellect.

Unfortunately, subsequent jurisprudence and policy initiatives have undermined the significance of this moment in Canadian copyright law: policy-makers have sought to expand the scope of copyright with little regard for the public interest or the public domain,[12] while the concept of balance has proved incapable of unifying conflicting views on the meaning and appropriate effect of the law.[13] Two factors have limited the impact of the theoretical shift effectuated by the Supreme Court. First, the *Théberge* balance left intact the notion that copyright is a reward for the author, essentially reaffirming the notion of the author's right, albeit a limited right that must be balanced with the public interest. The problem, of course, is that the concept of balance does not reconcile the protection of copyright with the public interest, but rather pits one against the other (such that, in a case of conflict, one or the other must ultimately prevail). The outcome of any balancing act will therefore depend on the particular interests that are weighed and the weight attributed to them. In this sense, the copyright balance is a framing metaphor, but not necessarily a basis for resolution or even a precursor to change.

The second and related problem is that the Supreme Court's articulation of the public interest goals of copyright law was like a seed dropped onto harsh and inhospitable soil. The traditional landscape of Anglo-Canadian copyright has long been occupied exclusively by the author-owner, creating an environment in which users' rights and the public interest are unlikely to flourish. Moreover, the advent of digital and network technologies has been casting a shadow over this landscape, making its occupants ever more determined to protect the property that they regard as their own. In this context, it is hardly surprising that policy-makers and powerful stakeholders have focused attention on the protection of owners' rights rather than nurturing the seeds of the public interest planted by the Supreme Court.

At the outset of this book, I claimed that we have arrived at a critical moment in our cultural life. New networked technologies present unprecedented opportunities for creative expression, critical engagement and participation in public discourse. If the copyright system is aimed at maximising creative opportunities, furthering the exchange of knowledge and preserving a vibrant public domain, then the potential of networked technologies to further the objectives of copyright is undeniable. But rather than advancing the potential of these technologies, copyright law is increasingly being employed and expanded in order to constrain their use, reinforcing the traditional norms of the analogue world.

In the case of *Robertson v. Thomson*, the Supreme Court of Canada's Justice Abella considered copyright's capacity to 'keep pace with technological developments to foster intellectual, artistic and cultural creativity', and stated that, in facing the challenges of regulation in this context, 'the public benefits of this digital universe should be kept prominently in view.'[14] The minority judgment continues: 'The Internet and new technologies have unleashed a remarkable array of new creativity, empowering millions of individuals to do more than just consume our culture, instead enabling them to actively and meaningfully participate in it.'[15] This statement holds the promise of a copyright system that respects and reflects the transformative possibilities of new technologies rather than resisting and constraining the emerging cultural practices that these technologies permit.

In order for this to occur, however, the recognition of copyright's public purposes now has to be harnessed and used to steer copyright law in a new direction. I have attempted to show, in this book, how copyright could (and why it should) be re-imagined in an instrumental mode and justified in relational terms that dissolve the conflict between author and user, owner and the public. In its re-imagined form, copyright will be better able to further the public purposes that justify its existence, and to advance the social values that these purposes reflect.

I began, in Chapter 2, by challenging the romantic conception of the author-figure, individualised, universalised and finally hypostatised in the role of copyright's original author. Invoking the deconstructionist critiques of postmodern and poststructuralist literary and cultural theory, I emphasised the historical contingency and specificity of the copyright's author, and the mythic nature of original creative genius. However, simply deconstructing the author offers only so much to the copyright theorist. First, the original author of copyright law clearly has enough life left in him in this postmodern era to occupy his central role (notionally, at least) in an ever-expanding, internationalised system of law; and second, the idea of the creative author with the capacity to make new meaning has an intrinsic appeal to those of us unwilling to succumb to postmodern fragmentation. The key, then, is to present an idea of the author as a socially constituted 'subject-in process',[16] but possessing sufficient subjectivity and agency to create meaning.

I argued, in Chapter 3, that feminist theory holds this key. Feminist literary theorists, caught in a dilemma between the stable author of unreconstructed modernism and the deconstructed anti-author of postmodernism, retrieved a version of the author-speaker through the concept of dialogism. While every utterance can exist only in relation to other utterances, the clash and struggle of language in the realm of cultural activity is a productive exchange that connects speakers, shapes social relations, and holds within it the capacity for change.[17] While every person necessarily exists in relation to others, the relational self is capable of exercising autonomy and shaping her reality through the construction of a personal narrative and participation in dialogic exchange.

What emerges from this discussion is an understanding of the author as a relational and socially embedded self who creates meaning from within a network of social relations. This reveals the dual nature of authorship, which encapsulates both our essential connectedness and our creative/critical capacity. The discussion also underscores the nature of authorship as relational and dialogic: rather than a solitary, unitary act, the act of authorship is part of an ongoing dialogue that forges connections through communication. Finally, the copyright interest is revealed as relational rather than individualisable: copyright structures relationships between authors and users, allocating powers and responsibilities amongst members of cultural communities, and establishing the rules of communication and exchange. We must therefore be attentive to the relationships of power and responsibility that it generates, and ask ourselves whether those relationships will foster the kind of creativity that we value.

The departure from copyright's traditionally individualistic conceptions of the author and authorship provides the first step towards copyright's re-imagination by introducing to copyright theory the central concepts of community, relationship and dialogue. However, such concepts have limited power in the face of individual claims to natural entitlement. The next step is to rid copyright theory of the concepts of 'natural rights' and 'property', which reduce intellectual expression to a 'thing' that is 'owned', and privilege the individual owner over the social good. To this end, Chapter 4 tackled the pervasive notion that authors have a natural right to own the fruits of their intellectual labours – a notion that leads many to regard the copyright system as no more than a legal mechanism designed to protect authors' rights.

I argued that a Lockean theory of natural entitlement, based on the right to reap the fruits of one's labours, offers an inadequate and inappropriate justification for the copyright interest. From within the confines of Locke's theory, copyright fails to satisfy the Lockean provisos that require 'no waste' and 'no harm'. Lockean copyright theory is further threatened by the notion that intellectual labour is never really individual but always interdependent and essentially collective; it is hard to see what portion of the intellectual product can be attributed to, and so appropriated by, the author alone. Moving outside of Locke's theory, I argued that deontological justifications of the author's right discount the role of the State (and so the public) in the creation of the copyright interest, which is then regarded as entrenched and fundamental, and given primacy over other interests and values. It is therefore a mistake to believe that Locke's theory can or should be used to rein in copyright's expansion.

The way that we conceive of authorship and the root of the author's right has significant implications for how we choose to define that right, and where we draw its limits. In Chapter 5, I examined the doctrine of originality that determines the existence and scope of the copyright interest, and explored the impact that different conceptions of copyright's nature and purpose can have upon the definition and implications of 'originality.' I suggested that, within a re-imagined model of copyright, we must recognise the functional and metaphorical nature of the originality requirement and define it in a way that respects the dialogic nature of authorship. I applauded the Supreme Court of Canada's definition of originality as non-trivial 'skill and judgment', primarily because it set aside the loaded concepts of 'labour' and 'creativity', both of which tend to define originality (and so the copyright interest) in relation to an author's perceived natural entitlement. At the same time, the test potentially captures the dialogic idea of authorship as a personal act of meaning-making using pre-existing texts and artefacts. Consistent with this dialogic idea, I suggested that the determination of originality should involve a contextual and relational assessment of both the original and allegedly infringing work, and the extent to which each of these contributes to the public purposes of the copyright system.

A dialogic theory of authorship also reveals the importance of downstream uses of the materials that define our cultural context; the copyright owner's interest, once granted, should not unduly interfere with the creative capacities and expressive activities of others engaged in the conversation of culture. As such, Chapter 6 considered the power that copyright currently wields to chill critical, transformative and socially useful reproductions of protected materials, particularly in light of the restrictive nature of the defences available to would-be users. Drawing upon recent Canadian jurisprudence, I demonstrated that the restrictive construction of fair dealing coincides with an overriding commitment to the author's right. The Supreme Court of Canada's endorsement of a large and liberal fair dealing defence in *CCH* was the direct result of its newfound concern with the public's interest and users' rights – a concern that acknowledges the integral, rather than exceptional, nature of fair dealing in the copyright system.

A copyright theory focused upon the enhancement of cultural dialogue must insist on the centrality of fair dealing to the purposes of copyright. It should also support the call for an inclusive US-style 'fair use' defence that does not restrict permitted uses to particular purposes, but examines more generally the contribution they make to the furtherance of copyright's goals. Finally, in the face of technical controls over the access to and use of digital materials, a re-imagined copyright model must protect the public domain, reinforce the limits of owner's control, and safeguard the rights and interests of the public in relation to locked-up content.

Chapter 7 proceeded to examine the relationship between copyright law, which grants exclusive rights over expression, and the human right of free expression. Through an analysis of Canada's infamous *Michelin* decision,[18] I argued that a commitment to the idea of copyright as private property prevented the Court from perceiving the connection between copyright's subject matter and the values inherent in the right to free expression. It did so by denying the nature of the plaintiff's work as a cultural text, reifying the boundaries of the owner's right, and obscuring the social values behind the copyright interest. Unable to perceive the significance of the defendants' expression as a dialogic response imbued with a new message, the court was blind to the speech implications of its decision, and the disservice that it did to copyright's purposes.

Finally, I suggested that the court's fundamental error (and one that is also found in the British and American jurisprudence) was conceiving of copyright and freedom of expression in individualistic rights-based terms. With an appreciation of the social values that underlie both copyright and freedom of expression – the value we attach to social interaction and relationships of communication – it becomes clear that these are not conflicting rights in need of resolution, but intrinsically connected affirmations of the same public goals. When copyright trumps the ideals of free expression, silences expression and clogs channels of communication, it undermines its own purposes and threatens its own legitimacy. As a limit upon expressive activities, copyright's justifiability depends upon its capacity to ultimately increase opportunities for qualitative cultural production and exchange in furtherance of the communicative ideal that underlies the free expression guarantee. The re-imagination of copyright in social and non-proprietary terms is therefore essential to its purpose and its premise.

The theme that runs throughout this book is the need for a re-imagination of copyright in terms that meaningfully depart from the normative assumptions of possessive individualism. In its re-imagined form, a relational theory of copyright casts the central constructs of copyright in a new light: the 'author' is not an isolated and independent being, but rather exists within a culture and a network of social relations; 'authorship' is not an isolated and independent act, but rather a dialogic process that constitutes the author in relations of communication; the intellectual 'work' is not an object of property, but rather an expressive contribution to an ongoing process of cultural dialogue; the audience and users of such works are neither passive recipients nor trespassers, but rather equal participants in the conversation of culture.

Thus reconceived, the protection that copyright grants to creators of intellectual expression is one means by which the State attempts to stimulate social engagement, dialogic participation and cultural contributions, all of which are aspects of the public good inherent in participatory community. From this perspective, the central doctrines of copyright, as well as the very notion of copyright itself, are instrumental legal constructs; we should seek to define them in the way that best serves the social aims and underlying values of a relational copyright model.

NOTES

1. John Dewey, *Democracy and Education* (New York: Macmillan, 1916) at 5–6. Cited in James W. Carey, *Communication as Culture: Essays on Media and Society* (New York: Routledge, 1992) at 22 [Carey, *Communication*]. Dewey's work has played a critical role in revealing the nature of communication as a social process 'whereby reality is produced, maintained, repaired, and transformed.' Ibid. at 22–3.
2. Carey, Ibid. at 25.
3. 'Culture' is defined in the Concise Oxford English Dictionary, 9th edn (Oxford: Clarendon Press, 1995): 'the arts and other manifestations of human intellectual achievement regarded collectively.'
4. While I refer to the cultural domain, it is important to note Carey's warning against the reification of 'culture.' See Carey, *Communication*, note 1 above at 65, citing Peter L. Berger and Thomas Luckmann, *The Social Construction of Reality* (Garden City, NY: Doubleday, 1966): 'When the idea of culture enters communications research, it emerges as the environment of an organism or a system to be maintained or a power over the subject. Whatever the truth of these views – and there is truth in all of them – culture must first be seen as a set of practices, a mode of human activity, a process whereby reality is created, maintained, and transformed, however much it may subsequently become reified into a force independent of human action.'
5. See Niva Elkin-Koren, 'Cyberlaw and Social Change: A Democratic Approach to Copyright Law in Cyberspace' (1996) 14 Card. A. & Ent. L.J. 215 at 232–3, describing the kind of social interaction by which social agents engage in 'meaning-making processes': 'This understanding of social dialogue includes everything from arts and sciences, to writing and reading a book, interpreting old texts, exchanging ideas about family values, searching information on a database, and creating and consuming artifacts.' Elkin-Koren explains, at 233: 'Through this process, social agents give meaning to the objective world and define their own identity.'
6. Carey, *Communication*, note 1 above at 87.
7. Ibid.
8. Rosemary J. Coombe, 'Objects of Property and Subjects of Politics: Intellectual Property Laws and Democratic Dialogue' (1991) 69 Tex. L. Rev. 1853 at 1864.
9. Marilyn Randall, *Pragmatic Plagiarism: Authorship, Profit and Power* (Toronto: University of Toronto Press, 2001) at 268.
10. Mark Rose, *Authors and Owners: The Invention of Copyright* (Cambridge, Mass.: Harvard University Press, 1993) at 106.
11. *CCH Canadian Ltd v. Law Society of Upper Canada* [2004] S.C.J. No 12., 1 S.C.R. 339.
12. Bill C-60, *An Act to Amend the Copyright Act*, first reading 20 June 2005; Bill C-61, *An Act to Amend the Copyright Act*, first reading 12 June 2008; Bill C-32, *An Act to Amend the Copyright Act*, first reading 2 June 2010.
13. The unanimity achieved in *CCH* was quickly lost in subsequent Supreme Court rulings on copyright. See *Robertson v. Thomson Corp.* [2006] 2 S.C.R. 363, 2006 SCC 43 and *Euro-Excellence Inc. v. Kraft Canada Inc.* [2007] 3 S.C.R. 20, 2007 SCC 37. In each of these cases, conflicting understandings of the balance and its relevance to the issues at hand resulted in conflicting judgments.
14. *Robertson v. Thomson Corp.* [2006] 2 S.C.R. 363, 2006 SCC 43, para. 79. Tempering this optimism somewhat, it should be noted that these statements the majority judgment was less concerned with ensuring that copyright not interfere with the advantages offered by new technologies: 'Media neutrality is not a licence to override the rights of

authors – it exists to protect the rights of authors and others as technology evolves.' Ibid, para. 49.

15. Ibid, citing Michael Geist, "Our Own Creative Land: Cultural Monopoly & The Trouble With Copyright" (Toronto: Hart House Lecture Committee, 2006), 9.
16. B.L. Marshall, *Engendered Modernity – Feminism, Social Theory and Social Change*, (Cambridge: Polity Press, 1994) at 108.
17. See Mary O'Connor, 'Subject, Voice, and Women in Some Contemporary Black American Women's Writing' in David M. Bauer and Susan Jaret McKinstry (eds), *Feminism, Bakhtin and the Dialogic* (Albany: State University of New York Press, 1991) 199 at 201.
18. *Cie Générale des Etablissements Michelin-Michelin & Cie v. C.A.W.-Canada* (1996), 71 C.P.R. (3d) 348 (FCTD).

Index